ARTFUL BREAKDOWNS

TOM INGE
SERIES ON COMICS ARTISTS

ARTFUL BREAKDOWNS

THE COMICS OF ART SPIEGELMAN

EDITED BY GEORGIANA BANITA
AND LEE KONSTANTINOU

University Press of Mississippi / Jackson

The University Press of Mississippi is the scholarly publishing agency of
the Mississippi Institutions of Higher Learning: Alcorn State University,
Delta State University, Jackson State University, Mississippi State University,
Mississippi University for Women, Mississippi Valley State University,
University of Mississippi, and University of Southern Mississippi.

www.upress.state.ms.us

The University Press of Mississippi is a member of
the Association of University Presses.

Manufactured in the United States of America

First printing 2023
∞

Library of Congress Control Number: 2022049567

Hardback ISBN 978-1-4968-3750-9
Trade paperback ISBN 978-1-43752-3968-3751-6
Epub single ISBN 978-1-4968-3752-3
Epub institutional ISBN 978-1-4968-3753-0
PDF single ISBN 978-1-4968-3754-7
PDF institutional ISBN 978-1-4968-37554

British Library Cataloging-in-Publication Data available

CONTENTS

Acknowledgments vii

Introduction: Up from the Underground:
Art Spiegelman and the Elevation of Comics 3
GEORGIANA BANITA AND LEE KONSTANTINOU

PART 1: MODERNISM AND FORM

Modernist Disruptions: Art Spiegelman as Experimenter,
Editor, and Critic 49
SHAWN GILMORE

A Ragpicker's Art: Spiegelman's Jazz Cosmopolitanism 68
ARIELA FREEDMAN

The Modern Void: Art Spiegelman's Aesthetics of Silence 86
GEORGIANA BANITA

PART 2: RADICAL POLITICS

Exploding Stereotypes: Spiegelman and Transgression 111
PHILIP SMITH

RAW Radicals: Art Spiegelman's Comic Politics 128
SARAH HAMBLIN

Art Spiegelman and 9/11 155
KENT WORCESTER

PART 3: MEDIATING MEMORY

Provisional Equanimity: Citation and Solace in Art Spiegelman's *In the Shadow of No Towers* 177
PATRICK LAWRENCE

Of Mice and Masks: Photography as Masking in Art Spiegelman's *Maus*. 192
LIZA FUTERMAN

Art Imitating Life: Traumatic Affect in Art Spiegelman's *Maus* and Holocaust Cinema 210
HARRIET EARLE

PART 4: COMICS HISTORY

Who Published *Maus*?. 231
COLIN BEINEKE

Ellis Island Art: Art Spiegelman's Place in the History of Immigration Comics. 251
CARA KOEHLER

Art Spiegelman's Faustian Bargain: TOON Books and the Invention of Comics for Kids. 272
LEE KONSTANTINOU

Appendix: Art Spiegelman's Primary Works. 290

About the Contributors 297

Index 300

ACKNOWLEDGMENTS

The authors would like to thank the contributors to this volume for their insightful and genuinely wide-ranging chapters. We are lucky to have worked with a series editor, David M. Ball, whose advice has been indispensable and enthusiasm for the book truly inspiring. For her guidance and commitment, we thank our editor at the University Press of Mississippi, Katie Keene. The highly efficient and professional Wendy Appelle at the Wylie Agency has helped this book come to fruition as the well-illustrated anthology it was always meant to be. We are, of course, indebted to Art Spiegelman himself for granting us permission to reproduce artwork he created over a span of 50 years, and to Nadja Spiegelman for providing the heartwarming cover image. We also appreciate the support of the anonymous peer reviewers who read our project in draft form.

Georgiana would like to thank her domestic motley crew, Rudolf and Tana, for encouragement and entertainment.

Lee would like to thank Julie and Eleanor for their patience as this project came to life. Thanks are due, as well, to Daniel Schwarz, who mentored Lee's first attempt to write about Spiegelman more than twenty years ago.

Grateful acknowledgment is made to The Wylie Agency LLC for permission to reproduce images from the following works:

Untitled from *Pipe Dreams* (Harpur College, SUNY Binghamton). Copyright © 1966 by Art Spiegelman.

"A Flash of Insight, a Cloud of Dust and a Hearty Hi-yo Silver" from *Witzend*. Copyright © 1967 by Art Spiegelman.

Maus I: A Survivor's Tale: My Father Bleeds History. Copyright © 1973, 1980, 1981, 1982, 1983, 1984, 1985, 1986 by Art Spiegelman.

Breakdowns: From Maus to Now: An Anthology of Strips by Art Spiegelman. Copyright © 1974, 1977, 2009 by Art Spiegelman.

"Cracking Jokes," originally published in *The Comics Revue* No. 1. Copyright © 1975 by Art Spiegelman.

Cover design for *Breakdowns: From Maus to Now*. Copyright © 1977 by Art Spiegelman.

Cover design for *Dead Men All Have the Same Skin*. Copyright © 1980 by Art Spiegelman.

RAW Volume 1, Issue 1: *The Graphix Magazine of Postponed Suicides*. Copyright © 1980 by Art Spiegelman.

RAW Volume 1, Issue 2: *The Graphix Magazine for Damned Intellectuals*. Copyright © 1980 by Art Spiegelman.

RAW Volume 1, Issue 5: *The Graphix Magazine of Abstract Depressionism*. Copyright © 1983 by Art Spiegelman.

RAW Volume 1, Issue 7: *The Torn-Again Graphix Magazine*. Copyright © 1983 by Art Spiegelman.

Maus II: A Survivor's Tale: And Here My Troubles Began. Copyright © 1986, 1989, 1990, 1991 by Art Spiegelman.

RAW Volume 1, Issue 8: The Graphic Aspirin for War Fever. Copyright © 1986 by Art Spiegelman.

"High Art Lowdown," review of the *High and Low: Modern Art and Popular Culture* exhibit at the MoMA. Copyright © 1990 by Art Spiegelman.

"Dead Dick" from *Lead Pipe Sunday*. Copyright © 1991 by Art Spiegelman.

Various covers for the *New Yorker*. Copyright © 1993, 1996, 1999, 2001, 2002 by Art Spiegelman.

The Wild Party: The Lost Classic by Joseph Moncure March. Copyright © 1994 by Art Spiegelman.

"Roll Up Your Sleeves, America!" from *World War 3 Illustrated*. Copyright © 1997 by Art Spiegelman.

In the Shadow of No Towers. Copyright © 2004 by Art Spiegelman.

Jack and the Box, currently collected in TOON Books. Copyright © 2008 by Art Spiegelman.

"The St. Louis Refugee Ship Blues," originally published in the *Washington Post*. Copyright © 2009 by Art Spiegelman.

Metamaus: A Look Inside a Modern Classic, Maus. Copyright © 2011 by Art Spiegelman.

Self-portrait from the *New York Times* (10/13/2013). Copyright © 2013 by Art Spiegelman.

WORDLESS! by Art Spiegelman. Copyright © 2014 by Art Spiegelman.

The Ghosts of Ellis Island. Copyright © 2015 by Art Spiegelman.

"Drawing the Line: Notes from a First Amendment Fundamentalist" from the *Nation* (150th Anniversary Special Issue, 3/23/2015). Copyright © 2015 by Art Spiegelman.

Cover for the *New Statesman* (5/19/2015). Copyright © 2015 by Art Spiegelman

ARTFUL BREAKDOWNS

Introduction

UP FROM THE UNDERGROUND

Art Spiegelman and the Elevation of Comics

GEORGIANA BANITA AND LEE KONSTANTINOU

As an art form the comic strip is barely past its infancy.
So am I. Maybe we'll grow up together.
—ART SPIEGELMAN, 1974

IN THE GRIP OF COMICS

It is hard to overstate the importance of Art Spiegelman as a creator, editor, and theorist of comics. He is arguably the most canonical cartoonist in comics history, and for good reason. His work has, by many accounts, brought a new sophistication and reflexivity to comics, and he has created an astonishing range of work in a variety of formats and styles across half a century. He has created bubble gum cards, expressionist drawings, children's books, avant-garde sketches, wordless lithographs, innovative cover art, graphic short stories, comics journalism, and a major graphic memoir. Spiegelman's Pulitzer Prize-winning *Maus*—his book about his parents' life in Nazi-occupied Poland and cross-generational Holocaust trauma—is regarded as one of the highest achievements of the form. His wrenching, intimate, and intellectually withering comics have challenged other cartoonists to engage in more formally ambitious work. His example and advocacy have, meanwhile, attracted critical attention not only to his own work but the medium as a whole. Yet like many recent cartoonists, Spiegelman has remained skeptical of the attention of academics and highbrow gatekeepers. Speaking of the popularity of the term "graphic novel," for example, Spiegelman has suggested that since the terms "graphics" and "novels" carry an allure of respectability, booksellers have used the neologism in the hope "that a double whammy of respectability would help make the stunted hunchback dwarf [of comics] look better by dressing it up in evening clothes."[1]

Notwithstanding this hesitation, Spiegelman has done more than anyone to bring legitimacy to his chosen medium. Some scholars have gone so far as to argue that *Maus* "created the very category of 'Greatest Comic Book of All Time' in the American context; prior to its success in the 'real world' of book publishing, such a concept was essentially meaningless."[2] At a time when no one quite knew what it meant to be a comics artist, Spiegelman mastered the contradictory art of crossing cultural registers, moving from low to high and back again, with surprising ease. His influence goes beyond comics. Spiegelman's cover illustrations for the *New Yorker*, for example, have expanded the role of the political cartoonist as public intellectual. And he has brought cartooning into dialogue with other genres and media, from music and photography to theater and dance.

At least as important as his comics is Spiegelman's lifelong work as an editor. The magazines he coedited with Bill Griffith—*Arcade*—and his wife Françoise Mouly—*RAW*—helped transform the perception of a long-marginalized medium. "Instead of making comics into a narcotic," Spiegelman observed, "I'm trying to make comics that can wake you up, like caffeine comics that get you back in touch with things that are happening around you."[3] His work as a comics editor has attracted audiences far beyond the cognoscenti in the arts and academic circles. Eliding easy distinctions between high and low, his vision of comics—both as a creator and as an editor—doesn't start from any notion of what capital-A Art should be, but with the possibilities of the medium itself. "Of course comics can be art," Spiegelman noted in 1979, "but so can pencil sharpening," although with enough artistic effort it might then "move over into the realm of whittling."[4]

Nonetheless, the advantage of the comics medium for Spiegelman lies partly in its disreputable status and history as popular entertainment: "It's a more fugitive medium," he explains, "it's born in the sawdust, you know, rather than fertile soil."[5] The hallmark of Spiegelman's cartooning is his versatility in shaping this sawdust. Suspicious of trademark styles, Spiegelman has decided his visual trademark will be that he has none. He has repeatedly stated that his ideal was never the always recognizable Hollywood-type star but the character actor, a vessel that humbly assumes the shape of its content; "the best way for me to proceed is not to try to be a star, but rather to be an actor . . . somebody who finds his way into each role and convinces you that he's that character."[6] When the formally pyrotechnic style of his underground comics became a trademark, the surprisingly conventional, narrative-driven *Maus* (serialized from 1980 to 1991) broke with expectations. By the late 1970s, many artists at the vanguard of comics were showing signs of ossification; "some of them," Spiegelman complained in 1980, "have fallen into riffs where essentially they do variations on exactly what they were doing ten years ago."[7] Paradoxically, though it marked a return to convention, *Maus* helped him escape the rut of the underground.

Across his career, Spiegelman has held fast to a broad vision of comics; "in their essence," he has suggested, comics "are about time made manifest spatially," forcing the reader into an awareness of "different times inhabiting the same space."[8] This is a loose framework, hospitable to endless variations in exactly how time and space interlock on the comics page. Cartooning is, for Spiegelman, an epistemology, a way of seeing. "Because they deal in essences, rather than nuanced description," comics reveal to him the way the mind works "in encoded, simplified images and concentrated verbal clusters."[9] Compared to literature, as a combination of word and image, comics comes "closer to the way the mind works than pure language."[10]

The deceptively simplistic style of *Maus* illustrates Spiegelman's vision most clearly. The characters in his memoir aren't portraits as much as schematics or blueprints, which the reader ultimately is responsible for giving shape to. Vladek as a rodent works as a stand-in for all persecuted Jews because his sketchy rendering aligns him with other similarly figured mice. Writing about *Maus*, Lawrence Weschler has suggested that the book's "ambiguity is of an almost crystalline precision."[11] Spiegelman treats cartooning as an art of condensation and expansion at the same time. History is compressed into easily disseminated visual packages, giving those visual packages the potential to deliver their meanings to a wider audience. Yet the mass audience Spiegelman targets must be primed "to stretch themselves to meet the work rather than to have the work poured down their sleeping, open gullets."[12]

Spiegelman's chosen style is always intended to support the story he wants to tell: "What I want to do is put myself at the service of whatever material I'm involved with and bring it out the best I can."[13] For every drawing, he relies on a hook—"a coat hanger, an armature" (plot, object, or event)—on which to hang his visual ideas.[14] In another interview, he insists "it's most important that each comic strip be a fully realized world, rather than that they're all obvious slices of the same masterwork."[15] Because "the best a work of art can do is give you some of these hooks with which one can try to come to grips with the ungrippable,"[16] different tools are required for different strips: the Rapidograph for "Don't Get Around Much Anymore," scratchboard tools and brush for "Prisoner on the Hell Planet." What holds this lifetime of work together, then, isn't so much a thematic continuity as Spiegelman's commitment to adapting the form of comics to a variety of contents, showing through his own distinguished example and the example of other innovative cartoonists that the medium has the representational versatility and emotional depth to address any subject.

NEW YORK I: CHILDHOOD, ADOLESCENCE, BUBBLE GUM

Art Spiegelman was born Itzhak Avraham ben Zeev in Stockholm, Sweden, on February 15, 1948, three years after his parents had reunited in the aftermath of their ordeals in the Nazi camps, and another three years before the family's move to the US. Socially and financially, the relocation triggered a decline. The Spiegelmans never regained the status they enjoyed in pre-war Poland, living modestly as a lower middle-class family in Queens. Vladek worked in the diamond district. Anja was a homemaker with insomnia and an addiction to sleeping pills. Young Spiegelman was raised to believe the world had little use for artists and even less for cartoonists. His father insisted he become a doctor or a dentist, pointing out that in the extermination camps, professors and lawyers would be the first in line to the gas showers.[17] Yet to Vladek's chagrin, Art was drawn to comics. He pored over *Batman* before he could read; and even though he quickly outgrew the superhero genre, it was clear early on that comics were his vocation.

Spiegelman was an omnivorous comics reader and something of a cartooning prodigy, already afire with ideas at a young age. "I wanted to be a cartoonist specifically from about the age of eleven," he recalls.[18] As a teen, he honed his skills by imitating other cartoonists, including *MAD* magazine alumni John Severin and Wally Wood as well as *Dick Tracy* creator, Chester Gould. The 1960s were the time of Spiegelman's apprenticeship. He spent much of the period studying underground comics while getting to know his own strengths and limitations. At fifteen, he was already a staff cartoonist at the *Long Island Post* while attending the High School of Art and Design in Midtown Manhattan. Under the pseudonym Artie X, he collaborated with Ronnie Hamilton, a Black classmate, scripting a strip called "Super Colored Guy" for a weekly Harlem newspaper.[19] With fellow aspiring cartoonist Jay Lynch, he contributed to self-published underground magazines like *Smudge*, *Wild*, and *Trump*. When the underground press movement started in the mid-1960s, he graduated to professional comics magazines. By 1966, he was doing sex-and-drugs comics for the *East Village Other* and handing out unsigned one-page comic strips to pretty girls on the street.[20]

For twenty years, however, Spiegelman's main source of income was the Topps Chewing Gum Company, for which he designed novelty trading cards. As a rule, Topps assignments occupied only two days a week, leaving five days for his own experiments. Spiegelman landed the job with the gum manufacturer when he wrote a precociously condescending letter to commend them for employing *MAD* cofounder Jack Davis, asking to see some original artwork that had run on the back of the company's trading cards.[21] Topps editor and art director Woody Gelman invited the teenage comic-strip obsessive to lunch,

Detail from "Memory Hole" (Soho, NYC 2005), *Breakdowns: From Maus to Now: An Anthology of Strips by Art Spiegelman.* Copyright © 1974, 1977, 2009 by Art Spiegelman.

gave him cartoons, and hired him. Of Gelman, Spiegelman would later recall: "He was a catalyst for a lot of what happened in the junk arena of culture that he championed. . . . He was working in these sub-subbasements of our culture, like animated cartoons and baseball cards and ephemeral publishing, and he both salvaged and preserved it and encouraged it into being."[22]

At Topps, Spiegelman produced parodies of consumer culture aimed at both children and their parents. He was the anonymous mastermind behind the successful series *Wacky Packages*, a *MAD*-inspired lampoon of advertising clichés, and *The Garbage Pail Kids*, crafted in the grotesque tradition of *MAD*-cartoonist Basil Wolverton. Both were essentially underground comic books in trading card format, less like Topps's popular fantasy series like *Mars Attacks* and more like a children's version of what would become *Arcade* and *RAW*: lurid, loud, self-conscious, envelope-pushing designs. James Manchin, State Treasurer in West Virginia from 1985 to 1989, famously tried to ban both *MAD* and *The Garbage Pail Kids* in his home state for their irreverent mocking of American institutions and for creating a generation of indiscriminate protestors.[23]

Ironically, when Spiegelman showed up for a Guernsey auction of original Topps cartoons and memorabilia, he could not afford to buy his own artwork and felt humiliated when winning bidders brazenly asked him to sign it.[24] The effect of pop culture's rise in art collector circles was to snag Spiegelman's early work out of his own hands. In later years, he learned to preempt this development by retaining copyright of his comics and exerting more influence in their curation. Jeet Heer in his sketch of Spiegelman's career fast-forwards through the years at Topps, dismissing young Art's early stabs at cartooning as "derivative and inferior."[25] Juvenilia is, of course, underwhelming, a necessary training ground for bigger and better things. But Spiegelman's Topps cards deserve more credit. At the least, Topps Gum placed its cartoon ads in high-circulation publications, including *Life* magazine, giving Spiegelman his widest exposure prior to *Maus*.

In 1966, Spiegelman enrolled to study art and philosophy at Harpur College (now SUNY Binghamton). No matter what courses he was taking, he would end up writing about comics, as in a 1967 art history class for which he submitted the essay "'Master Race': The Graphic Story as an Art Form." Published in 1955, one year before Alain Resnais released *Night and Fog*, Bernard Krigstein's "Master Race" was one of the earliest responses to the Holocaust by a Jewish artist. By the time Spiegelman's mother committed suicide in 1968, Art had already seen in "Master Race" how a cartoonist could use modernist techniques to transport the concentration camps into the urban present. Spiegelman met with Krigstein in the early seventies to discuss his college paper and was pleased when the elderly artist "entered into the analysis avidly, acknowledging a reference to Futurism in one panel, to Mondrian in another, denying a reference to George Grosz in yet another."[26] Thrilled to share the stage with these revered modernists, Krigstein resented being grouped with what he thought were lowly craftsmen like Kurtzman or Eisner.

At Binghamton, an early psychedelic capital, Spiegelman was not only exploring the connection between modernist form and comics history in his coursework, but also "taking LSD as casually as some of [his] contemporaries now drop antacids."[27] Under the influence, he was increasingly erratic and filled with self-destructive hubris. He lived in a forest cabin for a while, before being hospitalized in a mental ward, "wail[ing] in tune with the siren" on the way to the clinic.[28] After spending one month in the Binghamton State Mental Hospital, he decided to abandon his studies. Indirectly and tragically, Spiegelman's breakdown was a factor in his mother's death, which in turn launched his underground cartooning career.[29] It was at this time that his relationship with his father, who remarried a year later, became incurably fractious and fractured.

SAN FRANCISCO: THE UNDERGROUND

The dissolution of his family set Spiegelman on a path of personal development. When he relocated to San Francisco, he did so because he had swallowed the stories of hippie culture in *Time* magazine and the San Francisco *Oracle* "hook, line and sinker."[30] The people he hung out with in San Francisco could not think of anything else but comics. Spiegelman's mindset at the time was aptly reflected by his comics stand-in during this period: an "intense, long-haired, mustachioed, scrungy Zappaesque character," nothing like the fretful, sympathetic mouse-listener of *Maus*.[31] His conversations with Bill Griffith, the creator of Zippy the Pinhead, were never-ending, especially after both grew tired of the taboo-defying expectations of the West Coast subculture, of doing raucous cartoons for magazines like *Screw* and *Playboy*, and of getting both their drugs and their antiestablishment comics at the same head shops. Together, Spiegelman and Griffith plotted to redirect the hedonistic freedom of expression that underground comics had unleashed in the sixties and seventies by guiding cartoonists away from the eclectic, freewheeling approach dominating the San Francisco comics scene toward a more stringent sense of craft. To them, the dissipation and disorder of the underground meant that comics as a whole were under threat, so they crafted "a life raft for the underground cartoonists who were watching all of the underground comix not selling."[32]

Arcade: The Comics Revue, the magazine Spiegelman and Griffith cofounded, ran for seven issues from 1975 to 1976, publishing the likes of R. Crumb, S. Clay Wilson, and Justin Green in a format that aligned itself with satirical newsstand magazines. *Arcade* was partly meant to stave off the contamination of Marvel's magazine *Comix Book*, which Spiegelman was briefly involved with but abandoned when he realized he could not retain copyright to his work. At this point, he was looking for a vehicle through which he could retain creative control of his art and test the limits of the medium. He had already contributed to adult comics magazines from Print Mint and Kitchen Sink Press, including *Young Lust*, *Real Pulp*, *Bizarre Sex*, and *Sleazy Scandals of the Silver Screen*, so he had some practice in "get[ing] underneath the sanitized part of what comics can be."[33] With *Arcade*, he wanted to continue exploring his more sinister side in an arena that was free of prescriptions and taboo. Although *Arcade* emulated Kurtzman's magazines, which Spiegelman had contributed to in the 1960s, it distanced itself from the underground by remolding underground artists in *Arcade*'s more cultured image. Though bankrolled by the same publisher (Print Mint), for instance, *Arcade* and the bestselling *Zap* became polar opposites in tone and subject matter. The same artists—from R. Crumb to Spain Rodriguez—who were moonlighting with violent science fiction in *Zap* were also engaging in a more thoughtful nonfiction mode for *Arcade*.

"Maus," page 1, first published in *Funny Aminals* No. 1. Copyright © 1972 by Art Spiegelman.

Its West Coast countercultural ethos and East Coast elitism were an uneasy mix. While the underground sneered at *Arcade*'s pretentions, mainstream magazine readers were altogether indifferent. Spiegelman even managed to alienate contributing cartoonists by having to reject their work, if he did not find a place for it, or to ask for adjustments. The experience put him off being an editor at least for a while; among other things, he developed an ulcer and took to smoking four packs a day.[34] By the time he returned to New York, leaving Griffith in charge, *Arcade*'s life raft had capsized. Though this period ended in professional failure, two key specimens of Spiegelman's work originated during his time in San Francisco: the embryonic version of *Maus* published in *Funny Aminals #1* by Apex Novelties (1972) and "Prisoner on the Hell Planet," published in *Short Order Comix #1* (1973). Of the full-length graphic works he published in the 1970s, only a few—"Don't Get Around Much Anymore"

(1974), "Ace Hole, Midget Detective" (1974), "Little Signs of Passion" (1975), "Day at the Circuits" (1975), "Cracking Jokes: A Brief Inquiry into Various Aspects of Humor" (1975), "As the Mind Reels" (1975), and "The Malpractice Suite" (1976)—would make the cut for the *Breakdowns* anthology that marked the end of Spiegelman's underground phase. *The Complete Mr. Infinity* (1970), awarded the same Jewish writing prize *Maus* would win sixteen years later, *The Viper Vicar of Vice, Villainy, and Vickedness* (1972), and the illustrations to *Whole Grains: A Book of Quotations*, coedited with Bob Schneider in 1973, haven't been reissued since their initial print.

NEW YORK II: *RAW* AND *BREAKDOWNS*

"It was really in reading that strip," Mouly remembers of "Prisoner on the Hell Planet," "that I first got a sense of how extraordinary Art is. Brutally, ruthlessly honest, which is one way to get at the truth and, to me, the mark of a true artist."[35] Their first phone conversation revolved around "Prisoner" and lasted eight hours.[36] Spiegelman and Mouly were married three times: once in 1977 at City Hall to avert French-born Mouly's deportation, once again in Rego Park in a Jewish ceremony after Mouly had converted to please her father-in-law, and years later in 1998 with a ceremony that celebrated both their relationship and their careers in comics, with music provided by R. Crumb's amateur ragtime band. When she met Spiegelman, Mouly was interested in Raymond Queneau's mathematical axioms for literature and cared comparatively little for comics, but she gradually warmed to those aspects of comics that resonated with the French graphic arts. At the same time, Spiegelman was growing into a champion of the medium whose history he sought to reconstruct. The couple's first collaboration was a series of lectures titled "Language of the Comics," delivered at the Collective of Living Cinema in 1977, for which Mouly helped prepare the slides.[37]

In *Breakdowns*, published the same year, Spiegelman reprinted his early work, honed his editorial skills by curating his own comics, tinkered with new book formats, and mapped out possible avenues for the years ahead. The inventive material collected in *Breakdowns* probably wouldn't have received such an oversize, lavish treatment if Spiegelman hadn't shown more traditional talent in his sketches about the Shoah and his mother's suicide. In the words of Jeff Rund, who had just edited R. Crumb's *Carload O' Comics* and vouched for *Breakdowns* when its printing became too costly: "I don't understand two-thirds of the shit in this book, but anyone who could do that 'Maus' strip and the thing about his mother's suicide deserves a break."[38] It is significant, then, that the opening pieces of *Breakdowns* are "Maus" and "Prisoner." Taken together, these

Cover of *Breakdowns: From Maus to Now: An Anthology of Strips by Art Spiegelman*. Copyright © 1974, 1977, 2009 by Art Spiegelman.

works show Spiegelman attempting to shake up comics in two ways. On the one hand, the cartoonist broke down comics conventions with freewheeling formal play. On the other, he grounded his playfulness in the somber history of violence his parents barely escaped, a history his own psychological breakdown to some extent reenacted or echoed.

With *Breakdowns*, Spiegelman put out a serious-minded, experimental artifact into the world, thinking it would be enough if only three people cared or could make sense of it. Little more than three people ever did, and years later there was hardly a dent in the book's 3,500 print run.[39] The blues that followed this commercial failure prompted Spiegelman to revisit areas of his portfolio that felt more accessible. At the same time, and partly through Mouly's influence, Europe now seemed more than the distant colony of his parents' past. With *Maus*, he decided to inhabit it fully by rendering the story of the Holocaust through the eyes of his parents and by undertaking a series of travels to France, Belgium, Spain, and Italy to scout for comics talent.

It was as a vehicle for both his personal story of World War II and for a slate of European cartoonists like Joost Swarte, who found inspiration in industrial design, that Spiegelman and Mouly launched *RAW* magazine in 1980, two years after Mouly had founded her own publishing company, *RAW* Books and Graphics. The art of printing was in fact key to the magazine's aesthetic. In the late 1970s, to test Mouly's new printing press, the couple put out a series of mail books, essentially eight-page postcards, of which Spiegelman did one titled "Every Dog Has Its Day."[40] He also published a one-panel-a-page book, *Work and Turn*, in 1979. With baby steps at first, *RAW* Books soon progressed into a solid family business. Bankrolled by profits generated by printing a map and guide to SoHo, the project built on the success of creative bookmaking in the 1970s, while keeping comics intelligible to (and affordable for) broader publics outside the arts community. Though reluctant to participate in another magazine venture, Spiegelman again felt the need to have the last say on who and what got published, especially after unhappy stints as an editorial consultant for *Playboy* and *High Times*. Besides, he and Mouly wanted to showcase the work of their cartoonist friends and create a platform where Spiegelman's students at the School of Visual Arts could publish and learn.

Eleven issues of *RAW* were published between 1980 and 1991, as well as ten Raw One-Shot books, the latter appearing across the decade at an irregular pace of about one per year.[41] Because Spiegelman could be a harsh critic of his peers, a habit that had soured his relations to *Arcade*'s contributors a decade before, *RAW* benefited from the gentler guidance that Mouly provided to artists, who did not regard her as one of them and were therefore more amenable to her suggestions. Thanks to Mouly's dedication, the press also granted cartoonists the rare opportunity to publish in lengthier formats. Though they weren't conceived as graphic novels in the form we know them today, the Raw One-Shots expanded the emotional range of the medium by dwelling on individual images that shocked and unnerved the reader. In addition, *RAW* Books' handmade printing allowed the material to retain its aesthetic uniqueness even as it was being disseminated and marketed as mass art.

RAW cultivated both underground and "overground cartoonists," whom Spiegelman and Mouly challenged to pursue new artistic directions.[42] After all, the magazine was looking to draw together what Spiegelman would later call "odd bedfellows."[43] By and large, the selection favored cartoonists who could feel comfortable with the magazine's robust paper stock and formal elegance, who regarded themselves, in other words, as artists rather than entertainers. Important discoveries included Gary Panter, Chris Ware, and Charles Burns. *RAW* also moved away from the American tradition as Spiegelman and Mouly staked out global territory for the magazine. It was partly Mouly's French background that informed this international slant reaching far beyond the US and Europe. In an insert titled "Tokyo Raw," the magazine reproduced a rare English translation of Yoshiharu Tsuge's "Red Flowers," about a girl's first menstruation, which introduced US readers to the melancholy side of manga. Throughout its run, *RAW* brought both established and fresh voices as well as familiar and foreign work to American audiences, setting comics on a formally and historically introspective path. In line with *RAW*'s editorial agenda, Spiegelman's later projects would continue to seek large audiences for serious comics and foster interest in the medium's transnational history.

MAUS: COMICS ENTER THE MUSEUM

Maus and *RAW* could not be any more different. Whereas *RAW* laid bare the pasteboard and strings that went into making comics, the more immersive *Maus* was energized by its believable characters and propulsive narrative. Though anthologized in the magazine as a series of booklet inserts, Spiegelman's Holocaust story was more cohesive overall than the tonally diverse *RAW*. And yet the aesthetic of *RAW* had a major impact on how Spiegelman empaneled and designed *Maus*. He began work on the graphic memoir in 1978, at the age of thirty. The research itself did not take too long. "There wasn't a mountain of literature," he remembers, "I was able to do all my research in about three months."[44] A year later he travelled to Poland for some field work, since the full-fledged treatment of *Maus* required the kind of attention to detail that a short strip could afford to elide, but a book-length narrative could not. For many years *Maus* was a labor of love, appearing in installments that few were seeing and leaving Spiegelman unprepared, at the age of 38, for the unanimous acclaim that greeted the publication of the first volume in 1986. "I really thought of myself as kind of a cult artist," he noted years later, wistful of that lost anonymity, "somebody who had a small respectful following and who would then get discovered after he died of lung cancer at the age of fifty."[45] And yet, as a friend once quipped, Spiegelman had always acted as if he were already famous and felt confident in the value of his work, even when he expected it to be a message in a bottle rather than an instant success.[46] It is this confidence that fueled the sheer breadth and ambition of the *Maus* project.

Whereas in the proto-"Maus" and "Prisoner" strips Spiegelman struggled to express and exorcise feelings of devastation and loss, the book cast a wider net, probing the psychic mechanisms of exile, memory, and the intergenerational transmission of trauma. The approach resonated with the East Coast literati; *Maus*-in-progress was profiled in the *New York Times Book Review* and received an award before anyone (outside the magazine and festival circuit) had even seen the finished product.[47] Spiegelman was in therapy at this point. Because with *Maus* he set out to transcribe both the story and the pitfalls of telling it, therapy reinforced this aspect of the book. Spiegelman even included his therapist (Paul Pavel, an Auschwitz survivor) in Art's musings about the ethics of collaborative autobiography.

In 1985, upon reading an interview with Steven Spielberg about his upcoming animated film *An American Tail*—a story that used cats and mice to describe the European persecution of Jews—Spiegelman was "appalled, shattered"; "along comes this Goliath, the most powerful man in Hollywood," he noted of Spielberg, who would later anger him even more with *Schindler's List*, "just casually trampling everything underfoot."[48] He panicked and rushed to publish a first volume of *Maus* before the animated tale could scoop him. Had Hollywood not placed him under competitive pressure, *Maus* might have taken much longer to reach the bookshelves. What's more, it was partly through a fluke of history that the book appeared at all. The now classic graphic memoir earned its author an impressive pile of rejections from traditional presses like Knopf and Norton, which balked at the supposedly insurmountable tension between the book's lightweight medium and its somber subject matter. When Pantheon agreed to publish the first volume (reluctantly, as they were hoping to see the entire book first), they did so on the strength of the *New York Times* review coupled with the critical and commercial success of *RAW* magazine, whose official first print run of 5,000 copies (actually just 3,500 according to some sources) had already tripled.

When Pantheon published *Maus I* in September 1986, the memoir's popular success was nothing short of stratospheric. But if *Maus* appealed to such broad publics, it was also because Spiegelman addressed a book-reading audience rather than inveterate comics readers. The memoir became a surprising bestseller, selling close to 100,000 copies in the United States over just a year and a half. It was nominated for the National Book Critics Circle Award in Biography/Autobiography and garnered Spiegelman's second Joel M. Cavior Award for Jewish Writing.

As Holocaust nonfiction, *Maus* ranked among the first works to depict the genocide "without trying to extract hope or inspiration from it."[49] The mid-1980s marked a turning point in the perception of the massacres in Central and

Eastern Europe. In 1985, Raul Hilberg reissued *The Destruction of the European Jews* (first published in 1961) in a three-volume "revised and definitive edition," extending his focus on the bureaucracy of the genocide that implicated large numbers of Germans, while condemning the placatory actions of some Jewish leaders. Spiegelman's less-than-favorable portrayal of his father, Vladek, came at a propitious time, when the Holocaust narrative no longer needed perfect, virtuous protagonists. In 1979, one year after Spiegelman had started work on *Maus*, William Styron's *Sophie's Choice* sparked controversy around the perceived need to approach the Holocaust with reverence. Imre Kertész and Danilo Kiš had published semiautobiographical novels that humanized victims of the Holocaust, allowing them to defy readers' expectations, to be fallible and disappointing. Doing an animal comic about the Holocaust and being angry at one's survivor parents wasn't as shocking at it might have seemed a couple of decades earlier, when the first pages of *Maus* were drawn. The book version of *Maus* achieved a near-perfect blend of empathy with the survivors and estrangement from their damaged, posttraumatic selves.

Before he obtained a Guggenheim Fellowship in 1990 to complete the second volume, the years following the publication of *Maus I* were an extended press tour that made Spiegelman a household name. In 1987, a film crew asked him to pose awkwardly at Auschwitz for a ZDF/BBC documentary meant to introduce him to European audiences before the book was available in German (Spiegelman initially objected to this translation).[50] Like *Maus I*, the second volume was serialized before it appeared in book form. *The Jewish Forward* carried weekly installments in 1991 ahead of Pantheon's hardcover release in November. One month later, the canonization of the book was already in progress with the "Making *Maus*" exhibit at NYC's Museum of Modern Art. It was the first "enhanced book" in the history of comics, a hybrid release that Richard McGuire emulated when he published *Here* in tandem with the exhibit "From Here to Here: Richard McGuire Makes a Book" at the Morgan Library & Museum in 2014. What had started out in a Polish concentration camp museum in 1979 returned to a German art gallery in 1992 (Düsseldorf) as a haloed form of witness art. This circuit reveals as much about the rapid rise of comics as about the uniqueness of Spiegelman's project, which was a bona fide work of art—conceptually and aesthetically—long before it became a book of comics.

The publication of the two *Maus* volumes was almost immediately followed by the births of Spiegelman and Mouly's two children: Nadja in 1987 and Dashiell in 1992. By the time his two books and two children had entered the world, Spiegelman was spent. So, after the success of *Maus*, the cartoonist entered a holding pattern, a life of solitary, self-contained aftermath. Whatever may have caused Spiegelman's comics abstinence after *Maus*, it helped him free himself from the burden of expectation until he only had himself to please when it came to drawing. And once he stopped drawing comics, he started teaching them. In 1992, he taught a course on the history and aesthetics of comics at UC Santa Cruz, tracing the evolution of the medium using as props a slide-projector, pointer, and cigarettes. For an interview he gave around this time, he suggested the title "Art Spiegelman, Burnout."[51]

It's not difficult to recognize in *Maus* the moment when Art became an artist. Spiegelman, in other words, convinced the world of the artistry in *Maus* because he convinced himself first, not least by disavowing the success of his own book in the second volume of *Maus*, which consequently reads more like a reception history of the first volume than a new installment of Vladek's story. By distancing himself from his own achievement, Spiegelman gave himself the critical space to engage in a meta-appreciation of *Maus* that mirrors the perspective of its readers. From this moment on, Spiegelman's mind was permanently plastered in a mouse-print wallpaper, recognizable in nearly everything he produced post-1986. "At this point I'm carrying a 500-pound mouse on my back," he confessed with a mixture of pride and frustration, "which might even become my tombstone."[52] Spiegelman's main task thus became not producing new comics but commenting on his own masterpiece with Sisyphean persistence.

For over a decade, as he was coming up for air after the claustrophobia induced by his international fame, Spiegelman dedicated himself to retrospectives and making-of special features centered on, though not restricted to, *Maus*. Pantheon issued *The Complete Maus* in 1996, on the tenth anniversary of *Maus I*. Prior to this high-profile release, several exhibitions that detailed the *Maus*-maker's backstage secrets had already toured the US and Europe.[53] Pantheon's collected edition also had the positive effect of bringing other treasures of Spiegelman's oeuvre into the limelight. The international traveling retrospective *Comix, Essays, Graphics & Scraps* (1998) resulted in a lavishly designed best-of anthology that included at least one sample of nearly every Spiegelman project. This prismatic, archival volume suggested that comics could profit from reprints, reinterpretations, contextual framing, and the painstaking archeology previously restricted to the elite benchmarks of high art. Like modernist arts and writing, Spiegelman's comics work was an endlessly unfolding text whose laborious weaving and unmaking deserved intense examination. Some specimens were minor drawings, yet their cumulative claim was that a cartoonist could salvage as much valuable detritus as the best Joycean Scribbledehobble notebook.

At this stage of his career, Spiegelman was clearly more invested in exhibiting his work than in bringing out new material. In 2005, he was featured in the group exhibition "Masters of American Comics" at the Museum of Contemporary Art and the Hammer Museum in Los Angeles. A few years later, in 2009, he had his first solo exhibition that went beyond *Maus*, at Galerie Martel in Paris, later on tour in Milan. A new exhibition on *Maus* toured in Australia in 2004 (Jewish Museum of Australia, Victoria, and Migration Museum, Adelaide). A fitting bookend to this self-curatorial phase was the second documentary to profile the celebrity cartoonist, ARTE's *Art Spiegelman, Traits de Mémoire* (2010). McSweeney's 2009 publication of a facsimile edition of Spiegelman's private sketchbooks in three small volumes under the title *Be a Nose!* (in reference to a failed sculptor's frustration with his own lack of skill) consecrated the notion of comics as collectible modernist collages torn from the rib of personal history and extending far beyond the final page. Not incidentally, many of the color images in the sketchbooks read like exercises in the style of George Grosz circa 1920—mad cityscapes bursting with concave piles of buildings and people. Coupled with the material memory and nonlinear reading that Spiegelman had inaugurated with the multimedia footnotes to *Maus*, these glimpses into the exploratory stages of cartooning attached a new archival quality to the medium, a fascination with its B-sides, squiggles, and ephemera.

THE *NEW YORKER* AND SEPTEMBER 11

Spiegelman's post-*Maus* period favored single-page art and political topicality to the long-form historical narrative embodied by the two-volume memoir. For the now-celebrated cartoonist, it wasn't so much a conscious decision to change from one style to another as a subtle adjustment to personal circumstances and the vagaries of history. Spiegelman took up a job that carried scheduled responsibilities and found himself raising two teenagers, all while having to grapple with two unexpected military invasions and an unwelcome revival of nationalism. He started working as a staff artist for the *New Yorker* in 1992 and ended his affiliation with the magazine in the wake of the September 11, 2001, attacks. In fact, his stint at the *New Yorker*—bookended by the First Gulf War and the invasion of Iraq in 2003—is closely enmeshed with his experience of America's Middle Eastern policy and response to terrorism.

When the first plane hit the North Tower on September 11, 2001, Spiegelman and Mouly were heading out to vote in the city's Democratic mayoral primaries. The anguished parents immediately rushed to find Nadja at Stuyvesant High School, just four blocks from the towers, and Dash at the UN International school further uptown. The events of that day affected Spiegelman in ways that resonated with Vladek's memories of the Holocaust, but before he could gather his thoughts and make sense of his response, the *New Yorker* needed an appropriately themed cover. Spiegelman, Mouly, and David Remnick, editor of the *New Yorker* since 1998, had very different ideas for this historic design: Spiegelman drew a striking black-on-blue sketch to reflect the loss and grief on that clear September morning; Remnick, however, pressured by the trauma of the uncartoonable real, wanted to use a photo for the first time in the magazine's seventy-five-year history; Mouly meanwhile fancied a radical, all-black cover. The winning image—a black silhouette of the towers against a black background—was a fitting compromise. It certainly suited the haptic sensibility of both Mouly and Spiegelman, who always regarded comics as a gestalt experience addressing all the senses and now had to make sure the nearly identical shades of black formed a palpable contrast. The success of the 9/11 cover, one of the most memorable representations of that day and its aftermath, was again, much like *Maus*, hardly anticipated or intended. The optical illusion had been Mouly's idea, even though she credited only Spiegelman for the design; they had conceived that image together, the same way that *RAW* had sprung from both their minds.

By the time the towers fell, Spiegelman had been drawing political covers for the magazine for years (he contributed a total of 39). When he came on in 1992, the *New Yorker* retained little of the edginess that had infused it in the 1960s, when it had serialized Hannah Arendt's reporting on the Eichmann trial. Often derided as pedantic and insular, the *New Yorker* was a Caspar Milquetoast to Spiegelman's radicalism. Its sedate covers, which aspired to remain unmemorable and unstirring, could not contrast more with Spiegelman's preferences—both for his own work, in which covers stood out as much as content, and for the choices he made in his covers for literary works (he provided cover designs for novels by Boris Vian and Paul Auster), which could stand alone, independently of the book they packaged. It's easy to imagine what Spiegelman would have thought of the *New Yorker*'s covers in 1968, the year he was hospitalized for an LSD-induced meltdown and his mother died. "To look through the covers of the peak year of protest, 1968," John Updike writes in his introduction to *The Complete Book of Covers from the "New Yorker": 1925–1989*, "is to survey a world at peace with itself, of blooming cherry trees and sleeping dogs."[54]

Spiegelman was hired to break up this apathy when Tina Brown of *Vanity Fair* took over as editor. Brown decided to make herself more at home by bringing on Richard Avedon as first staff photographer, alongside two cartoonists: Spiegelman was one; the other, Edward Sorel, a political sketch artist and illustrator, was more in line with the *New Yorker*'s nonnarrative cover tradition. Spiegelman, by contrast, aimed to tell uncomfortable stories that readers could argue about. Updike rightly noted that African Americans were conspicuously absent in the *New Yorker*'s covers, even after the 1960s' bloody race riots, and Spiegelman seemed to share that sentiment when in 1993, two years after the Crown Heights riots in Brooklyn, the cartoonist created an interracial

Valentine's Day image featuring a Hasidic man kissing a Black woman—his first published cover for the magazine. Spiegelman admitted that the cover was "knowingly naive" and that tensions in Crown Heights could not "be kissed away," but he also hoped that "once a year, perhaps, it's permissible . . . to close one's eyes, see beyond the tragic complexities of modern life, and imagine that it might really be true that 'All you need is love.'"[55] Mouly, who encouraged his polemical style, brought other *RAW* contributors to the *New Yorker*. For Spiegelman, being only one in a large stable of cartoonists eased the pressure of worrying about how his ideas fit with the ethos of the magazine. What he opted for—and was allowed to publish—were potent covers that broke political taboos without outrageously disregarding mainstream rules of taste.[56]

Spiegelman enjoyed cartooning again not least because working for the magazine felt like one of those "holding actions and exploratory probes" that he preferred after the long stint on *Maus* had left him wary of commitment.[57] Aside from inflammatory covers, he published occasional comic strips and essays. In 1997, he contributed to *Six Nudes with Baguettes*, a collection of two-color postcards assembled with five other cartoonists, placing his subjects in concentration camps in a clear throwback to *Maus*. Spiegelman also brought his interest in comics history onto the pages of the *New Yorker* in the form of prose. Some essays he contributed were conventional book reviews of comics publications; among these, his obituary for Harvey Kurtzman stands out by being crafted as a comics essay. Other pieces were in the vein of Joe Sacco and Sue Coe, especially his comic strip on German xenophobia, based on a book tour to Rostock after a series of anti-immigrant attacks in the East German city in 1992. Over the years Spiegelman used many opportunities to pay homage to comics masters, including them in this way in the elevated cultural ranks the *New Yorker* represented. His poignant essay on the versatile voice and baffling suicide of Jack Cole—accompanied by a matching cover—was expanded into a book-length study in 2001. Compiled with graphic designer Chip Kidd, the book is an idiosyncratic riff on *Plastic Man* and his enigmatic maker. In keeping with Spiegelman's own return at the time to traditional cartooning venues like newspapers and magazines, *Jack Cole and Plastic Man: Forms Stretched to Their Limits* highlights the faded textures of Cole's strips printed on poor quality paper and the waxy pinup watercolors he contributed to *Playboy* in the 1950s. When Spiegelman decided not to renew his contract with the *New Yorker* in 2003, he did so partly because Remnick had declined to publish the anti-war cartoons Spiegelman was successfully placing in European newspapers.[58] Mouly remained in charge of the magazine's artistic look, which—in no small measure thanks to Spiegelman's contributions—had gained a reputation for its visual whimsy and acerbic politics.

"The Plastic Arts," *New Yorker* cover, 4/19/1999. Copyright © 1999 by Art Spiegelman.

In the Shadow of No Towers (2004), first serialized in the German weekly *Die Zeit* then issued in book-form by Pantheon, was Spiegelman's most high-profile work in this period. Whereas *Maus* dwelled on the trauma inflicted by the Nazi death camps on his parents, *No Towers* more straightforwardly chronicles Spiegelman's own struggle with the distress of being under attack. It is also an expression of his outrage at the Bush administration's policy on the Middle East and at the Patriot Act's infringement on civil liberties. The book draws its authority from the persona that Spiegelman had already established as a secondary witness to his parents' experience of World War II. In *No Towers*, he frequently compares the Nuremberg laws with the increase in anti-Muslim sentiment during George W. Bush's presidency. In many ways, then, decades after the retelling of his family history, Spiegelman was still animated by the energy that came from *Maus*, which carried his work through different permutations more or less evocative of that book.

LATE STYLE: FROM TOON TO TRUMP

What continues to attract Spiegelman to comics is, he has said, their ability to mimic the way the mind works. By lining up words and images, comics creates cognitive units that can be narrative-driven, impressionistic, or totally nonsensical. Being a cartoonist, then, requires at least a basic understanding of cognition, and Mouly in fact was enrolled in a neuroscience program before abandoning her studies when Dash was born.[59] Spiegelman's own interest in cognition drew his attention to the early developmental stages of childhood. Children often learn to decipher image stories before they are taught to read, but it's the formative moment when the two languages intersect that comics can capture especially well. If they work so effectively with children, it's not so much due to their young age as to their unformed linguistic skills. When Vladek was sketching the outlines of Nazi camps in *Maus*, he, too, was using cartoons as a primordial form of communication. When his memory and vocabulary failed, he took up a pencil and drew what he could recall, in broken lines and fuzzy detail. It's this quality of comics as a subliminal, barebones language that informed Spiegelman's interest in the sketches drawn by inmates in the Nazi concentration camps—austere images that left an imprint on the timorous, queasy shapes of *Maus*.[60]

It was therefore hardly surprising when, in the late 1990s, Spiegelman revisited his medium's hybridity by exploring children's comics. At that point, there was little rawness left in adult comics. On the other hand, comics for kids were, Spiegelman claimed, a dying breed in urgent need of a new life raft. Mouly and Spiegelman again manufactured one together when in 1999 they founded Raw Junior and the anthology series *Little Lit*, featuring senior *RAW* alumni like Charles Burns, Richard McGuire, and Chris Ware alongside renowned authors of children's books, among them Maurice Sendak, Daniel Handler a.k.a. Lemony Snicket, and William Joyce. In 2006, Penguin signed up to publish TOON Books, a series of comics Easy Readers, but before long, in 2008, Mouly launched TOON as an independent publisher. Although she was and remains the powerhouse behind TOON, Spiegelman wrote one of the early books (*Jack and the Box*, 2008). Echoes of *Maus*'s legacy percolate through other TOON Books, too: in Frank Viva's *A Trip to the Bottom of the World* (2012), for instance, in which a mouse sails to the Antarctic. For Spiegelman,

TOON Books was part of a larger shift, away from well-worn themes and more traditional forms of cartooning, toward projects that opened up the comics medium to new inter-art dialogues.

With "Hapless Hooligan in 'Still Moving'" (2010), a collaboration with the Pilobolus Dance Theater, Spiegelman incorporated elements of theater and dance in a performance that transformed the stage into a comics panel and vice versa. In *The Ghosts of Ellis Island* (2014), he paired up with the French artist JR to revisit the famous immigrant hospital facing the Statue of Liberty. For *WORDLESS!* (2014–)—a hybrid of PowerPoint comics history and musical

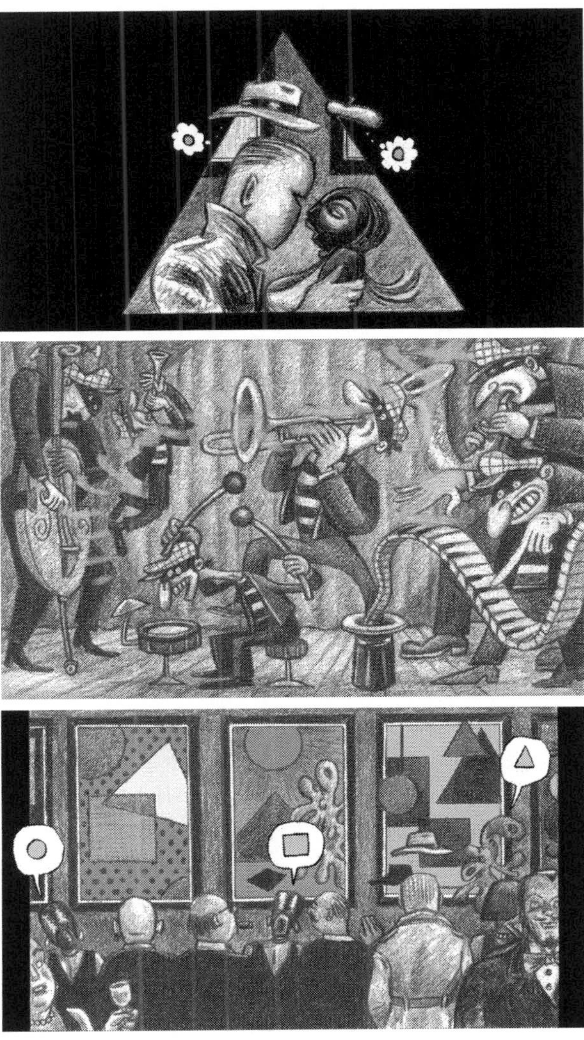

"Shaping Thought," from the performance *WORDLESS!* Copyright © 2014 by Art Spiegelman.

performance that included the new comic strip "Shaping Thought," Spiegelman toured college towns with the acclaimed jazz composer Phillip Johnston. He stood before a lectern outlining precursor styles and artists from both sides of the high/low divide who had influenced his work. The idea for *WORDLESS!* came when Spiegelman was invited by the Library of America to edit and preface its two-volume set of Lynd Ward's complete woodcut novels (which he did in 2010).[61] Putting Ward on a par with classic American authors not only confirmed that comics had finally arrived, but also prompted Spiegelman to unearth, champion, and recover obscure comics masterworks. In 2016, he paired with Abrams to edit and introduce Si Lewen's wordless epic *Parade* about the bloody wars of the twentieth century. Lewen, a Polish-Jewish refugee who fled to the US and later witnessed the liberation of Buchenwald as a Ritchie Boy in the US Army, died the same year.

With *MetaMaus: A Look Inside a Modern Classic* (2011) and *Co-Mix: A Retrospective of Comics, Graphics and Scraps* (2013), Spiegelman directed this new archival curiosity at himself, celebrating his life's work in a way that marked a natural close to his career. Only the election of Donald Trump in 2016 managed to bring him back from retirement. When his wife and daughter edited an anti-Trump comics collection in late 2016, to be distributed for free on Inauguration Day and at women's marches across the country, Spiegelman contributed a single-page (and single-word) panel in the style of political cartoonist Art Young, about whom he and Mouly penned an essay for the *New Yorker*.[62] He hasn't yet come out with a visual representation of Trump himself, but has been looking to Philip Guston's 1970s Nixon sketches for inspiration.[63]

THE RISE OF COMICS: NO SMOOTH SAILING

As a writer, graphic artist, editor, and publisher, Spiegelman personifies an era of comics history in which the art form tried to wrest itself away from its lower pedigree in the yellow press without, however, endorsing or reproducing the exclusionary logic of high culture. Yet to see in Spiegelman only the emblem of the celebrated artist who could never do anything wrong, was invariably greeted with wide acclaim, and branched out into new areas with immediate success, is to elide the less auspicious side of his career, or of any career, really, in the heavily antiprofessional, antiacademic field of comics.[64]

Some of Spiegelman's most exciting projects are the books he envisaged but never completed. One was an extended sequel to *Ace Hole, Midget Detective*, with the satire now directed at the Western genre. In many ways, that project would have meant treading water or going backwards artistically, so it is hardly surprising it never materialized, particularly after the mainstream acclaim of

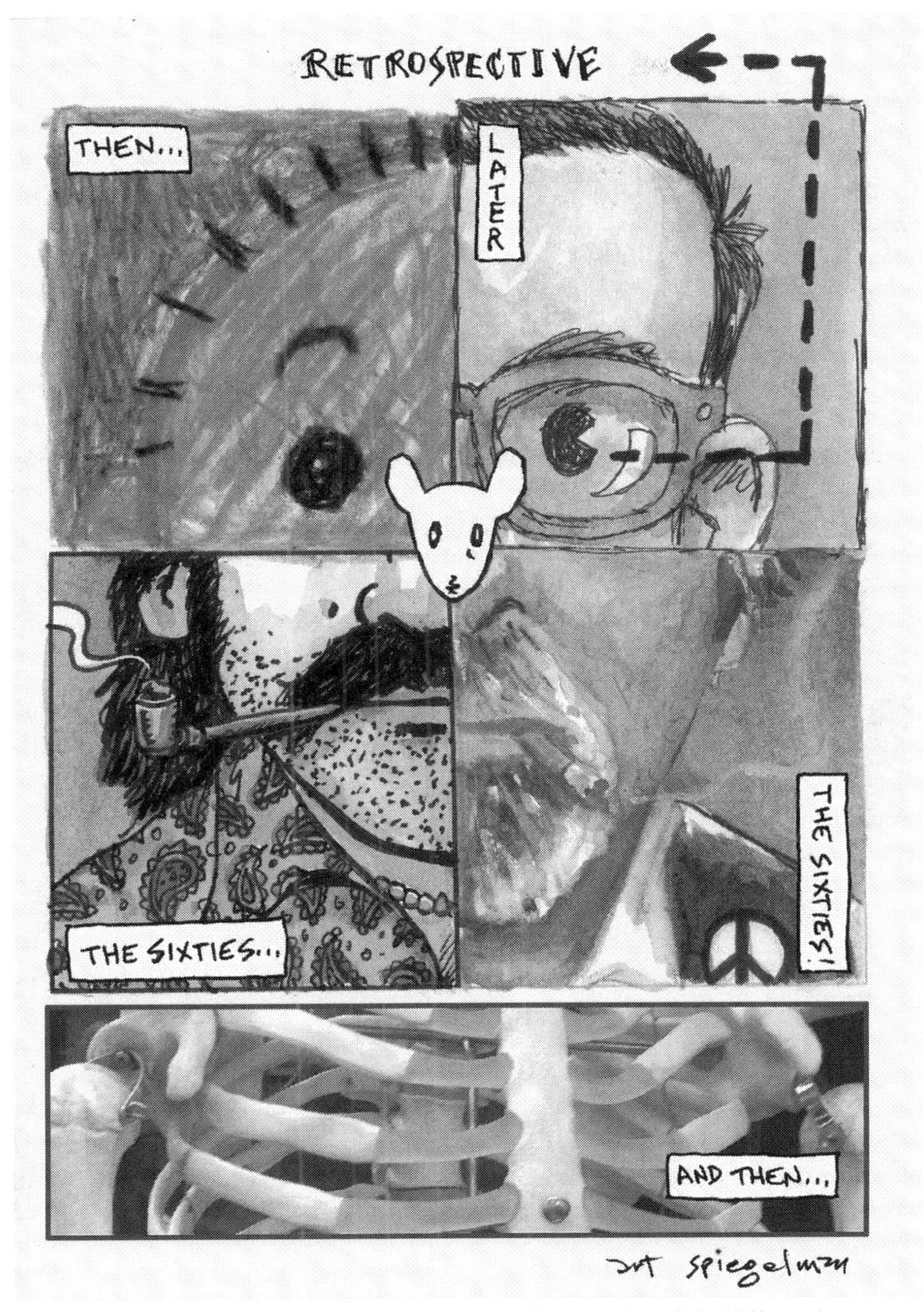

Self-portrait from the *New York Times*, 10/13/2013, on the occasion of a retrospective at the Jewish Museum in Manhattan. Copyright © 2013 by Art Spiegelman.

Maus. Another project that almost happened is *A Life in Ink*, the biography of a fictional cartoonist whose life spans the century-long history of the comics medium (1880–1980). Spiegelman planned to put his chameleonic abilities to use by recounting each section in a different format and style. Other projects that never fully gestated were editorial or art historical. In the 1970s, at the height of his experimental phase, Spiegelman set out to write a monograph on the nineteenth-century Swiss comics artist Rodolphe Töpffer, whose 1830s comic strips Mouly intended to translate. Conversely, Mouly was interested in translating essays by proto-surrealist French writer Alfred Jarry, with Spiegelman slated to illustrate them. Together, they also planned to retrieve and reprint various illustrations from European magazines including *L'Assiette au Beurre* and *Simplicissimus*.[65] While the influence of this material on their subsequent works is evident, neither the translations nor the editions of European comics ever made it into print.

In 1994, Spiegelman announced yet another book about the history and aesthetics of comics, flanked by separate comics projects documenting the rise of the medium. In fact, he has talked about this archeology of comics—one seeking to excavate, among other things, the formative influence of Töppfer's inventive caricatures—so many times in his interviews, that one could be forgiven for thinking he actually wrote it. Other projects have remained dormant for decades and may never fully materialize. Before the attacks of September 11, 2001, interrupted his routine and rearranged his priorities, Spiegelman was writing the story and preparing the sets for a music theater piece about comics censorship in the 1950s, entitled "Drawn to Death: A Three Panel Opera." The initially envisaged collaboration with composer and producer Van Dyke Parks didn't work out, however, and Spiegelman moved on to jazz composer Phillip Johnston, though in the end he and Johnston joined forces on something quite nonoperatic: the *WORDLESS!* multimedia tour.

It's conceivable that many of these projects simply got lost in the gap between the grand scale of Spiegelman's plans and the laboriousness required to bring them into the world. His perfectionism is also to blame. Both *RAW* and *Maus* were milestones—products of his desire "to get it right no matter what it took, as opposed to wanting to get it out and build on your former achievement in the next strip and hopefully, over time, leave a trail of other pieces of work that got you there."[66] Spiegelman has always wanted his works to be fully realized, with no trace of the temporary scaffolding that lent them structure and support at different stages. At the same time, his work often seems to emerge in defiance of his self-critical nature. The results are all the more precious for having escaped a mind so unwilling to let them go. Spiegelman has written at length about how for every cartoon he creates he is forced to surmount tremendous inner barriers, how every one of his panels materializes painfully from a pile of sketches, notes, drafts, and tryouts. Eking out a single page could take anything from two days to two months; *Maus* pages, for instance, took him about eight workdays each.[67] Being a comics celebrity has slowed him down even more, in addition to making him nervous about creating new work. "There are many wonderful cartoonists who are known to hundreds of people," he wistfully noted in the aftermath of his blockbuster success with *Maus*. "In some ways, I find their situation very enviable."[68]

Spiegelman's career path is indeed partly a function of the languid pace at which he produces new pages. His comics demand to be read slowly not least because they were a long time in the making. "I sweat these things out," he confessed to Lawrence Weschler, "one or two panels a day, a page maybe a week. And I was damned if I was going to put in all that work for a few chuckles."[69] For him, escapist stories, jokes, or science fiction fantasies are simply not worth the amount of work involved. It was for the same reason that after he considered serializing *Maus* in the monthly French magazine *A Suivre*, Spiegelman finally decided that *RAW*'s irregular publishing schedule would be a better fit for his methods. In not living by deadlines and spreadsheets, he imported the bohemian productivity cycles of the fine arts into the comics industry, which had long relied on a strict schedule of daily strips and on hand-to-mouth financial arrangements. The fact that *Maus* remains in print suggests Spiegelman's intuition was correct: in the sphere of art comics as in that of high modernism, scarcity pays better than continuous work, especially when the artist is ill-equipped for consistent production in the first place. A second *Maus* isn't needed to move the needle on Spiegelman's canonical standing. The uniqueness of the book—as a singular, unrepeatable "One Shot"—firmly entrenches its importance.

Spiegelman's irregular publications also tell us something about the cartoonist's struggle to work in a medium that was still closely associated with leisure. As he quipped in one interview, only half in jest: "I think all cartoonists start by drawing naked girls and blown-apart bodies and monsters on lined sheets of notebook paper when they should be doing their schoolwork."[70] In his sketchbook, he refers to some of his doodles as a way to avoid working on *Maus*. In the late 1970s, he was publishing *Ed Head* for Hefner's *Playboy* magazine as a relaxing diversion from his story of the Holocaust. The stop-and-start, unfinished quality of his career is emblematic of that moment in the history of comics when comics became a vocation, when doodling was no longer a welcome distraction from schoolwork; it *was* the schoolwork.

Having noted the obstacles posed by the lack of a high-cultural infrastructure for comics, we might also consider why the era that overlapped with Spiegelman's artistic peak was so propitious to comics. Spiegelman's comics arguably struck a chord with a burgeoning culture industry that aspired to integrate popular arts into the museums and merchandize previously unsaleable underground art. When they were flocking to Spiegelman's SoHo loft for "Comics 101"—a lecture designed to outline the history and promise of the medium—museum and art gallery curators were looking for the kind of amphibian, both niche and salable works, of which *Maus* counted as a prime example. Culture was emerging as an economic imperative in the 1980s and 1990s, spawning fresh agendas for creative industries dependent on consumer publics whose tastes were becoming newly omnivorous.

Informed by the climate and controversies surrounding the 1990 MoMA "High & Low" exhibition, art historian Thomas Crow in *Modern Art in the Common Culture* labeled this shared terrain simply "visual culture." To him, "a postmodern outlook can afford no exclusion of the Hollywood films, television productions, glossy advertisements, computer graphics, and all the other enticing visual products of the age."[71] Comics might easily be added to that list. Spiegelman embodies this paradox of comics culture to the extent that he comfortably inhabits both the organized universe of academia and art sponsorship (he was awarded an Honorary Doctorate of Letters by SUNY Binghamton and an Honorary Doctorate of Fine Arts by Rhode Island School of Design, along with a Guggenheim) and the post-underground alternative scene, forging a unique liminal position with his artisanal artifacts, offbeat lecture tours, and zany cross-art collaborations.

Finally, no overview of Spiegelman's six-decade career or of comics's vertiginous rise could ever be complete without due credit to the other constant in Spiegelman's career, besides *Maus*—the artistic companionship of his wife, Françoise Mouly. Gary Panter once described the comics power couple as "two super-intelligent people forming one mind."[72] Jeet Heer rightly notes that Mouly has been neglected. "For every article on Mouly," he observes, "there are at least a hundred profiles of her husband."[73] But far from being a footnote to her husband's success, Mouly's own accomplishments as a SoHo-based Sylvia Beach to Europe and America's emergent graphic arts helped entrench Spiegelman's impact on the medium and secure his legacy. His formal experiments would likely have been less daring if she hadn't been there to share his passion for fine art finesse and avant-garde flamboyance. *Maus* might not exist today if Mouly hadn't bucked the Marvel trend by founding *RAW*. Spiegelman's post-*Maus* material might well have been little more than a tired encore to his masterpiece if Mouly hadn't made waves as a visionary editor and tireless talent scout at the *New Yorker*. If nothing else, Spiegelman benefited from what their daughter, Nadja, in her family memoir focused on her mother, reverently described as "the buoying sensation that often came from being with her, that feeling of invincibility."[74]

And yet, even taking Mouly's inspiring, energizing presence into account and the ways in which Spiegelman's personal talent synced so marvelously with the history of his chosen medium, in the end comics might owe their upward mobility in no small measure to a streak of sheer good fortune. It wasn't the best who survived Auschwitz, Vladek exclaims in *Maus*, it was random! By a stroke of luck, he and Anja lived to see the end of the war. Another happy happenstance allowed Mouly to survive a suicide attempt in her youth, before moving to New York and meeting Spiegelman. As luck would have it, years later, Mouly would come across a copy of Spiegelman's graphic story of his mother's suicide and decide he was someone she wanted to meet. Some may begrudge Spiegelman the success that has followed him at every step since then, but his pages have come into the world through layers upon layers of private and historical serendipity.[75]

INFLUENCES: COMICS, LITERATURE, AND THE ARTS

Primary among Spiegelman's influences are the protocartoonists of nineteenth-century France. Both he and Mouly have raved about Gustave Doré's *The Rare and Extraordinary History of Holy Russia*, a piece of satirical propaganda composed of 500 illustrations published in 1854 at the height of the Crimean War.[76] When teaching the history of comics, Spiegelman lays particular emphasis on the pre-Code era, comics before 1910, and protocomics such as woodcuts.[77] As a comics historian, he has drawn attention to Wilhelm Busch's *Max and Moritz* (1865) as well as to the debut of *The Katzenjammer Kids* in William Randolph Hearst's *New York Journal* in 1897.[78] With Mouly in *RAW*, Spiegelman resuscitated European printmaking and illustration arts to trace their impact on US cartooning.[79] The European artists to whom he feels most indebted have left an imprint on distinct art forms—such as Töpffer, who influenced the symbolist iconoclast Alfred Jarry, the avant-garde poet Jean Cocteau, and Doré's wood engraving illustrations.

Among fellow cartoonists, key influences include Winsor McCay, Lionel Feininger, Harry Hershfield, George Herriman, Chester Gould, Will Eisner, Harvey Kurtzman, and Jack Cole. Spiegelman would later credit the McCay of *Little Nemo* and *Dreams of a Rarebit Fiend* in particular for teaching him the "architectonic rigor" he would apply in composing the pages of *Maus*.[80] From Kurtzman, he borrowed "very rigid approaches to panel breakdown, like dividing a row into two, three, or four, trying to keep an equal ratio. . . . each page being a unit of information and each row being a sub-unit of information as an organizational device."[81] In addition, it was the sexual compulsions of

R. Crumb's *Fritz the Cat* that opened up for him the prospect of "adult" comics, though his interest in the porno aspects of comics adulthood would be short lived. "Prisoner on the Hell Planet" was inspired by Justin Green's 1972 comic book *Binky Brown Meets the Holy Virgin Mary*. And, as he proceeded to work on his graphic memoir, drawing the same mice over and over again, he even found new respect for Carl Barks.[82]

Seen as literature rather than popular culture, Spiegelman's comics are an example of that wayward literary style which modernist literature scholar Ross Chambers has jestingly called "loiterature."[83] This poetics of digression goes back to Russian Formalism, whose theoretician, Viktor Shklovsky, in turn drew on the disordered fictional practices of eighteenth-century English novelist Laurence Sterne to describe the concept of artistic "defamiliarization."[84] Both Shklovsky and Sterne count among Spiegelman's influences. He cites Shklovsky's "Art as Technique" verbatim in his strip "Form and Content," but admires Sterne for a different reason, namely his ability to probe the limits of a genre, the novel, that was still tentative and unsettled—unlike Joyce, for instance, whose experiments were partly driven by fatigue with the form.[85] Spiegelman's "loiterature" also draws its vitality from the oppositional politics of the tumultuous late sixties.

He was formed as much by the death of his mother in 1968 as by the disturbances of the same year as a political moment that opened up spaces of reversal and leeway, which would go on to inform postmodern writing in the 1970s. The individual writers who stimulated Spiegelman over the years aren't as easy to classify. His tastes have been catholic, ranging from William Faulkner, Vladimir Nabokov, and French existentialism to the hard-boiled noir of Dashiell Hammett, Raymond Chandler, and James M. Cain.[86] Modernists receive the most nods in his interviews and are usually credited with a single, formative feature that found its way into his work: Gertrude Stein's "organized stuttering,"[87] Proust's multivolume projects,[88] Kafka's *Twilight Zone* quality.[89] In the early 1970s, on a trip to Los Angeles, Spiegelman also spent three "electric" days talking to SF legend Philip K. Dick.[90]

To be sure, Spiegelman's experimental tweaks of comics owed more to visual culture than to literature. Fine art influences are at their loudest in *Breakdowns*. "Nervous Rex: The Malpractice Suite" (1976), to name one example, blends the Milton Caniff noir style of mid-century comics with skewed assemblages of cubist provenance. The notion that the narrative space between the panels holds as much significance as the story inside—a concept that informs *Maus*, and which Scott McCloud popularized with *Understanding Comics*—also evolved from the encounter between painting and comics. When the painter Bernard Krigstein stumbled into the comics scene in 1926, he immediately became interested in what lay hidden in the gutter: "Look at all that dramatic action that one never gets a chance to see," he lamented. "It's between these panels that the fascinating stuff takes place. And unless the artist would be permitted to delve into that, the form must remain infantile."[91] Comics history might have taken a different path had Krigstein—who did not script his own comics—not been forced to adjust his sketches to the amount of text he was assigned to illustrate. Frustrated by the text to page-count ratio, Krigstein started to frantically subdivide the panels. His meticulous breakdown of the story resulted in a frenzy of precipitated action that highlighted slower sequences to create a technique that inspired Spiegelman's own play with narrative rhythm and visual cadence.

Other fine art influences were mediated by Mouly's coloring preferences: the austere palettes of Russian constructivism, or her interest in white space. She used both of them in *RAW* to shock comics out of their alignment with the garish underground, bringing the medium more in line with the black-and-white aesthetic of woodcut prints. Spiegelman suffers from amblyopia, which impairs his ability to see in three dimensions. The visual flattening and difficulty in judging depth that characterize this condition may, by way of compensation, have sparked his interest in depth of field, geometry, and lighting. In her memoir, *I'm Supposed to Protect You from All This*, Nadja Spiegelman recalls a visit to an Edward Hopper exhibition at Paris's Museum of Modern Art, during which her father took the time to explain to her the way light entered the canvas and how the carefully diagrammed lines drew the viewer into the painting.[92] And yet the clean, clear physical presence of Hopper's figures clashes with Spiegelman's coarser drawing style. What interests the comics artist is the moment "where things are flipping over"—not the realism of the Dutch masters or the drip painting of Jackson Pollock, but the pointillism of Georges Seurat, which marks the "lynchpin" between figurative art and textured surfaces.[93]

A major influence on Spiegelman was the cartoon illustrator Saul Steinberg, a Romanian-born Jewish émigré who drew his first cover for the *New Yorker* in 1945. Like Steinberg, Spiegelman has many arrows in his quiver that he can deploy on different occasions, sometimes even in the same picture, to dramatic effect. Steinberg praised the metapictorial quality of Spiegelman's 1999 *New Yorker* cover about police racism, calling the cartoon "a picture of a picture"—that is, a visual quotation that recasts familiar icons in new, disturbing ways.[94] It wasn't just Spiegelman's stocky New York police officer that created a meta-image by recalling idyllic turn-of-the-century urban comics. *Maus*, too, appropriated Nazi symbols in ways that retooled their violence to evoke the suffering of Jewish victims. The success of Spiegelman's symbolic negotiations rests, of course, on the political credibility of the vehicles in which they appeared. The anthropomorphic mice or the officer aiming at humanoid black targets in a shooting gallery could be seen as crude, racist agitprop if the respective covers did not visibly display the title of a liberal magazine (the

New Yorker) or, in the case of *Maus*, the name of a publishing house founded by émigré European Jews (Pantheon). Moreover, Pop artists like Warhol and Lichtenstein had proven that popular culture thrived on condensed imagery and logo-like emblems that nestled in the mind.

While many of Spiegelman's visual influences were derived from contemporary works, the soundtrack to Spiegelman's comics has always been jazz, whose piecemeal, improvisational aesthetic his drawings emulate on many levels. Of *RAW* magazine, he once noted: "To me it's like a nice piece of 1920s jazz. It's like these various riffs. It's this little pinball machine that's been set up for your eye to ricochet through."[95] While drawing *Maus* in his soundproofed atelier, Spiegelman would listen to the complete works of the Comedian Harmonists—a German ensemble from the late 1920s and 1930s made up partly of Jewish musicians, which got the group into trouble with the Nazi regime. The *Maus* playlist included other pieces from that era, by Cab Calloway and others, which were often used in *Betty Boop* film soundtracks.[96]

Spiegelman's stubborn refusal to sanction any film adaptations of *Maus* obscures the otherwise lasting impact of cinema on the themes and styles of his comics. Inspirations run the gamut, including films that left an imprint on Spiegelman's modernist style, such as the expressionist silent films of Fritz Lang; films he detested, like Steven Spielberg's *An American Tail*, *Life Is Beautiful*, and *Schindler's List*;[97] Claude Lanzmann's *Shoah*, whose tenor and detail shaped the fabric of *Maus*; and Buster Keaton's silent comedies, echoes of which he detected in Kurtzman's "impeccable timing" and "tight sense of structure,"[98] as well as in the dialogues and cinematic imagination of Milt Gross. In modern film, he admires associational arrangements that demand as much from the viewer as they do from the filmmaker. A key influence in this regard was the experimental filmmaker Ken Jacobs, one among a number of avant-garde film artists like Stan Brakhage and Ernie Gehr whose poetic craft relied on lyrical image sequences rather than conventional film prose.[99] Spiegelman was friends with Jacobs and Gehr in Binghamton, and even though he initially found their work "totally opaque," he learned to understand it.[100]

LEGACIES

Spiegelman's most lasting legacy has been in the genre of autobiographical comics. Chris Ware, Alice Bechdel, Marjane Satrapi, Emil Ferris, and many others have followed the trail that Spiegelman's confessional comics blazed four decades ago. Another key impact has been indirect, through the artists brought together and shaped by editorial projects like *RAW*. Spiegelman arguably made comics history when he discovered Chris Ware in a University of Texas student newspaper and asked him to draw for his magazine. The geographically dispersed comics community he and Mouly developed fostered the kind of cross-fertilizing exchanges that the Bloomsbury Group and the Hogarth Press once made possible for the modernist crowd. Though Spiegelman wryly referred to *RAW*'s first issue as a "Potemkin village"—a hollow façade that aimed to showcase a global comics scene well before any such thing truly existed—the comics world was a bustling city by the time the magazine closed its doors.[101]

As Spiegelman transitioned from bold, formally stark imagery to looser personal narratives, his own publishing efforts and the entire cohort of cartoonists around him were absorbed by the mainstream. The last three issues of *RAW* magazine were produced and distributed by Penguin Books, while Pantheon, which now co-published the *RAW* books edited by Mouly and Spiegelman, also embraced many of the magazine's alumni, including Ware, Burns, Panter, and Katchor, who went on to become masters of the medium in their own right. Spiegelman also supported Aline Kominsky-Crumb, Diane Noomin, MK Brown, and other women artists associated with *Weirdo* magazine—R. Crumb's competition to *RAW*—as well as with the Wimmen's Comix Collective. Spiegelman's cultivation of an inner circle, comprising the artists he agreed to publish in *Arcade* and *RAW*, sometimes drew the ire of fellow cartoonists.[102] And yet, despite the hard choices he had to make and which eventually put him off the business of editing, whatever attention he brought to the medium was something all of its practitioners benefited from, personally and as a group.

RAW itself would certainly not have enjoyed the same success and its contributors might have been less likely to find work at other venues if Mouly hadn't been appointed art director at the *New Yorker* in 1993 and gone on to greenlight many iconic cartoon covers, making the format not only acceptable but trendy. At *RAW*, it wasn't Mouly's role as colorist that left a mark on comics artistry; many wives had previously been recruited to do the coloring for their cartoonist husbands. It was the inspired style choices she made for the edgy magazine—after both she and Spiegelman had reluctantly worked as colorists for Marvel in the 1970s—that elevated the coloring craft to a genuine art form. The palette that Mouly used in Joost Swarte's cover for *RAW* Vol. 2, for instance, originated a style of muted tones that left a lasting imprint on the comics of Chris Ware.[103]

More circuitously, the success of *Maus* and Spiegelman's privileged position in U.S. publishing drew attention to the comics artists that informed his work and have since become, like Krigstein and McCay, the subjects of extensive biographies. Through his work and advocacy, Spiegelman has bestowed a new gravitas on the history of comics, cementing the idea that the medium has an archive well worth cataloguing. Spiegelman's fascination with the "language" of comics has always been accompanied by an interest in how comics became a language in the first place, who spoke it, and with what degree of skill.[104] This "intense historical consciousness, his awareness of how comics have evolved and where they need to go" has been the driving force behind Spiegelman's tireless advocacy of comics and cartooning.[105] As we pointed out earlier, he has never published a comprehensive history of comics. His "Comics 101" lecture was never meant to be exhaustive; in fact, it aimed to boil its subject down "to something that can be said while someone stands on one leg."[106] Yet scattered through his statements over the years are astute observations about the evolution of comics: about the temporal dimensionality that separates comics from cartoons; the origin of comics in the invention of the printing press; the entwinement of comics semiotics with the sign systems adopted by adherents of physiognomy like Töpffer.[107] In ways that confirm Spiegelman's cultural stature, even the most cursory of his observations has triggered substantial responses.

CRITICAL RECEPTION

More so than with other cartoonists, readings of Spiegelman's work have defied disciplinary boundaries. His comics are uncommonly intersectional partly due to the variety of his own experiences. The number of support groups he could join, he once quipped, is endless: second-generation Holocaust survivors, parental suicide group, frustrated artists, or mental hospital alumni.[108] As Spiegelman himself has pointed out, "*Maus* has been a beneficiary of identity politics."[109] The graphic memoir has generated more critical attention than any other work in the history of comics, and perhaps even in the history of Holocaust representation, and is frequently assigned in classes on postmodern literature, life writing, Jewish culture, immigration, twentieth-century history, and visual art.

What made *Maus* into catnip for academic readers also raised improbable expectations about Spiegelman's post-*Maus* career and misrepresented his core intellectual interests. Recognizing in the Holocaust memoir a masterpiece that transcended the low origins of the comics form, critics were eager to address the book as earnestly as possible in the contexts of Jewish culture, genocide, and literary ethics. Though sensitive and groundbreaking, much of this criticism approached *Maus* as essentially a novel or illustrated memoir that only happened to also be a comic book. Scholars rarely invoked the history of comics as an independent art form, instead assimilating *Maus* into what Spiegelman wearily called "a kind of official culture that may not allow it to live and breathe."[110]

Marc Singer has recently documented a similar process of critical deracination for Marjane Satrapi.[111] Even when it did acknowledge Spiegelman's place in comics history, the canonization of *Maus* threatened to paper over the medium's marginal cultural status. "Comics were never meant to be studied at school," Spiegelman said in 1994, "they were meant to be read while the teacher thought you were doing something else."[112] Spiegelman's post-*Maus* career, both as a cartoonist and as a comics historian, has been an uneasy response to the critical success of his memoir. Spiegelman sought recognition for his work and won it, but that recognition threatened to come at the expense of comics itself. To counter this effect, he sought to redirect the critical spotlight on comics, and again he succeeded, but he found that the newly canonized history of comics risked overlooking the subversive grit that made comics alluring in the first place.

Even as Spiegelman reinvented himself post-*Maus*, scholars continued to focus almost exclusively on that book, and understandably so. *Maus* was published just as four distinct areas of research—around the Holocaust, Jewish studies, visual culture, and memory—converged to forge an enduring narrative about the postwar cultural canon. When Maurice Halbwachs's *La mémoire collective* appeared in English in 1980, it ushered in the decade that witnessed the rise of Holocaust Studies. Because it appealed to scholars in all of these fields, it was inevitable that *Maus* would become a touchstone of late twentieth-century critical writing. On the one hand, then, soon after the publication of *Maus*, Spiegelman was inducted into the pantheon of Jewish American literature alongside Cynthia Ozick and Philip Roth, and into the cadre of leading US writers post 1945.[113] On the other, once academics had agreed on the composition of a comics canon, *Maus* became the centerpiece of that new canon, the highest standard against which all other graphic novels and memoirs have been measured.

The book looms large as the chief accomplishment of Spiegelman's career, a truth underlined by the fact that the only volume of essays on Spiegelman's work to date, Deborah Geis's 2003 critical anthology *Considering* Maus*: Approaches to Art Spiegelman's "Survivor's Tale" of the Holocaust*, centers on a single publication. That being said, Geis's collection gives an apt overview of the main directions in Spiegelman criticism. In her introduction, she notes that the writing of *Maus* coincided with a shift from documentary representations of the Holocaust through the eyes of its immediate survivors to the vicarious testimonies of their children, many of whom felt burdened by a responsibility they could not measure up to. These second-generation storytellers chose to set themselves apart from their parents by adopting a postmodern approach meant to suggest "that historical narratives are always fragmented, partial, and subjective."[114]

The anthology successfully assembles these fragments around three focal points: Spiegelman's autobiographical tools (from masks to animal metaphors and photography), the issue of comics as testimonial literature, and the socio-technological challenges of exposing *Maus* to new generations of readers. The chapters retrace the critical landscape of the 1990s that responded to Spiegelman's Holocaust testimony: autobiography and gender studies (Nancy K. Miller), psychoanalysis and trauma (Michael G. Levine), and the commodification of the Holocaust after *Schindler's List* (Michael P. Rothberg).[115] The capstone of *Maus*'s 1990s career in criticism was, of course, its inclusion in Marianne Hirsch's influential examination of visual culture and cultural recall, *Family Frames*.[116] This emphasis on the visual construction of Spiegelman's memoir would shape the critical consensus for years to come.[117] Before it was a celebrated comic book, *Maus* was included in the canon of visual history—as something that Lawrence Langer euphemistically called "pictorial literature"—marked by the fraught distinction between realist representation and imaginative discourse.[118]

After 2003, critics were consistently drawn to the figurative aspects of *Maus* and the artifices that allowed Spiegelman to talk of mice and men at the same time. Amy Hungerford in *The Holocaust of Texts*, analyzing the structure of remembrance in *Maus*, singles out depression as a "technology through which a person's identity transcends the limits of that person's current experience and personal past to encompass experiences—like the Holocaust—that are historically remote from the individual."[119] In this reading, *Maus* signals Art's attempt to replace his depressive melancholia with a narrative-based connection to the past. It's fair to say that while the subject of Vladek's memories informed earlier research on *Maus*, this later phase is characterized by a more Artie-focused metareflection on the transferability of memory and the moral pitfalls of grafting one person's experience onto the story of another.[120]

After the publication of *No Towers* in 2004, Spiegelman's account of 9/11 and its aftermath became one of two authoritative narratives, the other being Don DeLillo's novel *Falling Man*, that were discussed at length by a slew of studies on post-9/11 literary culture.[121] In the past decade, while Spiegelman scholarship continues to be published, almost none of it exceeds the framework established by *Maus* and *No Towers* as the fixed poles of Spiegelman's career.[122] This is partly because *Maus* and *No Towers* largely explore familiar, timeless themes related to history, memory, and trauma.

Yet a new set of questions and methods is emerging in Spiegelman scholarship. Bringing a sociological perspective to the comics field, Bart Beaty and Benjamin Woo show, for example, how *Maus* turned the hitherto meaningless notion of the greatest comic book into a plausible category; and they document how comics has become a repository of cultural capital.[123] Taking a longer perspective on Spiegelman's career, Philip Smith's 2015 study *Reading Art Spiegelman* sets out to decipher Spiegelman's strips as a "means by which he seeks to escape, mock, and oppose hegemonic rationality."[124] Smith detects in *Breakdowns* the antiauthoritarian impulse that allowed underground comics to push against the conformist, commodified pressures of the superhero and pulp mainstream. It's the first significant repositioning of Spiegelman's well-studied canon within a larger framework that includes his early career.[125]

The neglect of late Spiegelman probably has something to do with the expectations that *Maus* set. Many critics hoped Spiegelman would produce another comic on the order of *Maus*. Since the publication of Joseph Witek's volume of conversations in 2007, however, Spiegelman has quietly walked away from being a cartoonist, though he continues to cultivate a public persona, commenting on questions of concern to the worlds of comics, especially with his interventions in the Charlie Hebdo debates. Rather than draw another *Maus*, he has collaborated with performance and graffiti artists, toured with a jazz musician, and used his popularity to promote comics literacy to a new generation of readers. Very few of these efforts have drawn critical attention—an oversight that our volume seeks to redress.

OUR BOOK

If building the world of *Maus* was Spiegelman's obsession in the 1980s, after winning the Pulitzer Special Award in Letters, he could not wait to tear it down. "I'm left with redefining myself in a world that thinks of me as the *Maus* man," he lamented in an interview.[126] Similarly, our volume sets out to demystify the aura that *Maus* has bestowed on its creator in order to highlight important episodes of Spiegelman's career pre- and post-*Maus*. The title of our book—*Artful Breakdowns*—draws, of course, on the pun that Spiegelman inscribed in the title of his first comics collection. Importantly, the "breakdowns" in our title encapsulate our attempt to chart Spiegelman's oeuvre along a continuum that the intense focus on *Maus* has obscured. "Artful," meanwhile, is an attribute that Spiegelman himself would prefer to "arty," a word he bristles at due to its pretentious, "lifted finger" quality.[127] It is probably no coincidence that in the very last panel of his comic-strip introduction to the 2008 edition of *Breakdowns*, he cites from Victor Shklovsky's 1917 essay "Art as Technique": "Art is a way of experiencing the *artfulness* of an object. The object is not important."[128]

Broadly speaking, Spiegelman develops an art form for representing the act and experience of breakdown. At the same time, again and again, Spiegelman himself has broken down, in very public ways, in ways both literal and figurative, artfully. A breakdown, of course, also refers to the laying out of a simplified version of a comics page, placing narrative and script elements into a preliminary order. Our contention is that the tension between artfulness and breakdown, and between order and dissolution, never resolves itself in Spiegelman's oeuvre. It is not so much, as Philip Smith argues, that Spiegelman straightforwardly opposes hegemonic modes of rationality. Instead, Spiegelman's every effort to make sense of what Adorno called "damaged" life is constitutively doomed in advance. Spiegelman's singular talent can be located precisely in the way he turns his inevitable, iterated failure into the very form of his art. Rather than trace a series of developmental stages, telling a story in which Spiegelman moves seamlessly from underground obscurity to post-*Maus* triumph, our volume is organized in four parts—"Modernism and Form," "Radical Politics," "Mediating Memory," and "Comics History"—which investigate specific aspects of Spiegelman's comics cutting across different phases of his career.

Spiegelman's allegiance to a modernist aesthetic and his integrity as "fine" artist with faux mass-cultural credentials is explored in Part 1. In his opening chapter, Shawn Gilmore casts a wide net across Spiegelman's career as avant-garde cartoonist, editor, and historian to argue that a key impetus of his contributions on all these fronts is the desire to create striking assemblages in the tradition of modernist collage. The sheer range of modernist forms that Spiegelman has built on becomes apparent in Ariela Freedman's exploration of jazz as soundtrack and signature key for Spiegelman's improvisational renditions of cross-racial, lowbrow Americana. Taking her cue from Susan Sontag's contention that silence is one of modernism's key tools of innovation and protest, Georgiana Banita looks into how silence has supported Spiegelman's modernist project, from his early wordless cartoons and cover art to the multiple levels of speechlessness coursing through *Maus* and his late homage to woodcut artists of the interwar period.

With his chapter on Spiegelman's aesthetics of transgression, Philip Smith segues into the concerns of Part 2. By charting instances of provocation and subversion across Spiegelman's career, Smith suggests that critical accolades and popular appreciation never dulled the edge of Spiegelman's formal experimentalism, nor did they take the sting out of his cultural critique and non-PC outbursts of outrage. Yet it was *RAW* magazine, Sarah Hamblin shows in the following chapter, that most powerfully channeled Spiegelman's anticapitalist and anti-Reaganite positions—not in spite of its extravagant design, but as an extension of it. And it was with his vocally political cartoons after (and about) the September 11 terrorist strikes—Ken Worcester informs us—that Spiegelman articulated a set of progressive principles which aligned him with others on the Left who held similar antimilitarist views, while souring his relationship with the patriotic *New Yorker*.

Patrick Lawrence applies a different lens to Spiegelman's September 11 comics, one that organizes the essays in Part 3: the role of visual media in Spiegelman's memorialization of personal experience and world-historical trauma. The history of comics is imbued with nostalgia—for simpler times and truths, for the familiar faces of childhood heroes. By evoking early twentieth-century

Manhattan icons like Happy Hooligan or the Katzenjammer Kids, Lawrence suggests, Spiegelman devises a mode of consolation in times of turmoil that is unique to comics. Liza Futerman turns to another form of intertextuality—the presence of family photographs in *Maus*—to assert the authenticity of comics. Despite photography's much-touted facticity, she insists, in representing an event like the Holocaust, comics are better placed to convey the inaccessibility of the past. They do so by impressing the idea that any attempt to remove the masks we use to remember and understand the past will only reveal an even deeper layer of masks underneath, without ever uncovering an incontestable final referent. Of course, the medium most acutely confronted with issues of representability is cinema, and Harriet Earle makes the case that Holocaust cinema, particularly Alain Resnais's harrowing 1956 documentary *Night and Fog*, informed several techniques of mediating affect in *Maus*, from its drawing style to the indirect representation of violence.

The final section takes the measure of Spiegelman's work within a set of broader historical contexts: comics publishing, US immigration and ethnic history, and the debate about the emancipation of comics from their infantile beginnings to their current serious appeal. Colin Beineke makes an argument for a "book history" approach to comics when he casts doubt on what we thought we knew about *Maus*: that it appeared fully-formed as a two-volume graphic memoir in a collected edition from Pantheon Books. Its serialization as insert booklets in *RAW*, Beineke contends, reveals aspects about the book and especially its Jews-as-mice metaphor that are most revealing when read alongside the inserts' companion pages in the magazine. Cara Koehler reimagines the evolution of comics in relation to America's checkered history of racism and xenophobia. Taking Spiegelman's illustrations for JR's photography project *The Ghosts of Ellis Island* as starting point, she recognizes in Spiegelman's hybrid style and concern for the victims of US border politics the echoes of the medium's immigrant roots and of the little-studied conflation between comics' cultural marginalization and the ethnic or racial otherness of many of its iconic practitioners. What is also often overlooked is that while Spiegelman started out by advocating for comics as adult fare, in recent years he has written, edited, and published a wide variety of comics for children. Far from being a paradox, Lee Konstantinou suggests in the volume's closing chapter, by authoring children's comics Spiegelman proves that comics is no longer automatically accessible to children, but a serious genre with its own complex codes in need of painstaking initiation.

Spiegelman has worn many hats: cartoonist, editor, critic, historian. He crafted a medium-making graphic memoir that counts as the most seminal work in comics history, changing the way comics are drawn, read, and discussed. The way he applied himself to this task has transformed the world of comics. As one half of a powerful editor couple, a role that helped secure the legacy of his path-breaking book, he oversaw the formation of a bona fide comics scene in the United States. His work has transformed multiple fields far removed from the core concerns of comics scholarship, among them historiography, Holocaust Studies, and psychoanalysis. It did not come as a surprise when, in 2018, Spiegelman became the first cartoonist to be awarded the prestigious MacDowell Medal for an outstanding contribution to American culture and the arts, joining a preeminent roster of honorees including David Lynch in 2017 and Toni Morrison in 2016. Like Lynch and Morrison, Spiegelman is a recognizable, outspoken artist, an American icon who has created a new visual language for representing identity, and who has played a major role in elevating a whole medium.

Our detailed map of Spiegelman's life in comics and the editorial choices we have made testify to these achievements. Yet they also raise doubts about how inevitable his career path truly was, and whether the success he encountered along the way benefited his artistic sensibility or curtailed his potential. As it is, much of Spiegelman's work beyond *Maus* and *In the Shadow of No Towers*—including the material that is most indicative of his comics vision, such as *RAW*, *Breakdowns*, and his reflections on friends and mentors such as Schulz, Kurtzman, or Lewen—remains woefully underexplored. The number of comics, covers, and sketchbooks he has produced over the years far outstrips the amount of scholarship dedicated to them. His essays in particular, never collected in a single volume, remain criminally underused. That so many of his creations continue to surprise and puzzle us attests that his artistic project of modernist renewal and provocation has succeeded—and did so despite the trappings of canonization, celebrity, and wide cultural acclaim.

Notes

1. Andrea Juno, "Art Spiegelman," in *Art Spiegelman: Conversations*, ed. Joseph Witek (Jackson: University Press of Mississippi, 2007), 185.

2. Bart Beaty and Benjamin Woo, *The Greatest Comic Book of All Time: Symbolic Capital and the Field of American Comic Books* (New York: Palgrave Macmillan, 2016), 18.

3. Michael Silverblatt, "The Cultural Relief of Art Spiegelman: A Conversation with Michael Silverblatt," in *Conversations*, 126–27.

4. Alfred Bergdoll, "Art Spiegelman," in *Conversations*, 11.

5. Bergdoll, "Art Spiegelman," 11.

6. Bergdoll, "Art Spiegelman," 6–7.

7. Dean Mullaney, "*RAW* Magazine: An Interview with Art Spiegelman and Françoise Mouly," in *Conversations*, 21.

8. Silverblatt, "The Cultural Relief," 133.

9. Noami Epel, "Art Spiegelman," in *Conversations*, 146.

10. Graham Smith, "From Mickey to *Maus*: Recalling the Genocide through Cartoon," in *Conversations*, 90.

11. Lawrence Weschler, "Art's Father, Vladek's Son," in *Conversations*, 74.

12. Bergdoll, "Art Spiegelman," 12.

13. Mullaney, "*RAW* Magazine," 34.

14. Juno, "Art Spiegelman," 177.

15. Bergdoll, "Art Spiegelman," 7.

16. Bergdoll, "Art Spiegelman," 9.

17. Michael Fathers, "Art Mimics Life in the Death Camps," in *Conversations*, 124.

18. Bergdoll, "Art Spiegelman," 5.

19. Art Spiegelman, "On Loony Tunes, Zionism, and the Jewish Question," *Village Voice*, June 6, 1989: 21–22. See also Art Spiegelman, "Getting in Touch with My Inner Racist," *Mother Jones*, September/October 1997.

20. Roger Sabin, "Interview with Art Spiegelman," in *Conversations*, 97.

21. Jeet Heer, *In Love with Art: Françoise Mouly's Adventures in Comics with Art Spiegelman* (Toronto: Coach House Books, 2013), 35.

22. Dave Jamieson, *Mint Condition: How Baseball Cards Became an American Obsession* (New York: Atlantic Monthly Press, 2010), 116.

23. Art Spiegelman, "1986 Introduction," in *Harvey Kurtzman's Jungle Book* (Milwaukie, OR: Dark Horse Comics, 2014), 27.

24. Jamieson, *Mint Condition*, 136.

25. Heer, *In Love with Art*, 36.

26. Art Spiegelman, "Ballbuster: Bernard Krigstein's Life Between the Panels," *New Yorker*, July 22, 2002.

27. Spiegelman, "Getting in Touch."

28. Weschler, "Art's Father," 76.

29. "Was my commitment to the mental ward the cause of her suicide? No. Was there a relation? Sure. After the war, she'd invested her whole life in me. I was more like a confidant to her than a son. She couldn't handle the separation." (Ibid., 77)

30. Cited in Patrick Rosenkranz, *Rebel Visions: The Underground Comix Revolution 1963–1975* (Seattle: Fantagraphics Books, 2008), 98.

31. Rosenkranz, *Rebel Visions*, 70.

32. Sabin, "Interview," 98.

33. Silverblatt, "The Cultural Relief," 127.

34. Juno, "Art Spiegelman," 182.

35. Art Spiegelman, *MetaMaus: A Look Inside a Modern Classic,* Maus (New York: Pantheon, 2011), 95.

36. Heer, *In Love with Art*, 31.

37. Heer, *In Love with Art*, 44.

38. Cited in Art Spiegelman, "An Afterword," in *Breakdowns: Portrait of the Artist as a Young %@&*!* (New York: Pantheon, 2008), 34.

39. Heer, *In Love with Art*, 47.

40. The first of these reproduced comic strips by nineteenth-century French satirist and political cartoonist Emmanuel Poiré, who under the pseudonym Caran D'Ache coedited the satirical magazine *Psst . . . !*, made up entirely of editorial caricatures. It was a strange decision, since many of his cartoons were openly anti-Semitic. Mark Beyer did another one, "Manhattan."

41. *Jimbo* by Gary Panter (1982), *How to Commit Suicide in South Africa* by Sue Coe and Holly Metz (1983), *Jack Survives* by Jerry Moriarty (1984), *Invasion of the Elvis Zombies* by Gary Panter (1984), *Big Baby* by Charles Burns (1985), *Agony* by Mark Beyer (1987), *Hard-Boiled Defective Stories* by Charles Burns (1988). More One Shots followed in the 1990s: *Cheap Novelties: The Pleasures of Urban Decay* by Ben Katchor (1991), *X* by Sue Coe (1992), and Spiegelman's chain story graphic novel *The Narrative Corpse*, coedited with Robert Sikoryak (1998). The books were a mixed bag; some prefigured classics to come (by Burns and Katchor), others were less successful. The visual art of Coe's *X* fell short of Mouly's own expectations, and another series by Coe—*Porkopolis*, a muckraking-style feature on the multibillion-dollar farm food production industry based on her trips to fifteen slaughterhouses—never materialized in book form (though Coe released it as a pamphlet in 1989). Coe credits her time at *RAW*, and Mouly in particular, for their influence on this material, which would later be integrated into *Dead Meat* (New York: Four Walls Eight Windows, 1995) and *Cruel: Bearing Witness to Animal Exploitation* (New York: OR Books, 2011).

42. Mullaney, "*RAW* Magazine," 23.

43. Juno, "Art Spiegelman," 182.

44. Juno, "Art Spiegelman," 167.

45. Susan Jacobowitz, "'Words and Pictures Together,'" in *Conversations*, 155.

46. Chris Goffard, "The Man Behind *Maus*," in *Conversations*, 139–40.

47. It was the first time the *New York Times* was covering a work of comics, and an unfinished one at that; Ken Tucker, "Cats, Mice and History: The Avant-Garde of the Comic Strip," *New York Times Book Review* 90 (May 26, 1985): 3.

48. Weschler, "Art's Father," 72.

49. Ella Taylor, "The 5,000 Pound *Maus*," in *Conversations*, 192.

50. The German version of the documentary was released as *Art Spiegelman: Von Katzen und Mäusen* (dir.: Georg Stefan Troller, March 07, 1988, ZDF, 44 min). One year later, *Maus I* was profiled in *Comic Book Confidential*, a documentary on the history of comics (dir. Ron Mann, 1988, 90 min.), and received the Alfred Award for Best Foreign Album in Angoulême, France, the site of a comics festival that Spiegelman would attend (and draw poster art for) many times over the years.

51. Goffard, "The Man Behind *Maus*," 137.

52. Jacobowitz, "'Words and Pictures Together,'" 162.

53. One of these was *La Scrittura di Maus*, an exhibition that toured from 1994 to 1997. The New York Public Library's Centennial exhibition also included *Maus* as one of the 100 Books of the Century.

54. John Updike, foreword to *The Complete Book of Covers from the* New Yorker, *1925–1989* (New York: Alfred A. Knopf, 1989).

55. "Racial Theme of *New Yorker* Cover Sparks Furor," *Los Angeles Times*, February 9, 1993.

56. Notable covers include "Private Lives" (a face whose features are obscured by a keyhole, August 24 & 31, 1998), "The Low Road" (on the Monica Lewinsky scandal, February 16, 1998), and "41 Shots, 10 Cents" (on the Diallo shooting, March 8, 1999).

57. Juno, "Art Spiegelman," 172.

58. R. Crumb had a similar fallout with the magazine in 2009 over a cartoon on marriage equality. The *New Yorker* has continued to publish satirical comics on its cover—the go-to person

for the Obama and Trump eras has been Barry Blitt—though arguably with less of the artsy, edgy earnestness that Spiegelman could bestow on even the most obvious of his one-page gags.

59. Heer, *In Love with Art*, 78.

60. The drawings that informed Spiegelman's depiction of camp life included works by the Polish painter and draftsman Mieczysław Kościelniak and the Jewish Czech artist Alfred Kantor. See also Spiegelman, *MetaMaus*, 49–53.

61. Avishai Artsy, "Cartoonist Art Spiegelman Reveals His Influences in 'WORDLESS!,'" *Jewish Journal*, October 7, 2014.

62. Françoise Mouly and Art Spiegelman, "Art Young: A Cartoonist for the Ages," *New Yorker*, August 2, 2017.

63. Claudia Dreifus, "'Drawing Is Always a Struggle': An Interview with Art Spiegelman," *New York Review of Books*, April 13, 2018.

64. The quality and standing of Spiegelman's contributions to comics, while widely acknowledged, are by no means uncontested, although the self-deprecating stance he has adopted throughout his career has helped take the sting out of some critiques. David Clowes's lampoon of the comics industry, *Pussey!* (serialized in *Eightball* and collected by Fantagraphics in 1995) features a character modeled on Spiegelman who welcomes an aspiring young artist to his loft with the self-regarding preciousness of a kingmaker: "Welcome, my boy, to the editorial offices of Emperor's New Clothes Magazine. The moderne, avant-garde, neoexpressodeconstructivist Compendium of Comics (or, as I like to call them, KOMMIX). I am Gummo Bubbleman: Editor, Emperor, Enfant Terrible" (20). Harvey Pekar also famously took Spiegelman to task for his representation of his father, criticizing *Maus* for what he called its "*artificial, contrived, and pseudo-intellectual qualities*" (emphasis in original). Reprinted in "Blood and Thunder: Harvey Pekar and R. Fiore," *The Comics Journal*, March 22, 2013.

65. Bergdoll, "Art Spiegelman," 15.

66. Juno, "Art Spiegelman," 184.

67. Juno, "Art Spiegelman," 171.

68. Juno, "Art Spiegelman," 173.

69. Weschler, "Art's Father," 79.

70. Sabin, "Interview," 108.

71. Thomas Crow, *Modern Art in the Common Culture* (New Haven: Yale University Press, 1998), vii.

72. Heer, *In Love with Art*, 62.

73. Heer, *In Love with Art*, 8.

74. Nadja Spiegelman, *I'm Supposed to Protect You from All This: A Memoir* (New York: Riverhead Books, 2016), 364.

75. For a cynical perspective on Spiegelman's career, see Ted Rall, "The King of Comix," *The Village Voice*, July 27, 1999.

76. Mullaney, "*RAW* Magazine," 27.

77. Sabin, "Interview," 106.

78. Mullaney, "*RAW* Magazine," 29.

79. Spiegelman asks: "What about tracing comics back to Dada artists, German expressionists, Constructivists?" (Mullaney, "*RAW* Magazine," 31).

80. Silverblatt, "The Cultural Relief," 131.

81. Gary Groth, Kim Thompson, and Joey Cavalieri, "Slaughter on Greene Street: Art Spiegelman and Françoise Mouly Talk about *RAW*," in *Conversations*, 61.

82. Groth, Thompson, and Cavalieri, 61.

83. Ross Chambers, *Loiterature* (Lincoln: University of Nebraska Press, 1999).

84. The essay in which Shklovsky outlines this idea, "Art as Technique," was written in 1917, but did not appear in English until 1965.

85. Juno, "Art Spiegelman," 189.

86. Goffard, "The Man Behind *Maus*," 139.

87. Groth, Thompson, and Cavalieri, 60.

88. Weschler, "Art's Father," 73.

89. Jacobowitz, "'Words and Pictures Together,'" 154.

90. Juno, "Art Spiegelman," 178.

91. B. Krigstein, *Messages in a Bottle: Comic Book Stories* (Seattle: Fantagraphics Books, 2013), 261.

92. Nadja Spiegelman, *I'm Supposed to Protect You*, 206.

93. Groth, Thompson, and Cavalieri, 59.

94. Françoise Mouly, *Blown Covers:* New Yorker *Covers You Were Never Meant to See* (New York: Abrams, 2012), 9.

95. Groth, Thompson, and Cavalieri, 51. *RAW*'s musical sensibility for the interbellum era extends beyond jazz. R. Crumb's comic strip about blues musician Jelly Roll Morton counts among the magazine's most memorable highlights.

96. Epel, "Art Spiegelman," 151.

97. When asked by *The Village Voice* what he thought of *Schindler's List*, Spiegelman retorted that "the only thing the film conjured up for [him] was six million emaciated Oscar statuettes" (Taylor, "The 5,000 Pound Maus," 194). He despised the 1978 TV series *The Holocaust*, too, yet he watched parts of it with Vladek to trigger his father's memories of the camps (Sabin, "Interview," 113).

98. Art Spiegelman, "1986 Introduction," in *Harvey Kurtzman's Jungle Book* (Milwaukie, OR: Dark Horse Comics, 2014), 25.

99. Ken Jacobs was the one who pointed out to Spiegelman the similarities between representations of African Americans and of mice—their rhythms and body language—in early animated cartoons (Weschler, "Art's Father," 81).

100. Juno, "Art Spiegelman," 167.

101. Heer, *In Love with Art*, 106.

102. See the vitriolic takedown by Ted Rall in *The Village Voice*, in which Spiegelman is portrayed as godfather to a corrupt comics mafia; "King Maus: Art Spiegelman Rules the World of Comix with Favors and Fear," *The Village Voice*, August 3, 1999.

103. Heer, *In Love with Art*, 60.

104. Jacobowitz, "'Words and Pictures Together,'" 155.

105. Heer, *In Love with Art*, 7.

106. Taylor, "The 5,000 Pound *Maus*," 191.

107. Juno, "Art Spiegelman," 188–89.

108. Jacobowitz, "'Words and Pictures Together,'" 157.

109. Juno, "Art Spiegelman," 175.

110. Jacobowitz, "'Words and Pictures Together,'" 158.

111. Marc Singer, *Breaking the Frames: Populism and Prestige in Comics Studies* (Austin: University of Texas Press, 2019).

112. Jacobowitz, "'Words and Pictures Together,'" 158.

113. For a useful analysis of the canonization of *Maus* through its inclusion in the anthologies published by W. W. Norton, Inc., such as *Postmodern American Fiction: A Norton Anthology* (1st ed., 1997), *The Norton Anthology of Jewish American Literature* (1st ed., 2001), and *The Norton Anthology of American Literature* (7th ed., 2007), see Andrew Loman, "'That Mouse's Shadow': The Canonization of Spiegelman's *Maus*," in *The Rise of the American Comics Artist: Creators and Contexts*, ed. Paul Williams and James Lyons (Jackson: University Press of Mississippi, 2010), 210–34.

114. Deborah R. Geis, "Introduction," in *Considering* Maus (Tuscaloosa: University of Alabama Press, 2003), 3.

115. Absent from Geis's book is the strand of 1990s *Maus* criticism that explored Spiegelman's contribution to a postmodern historiography beset by "belated effects and partial recognitions"; Dominick LaCapra, *History and Memory after Auschwitz* (Ithaca: Cornell University Press, 1998), 154; see also Miles Orvell, "Writing Posthistorically: Krazy Kat, *Maus*, and the Contemporary Fiction Cartoon," *American Literary History* 4, vol. 1 (Spring 1992): 110–28.

116. Marianne Hirsch, *Family Frames: Photography, Narrative, and Postmemory* (Cambridge, Mass.: Harvard University Press, 1997).

117. See also Barbie Zelizer, *Remembering to Forget: Holocaust Memory through the Camera's Eye* (Chicago: University of Chicago Press, 1998).

118. Lawrence L. Langer, "A Fable of the Holocaust," *New York Times Book Review*, November 3, 1991.

119. Amy Hungerford, *The Holocaust of Texts: Genocide, Literature, and Personification* (Chicago: University of Chicago Press, 2003), 90.

120. The graphic form of the book came into sharper focus, as did questions pertaining to its religious/Jewish significance. See Stephen Tabachnik, "The Religious Meaning of Art Spiegelman's *Maus*," *SHOFAR: An Interdisciplinary Journal of Jewish Studies* 22, no. 4 (Summer 2004): 1–13. See also the catalogue published in conjunction with the exhibition *Masters of American Comics*, edited by John Carlin, Paul Karasik, Brian Walker, and Stanley Crouch.

121. See Kristiaan Versluys, *Out of the Blue: September 11 and the Novel* (New York: Columbia University Press, 2009); Katalin Orbán, "Trauma and Visuality: Art Spiegelman's *Maus* and *In the Shadow of No Towers*," *Representations* 97 (2007), 57–89; Georgiana Banita, *Plotting Justice: Narrative Ethics and Literary Culture after 9/11* (Lincoln: University of Nebraska Press, 2012); *Narrating 9/11: Fantasies of State, Security, and Terrorism*, ed. John N. Duvall and Robert P. Marzec (Baltimore: Johns Hopkins University Press, 2015).

122. See for instance Lopamudra Basu, "The Graphic Memoir in a State of Exception: Transformations of the Personal in Art Spiegelman's *In the Shadow of No Towers*," in *Drawing from Life: Memory and Subjectivity in Comic Art*, ed. Jane Tolmie (Jackson: University Press of Mississippi, 2013), 163–84.

123. Beaty and Woo, *The Greatest Comic Book of All Time*.

124. Philip Smith, *Reading Art Spiegelman* (New York: Routledge, 2016), 3.

125. International scholarship has followed a similar path, from readings that relied heavily on Holocaust scholarship to comics-oriented appraisals. Gerhard Richter in his interpretation of *Maus* manages to do both at once by conflating the Holocaust blues in Spiegelman's

second-generation account with the anti-aesthetic sordidness of early comics. (He uses the untranslatable German term *Katzenjammer* in reference to both cat trouble in Spiegelman's book and to the squalid style of *The Katzenjammer Kids*.) Gerhard Richter, "Holocaust und Katzenjammer: Lektüreprotokolle zu Art Spiegelmans Comic *Maus*," *Ästhetik des Ereignisses: Sprache, Geschichte, Medium* (München: Wilhelm Fink, 2005), 23–47. Even though we might expect German-language criticism to favor Holocaust-heavy readings of Spiegelman's work, it has gone to great lengths to argue that the comics form of *Maus* is what makes it so compelling as a work of Holocaust literature. Ole Frahm makes this point with particular fervor in his study of *Maus* as a work that illustrates both the Holocaust as a site of memory and the evolution of comics from the funny animals of yore to postmodern palimpsests of masked identities. Ole Frahm, *Genealogie des Holocaust: Art Spiegelmans* MAUS—A Survivor's Tale (Paderborn: Wilhelm Fink, 2006). The reception of *Maus* in other European countries continues to highlight its historical importance as a Holocaust text at the expense of its attributes as comics art. See, for instance, Simona Porro, *L'ombra della Shoah: Trauma, Storia e Memoria nei graphic memoir di Art Spiegelman* (Alessandria: Edizioni dell'Orso, 2012). In a French study of *Maus*, the cornerstones of the argument are provided by historians Peter Novick, Alison Landsberg, and Reinhart Koselleck. See Régine Robin, *La mémoire saturée* (Paris: Stock, 2011).

126. Jacobowitz, "'Words and Pictures Together,'" 162.

127. Sabin, "Interview," 99.

128. Spiegelman, "Portrait of the Artist as a Young %@?*!," in *Breakdowns* (New York: Pantheon, 2008), n.p. Emphasis in original.

Part 1

MODERNISM AND FORM

MODERNIST DISRUPTIONS

Art Spiegelman as Experimenter, Editor, and Critic

SHAWN GILMORE

SPIEGELMAN'S EXPERIMENTAL COMICS PAGE

Art Spiegelman's early career has been overshadowed by the critical focus on his masterwork, *Maus*, published in two parts in 1986 and 1991; by then, Spiegelman had been drawing comics for nearly twenty years. While the interest in the Pulitzer-Prize decorated memoir seems justified, it has left a gap in our understanding of both Spiegelman's pre-*Maus* work and his engagements with the legacy of modernist aesthetics, which played an important role in his artistic development. I address this gap in Spiegelman's critical reception to argue that in many of his early works, Spiegelman employs the key modernist aesthetic of formal juxtaposition to jar and unsettle, while simultaneously drawing new connections by means of what I term *visual parataxis*. This modernist strategy, latent in the formal logic of all comics, not only saturates Spiegelman's experimental phase in the 1970s, but also extends through his editorial and critical work into at least the early 1990s.

Spiegelman's use of visual parataxis varied across this period, as he moved between a series of related roles, from experimental comics artist to editor and cultural critic. In tracing Spiegelman's overlapping modernist efforts over twenty years, my aim is to show how he extended the logic of visual parataxis to radically reshape the possibilities of comics, their presentation, and their cultural cachet. First, I examine some of Spiegelman's early experimental comics, including "Don't Get Around Much Anymore" and "Ace Hole: Midget Detective," as well as his collection *Breakdowns* (1977), which brought many of these strips together. It was in these early works, I argue, that Spiegelman explored modernist notions of visual parataxis and unity, which he then expanded as part of his editorial and curatorial projects with *Short Order Comix*, *Arcade*, and *RAW*. In these magazines, published between 1973 and 1991, Spiegelman and his coeditors forged new structures for the comics magazine, creating unusual juxtapositions and establishing a variety of internal relationships between the works in each issue. I close with a consideration of Spiegelman's criticism of the Museum of Modern Art's 1990 "High & Low" exhibition, which took the form of a one-page comics essay published in *Artforum*. This piece assembled many of Spiegelman's concerns from the 1970s and 1980s, and attacked what he called "myopic" decisions made by the exhibition's curators. Along with Spiegelman's subsequent one-man show at the MoMA, this critique encapsulated his engagement with the forms of modernist juxtaposition that I identify throughout.

Spiegelman's attachment to the practice of visual parataxis was not an arbitrary choice, but, as I will show, combined his interest in the formal logic of comics—which relies on sequence and juxtaposition—with elements of modernist art, particularly the effects derived from the play of forms. In doing so, he not only set the stage for his later works, including *Maus* and *In the Shadow of No Towers* (2004), but also helped bring aesthetic theory to comics practice. After this period, partly due to Spiegelman's work as experimenter, editor, and critic, comics creators had to reckon with the radical ideas and formal practices he had established in his groundbreaking comics, magazines, and essays. To retrace Spiegelman's engagement with modernism, I turn to an early, one-page comic, "Don't Get Around Much Anymore," first published in *Short Order Comix* #2 (1974).[1] Here Spiegelman imagines the comics page as a space of experimental play, relying on the manipulation of sequence and juxtaposition to produce jarring visual effects.

MODERNIST COLLAGE: "DON'T GET AROUND MUCH ANYMORE"

"Don't Get Around Much Anymore" is a single-page comic laid out over five tiers of nearly nonnarrative panels that portray a man, alone in his one-room apartment. Formally, the page uses overlaid narration—the inner monologue of the main figure in the first panel—that is out of sync with the panels in which it is embedded. So, for example, the center panel contains two captions: "The sound doesn't work on the teevee . . . ," sending the reader one panel forward, while " . . . but I don't care. I own a record!" points one panel back. The captions eventually align with the images they accompany further down the page, until the last panel collapses these stray thoughts into a baffling final image: the television displaying a close-up on a smiling mouth, with what appears to be a second layer of lower teeth, angular and menacing, overlaid with the maudlin, "Did I tell you the refrigerator is empty?" referring back to the eighth panel

Detail from "Don't Get Around Much Anymore," first published in *Short Order Comix*, no. 2, currently collected in *Breakdowns*. Copyright © 1974 by Art Spiegelman.

at the center of the page. "Don't Get Around" plays with one of the expected formal properties of the comics page, namely that captions and panels stand in a clear relation to each other. Yet Spiegelman also challenges the notion of comics narrative itself. He does so by using paratactic techniques to burrow into the comics page, exposing the necessarily fragmented comics form as both challenge and opportunity.

The strip's last tier, for example, presents two panels that focus on a *Life* magazine article, followed by a return to the spiky smile on the silent television. Left by "whoever lived here before," these magazines are from the latter half of 1971, as indicated by the captions, which can be traced to an August 6 glossy profile of actress and singer Ann-Margret and a November 26 Melvin Maddocks review of Herman Wouk's *The Winds of War* (1971), respectively. The first of these traces Ann-Margret's career slump after early successes and her Oscar-nominated turn in the controversial film *Carnal Knowledge* (1971).[2] The centerpiece of the article is a two-page portrait of Ann-Margret "posing languorously" (as the photo caption explains) on a living room couch. She dons a black, full-length gown, goblet of wine hanging down, as she stares directly at the camera, alongside her cat. The pull quote on the same page, "I was a cartoon character—a joke," describes her recent reputation with critics.[3]

In "Don't Get Around," Spiegelman repurposes this article to challenge the vapid nature of magazine profiles. In panels twelve and thirteen, the comic pulls another line from the *Life* profile ("At last a star?—She still has doubts") and places it under a different reclining figure, this one a stylized version of a nude by Amedeo Modigliani—specifically *Reclining Nude* (c. 1919), which hangs in the Museum of Modern Art in New York.[4] The Modigliani is juxtaposed with the drawn reproduction of a Lark cigarette ad with its familiar slogan, "put [some] more flavor in your life," featuring a stark, chiseled man with a jutting cigarette over a striped background. These substitutions convert Ann-Margret to a modernist nude, ironically replacing the original portrait with an image of more substance, set against a contemporary advertisement. But Spiegelman goes even further: In his explication of "Don't Get Around" he writes that the "Modigliani print used to illustrate the Ann[-]Margret article also comes from a *Life* magazine advertisement."[5] By placing two advertising images side by side, Spiegelman further highlights the commercial impulse inherent in glossy magazines, with their mix of advertising and coverage of celebrities.

Panel thirteen repeats the image, doubling the Lark ad by adding another version at the top of the panel under a caption citing Maddocks's review of Wouk's *The Winds of War* (1971), a historical epic about the lead-up to World War II. Maddocks notes that the novel "is almost incorrigibly readable," but that the work's structure—juxtaposing military and global history with the stories of fictional characters caught up in the sweep of those events—is its ultimate problem: "All this public-private split-leveling of life has a fragmenting effect."[6] Spiegelman achieves his own "fragmenting effect" by nearly eliminating narrative progress, relying instead on visual contrast, symbolic repetition, and the disjunction of image and text throughout. By way of explanation, Spiegelman wrote in 1978 that he "had been studying a lot of cubist painters—Picasso, Braque, Gris—I suppose that affected the drawing. [My work] had developed along lines parallel to that of the graphic designers of the Twenties who had been exposed to the cubist experiments."[7] Spiegelman portrays his work here as an extension of and elaboration on modernist modes, including what he calls the "collage impulse, a tactic borrowed from Cubism," at play in panel five, which became "fundamental to the strip's pervasive references to media as extensions of experience."[8]

Throughout "Don't Get Around," Spiegelman does not just bring modernism to comics, he also builds on other experiments in underground comix, in particular on R. Crumb's "Bo Bo Bolinski: He's the No. 1 Human Zero—He's No Big Deal," which first appeared in the Print Mint single-issue adult zine *Uneeda Comix* in August 1970.[9] Crumb's one-page comic is arranged as a three-by-three grid of panels, featuring nine different perspectives on Bolinski, silent and cross-armed in his living room chair. Writing about this comic, Hillary Chute notes that "Crumb uses the most standard template for progression to in fact halt progression. He stops narrative time for comics, giving us a page of panels in which there is movement of perspective but not movement of time," allowing us to "see comics' experimental language as of a piece with Cubism, which sought to destroy fixed viewpoint."[10] Spiegelman in fact recalled in 1995 that he was fascinated by those moments in Crumb's work "where the panels of a page didn't move in time, [but instead] moved in space—so you'd just have a page that would be different pictures of the same thing. ["Bo Bo Bolinski" portrays] a guy sitting in a chair, and all it shows is movement in space, as if the page consisted of orthogonal projections showing the guy and the chair from different angles."[11]

COMICS AND VISUAL PARATAXIS

In "Don't Get Around," Spiegelman augments Crumb's use of "orthogonal projections" with a series of purposely juxtaposed images and captions that expose and challenge the formal logic of comics. In doing so, he employs the modernist aesthetic of visual parataxis, which allows him to call into question the presumptively causal relationship between successive comic-book panels. The artistry of "Don't Get Around" pivots on unexpected patterns that only partially conform to our expectations of panel-to-panel progression. Following Scott McCloud in *Understanding Comics*, we might identify these transitions as "moment-to-moment," "aspect-to-aspect," or "non-sequiturs."[12] McCloud's terms, however, don't quite fit the striking sequence of panels in "Don't Get Around," not least because they presuppose unusual concatenations of elements that are otherwise familiar and consistent, whereas Spiegelman draws together both moments and aspects. In fact, though we generally categorize the medium of comics as a subset of graphic narrative and often, following Will Eisner, as "sequential art," its formal logic has always relied on a more clashing type of visual parataxis.[13] And even though there are well-understood examples of visual parataxis outside of comics in, say, Picasso's juxtaposition of representational styles in the *Portrait of Gertrude Stein* (1906) or Eisenstein's method of cinematic montage, parataxis is not often discussed in comics studies.[14]

Parataxis is most clearly identified in the study of poetics and prose. In his masterwork *Mimesis* (1946), German philologist Erich Auerbach contrasts the use of hypotaxis, the favored mode of the classical epic, with parataxis, which more introspective writers and the "vernacular poets" gravitated towards.[15] Hypotaxis, which emphasizes hierarchies and causation, allows writers to produce the "copious and connected argumentation of which Homer's heroes are so fond," while parataxis and "its lack of connectives" can be used to "express the impulsive and dramatic, most often in matters concerned with the inner life."[16] Parataxis "becomes a weapon of eloquence" in the hands of certain writers, a way to avoid "rationally organized condensations [. . .] in favor of a halting, spasmodic, juxtapositive, and pro- and retrogressive method in which causal, modal, and even temporal relations are obscured."[17]

The disruptive potential of parataxis would be picked up by twentieth-century modernists to—in the words of literary scholar Susan Stanford Friedman—"describe the rupture of connective logic [. . .] evident in the radical juxtapositions of images or lyric sequences. Connections are suppressed, not immediately apparent, or even non-existent, to be formed in the mind of the reader through an interrogation of the possible correspondence or resonances between the disjunctive and the fragmentary."[18] It is this version that Spiegelman most firmly engages with. By applying modernist parataxis to the comics page, he produces "radical juxtapositions of images," with connections to be established by the reader or viewer. McCloud asserts that "comics *is* closure," in the sense that the reader feels compelled to connect two disparate comics panels in a sequence.[19] Visual parataxis, as deployed by Spiegelman, illustrates more fully what McCloud implies: that the logic of parataxis works on readers all the more effectively the stronger their impulse to fit what they see into closed-off patterns of meaning.

Through visual parataxis, comics also participate in the aesthetic method championed by many modernist projects, which Walter Benjamin in *The Arcades Project* (1927–1940) refers to as "dialectical images" composed of distinct components that encode coherent ideas, but which can only be understood in a gestalt apprehension of the whole, that is, of the parts and their relationship to one another. Proposed as a historical method, Benjamin's approach circumvents the beguiling linearity of narrative, challenging causal progression and requiring the reader or viewer to hold all aspects under consideration in a single unified pattern.[20] Though there is much to be said about the dialectical image in relation to comics, here it serves to clarify the modernist practice of parataxis: seeing the whole of a work as held together not by a predetermined sequential coherence, but by a notion of *modernist unity* rooted in the perception of the observer.[21]

CONNECTIONS AND DISORDER IN *BREAKDOWNS*

This new sense of the possibilities of comics is expressed across the ambitious collection of Spiegelman's early work, *Breakdowns: From Maus to Now, an Anthology of Strips* (1977), made up almost entirely of previously-published material from 1972–77, including "Don't Get Around." These pieces had all appeared in comic-book or magazine format—mostly in *Short Order Comix* or *Arcade*, both edited by Spiegelman—which meant that the art had been reduced in size, sometimes obscuring detail. *Breakdowns* overcompensated for this with its ample format (10" × 14"), meaning some pieces were printed at nearly twice their original publication size.[22] The book's size and cover, depicting various permutations of the color-separation process by which comics color is applied, invite the reader to consider the pieces anew, while the "breakdowns" in its title take on multiple meanings: not only the breakdown of comics color, form, and publishing standards, as well as the breakdown stage of comics drafting (during which the form of each page takes shape), but also the ways in which thematic content, with its emphasis on anxiety, neurosis, and the reception of the comics themselves, dovetails with formal concerns throughout the collection.[23]

Just after the publication of *Breakdowns*, Spiegelman acknowledged the paratactic nature of the book, noting: "it's most important that each comic strip be a fully realized world, rather than that they're all obvious slices of the same masterwork. I think that until I saw *Breakdowns* . . . , I didn't quite even know what my underlying themes were, or what connectives there were between strips, and *Breakdowns* made it clear to me and to other people as well, I understand."[24] These "connectives," as Spiegelman makes clear, extend beyond the titular interest in thematic "breakdowns" to the formal and stylistic experimentation underpinning the entire collection. *Breakdowns* was audacious, and fairly well-received in the comics community. John Benson, in *The Comics Journal*, noted that Spiegelman's "range becomes much more evident when the stories are collected together in one volume. *Breakdowns* really reveals a dimension to Spiegelman's work that was perhaps not obvious when the stories were published months apart in different publications."[25]

Critic Gilbert Choat, writing in *Alternative Media*, described *Breakdowns* as "an attempt to discover the essential comic strip, to find out what mechanisms the strip as such, as a form, possesses that give life and power to its successful incarnations." He found that Spiegelman's "urge to discover the quintessential dynamism of the comic strip has become inseparable from his stark material. These twin preoccupations . . . are exactly parallel to the artistic and philosophical problems and solutions of the great Modernists."[26] Choat explicitly compares Spiegelman's efforts to modernist masters, including Joyce, Picasso, Stravinsky, and Pound. In *Breakdowns*, as in modernism, "it became apparent that, as Wallace Stevens said, 'A great disorder is an order' . . . The collage process soon came to be seen as not intrusive, but essential . . . in Joyce's, Proust's or Faulkner's cluttered streams of consciousness, or the quintessentially modern collages of Dada, or the graphic and emotional 'breakdowns' of Spiegelman."[27] Choat's comparison is not an idle one and brings into focus the modernist impulses that surface throughout *Breakdowns*. Though each of the comics in the collection advances a distinct formal logic, they are held together by the "connectives" of visual parataxis and modernist unity.

THE GHOST OF PICASSO

The piece that most fully expresses this modernist connectivity is the longest comic in the collection, the eight-page "Ace Hole: Midget Detective." First published in *Short Order Comix* #2 (1974), "Ace Hole" is a pastiche of detective noir devices, pop culture iconography, and storytelling conceits, which follows its titular midget detective as he tries to track down a series of fake Picasso paintings.[28] Ace is put onto the trail of the forger Al Floogleman (a stand-in for Art Spiegelman), who is dispatched by the second page. Following the clues (the first, helpfully labeled "plot device"), Ace is led to an address at which he is assaulted and knocked into a dreamscape mimicking Winsor McCay's *Little Nemo in Slumberland*. His assailant is a woman he had seen earlier, Greta, whose angular, unproportioned figure recalls Picasso's *Les Demoiselles d'Avignon* (1907), accompanied by her man, Laurence Potato-Head, drawn as Mr. Potato-Head. After some more sleuthing, Ace engages in a violent confrontation with Laurence, killing him, and learns that Greta (a typical *femme fatale*) had set all of them up to get her hands on Laurence's money. Ace mounts his noble steed (a small dog) and attempts to ride off into the sunset, only to be ousted by the dog's owner, who forces him to walk alone down the street, muttering to himself.

While the story is straightforward, if farcical, its presentation is anything but. "Ace Hole" is full of visual and verbal allusions, each of which points to an intricate set of referents.[29] They begin with a headnote paraphrasing material from Gertrude Stein's *The Autobiography of Alice B. Toklas* (1933) on Picasso's love of American comic strips.[30] Then, when Ace is knocked out, he becomes Little Nemo, falling through Slumberland at the bottom of the second page (redrawn from the final three panels in the July 3, 1910 episode of Winsor McCay's *Little Nemo*), entering a dreamscape populated by both Picasso and Spiegelman himself. At the top of the third page, Picasso runs across a surrealist landscape, spouting aesthetic axioms, then posing as a reclining nude—in much the same mode as the Modigliani nude in "Don't Get Around"—atop a television that displays the slain Floogleman, who becomes Spiegelman himself left to cry a sea of tears. Over the third and fourth tiers, the Ghost of Picasso (drawn in a woodcut style) intones: "You have to have an idea of what you are going to do. But it should be a vague idea."[31] Two aesthetic ideals compete for Ace Hole's attention. We learned earlier that Floogleman had "been a small-change underground cartoonist," so the failed underground comics artist is left only to sob as Picasso pompously explains what true art ought to be.[32] This tension between high and low artistic claims frames the story's climax on page six. Laurence Potato-Head bursts in on Ace Hole and Greta, forcing Ace to fire his gun as the entire structure of the page shifts. In the third tier,

Detail from "Ace Hole: Midget Detective," page 6, first published in *Short Order Comix,* no. 2, currently collected in *Breakdowns*. Copyright © 1974 by Art Spiegelman.

Ace repeatedly thinks ". . . I squeezed my trigger! . . ." over an image of Bambi and Thumper from Disney's *Bambi* (1942), in a panel that combines a drawn version of Picasso's *Guernica* (1937) and a portion of the Comics Code, before returning to a close-up of Ace's face, gun still smoking in the foreground.[33]

The centerpiece of the page and scene is the complex *Guernica* panel. By including the relevant portion of the Comics Code, Spiegelman suggests multiple forms of critique.[34] For one thing, the panel obscures the moment of comic-book violence (Ace shooting Laurence) by substituting another image in its place and therefore adhering to the letter of the Code. But it does so by inserting a modernist depiction of atrocity, *Guernica*, which occludes the individual violence in the comic strip, but arguably enhances its impact through the large-scale abstraction of war. Further, the panel expounds the chief complaint at the core of underground comics: that the restrictive Comics Code (and mainstream comics culture more broadly) allowed for images of Bambi and high art, regardless of their implicit violence, while restricting the range of storytelling and aesthetic techniques possible in the comics medium. With "Ace Hole," Spiegelman offers a radical critique of the restraints on comics in a highly self-conscious style which, as Chute points out, itself "gestures towards a kind of proliferative Cubist narration."[35] This pointed artistic inversion marks Spiegelman's most explicit use of visual parataxis to explore both the possibilities of comics and the logic of modernist unity, all while using a genre-tinged narrative to deliver his critique of mainstream comics.

SPIEGELMAN'S EDITORIAL METHOD

Spiegelman's experimental work and the buildup to *Breakdowns* overlapped with his editorial duties on several magazines, where he employed similar techniques of paratactic juxtaposition and unity, using full comics (instead of panels) as the objects to be juxtaposed. Spiegelman was a serial editor, first on *Short Order Comix*, with two issues in 1973 and 1974, then as coeditor, with Bill Griffith, of *Arcade: The Comics Revue*, with seven issues from 1975 to 1976, and finally coediting *RAW* with Françoise Mouly, with eight issues in its first run and three more in its second, between 1980 and 1991. These efforts highlight a different mode of juxtaposition, with Spiegelman and his coeditors bringing together disparate artists, styles, and types of comics and prose to offer a variety of challenges to other magazines and collections available at the time.

Short Order Comix and *Arcade* replicated the format of previous underground comix collections but included more provocative and heterogeneous works. As Mike Kelly puts it: "These strips were not aimed at the drugged-out audience that enjoyed the adventures of the Freak Brothers or the erotical-comical funnies of R. Crumb; they required a more attentive audience."[36] Spiegelman and Griffith would position *Arcade* next to titles like the monthly humor magazine *National Lampoon* and *MAD* magazine, while making sure that each issue carried a table of contents and editorial (unusual for underground collections), which repackaged the comics within as features with clear titles and creators worthy of recognition.[37]

To give but one example, the third issue of *Arcade* juxtaposes underground comix by mainstay artists like R. Crumb, Justin Green, and Aline Kominsky in mixed formats and styles, an illustrated version of Coleridge's "Kubla Khan" by Manuel "Spain" Rodriguez, a two-page comic spread with no panel divisions by S. Clay Wilson, and a prose piece by Charles Bukowski, illustrated by R. Crumb, alongside a humorous three-page comic biography of H. P. Lovecraft, who ends up in the claws of his own creation, Cthulhu. Eschewing consistent themes and styles, these juxtapositions mix high and low aesthetics to create a cultural hodgepodge that presumes a good deal of readerly awareness. *Arcade* uses these contrasts to challenge the reader, moving away from the smooth transitions that precursor compilations—both commercial and underground—had relied upon. Griffith would later describe their editorial style in direct opposition to most underground comix: "Before *Arcade*, editors of anthology comic books would exercise a very light editorial control—that was never Art's personality. Neither was it mine, particularly, but Art was born to be an editor."[38]

The underground scene was in such advanced decline, however, that even *Arcade*'s curation and mixture of talents was not enough: "Our mission was to save underground comics," Griffith recalls, and "we really did want *Arcade* to be a magazine. As a matter of fact, Art eventually succeeded in that with *RAW*."[39] Spiegelman and Mouly created *RAW* to promote artistic comics in a glossy package that could appear on stands next to art and architecture magazines.[40] In his introduction to the collection *Read Yourself RAW* (1987), Spiegelman gives a sense of his and Mouly's editorial impulses: "Each artist had to have his own individual stylistic voice. . . . Although many of the artists didn't seem to have much in common with each other, either geographically or stylistically, they all seemed to recognize something in each other's work. It was elusive—maybe it was just the seriousness of their commitment to the comics form."[41] Spiegelman's emphasis here is on the assorted slate of artists and their enthusiasm about the possibilities of comics, which turned out to be *RAW*'s primary agenda, pairing artistic innovation with Spiegelman's and Mouly's hands-on editorial guidance.[42] The first eight issues were published between July 1980 and September 1986, in an oversized format, similar in proportions to *Breakdowns*.[43]

Its advertising aggressively positioned the magazine as "unReasonable, unAssimilated and unWavering," "Refined, Angry and Wired," etc. against the seemingly staid New York magazines of the day.[44] Mouly, who would go on in 1993 to become art editor at the *New Yorker*, reflected that "*RAW* was distinctly downtown, an avant-garde magazine of comics and graphics, far from the world of the *New Yorker*."[45] In much the same manner as *Arcade* but with more avant-garde panache, *RAW* juxtaposed a wide variety of artists and works in the vein of modernist parataxis. The stylistic differences were even starker, as Spiegelman and Mouly recruited European artists with bona fide modernist credentials alongside up-and-coming American cartoonists such as Ben Katchor, Chris Ware, and Gary Panter. As Jeet Heer puts it, "Mouly and Spiegelman sometimes highlighted the radical visual disjunction in their magazines by placing next to each other the pieces that had the sharpest visual contrast."[46] Illustrative of this technique is *RAW*'s fifth issue: "the centerfold is a Pascal Doury visual explosion, a scene of carnage that covers nearly the whole page with cross-hatched lines, followed by a sleekly minimalist Joost Swarte page—sequencing designed to produce aesthetic sparks."[47]

The frictional assembly of *RAW* became the stuff of legend and led to eight issues of uncompromising comics, art, and prose, often with a variety of tipped-in pamphlets, cards, or records inside each issue. One sequence from the eighth issue will serve as a particularly apposite example. After a few opening comics by Marc Caro, Kiki Picasso, and Kim Deitch, a small poem—a meditation on the atom bomb called "Alliteration" by Leo Gorcey—appears unexpectedly, with illustrations by Drew Friedman. This is followed by a twelve-page prose excerpt from Paul Boyer's *By the Bomb's Early Light: American Thought and Culture at the Dawn of the Atomic Age* (1985), accompanied by a variety of illustrations and cultural references. Next is one of Gary Panter's "Jimbo" comics, set in "the middle of a section of Dal-Tokyo [a future, terra-formed Mars] destroyed by a small homemade terrorist A-bomb. All is ashes and carnage."[48] And then, tipped-in, is chapter seven, "Mauschwitz," of Spiegelman's graphic memoir *Maus*. This gut-punch sequence, with its loose thematic focus on atomic weaponry, war, and genocide, mixes styles and narrative forms to suggest that no coherent through-line can be made or would suffice.

Much like Spiegelman's inclusion of *Guernica* in "Ace Hole," this sequence questions the easy elisions of *RAW*'s glossy contemporaries, which addressed the issues of the day in comparatively uneventful prose. Extending Spiegelman's preoccupation with modernism, *RAW* introduced new methods of thinking about the uneasy politics of modernist art, which would deepen his investment in the New York City art scene, particularly by engaging with the city's primary curator of modernist legacies, the Museum of Modern Art.

SPIEGELMAN AND THE MOMA: CONFRONTING THE ESTABLISHMENT

In October 1990, the Museum of Modern Art launched a major exhibition, "High & Low: Modern Art and Popular Culture," curated by art historian Kirk Varnedoe and *New Yorker* staff writer Adam Gopnik. The show was a massive undertaking, pairing major works from the MoMA's modernist collection—including Picasso, Miró, Magritte, and many others—with four "low" categories of art: graffiti, caricature, comics, and advertising. This radically paratactic experience was also accompanied by a large exhibition catalogue and a collection of essays. "High & Low" immediately came under fire from all sides, including those who thought that the "high" art typical of the MoMA was demeaned by the "low" art appearing alongside it, those who thought the selection rationale of the curators was questionable, and those who objected to the framing of the entire enterprise, focusing on the show's corporate sponsor, AT&T.[49]

Varnedoe and Gopnik clearly defined what they meant by "high" and "low," asserting that "high" art has a self-evident and unassailable position in art history: "We call their work 'high' art, not to glamorize it or quarantine it . . . but because these artists and their work are the primary material with which any history of art in this century must contend."[50] They further acknowledged that the newer categories of art occupy a contested place: "We call all these areas of representation 'low,' not to denigrate them out of hand . . . but to recognize that they have traditionally been considered irrelevant to, or outside, any consideration of achievement in the fine arts of our time—and in fact have commonly been accepted as opposite to the 'high' arts in their intentions, audiences, and nature of endeavor."[51] Taking this "high/low" opposition as both natural and insurmountable, the curators set themselves up for an impasse.

Spiegelman recalls his tepid reaction to the show, which "tried to grapple with the then-starting-to-be-fashionable issue of how the popular arts interacted with the more rarefied ones. Unfortunately, the show squandered the opportunity, merely ratifying the museum's long-held tastes and hierarchical predispositions."[52] A key problem was the misleading presentation of many comics that the show purported to display. The exhibition catalogue even contained a note that "many of the works reproduced in this book are not included in the exhibition of the same title."[53] Spiegelman took this as indicative of the underlying prejudices of the high art world: "The way I understood it at the time was, 'I guess the paintings win the wall and the comics win the catalogue.' The comics looked better because they were made for reproduction. For the most part the show seemed to condescend to the low-art artifacts."[54]

Spiegelman's retort to the "High & Low" show took the form of a one-page piece of comics criticism, "High Art Lowdown," published in *Artforum* in

December 1990.[55] Snidely noting that "this review of the MoMA's 'High & Low' show is not sponsored by AT&T," the comic proceeds to lay out an indictment of the curators' selections and critical bankruptcy of the exhibition. Spiegelman presents his argument in the styles of multiple artists whose works were exhibited in the show, including Roy Lichtenstein, Chester Gould, and George Herriman, among others. He also identifies many of the "Missing!" comics artists, including himself and "all his friends," though his critique is not just about the question of inclusion and exclusion.[56] A female figure in the style of Lichtenstein sobs to her putative creator: "Oh, Roy, your dead high art is built on *dead* low art! . . . The *real* political, sexual and formal energy in *living* popular culture passes you by. Maybe *that's*—sob—why you're championed by museums!" Dick Tracy, at the MoMA, reports: "I've searched high and low, chief—All I *see* here is their permanent collection. . . . They made myopic choices, not daring the risks that come with a 'risky' topic!"[57]

In the middle tier, redrawing Herriman's *Krazy Kat*, Spiegelman raises his main objection—that the show misunderstood its own fundamental question: "'High 'n' Low' is a question of class/economics, not aesthetics," recalling *Arcade*'s sequence of Coleridge, Bukowski, and Lovecraft, fifteen years earlier. The piece then shifts to a series of gags: that a Preparation H subway ad for hemorrhoid cream inspired Picasso to paint his famous, caricatured mask-like face for the *Portrait of Gertrude Stein* (1905–6); that the MoMA is the proverbial ostrich with its head in the sand; and that a more suitable piece of graffiti art to include would be a plea to donate the admission fees to "the homeless who live right next to the MoMA."[58] In a final speech balloon, Spiegelman compiles a jumbled list of categories under the title "Chop Suey" and claims that "the High and Low show is organized around similar principles!"

The critique here is multipronged, and its force derives from one of the most compelling versions of visual parataxis that Spiegelman would publish in this period. Not only do the various styles appear in sequence as a layered assault on the "High & Low" show; each visual example is one that Spiegelman redraws from an artist or artwork held up by the exhibition as "low art." Through his subversive response, he has turned the "High & Low" exhibits into an exhibition of his own, bringing his version of antihierarchical modernist parataxis to the fore and condemning thereby the elitist juxtapositions of the MoMA's curators. "High Art Lowdown" is, in many ways, the apotheosis of the experimentation, curation, and criticism that Spiegelman had been practicing throughout the 1970s and 1980s, now brought to bear on the vaunted institution of high art itself, the Museum of Modern Art.

Yet Spiegelman was not quite done with the MoMA, or with his interest in modernist modes. In fact, just a year after the "High & Low" exhibition, Spiegelman himself would have a solo show at the Museum of Modern Art in

Detail from "High Art Lowdown," review of the *High & Low: Modern Art and Popular Culture* exhibit at the Museum of Modern Art, published in *Artforum*. Copyright © 1990 by Art Spiegelman.

December 1991 and January 1992.[59] He did so as part of the Museum's "Projects" series, which a press release described as follows: "*Projects: Art Spiegelman* coincides with the publication of *MAUS II* . . . the installation includes all the original pages for both parts of *MAUS*, as well as ancillary sketches, preparatory drawings and layouts of individual sections, and source materials used by Spiegelman."[60] The show presented the final draft pages of both volumes of *Maus*, arranged at eye-level, alongside drafts and "breakdowns" displayed above and below each page, next to reference material that included tapes of Spiegelman's interviews with his father, Vladek.[61]

What we witness here is a version of modernist juxtaposition that sets Spiegelman's work in relation to itself, with drafts and references appearing alongside the final pre-print version of each page of *Maus*. Spiegelman would tell critic James E. Young: "If I had my way . . . this would be the text of *Maus*, replete with how I got to the so-called final panels."[62] In his "Project," in other words, Spiegelman acts as editor and curator of his own archive. Art critic and impresario Robert Storr, in an essay accompanying the show, identified the purpose of the installation in its attempt "to illuminate the final entity—a mass-produced work—by showing its complex genesis in the artist's mind and on the draftsman's page," and he pays particular attention to the multiple drafts behind each finished panel.[63] In the artist's own interpretation, Spiegelman's archive emerges as a unified modernist space, its totality drawn from the many pieces and visions of *Maus* held together dialectically, in much the same way Benjamin's *The Arcades Project* dissolves in an unfinished synthesis that privileges radical fragmentation over linear meaning.

At the time of his one-man show, the *RAW* project was wrapping up, *Maus II* was about to be published, and as the MoMA press release notes, "a Guggenheim fellowship and a nomination for the National Critics Circle Award are among the honors Spiegelman has received for *MAUS*."[64] He would soon win a special Pulitzer Prize, which symbolically ended this modernist-compiler-phase of his career. While Spiegelman would remain engaged with the legacy of modernism, his early period of experimentation, editorial work, and criticism—during which he extended the logic of visual parataxis and modernist unity to the compiler's art of comics—came to a close, having successfully expanded the scope and possibilities of the medium by elevating what had been there all along.

Notes

1. "Don't Get Around Much Anymore" was subsequently reprinted in *The Apex Treasury of Underground Comics* (1974), an early compilation.

2. P. F. Kluge, "Ann-Margret, Suddenly Blooming," *Life*, August 6, 1971: 30–35.

3. Kluge, "Ann-Margret," 33.

4. Amedeo Modigliani, *Reclining Nude* (c. 1919), Museum of Modern Art, 28 1/2 × 45 7/8" (72.4 × 116.5 cm), oil on canvas, object number 13.1950.

5. Art Spiegelman, "Don't Get Around Much Anymore: A Guided Tour," *Alternative Media* 10, no. 2 (Fall 1978): 9.

6. Melvin Maddocks, "Wouk at War in Slow Motion," *Life*, November 26, 1971: 16.

7. Spiegelman, "Guided Tour," 8.

8. Spiegelman, "Guided Tour," 8.

9. This piece is reprinted only a few pages before "Don't Get Around Much Anymore" in *The Apex Treasury* (1974).

10. Hillary Chute, "Graphic Narrative," in *The Routledge Companion to Experimental Literature*, ed. Brian McHale, Alison Gibbons, and Joe Bray (New York: Routledge, 2012), 412.

11. Gary Groth, "Art Spiegelman Interview," *Comics Journal* #180 (September 1995): 87. Spiegelman would recast this in 2008; as he recalls telling R. Crumb, "Panels can be inset into bigger panels to show different points in space simultaneously! Repeating panels can freeze the flow of time! Time is an illusion that can be shattered in comics! Showing the same scene from different angles freezes it in time by turning the page into a diagram—an orthographic projection!" Art Spiegelman, "Afterword," *Breakdowns: Portrait of the Artist as a Young %@&*!* (New York: Pantheon Books, 2008), n.p.

12. Scott McCloud, *Understanding Comics: The Invisible Art* (Northampton, MA: Kitchen Sink Press, 1993), 70–74.

13. Will Eisner employed the term "sequential art" in *Comics and Sequential Art* (Tamarac, FL: Poorhouse Press, 1985).

14. See for example Theodor Adorno, "Parataxis: On Hölderlin's Late Poetry," in *Notes to Literature, Volume Two*, ed. Rolf Tiedemann, trans. Shierry Weber Nicholsen (New York: Columbia University Press, 1992), 109–49. For a reading of modernist prose parataxis, see David Hayman, "James Joyce, Paratactitian," *Contemporary Literature* 26, no. 2 (Summer 1985): 155–78. On the connection to montage, see Henry Ebel, "Parataxis and Montage," in *After Dionysus: An Essay on Where We Are Now* (Rutherford: Fairleigh Dickinson University Press, 1972), 34–51.

15. Erich Auerbach, *Mimesis: The Representation of Reality in Western Literature*, trans. Willard D. Trask (Princeton: Princeton University Press, 1953), 118.

16. Auerbach, *Mimesis*, 107, 75, 71.

17. Auerbach, *Mimesis*, 166, 105.

18. Susan Stanford Friedman, "Cultural Parataxis and Transnational Landscapes of Reading," in *Modernism, Volume 1*, ed. Astradur Eysteinsson and Vivian Liska (Amsterdam: John Benjamins Publishing Company, 2007), 35–52, 37.

19. McCloud, 67. For a similar reading of these processes in poetry, see Barbara Hernstein Smith, "Thematic Structure and Closure," *Poetic Closure: A Study of How Poems End* (Chicago: University of Chicago Press, 1968), 96–150.

20. This is Benjamin's method in *The Arcades Project*, particularly in Convolute N, which most fully treats the notion of the dialectical image. This model, which was a point of contention between Benjamin and Adorno, is treated at length by Susan Buck-Morss in *The Origin of Negative Dialectics: Theodor W. Adorno, Walter Benjamin, and the Frankfurt Institute* (New York: The Free Press, 1977), 107, 143, 176, and in *The Dialectics of Seeing: Walter Benjamin and the Arcades Project* (Cambridge, Mass.: The MIT Press, 1989), 210–15, 218–51.

21. For another overview of this method, see Michael W. Jennings, *Dialectical Images: Walter Benjamin's Theory of Literary Criticism* (Ithaca: Cornell University Press, 1987).

22. Not all of Spiegelman's early works were included. For example, absent were his "Viper" comics, including "The Viper: Vicar of Vice, Villainy, and Vickedness!"—a five-page exercise in depravity, which sets up a new kid in the big city, one "Willie Wetback, Boy Immigrant," whom the Viper befriends, receives oral sex from, beheads, and then defiles; originally printed in *Bijou Funnies* #7 (November 1972). For a good overview of *Breakdowns* and its constituent comics, see Bill Kartalopoulos, "Comics as Art: Spiegelman's *Breakdowns*," *Indy Magazine* (Winter 2005).

23. A minor outlier is the three-page "Maus," which was first published in R. Crumb's *Funny Aminals* (1972) and is one of Spiegelman's most conventional underground comix.

24. Interview with Alfred Bergdoll, 1979, *Art Spiegelman: Conversations*, ed. Joseph Witek (Jackson: University Press of Mississippi, 2007), 7.

25. John Benson, "Art Spiegelman: From *Maus* to Now," *Comics Journal* #40 (June 1978): 36–37.

26. Gilbert Choat, "James Joyce, Picasso, Stravinsky, and Spiegelman," *Alternative Media* 10, no. 2 (Fall 1978): 7.

27. Choat, "James Joyce," 7.

28. "Ace Hole" was also reprinted in Marvel's *Comix Book* #1 (October 1974).

29. For more on how Spiegelman primes readers to recognize these allusions, see Thomas J. Roberts, "Popular Fiction in the Old Dispensation and the New," *LIT: Literature Interpretation Theory* 4, no. 3 (1993): 245–259.

30. Spiegelman quotes a paraphrase of Stein's *Alice B. Toklas*, taken from James R. Mellow, *Charmed Circle: Gertrude Stein and Company* (New York: Avon Books, 1974), 139.

31. Art Spiegelman, "Ace Hole: Midget Detective," *Short Order Comix* #2 (1974), 3.

32. Spiegelman, "Ace Hole," 1.

33. Spiegelman, "Ace Hole," 6.

34. For an overview of the Comics Code's origins and iterations, see Amy Kiste Nyberg, *Seal of Approval: The History of the Comics Code* (Jackson: University Press of Mississippi, 1998); the 1954 Comics Code is reprinted on pages 166–69.

35. Chute, "Graphic Narrative," 413.

36. Mike Kelly, "Art Spiegelman and His Circle: New York City and the Downtown Scene," *International Journal of Comic Art* 10, no. 1 (Spring 2008): 313–39, 318–19.

37. On the influence of *MAD* on Spiegelman's works, see Bill Kartalopoulos, "Borders, Breakdowns, and MAD-ness," *Indy Magazine* (Winter 2005).

38. Bill Griffith, "Politics, Pinheads, & Post-Modernism," *Comics Journal* #157 (March 1991): 50–98, 72.

39. Griffith, "Politics," 70, 72.

40. Mike Kelly, in "Art Spiegelman and His Circle," describes the social scene around *RAW*. See also the two-part oral history of *RAW* compiled by Bill Kartalopoulos in *Indy Magazine* (Winter 2005).

41. Art Spiegelman and Françoise Mouly, ed., *Read Yourself RAW* (New York: Pantheon Books, 1987), introduction, n.p.

42. For the cultural relevance of *RAW*, see Roger Sabin, *Comics, Comix & Graphic Novels: A History of Comic Art* (New York: Phaidon, 1996), 178–88; Patrick Rosenkranz, *Rebel Visions: The Underground Comix Revolution, 1963–1975* (Seattle: Fantagraphics Books, 2002), 252–53.

43. A second series of three issues appeared in a more conventional book format, published by Penguin in 1989–91, following on Spiegelman's success with the first volume of *Maus*.

44. Art Spiegelman, *Comics, Essays, Graphics & Scraps: From Maus to Now to Maus to Now* (New York: Raw Books & Graphics, 1999), 13.

45. Françoise Mouly, "Introduction," *Covering the New Yorker* (New York: Abbeville Press Publishers, 2000), 6–11, 9.

46. Jeet Heer, *In Love with Art: Françoise Mouly's Adventures in Comics with Art Spiegelman* (Toronto: Coach House Books, 2013), 68.

47. Heer, *In Love with Art*, 68.

48. Gary Panter, "Jimbo," *RAW* #8 (September 1986), 25–35, 25.

49. For an example of an unimpressed review, see Roberta Smith, "High and Low Meet on a One-Way Street," *New York Times*, October 5, 1990: C1, C25.

50. Kirk Varnedoe and Adam Gopnik, *High & Low: Modern Art and Popular Culture* (New York: The Museum of Modern Art, 1990), 15.

51. Varnedoe and Gopnik, *High & Low*, 16.

52. Art Spiegelman, *MetaMaus: A Look Inside a Modern Classic,* Maus (New York: Pantheon, 2011), 203.

53. Varnedoe and Gopnik, *High & Low*, 13.

54. Spiegelman, *MetaMaus*, 204. Spiegelman would propose a "Low/Low" show as a direct counterpoint to the "High & Low" MoMA exhibition, which would eventually lead to the 2005–06 "Masters of American Comics" show at UCLA's Hammer Museum and the Museum of

Contemporary Art; see Spiegelman's interview with Gene Kannenberg, Jr., 2002, in *Conversations*, 238–62, 242.

55. Art Spiegelman, "High Art Lowdown," *Artforum* (December 1990), 115. Spiegelman also participated in an interview walk-through of the exhibit, "Dore Ashton and Art Spiegelman Visit 'High and Low' at the MoMA," *Art International* 14 (Spring/Summer 1991): 60–64.

56. Spiegelman's work appeared in the exhibition catalogue, which included his and Mouly's cover of *Read Yourself RAW* and a page from the "Mauschwitz" chapter of *Maus*.

57. Gould also appears in the show's exhibition catalogue.

58. Subsequent reprints of this piece remove the text at the top and bottom of Picasso's Stein portrait, thus nullifying the joke.

59. For a review of the show, see Michael Kimmelman, "Examining How 'Maus' Evolved," *New York Times*, December 27, 1991: C3.

60. Press release, The Museum of Modern Art, "Projects: Art Spiegelman," December 1991, 1.

61. This setup would be repeated at later exhibitions of the *Maus* materials. An image of the gallery appears in *MetaMaus*, on page 204.

62. James E. Young, "The Holocaust as Vicarious Past: Art Spiegelman's 'Maus' and the Afterimages of History," *Critical Inquiry* 24, no. 3 (Spring 1998): 666–99, 692.

63. Robert Storr, "Making *Maus*," reprinted in Art Spiegelman, *Co-Mix: A Retrospective of Comics, Graphics, and Scraps* (Montreal: Drawn & Quarterly, 2013), 127.

64. Press release, 2.

A RAGPICKER'S ART

Spiegelman's Jazz Cosmopolitanism

ARIELA FREEDMAN

As Art Spiegelman's collaboration with the saxophonist and composer Phillip Johnston in the stage show *WORDLESS!* makes loud and clear, the soundtrack for comics has often been jazz. Spiegelman explains the conjunction in an interview by noting: "Jazz and comics both have intertwined histories of being whorehouse culture, as well as now having become symphonic, museum culture."[1] Perhaps even more revealing is his citation of Miles Davis's famous refusal to define or contain the genre—"I'll play it for you first and tell you what it is later."[2] Like jazz, comics mixes high and low registers. It is what the scholar of literature and music Alfred Appel in his book *Jazz Modernism* calls a "ragpicker's art": an aesthetic that samples the familiar and everyday by "alchemists of the vernacular who have 'jazzed' the ordinary and given it new life."[3] Jazz is also audience-based and improvisational, creating forms that are only complete in performance. In much the same way that the audience brings jazz to life, Scott McCloud, Spiegelman, and others argue that the reader helps complete a comic, closing the circle of artistic creation by filling in the gap between panels in the mind's eye.[4]

Jazz accentuates one of Spiegelman's most prominent themes over the last thirty years: the rejection of the dichotomy between the high and low in the arts. His work since *Maus* has repeatedly returned to the arts of the twenties and thirties, to the Jazz Age and its aftermath. *In the Shadow of No Towers* (2004) features tumbling cartoon characters from early newspaper comics. With *The Wild Party* (1994), Spiegelman illustrated and gave new life to the eponymous, largely forgotten 1924 Jazz Age poem by Joseph Moncure March. His collaboration with the dance company Pilobolus on the ballet animation *Hapless Hooligan in 'Still Moving'* (2010) is based on Frederick Burr Opper's popular comic strip *Happy Hooligan* (1900–1932). Also in 2010 Spiegelman edited and prefaced the Library of America's two-volume set of Lynd Ward's complete woodcut novels (1929–1937), which inspired and informed the 2013 performance of *WORDLESS!* with avant-garde jazz musician Phillip Johnston. In returning to the Roaring Twenties, Spiegelman evokes a threshold period in American history—postwar, pre-Depression—when popular arts including jazz and comics conspired to transform the landscape of an increasingly diverse and cosmopolitan America.

WORDLESS! in particular is both a show about musical lineage and a visual catalogue of influence. The performance features avant-garde comics by Frans Masereel, Lynd Ward, H. M. Bateman, Si Lewen, Milt Gross, and Otto Nückel to the accompaniment of jazz music that weaves in and out of Spiegelman's words. During *WORDLESS!* Spiegelman claims: "I needed to graft the high and low branches of my family tree together to climb out of the prison of little boxes that defined my medium."[5] Jazz is not simply a branch on that tree; it is a genre that echoes and emphasizes Spiegelman's attempt to figure out how to marry high and low, to syncopate his rhythms, and bend his notes. Jazz is both soundtrack and synecdoche for the improvisational and democratic American tradition that Spiegelman recovers and embodies. Indeed, comics and jazz were at the crux of the challenge to categories of high and low culture in the first decades of the twentieth century.

In bringing together his post-*Maus* engagements with jazz and comics, I will argue that Spiegelman's emphasis on Jazz Age fast living is nostalgic as well as elegiac. In his introduction to *The Wild Party*, Spiegelman seems to deny this, writing: "My own desire to illustrate *The Wild Party* grows from something beyond a yen for the innocent hedonism of the boop-a-doop and vo-de-oh-do twenties, although I confess to a powerful nostalgia for all the decades that precede my birth." Yet by the end of his essay he laments the distance between March's generation, "which swilled bathtub gin and had a wild party," and "our generation, which gulps Prozac and gets lost in used bookstores."[6] A closer look at the intersecting American traditions of jazz, cosmopolitanism, and comics will help unravel unacknowledged continuities in Spiegelman's career, linking *The Wild Party* with *In The Shadow of No Towers*, and his admiration for woodcut novels with his experimental cross-art collaborations.

MODERNITY AND THE JAZZ BANJORINE

The word "jazz" was first coined not as the name for a music genre, but as one of many labels for modernity. As Jed Rasula points out in a 1912 article in the *San Francisco Bulletin* titled "In Praise of 'Jazz': A Futurist Word Which Has Just Joined the Language," the term itself "was vaguely modernist, not specifically musical."[7] Beyond the Jazz Age of Fitzgeraldian cliché, jazz was one of the primary vernaculars of the avant-garde, especially in Europe, where both America and jazz were synonymous with modernity. In the words of Gilbert Seldes in *The Seven Lively Arts*, jazz was "the symbol, or the byword for a great many elements in the spirit of the time—as far as America is concerned, it is actually our principal expression."[8] At the same time, though jazz was referenced and incorporated into high modernist literary works, the genre's relationship to high modernism was primarily that of an outsider art during the twenties and thirties. T. S. Eliot could joke, "it is a jazz banjorine that I should bring [to a party], not a lute," but he was in danger of doing no such thing.[9] "The Waste-land" (1921) referenced ragtime and incorporated polyrhythm without being confused with the "primitivist" and popular music of the cabaret and dance hall. Jazz could be mined for its vitality and energy, but would not be included in the category of high art almost until the 1950s. As French composer Georges Auric said as early as 1920, "Jazz woke us up but from now on let us stop our ears in order not to hear it."[10]

In Fitzgerald's famous 1931 formulation, "the word 'jazz,' in its progress towards respectability, has meant first sex, then dancing, then music. It is associated with a state of nervous stimulation, not unlike that of big cities behind the lines of a war."[11] The initial association of jazz with transgression and underground culture—as Rasula points out, "after Prohibition became law in 1919, jazz and speakeasies were virtually synonymous"[12]—soon gave way to a climb towards what Fitzgerald calls "respectability" and what we might call cultural legitimation. Although the trajectory towards high culture was slow, it began early and detoured through Europe. In 1893, the Czech composer Antonín Dvořák, whose work often absorbed folk influences, proclaimed in the *Boston Herald* that "negro melodies . . . are the folk songs of America, and your composers must turn to them. . . . In the negro melodies of America I discover all that is needed for a great and noble school of music. They are pathetic, tender, passionate, melancholy, solemn, religious, bold, merry, gay, or what you will. It is music that suits itself to any mood or purpose."[13] Dvořák's praise provoked an interest in early blues and ragtime as the native arts of America.

If jazz tapped into an American tradition, it was also framed and precipitated by the dissonant and cosmopolitan melting pot of the city. As Rasula writes, jazz was "the first thoroughly cosmopolitan music of African-Americans,"[14] sped up by patterns of urbanization and by the Great Migration, which concentrated musicians in cities. Rasula calls jazz "the soundtrack of a threshold," though his claim surpasses the familiar argument that jazz served as background music. Jazz did not only accompany the modern city, it helped acclimatize the urban dweller to the experience of modernity, conveying "a practical image of jazz (as/and) modernism as a deliberate response to modernity as lived experience."[15]

Jazz channeled the energies of urbanization, but it also heightened them. Under its influence, Piet Mondrian's stately 1940 composition in red, blue, and yellow, *New York City I*, turned into 1942's joyfully kinetic *Broadway Boogie Woogie*, at once the map of a city grid and the synesthetic quickened tempo in "the unrelenting, hammering manner of boogie-woogie performances . . . the painting swings."[16] In this instance, the accessible populist radicalism of jazz pivots into conventionally highbrow forms like abstract painting, even as jazz itself becomes a highbrow pursuit. Seldes claims that syncopation, "which has so liberated jazz from normal polyphony . . . is one reason why Americans are often readier to listen to modern music than peoples who haven't got used to dissonance in their folk and popular music."[17] Jazz exemplified the modern, and in addition, it served as a gateway to other expressions of modernity.

LOWBROW CHAUTAUQUA: *WORDLESS!* AND *HAPPY HOOLIGAN*

Though comics were a European import, critics have often talked about comics and jazz in conjunction as examples of American popular culture *par excellence*. Seldes includes comics alongside jazz as two examples of the heterogeneous and vital public arts of America. Later on, with less enthusiasm, C. L. R. James cites "comics and the evolution of jazz" as part of "the deep social responses and evolution of the American people."[18] Seldes's book, *The Seven Lively Arts*—cited by Jeet Heer as "one of the first to consider the comics strip as a creative, expressive medium"[19]—argues that the study of the "lively arts" or of popular culture necessitates the abandonment of "two of the most disagreeable words of the language: high- and low-brow."[20] Writing in part as response to English art critic Clive Bell's casually racist 1921 article in the *New Republic*, "Plus de Jazz," which dismissed the genre as a "childish . . . horror of the Noble and Beautiful" marked by "jeers and grimaces,"[21] Seldes positions his work as defense and eulogy for the value of the popular arts. At the root of Bell's disdain for jazz was the dispersion of cultural authority: "What, I believe, has turned so many intelligent and sensitive people against jazz is the encouragement it has given to thousands of the stupid and vulgar to fancy that they can understand art and to hundreds of the conceited to imagine that they can create it."[22] By contrast, Seldes proclaims a "revolution" which announces not only the coming-of-age of the popular arts, but also the "expected—and wonderful—arrival of America at a point of creative intensity."[23]

If comics, vaudeville, and jazz were sometimes joined in the cultural imagination of critics, they also frequently accompanied one another in performance. Robert S. Petersen notes that "many early cartoonists worked the vaudeville circuit . . . where they would appear alongside a host of other variety acts."[24] In these "chalk talks," cartoonists including Rube Goldberg, Winsor McCay, Rudolph Dirks, and Milton Caniff would caricature audience members and play with drawings "that would evolve from one picture to another."[25] When Spiegelman refers to his *WORDLESS!* show as "Intellectual Vaudeville" and "Lowbrow Chautauqua," he is consciously referencing this performance tradition.

One of the conventional ways to distinguish between comics and animation has been to emphasize the difference between the stillness of the comics page and the illusion of seamless movement created on the screen. Spiegelman has himself described comics as "frozen boxes of time."[26] But cartooning and animation are proximate arts, and early cartoonists were quick to adapt their drawings to the new technologies of film. Winsor McCay was the most important figure in this transition; he introduced film into his live vaudeville performances, and later released the pioneering animated shorts "Gertie the Dinosaur" (1914) and "How a Mosquito Operates" (1912). In *WORDLESS!* Spiegelman channels McCay by animating cartoons from the twenties using QuickTime—a remediation that prompted some blowback from critics. In his *Paris Review* article on the show, Harry Backlund complains that Spiegelman never addresses "the huge contradiction of the show itself: he tells the crowd about the beauty of wordless novels, but the projections he shows in the interludes are not wordless novels at all. Set to Johnston's jazz and animated by a panning camera, the sequences have a new visual character, and a new sense of time. They effectively become silent films."[27]

But this very adaptation through movement pays homage to the vaudeville acts that mixed drawing and animation in order to stimulate and delight audiences in the teens and twenties. It is not so much that this strategy is new, as that it is old enough to have been nearly forgotten. As Spiegelman acknowledges in his catalogue of influences, the stylistic innovations of *WORDLESS!* are less invention than tribute. In the vaudeville *Gesamtkunstwerk* of jazz, animation, and lecture, he tips his hat to those pioneering cartoonists who turned their solitary art into performance and then made the pictures dance.

While some cartoonists experimented with vaudeville, others turned their work to different kinds of adaptation. In 1922, George Herriman's *Krazy Kat* was adapted into a jazz pantomime choreographed by Adolph Bolm, written by John Alden Carpenter, and performed by the *Ballet Intime* in New York. Bolm had been a key member of Serge Diaghilev's *Ballets Russes*, and though the *Krazy Kat* ballet achieved neither the notoriety nor the cultural impact of the *Ballets Russes* performance of Igor Stravinsky's *The Rites of Spring* nearly a decade earlier, it participated in the same modernist impulse to cross genres and media under the auspices of avant-garde performance. Spiegelman's collaboration with Pilobolus on a modern-dance and comics hybrid should be placed directly in the lineage of the *Krazy Kat* ballet, to the extent that both align comics with other arts in the style of *Gesamtkunstwerk* modernist fusion.

The *Krazy Kat* ballet was subtitled "A Jazz Pantomime for Piano," making Carpenter "one of the first composers to use the word 'jazz' in the title of a concert work."[28] What Carpenter "meant by jazz, then a newly coined term, remains open to speculation," the musicologist Howard Pollack wrote in 2012, and continued: "he seems to have had in mind an agglomeration of music that included jazzy popular song and jazzy dance band arrangements as well as the sort of improvised music by mostly black singers and instrumentalists that in time became known as real jazz."[29] Like Carpenter's arrangement, the soundtrack for *Hapless Hooligan* is eclectic and prominently features a number of jazzy pieces, including several by band leader Raymond Scott, whose music was licensed and adapted by Carl Stallings at *Looney Tunes* as backdrop to the exploits of *Daffy Duck*, *Porky Pig*, *Bugs Bunny*, and other Warner Bros. shorts. It is a matter of regret to some jazz musicians that the genre became famous in part as a soundtrack for kids' cartoons. In his autobiography, celebrated jazz trumpeter and educator Wynton Marsalis complains that jazz was "trivialized" by "associating it on screen with cartoons and sex scenes."[30]

But Marsalis's frustration is only the flip side of Spiegelman's more favorable, paradoxical observation that comics and jazz are at once "whorehouse culture" and "just for kids." The addition of music and movement "jazzes" Spiegelman's drawings and makes them shimmy. The full title of Spiegelman's modern dance collaboration, *Hapless Hooligan in "Still Moving,"* playfully highlights the tension between the static art of comics and the constant motion of the dancers. By the time he presents *WORDLESS!* Spiegelman seems to have fully embraced the fluidity of both music and cartoon animation. "Making 'Wordless!' has been a bit like taking sausages and turning them back into pigs," he says near the close of the show, adding: "We've tried to make our pigs dance without violating their true nature."[31]

JAZZ COSMOPOLITANISM: FROM *THE WILD PARTY* TO *IN THE SHADOW OF NO TOWERS*

Jazz and comics are historically connected, but they also share a plasticity that appeals to Spiegelman. In a 2014 interview about *WORDLESS!* Spiegelman the cartoonist praises Johnston the jazz musician as "a stylistic switch-hitter."[32] In another conversation, he clarifies:

> I would say that jazz has a suppleness that allows a lot of different kinds of things to fit into its idioms. In other words, these books are different

> from each other; I didn't want to do it all with [the] same tomato sauce. Each one has its own character, and Phillip has something that he does with the music he composes that's very analogous to—do you have any of my other work, besides *Maus*?[33]

There is an interesting slippage in this quotation, from the range of silent comics that *WORDLESS!* encompasses to the underappreciated variety of Spiegelman's own work, obscured by the gargantuan shadow of a tiny mouse. As the comics collected in *Breakdowns* make clear, before he developed the signature style of *Maus*, Spiegelman was a pastiche artist, a stylistic impersonator whose work ranged from the early alt-comix printed in *Arcade* and *RAW* to the neo-noir of "Ace Hole, Midget Detective." If *Maus* has been seen, even by Spiegelman himself, as the product of an artist finding his style and voice,[34] it is equally true that the stylistic consistency and autobiographical intimacy of *Maus* inhibited Spiegelman's broader artistic palette. By *Maus II*, his impatience is evident; he resists being contained by the towering achievement of *Maus* or in the straightjacket of his meta-expressionism and confessional approach.

When Spiegelman followed *Maus I* and *II* by reissuing and illustrating March's Jazz Age poem "The Wild Party," it was in a deliberate move to jazz up his own aesthetic trajectory. In their *Co-Mix* retrospective, the editors Tom Devlin, Jeet Heer, and Chris Oliveros explain that not only was Spiegelman "gripped by the evocative power and steamy nature of the story," but more than that, "having just released the second volume of *Maus*, Spiegelman was eager to do a book that was sexy, stylized and decorative—all qualities that the narrative of *Maus* didn't allow him to explore."[35] *The Wild Party* would not be a graphic novel but an illustrated volume, letting "the artist flex his muscles as a draftsman while also playing with a new way of merging words with pictures."[36] Poetry rather than prose, adaptation rather than autobiography, stylization rather than testimony—*The Wild Party* allowed Spiegelman to engage the glamour noir of Fitzgerald's Jazz Age while avoiding the repetition of a closer and more implicating historical violence.

Spiegelman begins his introduction to *The Wild Party* in the tone of a hard-boiled detective: "It was the spine that grabbed me."[37] The serendipitous discovery of the book in a used bookstore led to his discovery of the poem, "a hard-boiled, jazz-age tragedy told in syncopated rhyming couplets. It has the mnemonic tenacity, if not the wholesomeness, of a nursery rhyme, and to read it once is to get large shards of it permanently lodged in the brain."[38] Spiegelman cites the poem's influence on William S. Burroughs ("the book that made me want to be a writer") and Burroughs' dry response to the question of whether or not it is poetry—"Of course it's poetry. It rhymes."[39] Rather than emphasizing rhyme, Spiegelman frames the poem as a modernist mash-up, writing:

> *The Wild Party* is closer to "Frankie and Johnny" than to *Tristan and Iseult*, but March had been a protégé of Robert Frost's at Amherst, and knew his way around villanelle as well as around speakeasies. It owes as much to the language and sizzle of the tabloids, to the lyrics and rhythms of hot jazz and to the close-ups and cuts of silent films as it does to any earlier narrative verse other than off-color limericks.[40]

Here once again Spiegelman celebrates the vitality engendered by the hybridization of high and low in a work as indebted to classical poetry and early cinema as to true crime folksongs. Among other things, *The Wild Party* echoes Eliot's contemporaneous masterpiece "The Waste Land," especially the erotic languor and candlelit laquearia of the second section, "The Game of Chess." It evokes the unsentimental aestheticism of "The Love Song of J. Alfred Prufrock." It also has moments that mimic Frost at his pithiest, so closely as to ring the gong of plagiarism rather than the tinkling bell of influence. The ninth section of *The Wild Party* begins by intoning: "some love is fire; some love is rust/ but the fiercest, cleanest love is lust," a knock-off of Frost's poem, "Ice and Fire": "Some say the world will end in fire/ some say in ice/ from what I've tasted of desire I side with those who favour fire," published in *Harper's Magazine* in 1920.

In his review of the 1994 edition, the British literary and cultural critic Michael Wood compares Spiegelman's illustrations for *The Wild Party* to "dark Expressionist woodcuts, lurid, detailed, nightmarish" visions of the city.[41] But they are also indebted more particularly to the graphic tradition, especially the wordless novels of the twenties and thirties, such as Frans Masereel's *A Passionate Journey*, which narrates the life of an everyman in a modern city. Spiegelman's evocation of the woodcut technique creates a heavy chiaroscuro of light and shadow, although pen and ink, as opposed to the woodcut, no longer necessitates it; the sharply inked grain of the cross-hatched background is a nod and an homage to the heavier labor of the woodcut artist.

The Wild Party opens with a description of its two central characters, a "sexually ambitious" vaudeville dancer named Queenie and her lover, Burr, a sadistic clown with a history of violence against women. The pictures are darkly stylish; in the first full image, Queenie is held in the narcissistic infinite regress of two facing mirrors, dressed only in a rocket bra, tap pants, and knee-high stockings; her eyes are empty, pupilless slits. Occasionally, Spiegelman inserts cartooning emanata alongside his more sophisticated drawings: a lightning bolt on the cover to emphasize the deep dip of a couple dancing, and later on, a spurl above Queenie's head to signal irritation. The layering of the expressionist woodcut style and the broader, slapstick signaling of the emanata lightens the impact of the illustrations and claims their lineage in two

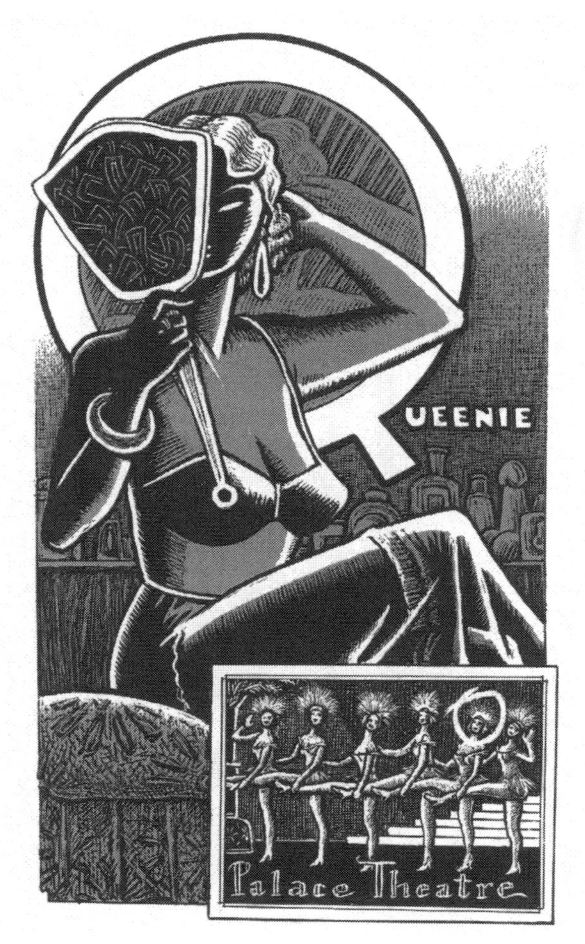

From *The Wild Party: The Lost Classic by Joseph Moncure March* (New York: Pantheon Books, 1994), p. 2. Copyright © 1994 by Art Spiegelman.

different traditions—the dramatic expressionist style of the woodcut novel and the humorous symbolia of the cartoon.

In part, the poem is well suited to comics adaptation due to the caricaturing broadness of its depictions. Following a dramatic fight, Queenie and Burr decide to host a party, and March exults in a catalogue of its disreputable guests. As Wood writes:

> The party is adorned with all kinds of supposed Twenties low-life: Madelaine True the lesbian; Jackie the bisexual; Eddie the boxer; Dolores the whore; the gay D'Armano Brothers. "And the usual two/Loud Jew/Theatrical managers." Dolores is said to be, in spite of her Spanish

> appearance, "somewhat Negro/And a great deal Jew." The casual racism is unpleasant even if it is, sadly, what we might expect; but it is not more unpleasant than the poem's use of its whole deck of stereotypes.[42]

March later regretted the farcical racism of his two long poems, "The Wild Party" and "The Set-Up," and released expurgated versions alongside a short memoir in 1968. Spiegelman returns to the unexpurgated version, in a defense of the original as "a perfect picture of its time."[43] If Spiegelman's insistence on the original text returns the language to its initial provocative charge, his illustrations sometimes manipulate and nuance the anti-Semitism and racism of the poem's descriptions, especially in his depiction of "the usual two/ Loud Jew/ Theatrical managers," who together "stood engrossed/ Bewailing high production cost."[44] In Spiegelman's drawing, which runs across the top of the page, the two managers face one another, mopping their brows and looking alarmed, plewds of sweat emanating from their brows. One of the managers could be straight out of a cartoon in the Weimar expressionist magazine *Der Sturm*: hooked nose, receding dark hair, spectacles, excess weight, hooded eyes, and blubber lips. But the other is drawn as a classic blonde, with a full head of hair, a trim figure, a bobbed nose, and a strong jaw. Spiegelman's drawing is an implicit, playful rebuttal of March's offensive stereotypes.

By contrast, Spiegelman blatantly plays up the misogyny of the poem. Nothing in Queenie's text description quite gets us to Spiegelman's image of her as an arch-narcissist pinned between two mirrors. His drawing of the "unlucky girl" "beat" by Burrs with "the heel of a shoe/ Til her lips went blue," so badly that it may have caused her "miscarriage/ Two days later"[45] is erotic, rather than violent: the strap of a slip sliding off a round shoulder, the skirt lifted to show a dark triangle of crotch. In one nude, Queenie has the blank small eyes and curly hair of Little Orphan Annie. More tellingly, none of the male characters are drawn in the nude. At the end of the poem, when Queenie and her new lover, Black, go to bed, she is naked except for her stockings, while he wears an undershirt and boxing shorts. This, too, is well within a comics tradition, from the Tijuana bibles that obscenely parodied popular comics strips, to the notoriously uneven exposure of male and female bodies in both comics and movies today.

If recovering the tradition of the Jazz Age is all in good fun, we ought not to gloss over the replication of racism and misogyny. Wood's impatience is justified: "We are manifestly slumming here; villanelle folk being cool in the speakeasy. This is what seems most hopelessly dated about the work . . . a time when nice white folks felt safe enough to play at risk, and when vice was easily defined and therefore (if you were a liberal) easily romanticised."[46] Perhaps we might revise Wood's sentence to note that it was also a time when nice white *men* felt safe enough to play at risk. The consequences for women were more drastic. Beyond the ragtime fantasy of the poem is a climate of everyday violence in which a woman is so badly beaten by her husband that she miscarries, while a fourteen-year-old girl brought to the party is nearly raped. In this context, Queenie's violence starts to look like self-defense.

The stylized violence of the poem builds up as the story continues. Spiegelman prefaces the later sections with candles melting away to track the time in the book and the burnout of the action. Shadows on the wall turn the party into a bacchanal, and as the characters get drunker and rowdier their faces become more grotesque and distorted, their smiles turned to grimaces. As the night grows later and the party becomes an orgy, Spiegelman mimics the anonymity of the protagonists in a panel that crowds body parts in fragments, and turns two kissing faces into a blurred, stretched monstrosity, in a technique reminiscent of the distorted faces that dissolve in the biomorphic canvases of British painter Francis Bacon.

The poem culminates in a betrayal and a murder. Queenie meets Black at the party. Instead of the blurred chaos of the orgy, they retreat behind the bedroom door, and their congress is described in a catalogue of metaphors that often served as filmic shorthand for the sex acts the movies could not show. Spiegelman riffs on this amusing indirectness with white paneled boxes of a burning fire, hammers clanging, a rough drawing of a train going through a tunnel, lightning flashing, a cannon erupting, and above that, as if in defiance of the censors, an unmetaphorical depiction of Queenie and Black having sex, complete with a detailed nipple. Burr walks in on them and there is an altercation; Black shoots his rival dead but even as Queenie is urging him to escape, "The door sprang open/ and the cops rushed in."[47] The clipped closing lines of the poem slam the door on the licentious scene, restoring law and order. Vice will be punished, virtue receives its reward; four years before the crash on Wall Street, the party is over.

In this Jazz Age poem, music itself plays a surprising role, not only as accompaniment for a pornographic fantasy of absolute loucheness in the 1920s, but also as an ecstatic and moving aesthetic experience that gives momentary respite from the inflamed intoxication of the party. The Brothers D'Armano, incestuous siblings whose introduction forms one of the nastier set pieces of stereotype in the poem—they are described as lisping, shrill-voiced, "powdered,/ rouged,/ sleek of hair:/ they must have worn/ pink silk underwear"[48] (curiously, Spiegelman draws them as drag kings, with tuxedoes, thin moustaches, and rounded, feminine faces)—agree to a musical performance late in the evening. The song they sing—"My Sweetie is Gone"—seems to be based on Bessie Smith's "My Sweetie Went Away," recorded on September 9, 1923, with the Down-Home Trio.[49] Though the Brothers D'Armano are ridiculed in the poem, the song transports them and their audience into ecstasy:

A chord rang out: turned blue, and ran
Through a syncopating vamp,
And the song began.
The verse was nothing—but the chorus was Art;
And its music was enough to tear you apart.[50]

The spell of the song brings a lull in the chaos of the party, its soul-tearing blues adding a tinge of melancholy to the gathering. Though Spiegelman does not visibly pick up on the cue, it is hard to imagine an artist as metafictionally self-conscious as he is failing to notice his own capitalized first name at the end of the fourth line. What do the D'Armano Duo, and by extension Spiegelman's own artful images, ultimately offer? Perhaps it is a moment of peace, a focusing of dispersed attention, or a surge of feeling in this hardened audience. Even later that night, a "white-faced youth, with a battered hat" sits in front of the Victrola and weeps as the record plays: "Each time it ended,/ He would look up startled: greatly offended./ He would then rise/ With streaming eyes./ Carefully,/ With a face of pain,/ He would start the same tune over again."[51] Spiegelman draws the youth in profile, with round button eyes and a weak chin, in contrast to the craggy-faced, lantern-jawed men who dominate the party. Behind the youth, in greenish shadow, are the collapsed bodies of the unconscious guests.

From *The Wild Party: The Lost Classic by Joseph Moncure March* (New York: Pantheon Books, 1994), p. 58–59. Copyright © 1994 by Art Spiegelman.

From *The Wild Party: The Lost Classic by Joseph Moncure March* (New York: Pantheon Books, 1994), p. 100–101. Copyright © 1994 by Art Spiegelman.

Michael Wood claims *The Wild Party* is a poem about the city. "What we are looking at in *The Wild Party* is the modern city: Berlin, Paris, New York; drink and sex and danger; life lived fast, and burning itself out, as all those candles, in the text and in the drawings, so ominously declare."[52] The city is not just any city; it is New York, which Spiegelman—a cosmopolitan rooted in Lower Manhattan—will later claim as his own. Spiegelman's Lower Manhattan exists in time as much as in space, from the ghosts of Sunday comics supplement stars to the far-off sounds of a wild party. When Spiegelman's version of "The Wild Party" was published in 1994, the city was undergoing change, as cities always are. But New York was about to change much faster. Beginning with Spiegelman's publication, *fin-de-millennium* New York found unexpected resonance in the Jazz Age of "The Wild Party," which was performed in two different New York theatrical productions during the 1999–2000 season; the following year, on September 11, the towers were hit. The Republican mayoral primary scheduled for that day was postponed, and Michael Bloomberg won in part on the promise of restoring stability in the wake of the terrorist attacks. The New York of the 2000s—post 9/11, post-Bloomberg—seemed as distant from the New York of the nineties as the New York of the nineties was distant from the New York of the twenties.

Nonetheless, in his response to the September 11 attacks, Spiegelman remained cathected to the art of New York in the twenties, now turning to Jazz Age comics. The unusual structure of *In the Shadow of No Towers*—half memoir, half archive—provides a kind of antidote to the crisis of 9/11 in the playful "ghosts of some Sunday supplement stars born on nearby Park Row about a century earlier," which return "to haunt one denizen of the neighborhood addled by all that's happened since."[53] Here, Spiegelman celebrates "old comic strips; vital, unpretentious ephemera from the optimistic dawn of the twentieth century,"[54] and he uses jazz as a metaphor for the hybridized and democratic power of comics in their parallel play between high and low. The "perpetual tug-of-war between vulgar and genteel culture in America has often been a fruitful one," Spiegelman writes in *No Towers*, "generating New Orleans whorehouse jazz on the one hand and Gershwin's *Rhapsody in Blue* on the other."[55] For jazz as for comics, the beginning of the twentieth century was a period of "open-ended possibility and giddy disorientation that inevitably gave way to the constraints that came as the form defined itself."[56] His is a political nostalgia—less an elegy for the past than an attempt to use the uninhibited art of the past as corrective to a narrowed and intolerant present.

Spiegelman declares himself a "rooted cosmopolitan" in *No Towers*,[57] and the creative fervor of the comics supplements and jazz bands of the twenties serves as a cultural background to the idealized New York of his imagination. These ghosts of the old New York contrast with the 9/11 breakdown described in *No*

Towers, which charts a city in physical and metaphorical collapse. Spiegelman's digitally mediated representation of the burning towers shows how distant post-9/11 New York is from the hand-drawn fantasies of the early Park Row Sunday pages. When it comes to the collapse of the towers, autography fails, and the iterative computer copy comes closest to representing a disaster that the nation encountered as televised and recursive. Spiegelman writes:

> The pivotal image from my 9/11 morning—one that didn't get photographed or videotaped into memory but still remains burned onto the inside of my eyelids several years later—was the image of the looming North Tower's glowing bones just before it collapsed. I repeatedly tried to paint this with humiliating results but eventually came close to capturing the vision of disintegration digitally on my computer.[58]

The attack on the towers is followed by jingoistic nationalism and militarism that alienate Spiegelman. His version of artistic catharsis marks a return to the promise of old New York, whose tumbling cartoon characters are both repetition of, and respite from, the falling bodies of the towers. In a gesture that serves less as haunting than as exorcism, Spiegelman recalls for us the cosmopolitanism of the Jazz Age, a nostalgic utopia that once foreshadowed a very different future.

In that sense, future research might explore *The Wild Party* and *In the Shadow of No Towers* as companion volumes. Each imagines a celebratory and endangered cosmopolitanism rooted in the brief years of postwar, pre-Depression America at one end, and in the aftermath of terror on the eve of the global financial crisis at the other. By the 1930s, the Jazz Age had ended, and the hybridity and miscegenation of jazz music became a sign of more than erotic transgression. Particularly in Europe, jazz signified racial impurity and democratic freedom, and as such was brutally suppressed. Fascist governments, whose musical tastes were haughtily classical and nationalist, outlawed jazz, which had once been the utopian soundtrack for a cosmopolitan identity. Spiegelman's own nostalgic return to jazz responds not only to the totalitarian era of the 1930s and 1940s, but also to the failure of post-9/11 America to embrace the immigrant culture that built both jazz and comics.

PASSING: JAZZ, COMICS, RACE

And yet, even the Jazz Age wild parties always left some people out. It is a telling slippage of the word "jazz" that it at once refers to a form of music developed by African American musicians and an era personified by rich white people on Gatsby's lawn. "Ragtime and jazz pioneered the infusion of dominant white culture by African Americans,"[59] as Rasula writes, but jazz was also marred by a history of appropriation. The founding role of African Americans in jazz was either regarded with racist horror by detractors—as in Clive Bell's lament at "the black and grinning muse"[60]—or was whitewashed by the involvement of white band leaders and musicians. Even Seldes, an early champion of jazz, regarded the "negro" contribution as spontaneous, primitive, and merely preliminary to the artistic sophistication of white jazz musicians like Gershwin.

The whiteness of the Jazz Age salon in March's poem (with the unhelpful exception of the Spanish/Jewish/Negro/Mexican harlot) is mostly accurate; while jazz in its cross-race appeal was imagined as a disruption of segregation, in fact segregation was routinely enforced. Discourse around the Jazz Age frequently fell into patterns of "negrophilia and negrophobia,"[61] both of which ultimately served to obscure the historical and aesthetic significance of African American musicians, just as Bessie Smith's original song disappears beneath the performance of the Brothers D'Armano. Wynton Marsalis makes a similar point when he notes that "the whole of jazz, black and white, was a refutation of segregation and racism,"[62] resulting in a color-blind ideal that was misused to belittle Black art: "But what happened time and time again when the negro won? He was denied, or his victory was attributed to 'natural talent.'"[63] "Musical idioms by African Americans are considered to be in the public domain,"[64] author and composer Charley Gerard writes in *Jazz in Black and White*, and argues in the same vein that the idea of jazz as a universal idiom appropriates and erases the particular contributions of African American artists.

Spiegelman is not entirely immune to this racial blindness. In *WORDLESS!* he uses the twin promise of jazz and comics to invoke "an Esperanto understood beyond the borders of language,"[65] and yet something is left out in this nostalgic and deracinating narrative of jazz and comics. Consider the African American George Herriman, creator of *Krazy Kat* and one of Spiegelman's heroes, who was born to a Creole family that hid its racial identity. Herriman's work was for Spiegelman the prime example of an art that "crossed all boundaries between high and low, between vulgar and genteel . . . a kind of art that made use of a jazz patois . . . of Yiddish as part of the language and Shakespeare as part of the language . . . and visuals that move through the Navajo blanket world of art deco and cubism and also with the pure doodle drawing implied by Töpffer taken to its highest expression."[66] Yet Spiegelman's Herriman has little to do with race, inhabiting instead a universal space in defiance of categories and boundaries. "Artists invent their own precursors," Spiegelman says, paraphrasing Borges, and his jazzy Herriman is the key predecessor to his own mashup of high and low, "beloved by intellectuals" but resistant to their categorizations. Even Spiegelman's fedora seems a tribute to the hat Herriman always wore as a way to disguise the telling kinkiness of his hair. But when Spiegelman quips during *WORDLESS!* that the title "graphic novel" was given to comics so "they could pass for white," his offhand gibe unintentionally obscures the ways that the history of comics includes much higher-stake forms of passing. In his next show about comics lineage, Spiegelman will hopefully tip his hat to this other silenced, if not wordless, element of comics history.

Notes

1. Jed Oelbaum, "Quit Thinking Like an Emoticon: An Interview with Art Spiegelman," *GOOD Magazine*, October 8, 2014.

2. Oelbaum, "Quit Thinking."

3. Alfred Appel, *Jazz Modernism: From Ellington and Armstrong to Matisse and Joyce* (New York: Alfred A. Knopf, 2002), 38.

4. Scott McCloud, *Understanding Comics: The Invisible Art* (New York: HarperPerennial, 1994), 63.

5. Harry Backlund, "The Silent Treatment," *The Paris Review*, February 13, 2014.

6. Art Spiegelman, *The Wild Party: The Lost Classic by Joseph Moncure March* (New York: Pantheon, 1999), viii.

7. Jed Rasula, "Jazz and Modernism: Reflections on a Zeitfrage," PhilosophyOfMusic.org: Approaches to Philosophy of Music: Continental, Analytic, Historical, Literary, and Multicultural, 2009.

8. Gilbert Seldes, *The Seven Lively Arts* (New York: Courier Corporation, 1957), 83.

9. T. S. Eliot, *The Letters of T. S. Eliot, Volume I: 1898–1922*, ed. Valerie Eliot (San Diego: Harcourt, 1988), 357. As Chinitz writes: "Eliot's deliberate association with the emerging American popular culture, and with its largely African-American roots, provided a way of laying claim to revolutionary cultural power while simultaneously acknowledging ambivalence about his relationship to it." See David E. Chinitz, *T. S. Eliot and the Cultural Divide* (Chicago: University of Chicago Press, 2005), 23.

10. Rasula, "Jazz and Modernism," 6.

11. F. Scott Fitzgerald, "Echoes of the Jazz Age," in *The Crack-Up*, ed. Edmund Wilson (New York: New Directions Publishing, 2009), 16.

12. Jed Rasula, "Jazz and American Modernism," in *The Cambridge Companion to American Modernism*, ed. Walter Kalaidjian (Cambridge: Cambridge University Press, 2006), 158.

13. "American Music. Dr. Antonin Dvorak Expresses Some Radical Opinions," *Boston Herald*, May 28, 1893. http://www.artsinteractive.org/DT/Pages/67.html.

14. Rasula, "Jazz and American modernism," 159.

15. Rasula, "Jazz and American modernism," 173.

16. Appel, *Jazz and Modernism*, 70.

17. Seldes, *The Seven Lively Arts*, 85.

18. C. L. R. James, "C. L. R. James on Comics," in *Arguing Comics: Literary Masters on a Popular Medium*, ed. Jeet Heer and Kent Worcester (Jackson: University Press of Mississippi, 2004), 142.

19. Heer, *Arguing Comics*, xii.

20. Seldes, *The Seven Lively Arts*, 349.

21. Clive Bell, "Plus de Jazz," *New Republic*, September 21, 1921: 94.

22. Bell, "Plus de Jazz," 95.

23. Seldes, *The Seven Lively Arts*, 84.

24. Robert S. Petersen, *Comics, Manga, and Graphic Novels: A History of Graphic Narratives* (Santa Barbara: ABC-CLIO, LLC, 2011), 100.

25. Petersen, *Comics, Manga, and Graphic Novels*, 100.

26. Art Spiegelman, "Dancing in the Dark! Some Notes on the Art of Collaboration," in "A Cartoon Odyssey: Ink-and-Paper Man Meets Lithe Bodies," by Stephanie Goodman, *New York Times*, July 9, 2010.

27. Backlund, "The Silent Treatment."

28. Howard Pollack, introduction to *Krazy Kat, a Jazz Pantomime for Piano: Original and Revised Versions*, by John Alden Carpenter (New York: Courier Corporation, 2012), v.

29. Pollack, introduction to *Krazy Kat*, v.

30. Wynton Marsalis, with Geoffrey Ward, *Moving to Higher Ground: How Jazz Can Change Your Life* (New York: Random House, 2008), 90.

31. Backlund, "The Silent Treatment."

32. Paul Constant, "Art Spiegelman and a Jazz Composer Bring Old Comics Back to Life," *The Stranger*, October 8, 2014.

33. Jed Oelbaum, "Quit Thinking Like an Emoticon."

34. Spiegelman has often described drawing *Maus* as a personal discovery. For instance, in a 2008 interview, he wrote of his reaction to an early, three-page take on *Maus*: "I knew, when I finished that piece, that I'd begun to find my actual voice as a cartoonist." Interview with Michael C. Lorah, "Talking Breakdowns with Art Spiegelman," October 29, 2008, http://www.newsarama.com/1404-talking-breakdowns-with-art-spiegelman.html.

35. Art Spiegelman, *Co-Mix: A Retrospective of Comics, Graphics, and Scraps* (Montreal: Drawn & Quarterly, 2013), 48.

36. Spiegelman, *Co-Mix*, 48.

37. Spiegelman, *The Wild Party*, v.

38. Spiegelman, *The Wild Party*, v.

39. Spiegelman, *The Wild Party*, vi.

40. Spiegelman, *The Wild Party*, vi.

41. Michael Wood, "It Rhymes," *London Review of Books*, April 1995, 23.

42. Wood, "It Rhymes," 23.

43. Spiegelman, *The Wild Party*, viii.

44. Spiegelman, *The Wild Party*, 32.

45. Spiegelman, *The Wild Party*, 7.

46. Wood, "It Rhymes," 23.

47. Spiegelman, *The Wild Party*, 111.

48. Spiegelman, *The Wild Party*, 30.

49. Bessie Smith, "My Sweetie Went Away," recorded on September 9, 1923, with the *Down-Home Trio*. Library of Congress National Jukebox.

50. Spiegelman, *The Wild Party*, 59.

51. Spiegelman, *The Wild Party*, 100–101.

52. Wood, "It Rhymes," 23.

53. Wood, "It Rhymes," 8.

54. Art Spiegelman, *In the Shadow of No Towers* (New York: Pantheon Books, 2004), 11.
55. Spiegelman, *In the Shadow of No Towers*, 12.
56. Spiegelman, *In the Shadow of No Towers*, 12.
57. Spiegelman, *In the Shadow of No Towers*, ii.
58. Spiegelman, *In the Shadow of No Towers*, 3.
59. Rasula, "Jazz and American Modernism," 160.
60. Bell, "Plus de Jazz," 94.
61. Rasula, "Jazz and American Modernism," 157.
62. Marsalis, *Moving to Higher Ground*, 95.
63. Marsalis, *Moving to Higher Ground*, 95.
64. Charley Gerard, *Jazz in Black and White: Race, Culture, and Identity in the Jazz Community* (Westport: Praeger Publishing, 1998), 6.
65. Backlund, "The Silent Treatment."
66. lacitebd (La cité internationale de la bande dessinée), "Une Histoire Personnelle de la BD par Art Spiegelman." *YouTube* video, 3:48, October 25, 2012.

THE MODERN VOID

Art Spiegelman's Aesthetics of Silence

GEORGIANA BANITA

ANTI-COMICS AND THE MODERNIST ARTWORK

"I weesh I waire dead!"—sobs Françoise Mouly in a four-panel autobiographical comic strip she and Spiegelman drew together in 1978, just one year after the couple had tied the knot.[1] "You will be! . . ." Art kindly assures her, "You'll have *worms* crawling in you!" Both look quite dead already, drawn in sharp cubist angles that make their movements appear stilted and machinelike. He, for one, would rather be rich than dead, Spiegelman unexpectedly confesses to his wife, leaving her with the uplifting thought that being both rich and dead is what they should really strive for. It's candid banter for sure, because up until *Maus* no one seemed to really die (i.e., decompose) in comics; and yet the abstract lines imbue the strip with a discomfiting grimness. Death and wealth amount in this vision to more or less the same thing—no longer being able to, or needing to, make comics. Spiegelman, however, is pointedly drawing an artful comic strip in which he and his coeditor wife appear to have teleported from a Picasso painting circa 1910, wailing about being dead.[2] There may be more dignified ways of depicting a solemn dialogue about mortality, but this comic goes full camp.

"The very aesthetics of the death wish," Susan Sontag wrote in her influential essay "The Aesthetics of Silence" (1969), "seems to make of that wish something incorrigibly lively."[3] Indeed the most dynamic aspect of Spiegelman's death wish vignette is the way it calls attention to its own reluctance to exist. "A Slice of Life"—as the strip is called, the narrative technique ironically made to sound literal and morbid—nicely sums up the vibrant spirit of negation that Spiegelman embraces in his comics. The most iconic of his works are known for their anemic tone, their pared-down, retromodernist style, and for a weary solipsism that accentuates the artist's own familiarity with death, which, due to the experience of his parents in Auschwitz and his mother's suicide, Spiegelman claims to understand implicitly. At the very least he has thought, written, and drawn about it more than most.

One of Spiegelman's favored strategies of negation is to use silence, which for a cartoonist means (nearly) wordless comics, as a way to sustain the threshold between mere communication and aesthetic form. To think about silence under the terms of the comics medium is to continue a debate of long concern to theorists of modernism. And because Sontag's reflections on silence date back to the time Spiegelman was honing his cartooning skills (the countercultural late 1960s), I turn to her for insights into the challenge of modernism to traditional—legible, focused—expressive art. This challenge is carried out by a set of diminishing effects whose ultimate end, well illustrated in Spiegelman's sliced self-portrait, is the stillness of death. As Sontag lucidly puts it: "The notions of silence, emptiness, and reduction sketch out new prescriptions for looking, hearing, etc.—which either promote a more immediate, sensuous experience of art or confront the artwork in a more conscious, conceptual way."[4] To the same extent that religious spirituality is rooted in the theology of God's absence and silence, she explains, modern art aspires toward a demystified, self-estranged anti-art that replaces subjectivity with detachment, design with fortuity, and speech with silence.

Sontag delineates several aspects of aesthetic silence that are also constitutive of Spiegelman's comics practice. What she has in mind, it must be noted, is not simply the decision to be literally quiet. "Modern art's chronic habit of displeasing, provoking, or frustrating its audience"[5] also counts as a means to abolish the consoling effects of speech. It's easy to see how her words resonate with Spiegelman's attitude to the language and audience of comics. Rather than commit to a softer, more classical use of silence "as a zone of meditation, preparation for spiritual ripening, an ordeal that ends in gaining the right to speak,"[6] Spiegelman unapologetically subscribes to the modernist notion that "the power of art is located in its power to *negate*."[7] As we shall see, the cartoonist does not merely raise a sharp needle to the conventional word balloon, he dismisses it entirely as a farce, a pointless exchange with no capacity for transcendence.[8]

It will be the argument of this chapter that Spiegelman enlists the artistry of wordless comics as a force against legibility, with the aim to counter an all-too-easy—and therefore potentially insincere or unearned—access to the past, be it personal or collective, and to the meaning of modernist art. To prove this point, I address several broad developments in Spiegelman's career as well as engage individual works in detail, especially lesser-known art, as a way of furthering their reception. Moving across a chronological axis, my first claim will be that Spiegelman's underground work is, to borrow a phrase from Sontag, "noisy with appeals for silence"; that it displays what she would have called "a coquettish, even cheerful, nihilism,"[9] which flouts formal expectations with no higher purpose than to simply disorient the reader and deride commercial comics. Second, I contend that with *Maus*, Spiegelman abandoned the contrived hilarity of his pantomimic cartoons to explore more varied wordless effects. Beyond debating the idea that nothing of any value can be said after and about the Holocaust, *Maus* crafts memorable uncaptioned panels that push the limits of what silence can signify when what is missing is not just words, but their unique container in comics: word balloons. Finally, with his editing projects of the 2010s, Spiegelman traced the origins of the graphic novel to the woodcut stories of expressionist lithographers like Lynd Ward—and the impetus of his own silent comics to the antiwar aesthetic of interbellum illustration art. Framing my premises is the idea that silence as a mode of comics expression and self-fashioning is instrumental in situating Spiegelman within a modernist canon. His recurring predilection for the silent comics panel puts Spiegelman in the company of modernist icons such as Beckett and Kafka, not merely by virtue of what he does with it on the page. Equally important is the way Spiegelman has rationed his output over the years to reflect the high modernist value of manufactured scarcity cultivated by T. S. Eliot and others.

NOVOCAINE DREAMS: THE 1960S

Spiegelman often utilizes silence to communicate a feeling that defies language, requiring instead a kind of telepathy that draws the reader into the panel even without the benefit of captions. I do not mean Spiegelman's wordless Tijuana bibles, whose purpose was to raise a puerile, electrifying ruckus among the handful of hippie friends reading them, but the genuinely downcast experiments commissioned by artists like Wally Wood, one of *MAD*'s founding cartoonists. Spiegelman already dispensed with any superstitions about the need for words in comics with some of his earliest strips, in which he not only omitted the captions, but used a style that made them seem altogether redundant.

The first, an untitled strip from 1966, is a droll 16-panel comic on an utterly serious subject—what we may call the etiology of fear.[10] In each panel, a flabby, juvenile-looking character (probably not unlike Spiegelman circa 1966) cowers anxiously in a corner because sharing his space is a monstrous object, a different one in every panel. Some are obviously dangerous (a roaring dinosaur, an octopus, a handgun, a knife, the devil), others more ambiguously scary (a large pair of breasts, a floating eye, a gap-toothed mouth). In the third-to-last panel,

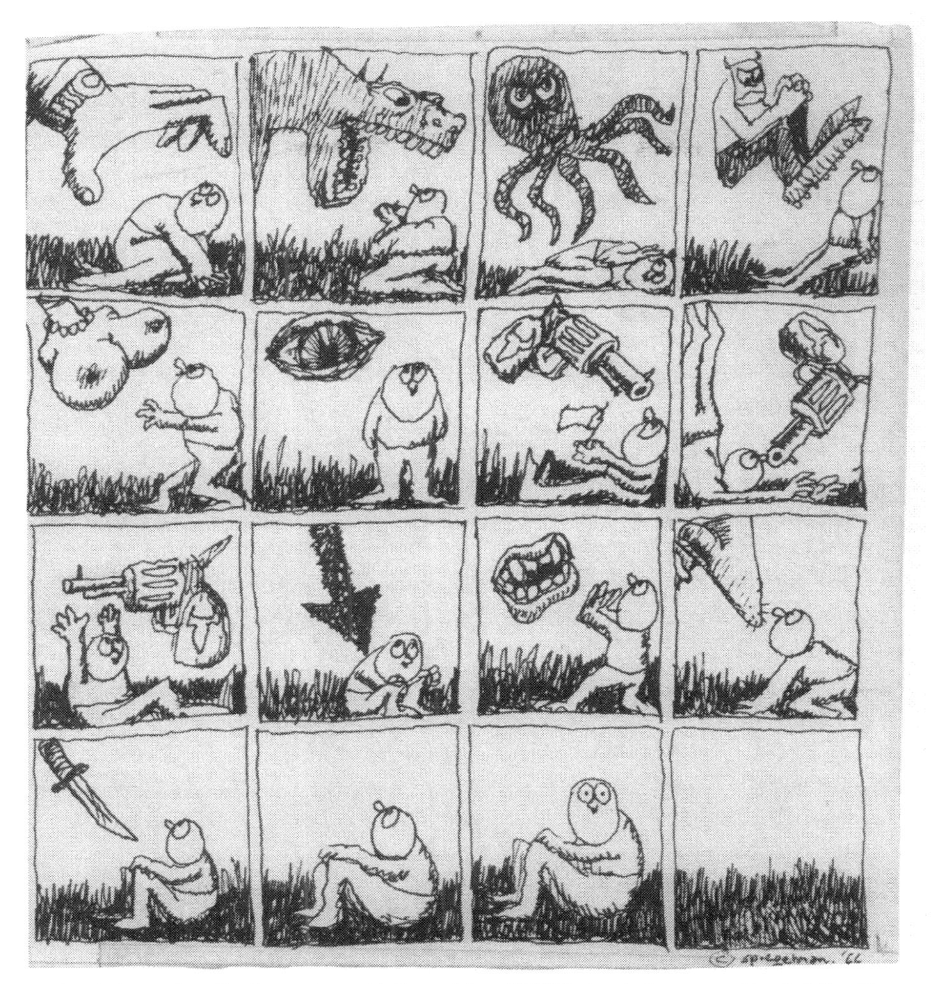

Untitled image from *Pipe Dreams*, the weekly Harpur College (SUNY Binghamton) newspaper. Copyright © 1966 by Art Spiegelman.

the figure finds himself mercifully alone. He also looks even doughier than usual and softer around the edges, as if he's been gaining weight. It becomes clear in the penultimate panel that he is indeed thriving as sole occupant of his space, with only a patch of grass to lie in, and he cannot repress a goofy smile in our direction. By the last panel he has vanished completely, with nary a dent in the grass. Despite the minimalist narrative and drawing style, Dough Boy's disappearing act has a chilling effect that adumbrates the formal and semantic logic of Spiegelman's later wordlessness in two ways. For one, what inhibits verbal expression in this strip is a sense of dread; the protagonist is literally stunned into silence. What we also find here in embryo is Spiegelman's position on how art, and comics in particular, accommodates suffering. It is only by opening up to the horrific, to violence, and to shame that we earn our place within the panel, and on top of the grass rather than beneath it.

Many of Spiegelman's pre-*Arcade* comics are replete with similar images that tear apart the relation between the body, consciousness, and language: the disembodied mouth, for sure, but also moments of overt discomfort with the conventions of captioning: "It's hard to get used to having a balloon come out of your mouth whenever you talk!" laments Spiegelman's alter-ego Skeeter Grant in an eponymous strip published in 1972.[11] In "Alienation Blues" (1970), a series of despondent drawings is captioned with the tongue-in-cheek, flowery pronouncement, "And somewhere beneath the Novocaine numbness there are still the echoes of joy and pain!" stretched over two panels separated by two intercalated minipanels in lieu of word balloons ("Life is a sickness," intones an obese Buddha; "Drink plenty of fluids and stay in bed," advises Little Nemo).[12] In the title panel, miniature Spiegelmen float around, encased in wordless balloons of varying sizes.

The overall effect is an antithesis of sequential comic-making, a catalog of non sequiturs that cleaves the faith in story-*telling* and resolution on which comics typically depend. Spiegelman's strips of this period do not advance toward comic relief because relief is perceived from the outset as a lie. The same "Skeeter Grant" skit mentioned above, which recounts a dream in which the author gets stuck in a comic strip with a tin can glued to his head—Happy-Hooligan-style—is almost embarrassed about its punchline ("Relax, buddy boy, it's just the style you're drawn in."). "The Baron Desert," a homophonic parody about a barren desert and a cyclist who "peddles" (pedals) without using his hands or legs, having lost them in a war, and therefore ends up on the ground more often than upright, affixes an equally absurd punchline to its last panel ("But he meets a lot of people!").[13] In this Graveyard City, where high-rises are shaped like tombstones, it is not worth speaking much at all; and whatever does get said is likely to be misunderstood.

Spiegelman came into his own as a bona fide silence artist with "A Flash of Insight . . ."—which Wally Wood called the "three-page *thing* about masturbation"—published in 1967, one year before Spiegelman experienced a psychotic episode that landed him in hospital and ended his university studies.[14] The strip's surreal effect derives from its inarticulate world (masturbation is a solitary, generally quiet pursuit) and the night of preconsciousness in which its black-heavy panels are set. No sequence of words can logically describe what happens between the first and the last panel. Suffice it to say that the strip plays with sequential continuity; as we progress from one panel to the next, we remain at the same location, just panning across rather than fast-forwarding in space or time. By the penultimate panel, the Masturbator, now trapped inside a mouth

Detail from "A Flash of Insight, a Cloud of Dust and a Hearty Hi-yo Silver," first published in *Witzend*. Copyright © 1967 by Art Spiegelman.

that opens and shuts at nondefined intervals, hangs limply between the rows of pebble-shaped teeth. He vanishes entirely in the last panel, a black monolith.

The recurrence of the blank panel contains clues to Spiegelman's struggle at this time to place high literature, high art, and lowbrow funnies in relation to each other. It is significant, then, that his sketchbooks are filled with references to modernist writers such as Aldous Huxley and William Faulkner, who mounted their modernist interventions on the ability of literature to capture sense experience.[15] For Spiegelman, in contrast, the achievement of comics done with the right dose of iconoclasm rests in their ability to free us from the burden of experience and meaning altogether. "Play with your cells and become your own food!" says the title of a widely reprinted leaflet Spiegelman drew in 1967.[16] For the Spiegelman of the Flower Power era—self-absorbed and self-defeating, purposefully unfunny and outré—comics sought to redirect their energies inward. Their single recognizable premise is the fading of the artistic referent (body, language, consciousness, humor as a mainstay of social life) and the impermanence of whatever "flash of insight" might be gained from art.

In these early works, Spiegelman comes up with a repertory of objects otherwise obscured by the codes of comics speech—mouths in particular, but also word balloons—on which he lavishes extravagant attention. In other words, by peeling back comics clichés, he is allowing other *things* to speak. Similar techniques crop up in strips published a decade later. "Drawn Over Two Weeks While on the Phone" (1980) features speech balloons, but inside them are single geometrical shapes instead of words.[17] In the final panel the circle, square, and triangle take center stage, having banished the comic's living protagonists into word bubbles; the figures even reshape three panels in their own image. Despite the sense that important messages are exchanged in this strip (and the fact that Spiegelman ostensibly drew the cartoon while actively on the phone, presumably not just breathing into the receiver), not a single word is uttered. Here as in the other silent comics discussed above, the panels are concatenated by free association, as if stringed together by an anxiously racing mind.

SILENT SCREAMS: *BREAKDOWNS* AND COVER ART

For the frontispiece drawing in *Breakdowns*, Spiegelman used the 1973 single-panel, nearly wordless comic "Auto-destructo," in which a Rube Goldberg machine comments on the pointlessness of commercial comics.[18] A lengthy legend explains the steps by which a number of cartoon staples (cat, mouse, dog, cannonball, candle) sets into motion an elaborate contraption whose only purpose is to perpetuate itself—much to the despair of observer S., who would rather take an overdose of sleeping pills than watch the spectacle all over again. On the opposite page, a brief introduction to the anthology cites Murat Bernard "Chic" Young, creator of the vapid "pretty-girl" strip *Blondie*, to illustrate the kind of commercial cartoons Spiegelman had in mind: "It is up to the careful comic artist to see that he offends no one, hurts no group and that his strip is all in good clean fun. . . . All in all, drawing comic strips is very interesting . . . in a dull, monotonous sort of way."[19] The drawings that accompany the quote align two virtually identical panel sections to describe the lack of variety typical of standard comics.

In contrast to this dull procession, a fragment of the "Prisoner on the Hell Planet" strip featuring Spiegelman's haggard likeness as a camp inmate, a Star of David, frantic expressionist lines, and the word FUN (as in funeral) at strange, disquieting angles articulate Spiegelman's vision of anti-comics: a visually and vocally impoverished art that draws attention to itself, not because it has something to say, but because not being able to speak is part of the modern human condition. "Oy Vey" are the only words uttered in "Auto-destructo," and the only visible item not involved in the devious fun-machine is a rendition of Edvard Munch's 1893 expressionist composition *The Scream*, hanging crookedly on the pastel-colored wall.

Spiegelman's repertoire over the following two decades would be governed by a perverse vision of comics' morbid "fun," expressed by two of his most recognizable devices. One is the disconnect between dialogue-free panels and the narrative captions attached to them (he brought this strategy to perfection in the 1973 strip "Don't Get Around Much Anymore").[20] The second denotes his preference for metanarrative plots placed atop a series of panels that stand in tension with the story they purportedly tell ("Little Signs of Passion," 1974; "New York Journal," 1975). Other strips he drew in this era dramatize dreamlike states in which language and logic are suspended, leaving us with enigmas that reverberate on a nonreferential, psychic level. "Real Dream" (1975), for instance, presents a "revolting" scene centered around an obese party hostess holding a large sausage to her groin and vomiting profusely.[21] "Doctor Shpiegelmann," presumably Art's Jewish consciousness, volunteers outrageous interpretations of the dream's traumatic symbols; the vomiting signifies the uprising in the Warsaw Ghetto, etc. The punchline, "We must never forget the 6 million," suggests that Spiegelman's defiance of ordinary language is leavened with the fear that by not giving voice to the "revolting display" of reality, we forgo necessary objections to history's brutal Goldberg machines.

The wraparound covers that Spiegelman drew for the Zweitausendeins German-language editions of Boris Vian's collected works in the 1980s are cut from the same cloth.[22] Though covers are not in themselves wordless comics, in the sense that the book title provides an explanatory or discordant caption, Spiegelman's covers have always visibly refused to simply record a straightforward narrative. For Vian's 1947 crime novel *The Dead Have the Same Skin*, he revisited *The Scream*, whose black-and-white effigy is pasted over every single one of a building's close to thirty windows. The anguish of the curved body in Munch's painting pierces the purple sky, providing an apt backdrop for the central attraction of the noir-inflected design: the locked gazes of a white, square-jawed sleuth and a black-skinned damsel on the front cover, mirrored on the back by the same image in which the races have been swapped.

Cover for Boris Vian's *Tote haben alle dieselbe Haut* (*The Dead All Have the Same Skin*). Copyright © 1980 by Art Spiegelman.

The Dead All Have the Same Skin is a narrative of racial passing that unravels when the protagonist's past catches up with him. It's a serious subject, but in Vian's hands it becomes lurid and surreal. The novel's unfortunate hero, Dan Parker, a bouncer in a New York nightclub, harbors the false conviction that he was born into a Black family. A blackmailer catches wind of this illusion and threatens to expose him, whereupon Parker murders the blackmailer and commits suicide. Munch's elastic eye-hook head, partly inspired by the petrified expression of a Peruvian mummy, is reminiscent of an open-mouthed skull.[23] Given the novel's racial ambiguities, it's easy to see that Spiegelman's cover image aims to imply that race is only skin-deep and everyone's bones are the same color. Moreover, even in this cover image for a fun novel, Spiegelman theorizes the dilemma of being, like Vian himself, a poète maudit, a dreamer forced to dabble in commercial fare while continuing to protest against the leveling of art by creating self-conscious, opaque works. For the other Vian covers, Spiegelman went all out with florid, incoherent assemblages and raucous imagery inspired by Vian's own idiosyncrasies and their shared passion for jazz.[24] The tension between the books' superficial pulp content and their destabilizing inner workings is essential to the effect Spiegelman is after.

The most obviously captionless comics Spiegelman has produced are his thirty-nine covers for the *New Yorker*, which he joined in 1992 with a mission to make the venerable weekly brasher and more groundbreaking. Despite the lack of dialogue, however, the covers count as Spiegelman's most talkative, conversation-starting products since *Wacky Packages*. If at all present, their critique of comics language is confined to their often-quirky titles, included only in the table of contents for the respective issue. Covers like "Guns of September" (children getting off the school bus, packing lunch boxes and automatic weapons) or "41 Shots, 10 Cents" (a white police officer aims at black targets in a shooting gallery) address hot-button issues with the kind of genteel irony befitting a medium that has finally arrived. After all, a *New Yorker* cover is not the ideal place to upend the orthodoxies of your medium or land porn and disability gags on the coffee tables of urban sophisticates. That being said, the covers arguably prodded Spiegelman toward a greater economy of language. "I tell artists that their image isn't ready until it can be shown without a caption," Mouly points out in *Blown Covers*, the collection she edited of the cover ideas that did not make it into print.[25] Indeed the best images—and the best of Spiegelman's comics—cut to the core of a problem in ways that make words appear powerless or redundant.[26]

SEVEN TYPES OF SILENCE IN *MAUS*

"I was drawing the most perverse and violent atrocities I could," Spiegelman would recall of his underground phase, "but not even consciously connecting them to all the atrocities in my own life and background."[27] That connection came with *Maus*, where personal suffering became enmeshed with what David Patterson in his 1992 study of the Holocaust novel called "the shriek of silence."[28] Silent are the voices of the Spiegelmans lost in the war and of the world that has grown over the memory of the Holocaust. "It's so peaceful here at night," Mouly says in *Maus II*, glancing thoughtfully into the night sky after listening to another episode in Vladek's story. "It's almost impossible to believe Auschwitz ever happened."[29] The moment of silence, almost a cliché in Holocaust history and art, collects a multitude of meanings, from the extended silence of survivors in Claude Lanzmann's *Shoah* to Adolf Eichmann's speechless passivity before witnesses in his Jerusalem trial. Elie Wiesel puts it especially well in his novel *The Testament* (1981) when he writes, "The philosophers are wrong: it is not words that kill, it is silence. It kills impulses and passion, it kills desire and the memory of desire. It invades, dominates, and reduces man to slavery. And once a slave of silence, you are no longer a man."[30] Wiesel's words carry a vivid encouragement to speak as a way to counterbalance the silence of oppression and forgetting. In *Maus*, silent moments operate on multiple levels to emphasize several themes: the duration of pain, the indifference of criminals, the lethargy weighing everyone down, and the lack of communication in the

Nazi camps and at other sites of war, aside from shouted orders and physical abuse. Often the *Maus* panels are simply suffused in a sort of underwater silence, inevitably punctuated by the bubble of voices swimming to the surface to make themselves heard.

The scholarship on *Maus* that pays attention to the book's silent aesthetics tends to pivot on the notion that the genocide was so inconceivable that only silence should count as a defensible way of engaging with the past century's gravest crime—a powerful point that the book indeed makes, repeatedly. But it does not do justice to Spiegelman's artistry to see in his work merely an apologetic placeholder for the unrepresentable. By privileging silence over words in such a wordy medium, Spiegelman shows that far from being a questionable form in which to address the Holocaust, artful comics present new ways of tackling an old problem. I identify seven types of comics silence that mirror key questions raised by *Maus*, from the familiar debate around representability and the ur-silence of the mother's burnt diaries; through the silence of depression, of the camp itself, of the war in general, and of guilt about its outcome; to the silence of the objects that accompanied Vladek through the camps and are now used to craft a makeshift captionless museum of mass murder.

Firstly, *Maus* appears to merely rehearse the idea that silence serves us best in remembering past atrocities. In a powerful scene in *Maus II*, Pavel, Spiegelman's psychotherapist in the book (and in real life) suggests that the best way for survivors to honor the silence of those who did not live to tell about their experiences is to refrain from giving their own accounts: "the victims who died can never tell THEIR side of the story, so maybe it's better not to have any more stories."[31] Pavel's conclusion is not self-evident, and yet Art appears to agree. The three panels that document their conversation are both amusing and uncomfortable because they expose the contradiction at the heart of the book. Art begins by quoting Samuel Beckett's adage, "Every word is like an unnecessary stain on silence and nothingness," informed by the existentialist critique of language that Jean-Paul Sartre in 1945 referred to as "the literature of silence."[32] A completely wordless panel follows, after which Art interrupts his silent immolation with the quip: "On the other hand, he SAID it."[33] Pavel one-ups him with a self-referential remark of his own: "Maybe you can include it in your book"—and Spiegelman does.[34]

Michael Levine takes this paradox to mean that Spiegelman "uses the verbal and visual language of the text as *contradictory* stains to *sustain* the very silence they taint."[35] Levine's argument groups words and comics together as equally beholden to a logic that puts them at variance with the silence extolled by existentialism and the avant-garde. While drawing comics certainly amounts to more than leaving the page blank, it seems to me that Spiegelman is able to use comics—and wordless panels especially—to perform or recreate moments of complete silence. The brief exchange about Beckett can be read in the same vein. Spiegelman impresses on readers the importance of silent remembrance not by confronting them with an empty panel (which he might have done earlier in his career), but by trapping them in a room where nothing happens, no one says anything, and the silence cuts even deeper because the referent is there even though it is not named. We are left with Pavel and Art sitting quietly in their armchairs, with only a closed window, curtains, and upholstery to look at (the bookcases are behind Art, so we cannot see them), while we measure the meaning and effect of silence.

Secondly, it's a part of the memoir's contentious ambiguity that Vladek is not only a victim of the Holocaust, but also a censor to his wife's memory and voice. Even though Vladek mentions "beautiful letters" she wrote to him in eloquent Polish during their courtship,[36] her voice does not reach us directly. We also learn that she translated communist messages into German, which to her husband meant that she was "involved in conspirations!"[37] Yet nothing is known about these messages beyond the fact that she translated them, which only compounds the myth of Anja's personal worldview. Art clings to these scraps of information to outbalance the futility and despair he feels in the wake of her suicide. Vladek asks Anja to put an end to her political involvement if she wants the marriage to continue, and she does—"she was a good girl."[38] It's clear that Vladek silenced her, long before he burned her diaries, by refusing her a separate consciousness, conviction, or narrative. Unsurprisingly in this context, Anja often appears in silent scenes and is a silent bystander in many others that feature dialogue between other characters. Hunkered down in a bunker with Vladek, Miloch, Miloch's wife, and their baby boy, "the whole day and night Anja sat writing into her notebook."[39] The moments Anja spends talking/writing to herself highlight the indifference of others to what she had to say, and keeping these panels free of dialogue is perhaps Spiegelman's attempt to honor her memory.

Third, Anja's speech is further impaired by her depressive mood; she asks to die, disregards Vladek's words of encouragement, and even when she does talk, her language is closer to silence than to actual interaction. Spiegelman and Mouly have spoken openly about their own bouts with depression that do not so much cripple them as they inform their art and personalities. Starting with "Prisoner on the Hell Planet," Spiegelman's scrutiny of depression—both his mother's and his own—is inextricable from the expressionist style that he ultimately rejected in the book-length *Maus*. And yet traces of psychic breakdown remain in evidence, manifesting in a collapse of language or lack of vigor. "I just don't want to live,"[40] Anja proclaims after Richieu's birth and is taken to a Czech sanatorium. It is 1938. Significantly, the moment coincides with the first appearance of the swastika and a surge of anxiety among Jews as stories of pogroms, arrests, and dispossession emerge from Germany. Personal crisis, then, points to larger social perils and we are asked to read the silence that engulfs Anja's life as a correlative to the silencing of the Jewish population, a parallel later reinforced by Art's accusation that his father's burning of Anja's diaries amounts to nothing short of murder.

The fourth level of silent discourse in the book revolves around the camp. Giorgio Agamben, in his authoritative analysis of detention practices, notes that "One of the essential characteristics of modern biopolitics . . . is its constant need to redefine the threshold in life that distinguishes and separates what is inside and what is outside."[41] The animal metaphor that pits cats against mice already goes a long way toward tracing that difference between powerful insider and abject outsider. Yet the distinction between who is a citizen and who is disposable also depends on whether or not one is permitted to speak. In one panel Vladek reclines against a wall, head slouched over the knees, underneath a small window. His face is featureless, literally blank; another shadow nearby suggests he is not alone, but the lack of dialogue points to a deafening silence. The panels that describe the shower room and ovens are even more deserted and quiet. Closely hatched pencil strikes obscure the small window in the shower room door and the mouth of every oven.[42] The elevated angle provides an in-depth view of the rooms, opening up the space and amplifying its silence.

Another remarkable detention sequence concerns the seamstress Miss Stefanska, who receives from Anja a package of communist papers, though she is not aware of its content. Polish police find it and arrest Miss Stefanska, who goes on to spend three months in jail. A small panel shows her seated solemnly in her cell, glasses perched on her nose as if she has just temporarily been called away from her working table. White prison bars conceal our view of the panel and hers through the window. Hands gathered peacefully in her lap, Miss Stefanska appears to be spending her prison stint paralyzed with incomprehension, resigned to her lot, and unwilling or unable to protest. There is not a single image in the memoir of a silent Anja wasting away in the camp as the years go by, which is why this analogous scene of incarceration is worth closer attention. As suggested by the slightly tilted panel, Miss Stefanska's captivity stands at an uncomfortable angle to the main story, unless we read in her desiccated condition the same feature of the camp that would claim Anja's life over twenty years later: the inertia and illogic of captivity that allow it to endure long after the prison gates have opened or been smashed down.

The fifth type of silence is also the most prevalent. Many of the war scenes in *Maus* do not contain much dialogue and only brief narration from Vladek, which is crammed into narrow boxes that hew close to the panel edges. The panels set in the bunkers of Srodula introduce a different kind of silence—the nervous noiselessness of the cellars where Jews are hiding to evade detection

From *Maus I: A Survivor's Tale: My Father Bleeds History* (New York: Pantheon, 1986), p. 111. Copyright © 1973, 1980, 1981, 1982, 1982, 1984, 1985, 1986 by Art Spiegelman.

and deportation. In a panel that describes the arrival of German troops with their sniffing dogs, the silent intensity of the search and the muffled apprehension of the bunker dwellers become palpable on the page.[43] A large framing panel in which we glimpse slices of a moonlit landscape encloses three interior panels that seem even quieter for being encased in this way. In the first, soldiers and dogs search through coal crates, in the third they descend into the cellar, pointing flashlights at mounds of coal. Sandwiched between them is a smaller panel in which three figures huddle quietly, with a fourth pressing an ear against the door. The gutter separates the hidden figures from their pursuers like a protective wall. Rather than simply forgo captions for decorative effect, these silent panels in *Maus* utilize silence as part of the comics' visual mise en scène (or, in this case, mise en abyme).

Even though the silence of fear is especially poignant in indoor scenes, the outdoor sequences in *Maus* that recount Vladek and Anja's nighttime travels on foot through the countryside also lack dialogue. We find a typical example at the bottom of page 135 in *Maus I*, interposed like a suspended photograph between Artie, seated on the left with his notebook and recorder, and Vladek on the right; "It was still dark outside," the father recalls. "We didn't know where to hide ourselves . . ." In the silent panel, two small figures follow a swastika-shaped trail into the woods. Father and son provide exposition and comment on what unfolds before us like a silent film of the Holocaust, a format into which the entire memoir could have been pressed, considering that much of the dialogue can be elided without significant narrative loss. Panels like these are not so much spoken comics that have jettisoned all speech, but dramatic inserts meant to stand out and remain unassimilated. The position of this silent panel in-between father and son is significant because it also casts doubt on the authorship of *Maus*, insisting that the most powerful images in the book belong as much to the Holocaust survivor as to his son. The wordlessness of these images locates their origin in two distinct imaginations that clash and clamor for attention, which is why they are most effectively co-mixed and distilled on the silent page.

When silence sets in, the panels' formal design and texture come more clearly into view. The tight crosshatching is reminiscent of prison bars, a shading and faceting effect that works especially well in wordless panels where the dense lines form a dark area fully enveloping the figures trapped inside. The last three panels on page 144 of *Maus I* are typical of this progression. As Vladek and Anja look for shelter to pass the night, a seemingly safe construction site beckons. When Vladek lowers himself into a foundation trench, the panel centers on his suspended body from the standpoint of someone who might be suspicious of their presence. The extreme angles and canted shots suggest impending violence. "And here we waited a cold few hours for the day," we read in a caption placed just outside the last, wordless panel in which the Spiegelmans snuggle against the wall. The moiré patterns of the background ripple more intensely in the proximity of their bodies as if warmed by their body heat. This feature runs through many of the book's wordless moments; whenever humans become silent, their surroundings come to life.

The sixth kind of silence that Spiegelman avails himself of confirms the connection between the formal representation of silence through wordless panels and the psychological effects of silence as refusal or rebuke. Silence can signify the collapse of resistance, of conscience, of the most basic humanity, or the defeat of language and with it of human reason. Because the implications of silence are so grave and so damning, drawing and reading wordless panels raises questions of complicity for both Spiegelman and his readers. When Vladek recalls how the cattle carriages came to a stop after the evacuation of prisoners from Auschwitz—back into the Reich towards Dachau, in February 1945—the silence that descends on the panels describes the breakdown of both people and machines. Trains were often used in Eastern Europe, which did not have a camp system, to kill passengers left to starve inside, sometimes while the trains kept moving through the countryside.[44] Spiegelman's silence calls attention to the invisible violence at play in the way the Holocaust was carried out and in the reasons why it continues to defy figuration. What's more, the train panels go against the logic of narration, as they zoom in on the carriages instead of tracing their movement in serial succession. The uncomfortable duration of this sequence traps the reader inside the crime scene and uses silence on multiple levels to evoke the utility of carriages as stealthy weapons of mass murder; to underscore the challenge that these death machines posed for the prosecution of the perpetrators; and to remind us of the ways in which any artistic reconstruction of violence runs of risk of reproducing it.

I have kept the most understated form of silence for last. It is the wordlessness of things, which play a larger part in *Maus* than has been acknowledged so far.[45] From the moment Richieu jumps to embrace his father—recently released from a POW camp—and winces when he feels the cold buttons of Vladek's coat, *Maus* shows an unusual attention to inanimate things. Not only do they add texture to the story, they also document a war in which people were indistinguishable from objects. As chattel, labor force, disposable ash, or fuel, when the victims of the Holocaust were dispossessed by the Nazi state, they became themselves possessions, and were compelled to trade in material property to better their lot in the ghettos and the camps. Many silent moments in the book go back to the objecthood that the inmates of Auschwitz were reduced to. "He's more attached to things than to people," Vladek's second wife, Mala, herself a Holocaust survivor, explains to Art with tired exasperation.[46] Despite his deeply ingrained OCD behavior, there is evidence in the book that Vladek treasures things partly because to him, for a long time, material objects were in fact equivalent with people, and could even save lives in an environment where property determined human worth.

Vladek gathers trash everywhere he goes, even out on the street. When he finds a piece of telephone wire, he picks it up, insisting to Artie that it's hard to find and always useful. It's as if the countless human selections Vladek witnessed have made it impossible for him to consider an item, however small, totally useless and therefore discard it. Vladek has been judged harshly, not least by his own son, but that may be less a testament of character than the result of Spiegelman's artistic priorities. Vladek is a hoarder who spends a lot of time interacting with his precious collections; he handles, among other things: wires, war treasures, pills, and nails. Spiegelman makes short shrift of drawing these because he is less interested in figurative drawing and more focused on narrative progression. Completely silent panels in *Maus* are therefore more strikingly blank than a wordless panel in Chris Ware, for instance, where sharply drawn objects tell stories of their own.[47] Instead, because Spiegelman does not clutter his panels with things, when his characters are alone or quiet he fills the air around them with frantic crosshatching. Wordlessness for him is hard, and hard-earned.

ANTIWAR ART AND THE WORDLESS NOVEL

Among Spiegelman's works, *Maus* comes closest to a literary novel; yet it is also, in parts, a memoir in pictures. Taken together, the title panels to the two volumes form a woodcut novel in the tradition of Frans Masereel's and Lynd Ward's picture stories—"obscure precursors of today's graphic novels that briefly flourished between the two World Wars."[48] Despite the prominent headlines inside the title panels, the images exude the starkness we have come to associate with the woodcut genre and many of its characteristics: the focus on a sparsely drawn foreground without depth of field; the mythological simplicity of figures and poses; fetishized physical features; and the implication that the scene is not artificially turned to mute so much as it captures a prolonged state of paralysis.[49] If there was any doubt about the original sources of inspiration for the artwork of *Maus*, these panels certainly remove it.

For the purposes of a silence-based approach to Spiegelman's work, the central place of 1920s and 1930s woodcut art in his aesthetic practice and theory is especially salient. And given that silence in his comics is often allied with atrocity and war, it is not surprising that Spiegelman's influences from the modernist heyday of wood engraving are also linked to war. In 2010, Spiegelman edited and prefaced the Library of America edition of Lynd Ward's wordless novels, emphasizing Ward's antiwar stance and his impact on the visual syntax of comics storytelling. In 2016, he edited, designed, and wrote a brief introductory note to the Library of America's remastered accordion-fold reprint of Si Lewen's antiauthoritarian wordless epic *The Parade* (1957). And in 2014, he toured with his talk *WORDLESS!* alongside jazz composer and saxophonist Phillip Johnston, whom Spiegelman had done cover art for in the 1980s—an apt choice, given that Johnston has composed modern scores for silent films.

The introduction Spiegelman wrote for the Ward collection comments on the high expressionism of wood engravings at some length and with great incisiveness. Ward's predilection for novels in woodcuts, Spiegelman suggests, is secondary to his broader "concern with visual qualities that just 'are,' and are their own justification for being."[50] Spiegelman refrained from glossing too extensively on the books, in an attempt to "honor Ward's intention to keep his narratives available to each reader's subjective interpretation—uncontaminated by nailing it to a cross of explanatory language."[51] This is not to say that Ward's novels lack explanatory power. While silence (i.e., the trauma of war and other cataclysms) may be the origin of picture stories like Ward's, it is not the outcome or purpose of the artwork itself. Against the faithlessness and machine aesthetic of modernity, artists like Ward and Spiegelman forge connections of recognition and intelligibility as a replenishing counterforce to the aftermath of two world wars. Spiegelman's insistence that Ward's novels "are filled with language," that they put forth complex, lucid statements—albeit "in the reader's head rather than on the page"[52]—enables us to see his own work differently.

From the silent-scream motifs of the pre-*Maus* period to the erasure of voices in *Maus*, Spiegelman's art demands a conscious engagement with language and indirectly also with the rhythms and effects of comics locution. In the process of what Spiegelman refers to as the "subvocal translating of images into words,"[53] readers are pressured to compose a new internal language both commensurate to the violence depicted on the page and intelligible to themselves. By this operation, the comics are no longer or not simply silent, because their silence has been transferred to, and overcome by, the act of reading. As a result, even in comics strips that are not literally silent, by using surrogates of silence—a pared-down dialogue, or prose that is too polished and arch, too linear and neatly organized ("And somewhere beneath the Novocaine numbness there are still the echoes of joy and pain!")—Spiegelman invites the reader to linger on each composition and mentally transcribe its implicit idiom.

Interestingly, since *Maus*, silence has arguably become a part of Spiegelman's approach to comics more generally. Over the past three decades he has produced comparatively little work, most of it in formats that veer away from the crammed captions of *Maus* toward larger pictorial canvases. One of these is *In the Shadow of No Towers* (2004), which asks emphatically to be seen as a book not least due to its expressive "empty" cover, borrowed from the *New Yorker*, and the elaborate dialogues it stages between old and new comics.[54] It is easy to see what still excites Spiegelman about the medium, going back to Happy Hooligan and the Katzenjammer Kids: their attention to the everyday, the banal, to that which goes, quite literally, without saying. French writer Georges Perec, writing in the tradition of fellow OuLiPo member Raymond Queneau—a favorite with both Spiegelman and Mouly—called this quotidian, background noise the "infra-ordinary."[55] *No Towers* zooms in on many details of American life in the twenty-first century, as the nation became embroiled in three wars (Afghanistan, Iraq, and the War on Terror), including many scenes whose significance has been dwarfed by the spectacle of terrorism. "Her inner demons had broken loose and taken over our shared reality," Spiegelman writes in the caption to one of the few dialogue-free panels in *No Towers*, a hellish vision of what the rants of a racist homeless woman in his neighborhood might look like if Marc Chagall had produced a painting about planes plowing

Art for *In the Shadow of No Towers*. Copyright © 2004 by Art Spiegelman.

into towers.[56] Whatever inconspicuous detail he sets his sights on, Spiegelman manages to apply a magnifying glass to its insidious effects in wordless forms that stop readers in their tracks. Only this time, the silence is the silence of nightmares and Spiegelman's response to it more overtly political. When he turns to confront the woman—for the first time now, though he has heard her many times before—it is clear that the silent treatment just will not do anymore.

Since his political cartoons on the Charlie Hebdo attack, Spiegelman has drawn very little, most prominently a four-panel lament on Donald Trump for the comics collection *Resist!* coedited by Mouly and Nadja Spiegelman in 2017. Yet the fact that he has held back over the past decade does not diminish his achievements. "On the contrary," Sontag might say, "it imparts retroactively an added power and authority to what was broken off—disavowal of the work becoming a new source of its validity, a certificate of unchallenged seriousness."[57] For Spiegelman, comics have always been an exercise in endurance and asceticism. "Drawing really comes hard to me. I sweat these things out—one or two panels a day, a page maybe a week," he explained in an interview.[58] The inevitable silence that falls on such drawn-out work sessions leaves an imprint on the page and gives Spiegelman's comics their transcendent quality.

I have suggested silent comics as a new approach to Spiegelman's visionary redrawing of the medium's bounds. And while there is ample reason to believe that silence holds an essential stake in Spiegelman's modernist project, what silence is and how Spiegelman understands it turns on a range of issues I could only allude to here. A more extensive analysis of Spiegelman's silent comics ought to address the influence of psychotherapy on his exploration of the unconscious and on his discontent with language as an impediment to self-knowledge. It should also explore to what extent Spiegelman's multilingual family life (with his Polish-speaking parents and his French wife) impressed on him the idea that individual words are nothing but an accident of history, and thereby prompted him to rethink the use of language in comics. The upshot of both circumstances—his therapy and his cosmopolitanism—is not so much the desire to withdraw into a complete void, far beyond the frontiers of discourse, but something more dialectical. Silence does foster thought, Sontag writes, even though it "must appear from the perspective of traditional thinking and the familiar uses of the mind as no thought at all."[59] Instead, silence becomes "the emblem of new, 'difficult' thinking"—much the same way that Spiegelman became the artisan of "difficult" comics.

Notes

1. Art Spiegelman (and Françoise), "A Slice of Life, with Art and Françoise . . . ," one tier, *Snarf* no. 8 (1978). Reprinted in Art Spiegelman, *Co-Mix: A Retrospective of Comics, Graphics and Scraps* (Montreal: Drawn & Quarterly, 2013), 35.

2. The discontinuity of form and the planar faceting of the two human figures in this strip clearly recall the physical fragmentation of the body typical of early Cubism. On the intersection of Cubism and other artistic styles with comics art, see Craig Yoe, *Arf Museum* (Arf Books in association with Fantagraphics Books, 2006). Spiegelman discusses his Cubist influences in the afterword to the 2008 edition of *Breakdowns*. See Art Spiegelman, "An Afterword," in *Breakdowns: Portrait of the Artist as a Young %@&*!* (New York: Pantheon, 2008), n.p.

3. Susan Sontag, *Styles of Radical Will* (New York: Farrar, Straus and Giroux, 1969), 12.

4. Sontag, *Styles of Radical Will*, 13.

5. Sontag, *Styles of Radical Will*, 7.

6. Sontag, *Styles of Radical Will*, 6.

7. Sontag, *Styles of Radical Will*, 8.

8. Spiegelman has not explicitly talked about wordless panels in his work, but he admires cartoonists who use them. For an article that Françoise Mouly penned for the *New Yorker* in 2016, Spiegelman counts two wordless one-page strips by R. Crumb (from *Bo Bo Bolinski*) and Milt Gross (his comics review of *Grapes of Wrath* from 1939) among his favorite "one-page graphic novels." See Françoise Mouly, "Eyeball Kicks: Art Spiegelman on One-Page Graphic Novels, *New Yorker*, August 22, 2006.

9. Sontag, *Styles of Radical Will*, 12.

10. Published in *Pipe Dreams*, the weekly Harpur College (SUNY Binghamton) newspaper, in 1966, reproduced in Art Spiegelman, *Co-Mix*, 15.

11. Art Spiegelman, "Skeeter Grant," *Sunday Paper* (a short-lived weekly broadsheet), 1972; reprinted in Spiegelman, *Co-Mix*, 19.

12. Art Spiegelman, "Alienation Blues," *Phucked-Up Funnies* (a large-format comics insert edited by Spiegelman and included in the 1970 Harpur College Yearbook), 1970. Reprinted in Spiegelman, *Co-Mix*, 18.

13. Art Spiegelman, "The Baron Desert," *East Village Other* (1968); reprinted in Spiegelman, *Co-Mix*, 18.

14. Art Spiegelman, "A Flash of Insight, a Cloud of Dust and a Hearty Hi-yo Silver," *Witzend* (Wally Wood's proto-underground magazine), 1967; reprinted in Spiegelman, *Co-Mix*, 20.

15. Art Spiegelman, *Be a Nose! Three Sketchbooks* (San Francisco: McSweeney's, 2009): 1979 Sketchbook, Plate 4; 1983 Sketchbook, 78.

16. Spiegelman, *Co-Mix*, 20.

17. Art Spiegelman, "Drawn Over Two Weeks While on the Phone," *RAW*, v. 1, no. 1 (Fall 1980): 27.

18. Spiegelman, *Breakdowns*, 2008. On the workings of the Rube Goldberg machine, see Michael North, *Machine-Age Comedy* (Oxford: Oxford University Press, 2009), chapter 3: "Goldberg Variations."

19. Lawrence Lariar, *Careers in Cartooning* (New York: Dodd, Mead, 1950), 54.

20. On "Don't Get Around," see Philip Smith, *Reading Art Spiegelman* (London: Routledge, 2018).

21. Art Spiegelman, "Real Dream," *Breakdowns*, n.p.

22. Reprinted in Spiegelman, *Co-Mix*, 32–33.

23. See Edvard Munch, *The Freeze of Life: Essays*, ed. Mara-Helen Wood (London: National Gallery Publications, 1992), 50. Countless skulls appear in Spiegelman's sketchbooks and his covers for Boris Vian; even more memorable is the Hitleresque cat-skull on the covers of the two *Maus* volumes.

24. A tamer version of this frenzy animates the 2006 wraparound cover for Paul Auster's *New York Trilogy*. See Spiegelman, *Co-Mix*, 94.

25. Françoise Mouly, *Blown Covers:* New Yorker *Covers You Were Never Meant to See* (New York: Abrams, 2012), 15.

26. With other, more offbeat covers and poster art of the post-*Maus* era, especially for music albums (the collection of songs by the satirical 1940s and 1950s musician Spike Jones, a compilation of Nazi-banned compositions called *The Music Survives!* and covers for two albums by the now-defunct band The Microscopic Septet, founded in 1980 by Phillip Johnston), Spiegelman moved away from the visual one-liners and pulp style of the *New Yorker* artwork to craft properly avant-garde images once more.

27. Art Spiegelman, *MetaMaus: A Look Inside a Modern Classic,* Maus (London: Viking, 2011), xx.

28. David Patterson, *The Shriek of Silence: A Phenomenology of the Holocaust Novel* (Lexington: The University Press of Kentucky, 1992).

29. Art Spiegelman, *Maus II: And Here My Troubles Began* (New York: Pantheon, 1991), 74.

30. Elie Wiesel, *The Testament* (New York: Schocken Books, 1981), 209.

31. Spiegelman, *Maus II*, 45.

32. Jean-Paul Sartre, *Situations, I. Essais Critiques* (Paris: Gallimard, 1947), 271. For a post-modern, post-humanist usage of the term, see Ihab Hassan, *The Literature of Silence: Henry Miller and Samuel Beckett* (New York: Knopf, 1968).

33. Spiegelman, *Maus II*, 45.

34. Moments like these, which testify to Spiegelman's effort to represent silence without silencing the victims of mass murder, are symptomatic of a larger conundrum for which Lyotard provides a useful formula. No amount of detail or testimony can adequately represent the atrocity, he insists in *Heidegger and "the Jews"*; the enormity of the crime must therefore be registered in silence, or rather in the memory of a silence that no concept or phrase can ever drown out. Jean-François Lyotard, *Heidegger and "the Jews"* (Minneapolis: University of Minnesota Press, 1990).

35. Michael G. Levine, *The Belated Witness: Literature, Testimony, and the Question of Holocaust Survival* (Stanford: Stanford University Press, 2006), 76.

36. Spiegelman, *Maus I*, 17.

37. Spiegelman, *Maus I*, 27.

38. Spiegelman, *Maus I*, 29.

39. Spiegelman, *Maus I*, 123.

40. Spiegelman, *Maus I*, 31.

41. Giorgio Agamben, *Homo Sacer: Sovereign Power and Bare Life* (Stanford: Stanford University Press, 1998), 131.

42. Spiegelman, *Maus II*, 71.

43. Spiegelman, *Maus I*, 111.

44. "Deportation Rumanian style consisted in herding five thousand people into freight cars and letting them die there of suffocation while the train travelled through the countryside without plan or aim for days on end." Hannah Arendt, *Eichmann in Jerusalem: A Report on the Banality of Evil*, 1963 (New York: Penguin, 2006), 191.

45. Most discussions of objects in *Maus* concentrate on Art's cigarettes as metaphors for the conflagration of the Holocaust. I engage with these elsewhere, see Georgiana Banita, *Plotting Justice: Narrative Ethics and Literary Culture after 9/11* (Lincoln: University of Nebraska Press, 2012), 75–92.

46. Spiegelman, *Maus I*, 93.

47. I have analyzed Chris Ware's use of silent panels elsewhere. See Georgiana Banita, "Chris Ware and the Pursuit of Slowness," in *The Comics of Chris Ware: Drawing Is a Way of Thinking*, ed. David M. Ball and Martha Kuhlman (Jackson: University Press of Mississippi, 2009), 177–90; "The Silent Sublime" [Review of Chris Ware's *Building Stories*], *The Comics Journal*, October 22, 2012; and "'A Diary of Time Itself': An Academic Roundtable on Chris Ware's *Rusty Brown*," *The Comics Journal*, March 23, 2020.

48. Art Spiegelman, "An Early, Wordless Graphic Novel about Mankind's Appetite for War," *New Yorker*, October 25, 2016.

49. *RAW* also published a portfolio of four stone lithographs by Spiegelman in an edition of 30 in 1992. Their style is evidently indebted to woodcut art. See Spiegelman, *Co-Mix*, 46.

50. Art Spiegelman, "Reading Pictures: A Few Thousand Words on Six Books Without Any," in Lynd Ward, *Prelude to a Million Years, Song Without Words, Vertigo*, ed. Art Spiegelman (New York: Library of America), xi. Spiegelman's essay is best understood alongside David M. Ball's detailed investigation into the complicated position Ward occupies between literature,

comics, and art history. See David M. Ball, "Lynd Ward's Modernist 'Novels in Woodcuts': Graphic Narratives Lost Between Art History and Literature, *Journal of Modern Literature*, vol. 39, no. 2 (2016): 126–43.

51. Spiegelman, "Reading Pictures," xv.

52. Spiegelman, "Reading Pictures," xvi.

53. Spiegelman, "Reading Pictures," xvii.

54. Art Spiegelman, *In the Shadow of No Towers* (New York: Pantheon, 2004). Another is *The Ghosts of Ellis Island* (2015), a collaboration with French photographer JR.

55. Georges Perec, *Species of Spaces and Other Pieces* (New York: Penguin, 2008), 210.

56. Spiegelman, *In the Shadow of No Towers*, 6.

57. Sontag, *Styles of Radical Will*, 5–6.

58. Lawrence Weschler, "Art's Father, Vladek's Son," in *Art Spiegelman: Conversations*, ed. Joseph Witek (Jackson: University Press of Mississippi, 2007), 79.

59. Sontag, *Styles of Radical Will*, 17.

Part 2

RADICAL POLITICS

EXPLODING STEREOTYPES

Spiegelman and Transgression

PHILIP SMITH

Jonathan Safran Foer recalls visiting Art Spiegelman's studio in New York and being stunned by the number of work surfaces he found there: "There must have been half a dozen desks throughout the office. How could one person, I wondered, need so many surfaces? Where is the army of Art Spiegelmans?"[1] While, as this volume attests, there are many connections to be made between different parts of Spiegelman's oeuvre, each of his works is stylistically distinctive from the others. A page from *Breakdowns* is immediately distinguishable from a page in *The Wild Party*, which is, in turn, completely different from a page in *Open Me . . . I'm a Dog!*, or in *Co-Mix*, *MetaMaus*, etc. Indeed, even individual narratives within particular works are often, themselves, distinct from other elements. Consider, for example, the deliberately jarring inclusion of "Prisoner on the Hell Planet" within the pages of *Maus*, or the collage of registers which make up each page of *In the Shadow of No Towers*.

Foer's question, then, is apt. Rather than conceiving of a single Art Spiegelman who has followed a linear path of stylistic development, it might be more useful to imagine an army of Spiegelmans—including Spiegelman the children's book author, Spiegelman the editor, and Spiegelman the comic book historian. Each of these figures has his own palate, his own artistic and political sensibilities, and perhaps even, as Foer suggests, his own desk. In this chapter, I wish to reconcile two seemingly contradictory Spiegelmans, each of whom embodies a distinct political and artistic ethic: the Spiegelman of the underground, on the one hand, and the Spiegelman who enjoys commercial success, critical recognition, and the patronage of major publishers, on the other.

The discourse that frames this discussion concerns the legitimization of comics as an art form versus the subversive potential of the underground comix scene. There are two, by no means mutually exclusive, stories we can tell about the evolution of underground and alternative comics. The first is one of progress; by emphasizing the craft of comic book creation, early and late underground cartoonists, among them Spiegelman, Bill Griffith, or the Richard McGuire who published the comic strip "Here" in Spiegelman's *RAW* (1989), engaged directly with the rhetoric, particularly prevalent during the 1950s, which declared comics to be a "low" form of art. Their comics, and Spiegelman's *Maus* specifically, have changed the perception of the medium in US culture. The hard-won awards and exhibitions, as well as the increased sales that come from reviews and widening readerships, have served to fund comic book production and to grow the audience for comics. The cultural kudos have also motivated early-career comic book creators, brought comics into teaching at all education levels, and built an archive and history of the medium.

An alternate narrative is that modern "alternative" comics have sacrificed the subversive power of their underground forebears in order to pander to the tastes of newspaper reviewers, gallery owners, academics, advertisers, and other arbiters of culture. Veteran creator R. Crumb has been particularly vocal in his resistance to his works being co-opted by more regulated media. He told one interviewer: "It's all bullshit . . . the fine-art world, the myth of the creative genius artist."[2] In the same interview, in what seems like a direct comment on Spiegelman's career path, Crumb explains that with few exceptions he refused to work for the *New Yorker* because doing so would restrict his creative freedom.[3] When the *New Yorker* editor David Remnick declined to publish a provocative cover Crumb had done on gay marriage, Crumb cut ties with the magazine. He rejects any scenario which involves someone "standing over us saying 'You can't draw this.'"[4]

Such a narrative casts the fall of the underground as a process of suppression and co-optation. In Britain in the early 1970s, the creators of the underground titles *Oz* and *Nasty Tales* were arrested for obscenity, while in New York, *Zap Comix* was declared obscene and taken to court in 1972. In 1973, *Air Pirates Funnies* suffered a similar fate.[5] A far more insidious method by which the center has contained and controlled the protest and critique presented by the underground, however, is by absorbing it. Since the 1970s, Roger Sabin argues, the underground comix movement has been "anaesthetized and co-opted into mainstream culture."[6] The most celebrated of the "alternative" cartoonists working today, such as Chris Ware and Richard McGuire, tend to be those who largely prefer (now uncontroversial) innovative execution over controversial content.

Scholars including Sabin, Charles Hatfield, Paul Williams, and James Lyons have similarly argued that a subversive ethic and critical recognition may be somewhat divergent goals.[7] The oft-quoted signs of legitimacy, such as awards, exhibitions, reviews, and publication in major literary magazines, introduce greater levels of regulation into comics practice and threaten to disincentivize artists from exploring marginalized and taboo subjects. This problem is tied to commercial and technological transformations, including changes in the modes of comics production and distribution. Unlike the radical underground comix scene of the 1960s, which used small presses or hand-printed means of production and mail order for distribution, many successful alternative cartoonists are now dependent on the support of major publishing houses, galleries, and magazines. These entities act as gatekeepers to publication and recognition and are thus able to regulate which comics and creators enjoy critical and commercial success.

Cartoonists, to paraphrase Crumb, must choose either to be declawed and critically petted, or to be outspoken in obscurity. Marjane Satrapi publishes commentary and comics in the *New York Times* and the *New Yorker*, while Crumb's diegetic incarnation masturbates out of a window, albeit in the rarified halls of the David Zwirner Gallery. David M. Ball's image of "an entire generation of graphic novelists who aspire to the status of literature" may be a utopian vision or a nightmare depending on one's beliefs about the relationship between transgressive art, economics, and cultural capital.[8] Both positions, Hatfield argues, are problematic, and they both fail to reach a "middle" audience; but they do provide "the inescapable setting for any discussion of comic books as literature."[9] Like most artists, Spiegelman has negotiated a position between the twin drives for legitimacy and creative freedom.

In what follows, I seek to show that the commercially successful and critically acclaimed Spiegelman of the post-*Maus* era and the transgressive Spiegelman from the world of underground comix are not as distant as the dichotomy described above might suggest. I argue that Spiegelman has maintained, throughout his career, a commitment to boundary-crossing in its various forms, and that his capacity for profanity as cultural critique has continued—not in spite of, but through changing models of distribution and greater interactions with the critical and commercial establishment.

For the purposes of this argument, I understand the necessary and sufficient condition of transgression (etymologically "boundary crossing") in a work of art to be its defiance of social convention. For a text to qualify as transgressive in a homophobic society, for example, it would be sufficient for it to contain positive representation of LGBTQ+ identities. In other words, a text can be understood as transgressive only in relation to the mores of the culture in which it is produced. In this sense, I concur with Julian Wolfreys that transgression is subjective, polysemic, and ever-changing.[10] As boundaries are negotiated, so, too, are the questions of what exists within and outside of those boundaries. Texts which were considered transgressive in Victorian England, for instance, can seem positively mundane to modern readers.

While transgression in this broad definition may be challenging, it need not provoke anger, horror, or nausea in its audience. In the modern era "the transgressive text," Wolfreys contends, "is not the one that shocks . . . Nothing is more banal, predictable or quotidian."[11] Nor is it necessary or sufficient that a transgressive text be produced without the interference of gatekeepers. It is possible, in fact, within the terms I have laid out, for transgression to exist and even thrive within policed environments. In order to maintain his commitment to the profane, Spiegelman, I propose, has constantly renegotiated his relationship to the cultures he has been in dialogue with throughout his career.

THE UNDERGROUND

Most of the cartoonists grouped under the "underground" banner were mostly in their early adolescence during the 1950s, when a large-scale social movement—including church groups, academics (most famously, though certainly not exclusively, Dr. Fredric Wertham), and parents' organizations—accused comics of causing juvenile delinquency and the retardation of reading abilities. One result of the anti-comics campaign was the Comics Code Authority [CCA], a form of self-policing among comic book creators which severely curtailed the subject matter and imagery that could be shown in comics. The generation of comic book readers who were children during this period came of age in the 1960s, when the antiauthoritarian counterculture movement was on the rise. As a result, many in this emergent cohort of comic book creators, Spiegelman included, deliberately defied the political conservativism of the generation that preceded them.

And yet, even when producing his works independently, Spiegelman has always been funded, albeit indirectly, by commercial publishers. He enjoyed a long career with Topps Gum from 1966 to 1989, and with "*Playboy* Funnies" from 1977 to 1983. At the same time, he produced independent work in line with the underground movement and, in that sense, embodied a do-it-yourself spirit and an aesthetic commitment to transgression. The first wave of the underground addressed themes of taboo sex (including incest, bestiality, free love, and rape) as well as drug consumption, radical politics, and extreme violence. Early underground comics often included deliberately misogynistic and racist caricatures such as, most iconically, R. Crumb's character Angelfood McSpade (1968). Sabin describes the revolutionary aesthetic of the underground as follows:

> [The CCA] stipulated "no sex," so the comix reveled in every kind of sex imaginable; the Code stipulated "no violence" so the underground

> took bloodshed to extremes; above all the code stipulated "no social relevance" yet here were comics that were positively revolutionary.[12]

In addition to their subversive content, underground cartoonists used a new business model—selling by hand, by mail order (as was the case with the 1977 version of Spiegelman's *Breakdowns*), or in head shops. The economics of the underground, as Sabin argues, was perhaps as revolutionary as the content. The underground comix movement sought not only to liberate the subject matter of comics from the highly restrictive standards of the CCA era, but to bypass the sales models which had underwritten the CCA practice. In other words, the direct sales model of the underground was revolutionary irrespective of the comics' content, because it sidestepped the distributors who gave the censorship of the CCA its potency.

Spiegelman's early work—some of which the established artist later published with Drawn & Quarterly (pages 14–26 of *Co-Mix*) and Pantheon (the afterword to the 2008 edition of *Breakdowns*)—belongs to the first wave of the underground.[13] Spiegelman describes his comics at the time as follows:

> I tried to absorb what Crumb and the other underground cartoonists I admired were up to by badly imitating them all. It made for some very embarrassing work: standard stabs at erotica and transgressive humor, as well as grotesque exercises in taboo breaking that feature patricide, necrophilia, and other misguided eruptions of violence on paper. One of these strips "climaxed" with a character of mine, fucking a young boy's severed head in the neck. I wanted to draw the most disturbing images I could think up.[14]

As I have argued elsewhere, the underground's inclination toward shock remains visible in *Breakdowns*, which often includes grotesque sexual content and nudity ("Real Dream: Hand Job," "Cracking Jokes," "Little Signs of Passion," "Spiegelman Moves to N.Y. 'Feels Depressed,'" "Real Dream," "The Malpractice Suite," and "Ace Hole"), sexual puns ("Hand Job," "Ace Hole," etc.), and racist caricatures ("The Malpractice Suite" and "Real Dream: The Sleep of Reason").[15] The first edition of *Breakdowns* had a print run of just 3,500 copies from the small independent publisher Belier Press and was advertised for sale by mail order in *RAW*—a magazine which, itself, was self-published by Spiegelman and his wife Françoise Mouly, with an original run of 3,500 copies.[16] An iconoclastic, self-promoting entrepreneur, Spiegelman was thus an archetypical comic book creator. The print run for *Breakdowns* was small and sales were low, but Spiegelman was under no pressure to adjust his content to the palate of anyone other than the underground's small readership—a readership, it should be noted, scarcely larger than the number of creators.

As Spiegelman's artistic voice developed, so too did his philosophy of transgression. He came to distinguish between shocking images that challenge their audience and those which reinforce existing prejudices. He writes of one of Crumb's racist parodies:

> My problem with the strip was that it wasn't virulent enough. And my proof of that is that it was able to be co-opted and reprinted in a neo-Nazi magazine with no problem. If he had done his job as a satirist well, then it would not have been able to be looked at without anger by the presumed target—the presumed target being the racist, rather than the blacks and Jews.[17]

In his essay "Little Orphan Annie's Eyeballs," which appears in *Comix, Essays, Graphics & Scraps*, Spiegelman similarly argues that while he is suspicious of Lenny Bruce's "inoculation" theory (i.e., by occupying a word we strip it of its power), he feels that removing taboo words from our vocabulary does little to rob them of their poison. "I'm wary of the process that imposes a new vocabulary as a means of changing the concepts themselves (like 'retarded' for 'moron,' or even 'graphic novel' for 'comic book.') We don't need more gentile synonyms. We need to examine and redefine the words we inherit."[18] His solution, then, is not a cleaner vocabulary or inoculation through repetition, but an open conversation about the capacity of particular words and images to offend. We need transgressive works, he argues, because they help us understand the nature and form of prejudice.

CROSSING THE HIGH-LOW BOUNDARY

The fact that Spiegelman's early works embody an underground commitment to transgression leaves us with the question of how he nevertheless came to be embraced by the artistic and cultural mainstream. If his work were truly committed to occupying and defying stereotypes, then surely it would never have found traction among middlebrow intellectual and artistic circles to begin with. To explain Spiegelman's adoption by arbiters of culture, I propose that underground comix, and Spiegelman's early works specifically, contained a second strand of *formal* transgression alongside their thematic commitment to blatant offense. Until the success of *Maus*, virtually all texts that treated comics as a sophisticated art form were, themselves, formally transgressive. George Herriman's *Krazy Kat* (1913–1944) violated artistic norms long before the underground era, because it introduced beautiful surreal landscapes and verbal creativity that were antithetical to dominant perceptions of the medium. The boundary crossed by works in this vein was that between "high" and "low" art.

Like the thematic experiments in taboo that defined the first wave, the challenge issued to arbiters of culture—concerning the place for comics art in modern society—can also be traced to the same mid-1950s rhetoric that dismissed comics as intellectually vapid and even dangerous. Spiegelman's work in *Breakdowns*, as well as embodying the shock aesthetic of the early underground, signaled a stylistic evolution toward more structurally experimental works, articulating a desire to both question and revel in the outlaw status of the medium. Bill Griffith, who coedited *Arcade* with Spiegelman, asserts that their work at the time was a "conscious effort to move away from the stifling and limiting themes of the early underground—sex, dope, violence etc. The need for that sort of catharsis had passed . . . we wanted to get on with the business of being artists."[19] This was not a shift away from the antiauthoritarian ethic of the underground, but an evolution of its revolutionary spirit.

Beyond a mere exercise in taboo-breaking, then, *Breakdowns* can also be read as a thesis on the legitimacy of comics as an artistic medium. Spiegelman's argument relies not only on formal experimentation such as panel transition types ("Skinless Perkins" and "Don't Get Around Much Anymore"), multipath narratives ("Day at the Circuits"), and diegetic expansion ("Little Signs of Passion"), but on a broad historiography of the form including quotations from Rube Goldberg ("Auto-Destructo"), Rex Morgan M.D. ("The Malpractice Suite"), Chester Gould ("Ace Hole"), and Winsor McCay ("Ace Hole"). In breaking down the tools of the comic book, Spiegelman also provides a visual archaeology of those tools. Quotation in *Breakdowns* serves to connect the contents of the collection with Spiegelman's artistic forebears, and to elucidate a history of artistic experimentation already present in the works of the medium's American pioneers. The range of quotations in *Breakdowns* does not, however, end with the comic book form. Spiegelman also references Pablo Picasso ("Ace Hole"), Walt Disney ("Maus"), Jack Woodford ("Little Signs of Passion"), iconic Holocaust photography ("Maus"), Edvard Munch ("Prisoner on the Hell Planet"), and, in the 2008 edition, James Joyce ("Portrait of the Artist as a Young %@#$!"), thereby blurring the boundaries between "high" and "low" art. Despite this emerging dichotomy, *Breakdowns* embodies the taboo-breaking aesthetic of the underground, while mounting a treatise on the capacity of comics to perform sophisticated cultural work. In *Breakdowns*, the "high" and "low" arts are not mutually exclusive, but mutually constitutive.

Spiegelman continued his campaign against the traditional classification of comics as "low" art with *RAW*, a comic book magazine which sought to, in Witek's words, explore "the formal boundaries and conceptual overlaps between comics and other visual narrative arts."[20] In many regards, *RAW* was the bridge between the underground aesthetic of edginess and the new, "alternative" era of artistically and emotionally sophisticated (and more widely palatable) comics. The argument against distinctions of "high" and "low" media was generally a gesture of tragic recognition rather than an expectation of cultural change. "Comics as a medium for self-expression? Oh John, you're such a fool!" reads an advertisement for *RAW*. Most famous among the comics to appear in *RAW*, of course, was Spiegelman's own serialized *Maus*—his clearest articulation of comics' potential as a medium. Not coincidentally, among his comics for adults, *Maus* is also the work which has generally been regarded as the least overtly offensive.

This is not to say that *Maus* did not cause any offense—several cartoonists and critics have voiced serious concerns over the graphic memoir. In 1986, after the first volume of *Maus* was published, fellow creator Harvey Pekar criticized *Maus* for presenting an unflattering (or, at best, mixed) portrayal of Poles, for the use of unnecessarily emotive cartoons over photographic realism, for dwelling on Vladek's personality flaws, and for Artie's generally insensitive treatment of his father.[21] Walter Benn Michaels accuses Spiegelman of dividing modern America's racial landscape into Jews and non-Jews, and homogenizing all other ethnic groups into the category of "dog."[22] *Maus* also attracted negative attention in Poland for its portrayal of Poles as pigs, and in German newspapers for attempting to reduce a historical subject of such immensity to the seemingly trivializing comic book form.[23]

For a widely read work that engages with a politically charged subject, the fact that *Maus* received some criticism is hardly surprising, nor are these unfavorable reactions a reason for us to assume that in writing *Maus* Spiegelman *intended* offense. Certainly, as has been argued exhaustively over the last twenty-five years, *Maus* engages with racist imagery found in anti-Semitic propaganda.[24] It does not do so, however, in ways that seem complicit with its source. Gone are the hook-nosed anti-Semitic cartoons and scenes of grotesque violence.[25] Indeed, the playful antiauthoritarian tone of the early underground would have been entirely at odds with the subject matter. *Maus*'s audacity and its transgression lies not in its content, then, but in its ambition. *Maus* came at the end of a series of editorial and creative projects in which Spiegelman sought, under the somewhat broader banner of transgression discussed above, to challenge the traditional status of comics as "low" art. The impetus of these projects was entwined with the larger project of transgression in underground comix and would have remained so—were it not for the fact that the gamble actually paid off.

TRANSGRESSION AFTER *MAUS*

The publication of *Maus* coincided with, if not the end, then certainly the slowing-down of the underground comix scene. In what at the time seemed an utterly bizarre, seismic cultural shift, *Maus* received a glowing review from celebrity critic Ken Tucker in the *New York Times Book Review*.[26] The publishing house Pantheon, which had previously shown no interest in working with Spiegelman, agreed to publish the first volume of *Maus*. Comic book fans and creators were unexpectedly receiving some of the legitimacy they had campaigned for. In retrospect, of course, we can see that a number of historical factors led to this—*Maus* arrived at a key moment as large-scale conversations around the Holocaust were taking place.[27] It also coincided with Frank Miller's *The Dark Knight Returns* and Alan Moore and Dave Gibbons's *Watchmen*—two comics which also seemed conclusively to prove that the medium was capable of sophisticated storytelling—as well as with the earliest forms of comics criticism such as Ariel Dorfman and Armand Mattelart's *How to Read Donald Duck* (1971). Nonetheless, at the time, for a comic that had originally been self-published in a magazine with a print run of just 3,500 copies, the astronomical success of *Maus* was completely unprecedented.[28]

Following his challenge to arbiters of culture about the place for comics in literary and artistic hierarchies, Spiegelman found himself suddenly embraced by the same establishment that the underground had defined itself against. "I'd arrogantly assumed my work would be read posthumously," he told Hillary Chute in *MetaMaus*.[29] One immediate consequence of this success was that he ceased to use the independent means of publication typically associated with underground comix. Quite simply, the underground lacked the infrastructure to deal with success on such a scale. The first collected edition of *Maus I* was published by Pantheon in 1986—a significantly larger publishing house than Belier Press, and much larger than Spiegelman's own home-printing operation. He received a National Book Critics Circle Award in the same year. Pantheon also published the first volume of *Read Yourself RAW*, a collection of comics from *RAW* magazine, in 1987. Only two years later Spiegelman's work, beginning with *RAW Vol. 2*, was released by the publishing giant Penguin. Spiegelman went on to receive a Guggenheim Fellowship in 1990, a Pulitzer Prize in 1992, and was honored with a solo exhibition at New York's Museum of Modern Art also in 1992. He joined the staff of the *New Yorker* in the same year. Penguin followed *Maus* with a series of other graphic novels, lending the titles it published, and the medium as a whole, a degree of legitimacy which comics had not previously enjoyed.

The success of *Maus* was intoxicating not only for Spiegelman, but for the underground comix community as a whole. Prior to *Maus* few comics had

Detail from "Drawing the Line: Notes from a First Amendment Fundamentalist," the *Nation*, 150th Anniversary Special Issue 3/23/2015. Copyright © 2015 by Art Spiegelman.

received significant interest from either the mainstream media or the academic establishment. While a large portion of the response to *Maus*'s success was celebratory, there were many who, perhaps driven as much by hubris as a desire to defend the underground's history of independence, greeted it with cynicism. Douglas Wolk complains that "[f]or those of us who've been passionate about comics for ages, it's hard not to resent *Maus* a little for being a lot of other people's sole idea of what art comics are like."[30] In 1991, French cartoonist Lewis Trondheim produced a parody of *Maus* titled *Emmaüs* in which Artie reluctantly decides to tell his father's story as a comic book only when he learns that the rights to the story in all other media have already been sold.[31] Trondheim seems to offer, in line with the self-flagellation that was a core theme in *RAW*, a tragic recognition of the low standing afforded to comics in 1990s culture. A comic that skillfully dealt with adult themes, he seems to suggest, was treated rather like a dog (or, more appropriately, a mouse) that could talk. Critics were not impressed that it spoke well, but rather that it spoke at all. Implicit in Trondheim's argument is the suggestion that pandering to the tastes of the artistic establishment is an unnecessary act of submission.

It is tempting to read the recurring instances of taboo-breaking in Spiegelman's work from the 1960s and 1970s as a kind of adolescence. The problem with such a reading, however, is that Spiegelman's later work shows the same proclivity for transgression as his earlier period. In the 2015 full-page comic strip "Drawing the Line: Notes from a First Amendment Fundamentalist"—written for, but never published by, the *New Statesman* in their issue on "Saying the Unsayable"—Spiegelman shows a picture of Artie (the protagonist of *Maus* also featured by *In the Shadow of No Towers* and several one-off comics) holding two magazine covers. One of them flaunts a smiley face and the caption "have a nice day," the other shows the same smiley face wearing a squiggly turban and labeled "Mohammad." In the ensuing panels, Artie explains the juxtaposition:

> "Desire Not to Offend" is a euphemism for Mortal Fear! AK-47s give far too much veto power to the afflicted . . . and hiding behind a smug PC phrase adds insult to the deadly injury prompted by the original cartoon "insult" [. . .] juvenile rebelliousness is part of cartooning's DNA! Me? . . . I'd rather use cartoon language to EXPLODE stereotypes than reinforce them.[32]

Spiegelman pulled his censorship-themed cover from the *New Statesman* because the magazine reneged on its agreement to carry "First Amendment Fundamentalist." The strip was a response to the January 7, 2015, murder of

Withdrawn cover for the *New Statesman's* special issue on "Saying the Unsayable," guest editors Neil Gaiman and Amanda Palmer, 5/19/2015. Copyright © 2015 by Art Spiegelman.

twelve people and the injuring of eleven others in the offices of French satirical newspaper *Charlie Hebdo* by gunmen who identified themselves as members of a branch of al-Qaeda. The attack was, al-Qaeda spokesmen claimed, retaliation for the magazine's irreverent depiction of the Prophet Mohammed. Spiegelman, along with many of his colleagues, drew cartoons which included images of the Prophet Mohammed as a stance of defiance. In the final panel of this strip, Artie is petting a rat with a humanoid face bearing a Star of David. The image invokes a 1940s anti-Semitic poster from occupied Denmark in an unsubtle reference to Spiegelman's own willingness to confront anti-Semitic imagery in *Maus*.[33]

This commitment to transgression is a recurring feature in Spiegelman's later work. In 2006, almost three decades after the first edition of *Breakdowns* was published, Spiegelman created a series of cartoons in response to an anti-Semitic cartoon contest run in the Iranian newspaper *Hamshahri*; these cartoons, which appear in *MetaMaus*, were eventually submitted to the *New Yorker* and *Harpers*.[34] One such cartoon shows two men, both drawn in the style of racist caricatures with, to use Spiegelman's words, "a hooked line for a nose and large animated hands."[35] The men are identical, save that one wears a keffiyeh (an Arabic head scarf) and the other does not. The man wearing the keffiyeh addresses the other: "That's funny . . . You don't look Jewish."[36] The cartoon not only embodies offensive imagery, but calls it into question, suggesting that the perceived ethnic differences between Israeli Jews and their Arab neighbors

Cartoon created in response to an anti-Semitic cartoon contest run in the Iranian newspaper *Hamshahri*, reprinted in *MetaMaus: A Look Inside a Modern Classic,* Maus (New York: Pantheon, 2011), p. 102. Copyright © 2011 by Art Spiegelman.

"Valentine's Day," *New Yorker* cover, 2/15/1993. Copyright © 1993 by Art Spiegelman.

are less distinct than political rhetoric might suggest. Spiegelman also wrote a letter to the jury, commending certain entries to an Israeli anti-Semitic cartoon contest that appeared in response to the *Hamshahri* competition. "I guess the best Jewish cartoonists were just too busy grubbing for money to bother entering a contest where the crummy first prize is a box of *matzohs*," he writes.[37] Spiegelman's sketchbooks, published by Drawn & Quarterly in 2014, feature the recurring image of a large-lipped African man wearing tribal dress, the mock cover of a Nazi-themed romance comic, and, in one sequence, a severed phallus bouncing its way across the page.[38] Perhaps most famously, Spiegelman created the controversial 1993 Valentine's Day cover of the *New Yorker* that showed a Hasidic Jew and a Black West Indian woman locked in a kiss. These instances suggest an ongoing fascination in Spiegelman's work with the power and necessity of transgressive imagery.

Clearly, then, even as he engaged in a project of self-canonization, Spiegelman has maintained his commitment to the taboo-breaking ethic of the underground. Indeed, rather than being cowed by artistic and cultural norms, his desire to challenge political orthodoxies around identity and race, and to explore controversial subjects like anti-Semitism or violent extremism, have often put him at odds with publishers. Spiegelman seems to wear this rejection as something of a badge of honor that cements his credentials with both the world of "high" art and the "alternative" underground. The 1993 Valentine's Day *New Yorker* cover appears in *Co-Mix* and is accompanied by the caption: "This was the first of many Spiegelman covers which would cause an outcry. Some proposed covers never made it to the newsstand because they were deemed 'too outrageous' by editors."[39] The book itself carries several covers originally created for the *New Yorker* which, prior to *Co-Mix*, had gone unpublished. One such cover, perhaps an homage to Crumb's incest-themed cartoon "The Family That Lays Together Stays Together," shows a pregnant mother walking beside her pregnant daughter, who pushes a pram containing a pregnant infant, who holds a pregnant doll.[40] Notoriously, many US newspaper and magazine publishers, the *New Yorker* included, also refused to carry the original pages of *In the Shadow of No Towers* because Spiegelman's message ran counter to the bellicose political rhetoric of the time; the comics were first published, instead, in European newspapers.[41]

The fact that these rejected works have appeared online, in lavish collected editions, and established European venues demonstrates that Spiegelman has not compromised his high-art ambitions. Rather, these rejections serve, if anything, to add to his artistic capital.[42] Nor do they limit the public visibility of his work. The advent of the internet has provided Spiegelman with an alternative means of distribution outside of mainstream media channels. Prior to the publication of *Co-Mix*, one could find Spiegelman's rejected *New Yorker* covers online.[43] Before the *Nation* included it in its 150th Anniversary Special Issue in 2015, the internet was the only place where one could read Spiegelman's "First Amendment Fundamentalist" strip. Spiegelman is not a webcomic creator by any means, but he has continued to find ways to distribute his work outside of mainstream, policed spaces.

In this chapter I have sought to show that Spiegelman has maintained, throughout his career, a commitment to both formal and political transgression. This mode of transgression has ranged from the grotesque styles of the early underground to images that question the boundaries of offense, to nuanced assaults upon the classification of comics as "low" art, to scathing indictments of political correctness in the American press. Crucially, Spiegelman has continued to create transgressive works despite unparalleled commercial and critical success. Rather than curb his desire to "explode stereotypes," his relationship with editors, academics, gallery owners, and reviewers has offered him a means to accrue artistic capital through rejection.

Rejected Mother's Day idea for *New Yorker* cover, 4/15/1996. Copyright © 1996 by Art Spiegelman.

The fact that Spiegelman has maintained his creative independence despite cultural co-optation does not mean that his career path is either typical or replicable. While, as Spiegelman demonstrates, creative and financial independence is neither necessary nor sufficient for transgression to occur, the two often exist together. It is germane to this discussion, then, that Spiegelman is not alone in using the internet as a means to bypass editorial prohibition. Online distribution comes in many forms with varying degrees of editorial control or barriers of access, including zero. The ability to publish independently and to sell merchandise directly to fans has allowed some cartoonists (albeit a minority) to achieve financial stability without awards, grants, a job at the *New Yorker*, or the backing of a major corporation. To offer just one example, in March 2013, independent comics artist Aaron Diaz, creator of the webcomic *Dresden Codak* (2005–present), raised $534,994 to produce a print copy of his work entirely through fan support. Online distribution thus offers a means by which comic book creators might replicate, if not Spiegelman's uniquely transcendent career, certainly the do-it-yourself independent spirit of the early underground and maintain comics' capacity to cross boundaries.

Notes

1. Jonathan Safran Foer, "Art Spiegelman," in *Masters of American Comics*, ed. John Carlin (New Haven: Yale University Press, 2005), 297.

2. Ted Widmer, "Interview: R. Crumb, The Art of Comics No. 1," *Paris Review* 193 (Summer 2010).

3. R. Crumb has not been entirely resistant to critical recognition, although, one might argue, his art has always been presented on his own terms. His works have appeared in art galleries since the 1970s including, in 2012, at Paris's prestigious *Musée d'Art Moderne*.

4. Qtd. in Roger Sabin, *Adult Comics: An Introduction* (London: Routledge, 1993).

5. The trials were, in some regards, the beginning of the end. Lawyers' fees were expensive, paper costs were rising, head shops were closing, and the end of the Vietnam War meant that the counterculture movement lost its unifying directive. The underground did not die out completely—*Knockabout* continued to publish through the 1980s and Drawn & Quarterly "picked up where *Weirdo* left off" (Sabin 98), publishing experimental and edgy works. By the 1980s, however, the underground comix movement had inarguably lost its momentum.

6. Sabin, *Adult Comics*, 49.

7. Charles Hatfield, *Alternative Comics: An Emerging Literature* (Jackson: University Press of Mississippi, 2005); Roger Sabin, *Comics, Comix and Graphic Novels: A History of Comic Art* (London: Phaidon, 1996); Paul Williams and James Lyons, "Introduction," in *The Rise of the American Comics Artist: Creators and Contexts*, ed. Paul Williams and James Lyons (Jackson: University Press of Mississippi, 2010), xi–xxiv.

8. David M. Ball, "Comics Against Themselves: Chris Ware's Graphic Narratives as Literature," in *The Rise of the American Comics Artist: Creators and Contexts*, ed. Paul Williams and James Lyons (Jackson: University Press of Mississippi, 2010), 120.

9. Hatfield, *Alternative Comics*, xii.

10. Julian Wolfreys, *Transgression: Identity, Space, Time* (London: Palgrave Macmillan, 2008).

11. Wolfreys, *Transgression*, 12.

12. Sabin, *Adult Comics*, 171.

13. Art Spiegelman, *Co-Mix: A Retrospective of Comics, Graphics, and Scraps* (Montreal: Drawn & Quarterly, 2013).

14. Art Spiegelman, *Breakdowns* (New York: Pantheon, 2008), 71.

15. Philip Smith, *Reading Art Spiegelman* (New York: Routledge, 2015).

16. Hillary Chute, *Disaster Drawn: Visual Witness, Comics, and Documentary Form* (Cambridge, Mass.: Harvard University Press 2016), 186.

17. Art Spiegelman, "Art Spiegelman Interview," *The Comics Journal* 181 (1995): 135–36.

18. Art Spiegelman, *Comix, Essays, Graphics, and Scraps* (Selerrio Editore—La Centrale dell'Arte, 1999), 18.

19. John Carlin, *Masters of American Comics* (New Haven: Yale University Press, 2005), 128.

20. Joseph Witek, *Comic Books as History: The Art of Jack Jackson, Art Spiegelman, and Harvey Pekar* (Jackson: University Press of Mississippi, 1989), x.

21. Harvey Pekar, "*Maus* and Other Topics," *The Comics Journal*, 113 (1986): 54–57.

22. Walter Benn Michaels, "Plots Against America: Neoliberalism and Antiracism," *American Literary History* 18, no. 2 (2006): 288–302.

23. Art Spiegelman, *MetaMaus: A Look Inside a Modern Classic,* Maus (New York: Pantheon, 2011), 122–25.

24. For a summary, see Philip Smith, "Spiegelman Studies: *Maus*," *Literature Compass* 12, no. 10 (2015): 499–508.

25. See Smith, *Reading,* for a discussion of violence (and the lack thereof) in *Maus.* See also the chapter by Ariella Freedman in this volume for a discussion of the moveable border between cartooning and racist caricature in Spiegelman's illustrations to Joseph Moncure March's *The Wild Party.*

26. Arie Kaplan, *From Krakow to Krypton: Jews and Comic Books* (Philadelphia: The Jewish Publication Society 2008), 172.

27. Ian Gordon, "Making Comics Respectable: How *Maus* Helped Redefine a Medium," in *The Rise of the American Comics Artist: Creators and Contexts,* ed. Paul Williams and James Lyons (Jackson: University Press of Mississippi, 2010), 183.

28. For more on the impact of *Maus,* see Andrew Loman, "That Mouse's Shadow: The Canonization of Spiegelman's *Maus*," in *The Rise of the American Comics Artist: Creators and Contexts,* ed. Paul Williams and James Lyons (Jackson: University Press of Mississippi, 2010), 210–34.

29. Spiegelman, *MetaMaus,* 79.

30. Douglas Wolk, *Reading Comics* (Boston: Da Capo Press, 2007), 342.

31. Louis Trondheim, "Emmaüs," *Rackham Poutch* (Paris: Rackham, 1991), 39.

32. Art Spiegelman, "Drawing the Line: Notes from a First Amendment Fundamentalist," *Nation,* 23 March 2015.

33. Spiegelman, *MetaMaus,* 115.

34. Spiegelman, *MetaMaus,* 102–3. This sinuous line of publication, from rejection to promulgation in high-prestige venues, is shared by *In the Shadow of No Towers.*

35. Spiegelman, *Comix, Essays,* 17.

36. Spiegelman, *MetaMaus,* 102.

37. Art Spiegelman, "Letter to the Jury," *Modern Fiction Studies* 52, no. 4 (2006): 783–87.

38. Art Spiegelman, "Art Spiegelman," in *Drawn and Quarterly: Twenty-Five Years of Contemporary Cartooning, Comics, and Graphic Novels* (Montreal: Drawn & Quarterly, 2015), 693, 695, 698–99.

39. Spiegelman, *Co-Mix,* 54.

40. Spiegelman, *Co-Mix,* 57.

41. Sven Cvek, *Towering Figures: Reading the 9/11 Archive* (Amsterdam: Rodopi, 2011).

42. Philip Smith, "Digital Media and the Comic Book," in *Critical Insights: The American Comic Book,* ed. Joseph Sommers (Salem: Grey House Press, 2014), 153–69.

43. Killian Fox, "The Covers the *New Yorker* Rejected," *Guardian.com,* April 29, 2012.

RAW RADICALS

Art Spiegelman's Comic Politics[1]

SARAH HAMBLIN

Few would disagree that the praise heaped on Art Spiegelman and Françoise Mouly's comics anthology magazine *RAW* is well deserved. *RAW* has been hailed as a "revolutionary,"[2] "groundbreaking,"[3] and "seminal"[4] publication that ushered in the alternative comics culture of the 1980s and launched the careers of some of today's most celebrated graphic novelists. As the first American venue dedicated to publishing avant-garde artists and international comics auteurs, *RAW* connected underground comix with the new generation of experimental artists committed to exploring the boundaries of the medium and changing the way comics were perceived. Yet despite its importance, *RAW* has received little sustained critical attention. Although mentioned in almost every history of the medium, *RAW* usually only merits a brief appraisal that reaffirms its pivotal role in the evolution of comics, before transitioning into a discussion of the most famous work that it serialized: Spiegelman's *Maus*.[5]

These potted histories uphold the same basic narrative, positioning *RAW* as a response to the narrowing scope of nonmainstream comics culture in the late 1970s. While underground comix still dominated the alternative scene, they had lost their radical edge, as scores of derivative titles reduced the underground to a series of tired clichés. The handful of independent publishers that survived struggled to find an audience in a market dominated by DC and Marvel. Inspired by European comics, Spiegelman and Mouly created *RAW* as a venue for new artists who were producing challenging work that did not fit the current underground mold. *RAW* showcased European auteurs, including Jacques Tardi, Joost Swarte, Kiki and Loulou Picasso, Javier Mariscal, Ever Meulen, and Pascal Doury. It also endeavored to include work by artists beyond the European canon, including José Muñoz and Carlos Sampayo (Argentina), Chéri Samba (Congo), Vitaly Komar and Alexander Melamid

(Russia), and, in a special feature dedicated to Japanese manga in *RAW* Vol. 1, Issue 7, Teruhiko Yumura, Yosuke Kawamura, Shigeru Sugiura, and Yoshiharu Tsuge. In addition, *RAW* included historical strips by avant-garde artists who were positioned as forerunners to the adult comics tradition. These figures included Winsor McCay, George Herriman, Milt Gross, and Basil Wolverton, and more esoteric artists such as Gustave Doré, Boody Rogers, Fletcher Hanks, and the nineteenth-century Russian-French satirist Caran D'Ache (Emmanuel Poiré).

The majority of *RAW*, however, was dedicated to new American artists, many of whom were affiliated with the New York School of Visual Arts, where Spiegelman was teaching. Others came from the Collective for Living Cinema in Lower Manhattan, where Spiegelman lectured on comics. Although they are today some of the most celebrated names in graphic literature, at the time, these artists—among them Mark Beyer, Charles Burns, Chris Ware, Gary Panter, Sue Coe, Lynda Barry, Ben Katchor, Mark Newgarden, and Carol Lay—were little known and out of step with both underground and mainstream circles. Much like the contemporary international artists that *RAW* attracted, these American cartoonists were producing experimental work that showcased the medium's versatility, exploring the relationship between comics and other art forms.

The dominant historical account emphasizes *RAW*'s formal innovations and recognizes in it the outcome of the underground's commitment to comics as a means of self-expression. *RAW*, in this reading, reoriented the underground's investment in individual expression away from countercultural politics toward, as Bart Beaty argues, "a particular comics lineage that was at once international, highly formalist, and . . . irreverently outside the mainstream of American comics publishing."[6] This self-consciously intellectual approach is associated with an aesthetic tradition that eclipses political engagement, positioning *RAW* against radical political comics. As Arie Kaplan puts it: "Eschewing the overwhelmingly political bent of *World War 3 Illustrated*, *RAW* championed personal artistic expression."[7] In both form and content, then, *RAW* is seen as a sophisticated, high-art engagement with the concept of comics itself, unconcerned with the radical politics of either the earlier underground scene or its politically engaged contemporaries.[8]

Spiegelman's work is frequently tarred with the same apolitical brush. As a figurehead of comics' aesthetic revolution and a Pulitzer-Prize winning memoirist, Spiegelman is often categorized as a capital-A Artist invested in aesthetic innovation and narratives of personal experience, rather than radical politics.[9] "Prisoner on the Hell Planet," *Maus*, *Breakdowns*, and *In the Shadow of No Towers* are all autobiographical works that detail Spiegelman's anxieties and explore the psychological response to trauma. Like *RAW*, Spiegelman himself is therefore seen as emblematic of a larger alternative comics culture that is more inclined toward formal experimentation, individual expression, and personal responses to world events than toward political commentary or radical politics.

This chapter aims to show the opposite, arguing that while *RAW* did spearhead an aesthetic revolution, this revolution did not come at the expense of political radicalism. Rather, *RAW*'s stylistic experiments link formal innovation with radical cultural critique. In their role as editors, Spiegelman and Mouly pursued anticapitalist and anti-Reaganite positions through the artists they published and the thematic focus of each issue. At the same time, radical politics informs both the form and content of Spiegelman's own contributions to *RAW*, as well as the design of the magazine itself. As editor and contributor, then, Spiegelman privileges certain political aesthetics—neosincerity, détournement, punk, and New Wave typography—to critique Reagan-era neoliberalism and to promote a critical engagement with image culture that works to reaffirm comics as a site of resistance. In examining *RAW*'s place within the radical comics tradition, this chapter documents a political sensibility that has been overlooked in discussions of *RAW* and of Spiegelman's work more generally to argue that *RAW*'s avant-garde aesthetic is not in opposition to its radical politics, but at its center.

RAW CONTENT: EDITORIAL RADICALISM

By their nature, anthologies represent a range of voices, so it would be inaccurate to claim that *RAW* expresses a unified politics or style. Indeed, one of the goals of *RAW* was to showcase a variety of alternative comics and to break with the limited visions of underground and commercial comics that preceded it. Taken as a whole, however, the publication firmly sits within the radically political comics tradition. Indeed, Spiegelman himself has commented on the way that oppositional politics permeates the overall content and tone of *RAW*:

> Although I've never been as committed politically to any kind of programmatic assault on the culture, it just came with the territory of growing up with the underground newspapers and comics. And it just never seemed that separate, the culture and the politics. Look through the underground comics you'll find lots of stuff that wasn't political but somehow seems vaguely informed by a repulsion with Nixon and the Vietnam War, no matter what else was going on. It remains true here.[10]

Thus, while radical politics does not emanate from every single piece collected in *RAW*, it nevertheless remains a central component of the publication. As Bart Beaty notes, the anthology evinces an "extremely consistent and singular editorial vision" resulting from Spiegelman and Mouly's hands-on editorial style.[11] Under their guidance, *RAW* maintained a remarkable consistency that reflected Spiegelman's larger political agenda.[12]

The magazine often spoke explicitly to political issues, including racism, the plight of the working class and migrant workers, animal rights, environmentalism, gentrification, imperialism, Reaganism, anticommunist hysteria, nuclear proliferation, and early manifestations of neoliberal capitalism. The sheer number of pieces in *RAW* that address these issues is so extensive that it precludes a detailed discussion of each strip. Central to *RAW*'s radical core is the overall mode of critique that such pieces favor. The vast majority tackle issues fundamental to American culture, casting them as systemic rather than personal. At the same time, the anti-Reaganism that forms a key pillar of *RAW*'s radicalism is framed in broadly Marxist terms, where neoliberal capitalism operates as a kind of rhizomatic structure that intersects with multiple systems of oppression. Working in this vein, Andrew Tyler and Sue Coe's "This Little Piggy Went to Market" (Vol. 2, Issue 2) addresses animal abuse, toxic masculinity, and environmental degradation as problems endemic to the logic of surplus value. Similarly, Mouly's "Food for Thought" (Vol. 1, Issue 3) ties its criticisms of convenience food and advertising to the corporatization of farming and to the monopoly that runs the food chain, while Lynne Tillman's "Living with Contradictions" (Vol. 1, Issue 4) roots a feminist critique of marriage in the capitalist logic of commodity culture. The consistent anticapitalist perspective and repeated emphasis on systematic modes of oppression position *RAW* within the tradition of radical rather than liberal critique.

Spiegelman and Mouly's political focus extends beyond simply accepting pieces that address political subjects from a broadly anticapitalist perspective. Indeed, the structure of the magazine issues itself emphasizes political questions. Each issue is organized around a theme encapsulated in its sardonic strapline, which often highlights a systemic political problem. In some cases, Spiegelman and Mouly invited artists to contribute something on a particular theme—Vol. 1, Issue 8 includes a section on thermonuclear war, for example, while Vol. 2, Issue 1 features pieces that explore communist nostalgia. In other instances, Spiegelman and Mouly used their editorial position to engage specific political debates. One of the most well-known examples of this is Spiegelman's refusal to print Drew Friedman's "Comic Strip" in *RAW* Vol. 1, Issue 2 unless Friedman included a supplementary page ("A Real-Life Situation") that drew attention to his own use of problematic racial stereotypes and their prevalence in American comics history. Spiegelman also required Charles Burns to incorporate an image of Reagan in his cover for *RAW* Vol. 1, Issue 4 in order to link the administration's nuclear policies with the deathly wasteland and mutant version of American family values the cover depicts.[13]

A similar sentiment is expressed in Spiegelman and Mouly's decision to illustrate an excerpt from sociologist Lloyd deMause's *Reagan's America* with drawings by Sue Coe that were created independently of the text ("Radioactive Guilt: Ritual Sacrifice in Reagan's America" in Vol. 1, Issue 7).[14] DeMause's text relates how Reagan manufactured a culture of fear and hysteria through the repetition of a narrative of impending external threat and economic precarity. DeMause presents the acceptance of this paranoid world view as the function of the country's damaged psyche, whereby American foreign policy is tied to a savage free-market ideology that results in "surplus destruction." Coe's surrealist illustrations, which Spiegelman and Mouly describe as "visual tangents rather than as illustrations per se,"[15] draw out the psychological underpinnings of deMause's text to highlight the distorted nature of America's national psyche. Coe's twisted images of motherhood in this context expose the disastrous effects of Reaganomics—which deMause likens to the self-destructive logic of Aztec sun-god sacrifice—while her bleak landscapes and emaciated bodies become harrowing representations of a possible future.

At the same time, Spiegelman and Mouly's design for the piece, especially the choice of pull quotes and their placement next to certain illustrations, explicitly highlights the editors' own critical point of view. By placing the quote, "'The victims of Reaganomics' is not a purely metaphorical phrase . . . 150,000 deaths can be attributed to the effects of Reaganomics," next to Coe's illustration of a man spray-painting "jobs not guns," Spiegelman and Mouly make the point that Reagan's military spending works in tandem with America's obsession with gun ownership to divest both money and attention away from issues of un- and underemployment. Coe's German Expressionist style links the economic crisis of the 1980s to the Great Depression and the urban pessimism of film noir, while the text's emphasis on nuclear proliferation, and the high death toll referenced in the pull quote, imply an impending holocaust. These and other design choices show that Spiegelman and Mouly were instrumental in shaping *RAW*'s political tone and furthering its systemic critique of American economics and politics.

Spiegelman's choice of historical artists also pursues political ends, this time by situating *RAW* within a larger radical history. Alfred Jarry, Théophile Alexandre Steinlen, and Frans Masereel—all reprinted in *RAW*—were left-wing radicals who produced political comics. Jarry's satirical prose piece "Hommages Posthumes" (Vol. 1, Issue 1) exposes the hypocrisy of bourgeois society. Steinlen created hundreds of political cartoons, published under the pseudonym Jean Caillou, that focused on the experiences of the working class. Steinlen's "Cats," which Spiegelman republished in *RAW*, Vol. 1, Issue 8, can also be read as an allegorical commentary on class relations, as an average mouse finds itself the unwitting plaything and eventual prey of three well-kept house cats. Likewise,

Masereel, whose work is reprinted in several issues of *RAW*, contributed to populist leftist and pacifist publications and his work was widely distributed in communist countries due to its socialist themes.[16] Moreover, *RAW* also visually alludes to the publications in which these historical pieces were originally printed. Masereel's "Back to the Front," printed in the "Raw Gagz" section of *RAW* Vol. 1, Issue 8, was originally published in the populist left-wing publication *PM*. The "Raw Gagz" section of this issue also includes a Stuart Davis image from the leftist periodical *The Masses*. The image, "Some *Masses* Artists Seeking Inspiration," is here retitled "Some *RAW* Artists Seeking Inspiration." In tweaking this title, the editors suggest that *PM*'s and *The Masses*'s linkage of formal innovation and political radicalism serves as a model for *RAW*'s own radical aesthetic.

Spiegelman and Mouly's editorial hand is also visible in the magazine's rebuttals to censorship and to the conservative attitudes that were gaining traction during the 1980s. In *RAW* Vol. 1, Issue 5, Spiegelman and Mouly blocked out the explicit images of genitalia in Pascal Doury's "Theodore Death Head," fearing that stores carrying the issue would risk being raided. Instead, they offered readers a mail-in sticker sheet of the omitted penises that they could then affix themselves, in an attempt to highlight the absurdity of censorship laws. Spiegelman and Mouly also discuss censorship in their editorial for *RAW* Vol. 1, Issue 4, which details the production difficulties for the issue's insert—a flexi disc montage of Reagan's speeches by sound scholar Douglas Kahn. The American company contracted to press the disc refused to do so. Citing the risk of a defamation lawsuit, they demanded that Spiegelman and Mouly secure written permission from Reagan himself before proceeding. The disc was eventually pressed overseas, provoking Spiegelman and Mouly to condemn, in their editorial, the repression of dissenting political opinion in America: "Meanwhile, back in America, the Fifties are alive and well. And it's not just Rockabilly."[17]

The critique of censorship can, in fact, be traced back to the first issue of *RAW*, which opens with a translation of Alfred Jarry's "Hommages Posthumes." Jarry's piece defends the necrophiliac gravedigger, Honoré Ardisson, to expose how the law shores up not justice, but a bourgeois moral and social order. In choosing Jarry—a figure who was no stranger to censorship—as the opening artist for the magazine, Spiegelman and Mouly place censorship and laws regarding freedom of representation at the forefront of *RAW*'s political investments. This critique of censorship is a cornerstone of *RAW* and Spiegelman's radical politics, something Spiegelman reaffirmed in absolute terms in his exploration of the Danish Muhammad cartoon controversy several decades later.[18]

RAW SUICIDE: THEMATIC RADICALISM

While overtly political content is easy to find in *RAW*'s pages, its more general thematic preoccupations similarly evince *RAW*'s political commitments. Indeed, along with the blunt criticisms of Reagan's economic and militarist policies, perhaps the most compelling example of *RAW*'s radicalism resides in one of its purportedly most depoliticized themes: suicide. Next to Cold War anxieties and anti-Reaganism, suicide is the most common theme across *RAW*'s eleven issues. For critics like Jeet Heer, this preoccupation is evidence of the magazine's investment in personal experience, as it expresses Spiegelman's and Mouly's own battles with clinical depression: "Mouly and Spiegelman made their personal obsession with self-annihilation part of the governing gestalt of their journal . . . *RAW* was quite literally a way for the couple to stave off death and do something meaningful with their lives."[19] In *RAW*, however, suicide moves beyond individual psychological trauma.

From the first issue, the subject of suicide is connected to a larger critique of the alienation of modern life. As Spiegelman puts it: "In a sense, suicide is like a case of terminal alienation. And alienation in its less terminal stages seems like the only appropriate response to me to the society I'm living in."[20] The existential despair expressed throughout *RAW* is therefore more than simply the expression of a personal neurosis. It is also part of the magazine's larger challenge to the rationality of mass consumption. At the same time, the magazine's preoccupation with suicide resonates with Cold War anxieties about nuclear escalation as a form of mass suicide. Indeed, the title of *RAW* Vol. 1, Issue 1, "The Graphix Magazine of Postponed Suicides," suggests this link. Spiegelman and Mouly saw the phrase "postponed suicide," adapted from Emil Cioran's quip that "every book is a postponed suicide," as an affirmation of life, but the expression also alludes to the resurgent threat of nuclear annihilation under Carter and then Reagan.

Spiegelman's cover design for *RAW* Vol. 1, Issue 1 reflects this preoccupation with suicide as a multifaceted emblem of alienation, of the capitalist indifference to suffering, and of the dangers of nuclear proliferation. The cover depicts a man sitting in a luxury high-rise apartment reading *RAW*, while a tipped-in color image shows another man outside his window plummeting to his death. The cover separates the two men: The one inside is drawn in black-and-white, he is stationary, and framed only by the borders of the page; the man outside is in color, moving, and framed by the window. The color image has been hand-glued to the page, which gives it additional depth to further separate the two men in a maneuver that implies a class distinction. The man in the apartment is well dressed and his home displays the trappings of luxury. These separations reflect the indifference of the wealthy to the suffering of others, an indifference

Cover of *RAW* Volume 1, Issue 1, *The Graphix Magazine of Postponed Suicides*. Copyright © 1980 by Art Spiegelman.

highlighted by the men's stance and the directions of their gazes. While the falling man is facing forward and looking through the window directly at the reader, the man in the apartment stares down at the magazine, his back turned and his posture relaxed. Moreover, the imposing buildings in the color image, along with its contrasting colors and distorted forms, evoke the aesthetic of German Expressionism. The cover thus echoes the anxieties brought on by the modern metropolis, foregrounding the violence of class exploitation.[21]

At the same time as it expresses the logic of class difference, the tipped-in image also links suicide to nuclear war. The tilted buildings and burnt color palette suggest an explosion, while the use of shadow on the falling man's face and the diagonal rays on the building's windows imply a bright explosion akin to a nuclear detonation. The clawed hands of the falling man also bring to mind fears of deformity and mutation at the heart of other strips in *RAW*, especially those of Charles Burns. In this register, the indifference of the man in the apartment to the destruction outside his window can be seen as a commentary on American attitudes to nuclear proliferation. As Paul Boyer's piece in *RAW* Vol. 1, Issue 7, explains, the United States has continued to defend its use of the atomic bomb in Hiroshima and Nagasaki despite the devastation it caused and evidence that it was unnecessary. While American public opinion supported the escalation of Cold War defense systems, including an expansion of the nation's nuclear arsenal, Spiegelman's cover invites us to regard such policies as a form of suicide, be it directly through the nuclear war that the color image alludes to, or indirectly via policies that divert funds to military spending and away from vital social programs. In this one image, then, *RAW* establishes a multilayered preoccupation with suicide that will go on to dominate its entire run. The cover imbricates suicide in two of *RAW*'s most dominant radical critiques: of the violence of class difference and of the self-destructive logic of nuclear proliferation.

RAW FORM: AESTHETIC RADICALISM

The editorial principles and thematic frameworks that structure *RAW* work together to position it within the radical comics tradition. Yet its commitment to this tradition extends beyond content to permeate the form and style of the magazine itself. *RAW* draws on multiple political aesthetics—neosincerity, détournement, and punk design—to further mount a radical critique of the rising conservative Christian Moral Majority movement and the concomitant repressive turn in American culture. As such, *RAW*'s design, one of the magazine's most celebrated features, is more than formalist experiment.[22] Rather, its avant-garde investments attempt to reestablish comics as a site of resistance to commodity culture and to the conventional styles favored by the increasingly commercialized art market of the 1980s. Indeed, the decade ushered in a new conservatism in US culture and politics as well as in art. Reagan's neoliberal economic policies were accompanied by an alliance with conservative Christians opposed to the socially progressive movements of the 1960s, including feminism and reproductive rights, gay pride, sexual liberation, and civil rights. In a climate saturated with 1950s nostalgia, American culture succumbed to materialism and conspicuous consumption, anticommunist hysteria, ultrapatriotism, and neoliberal self-interest. *RAW* challenged this cultural conservatism formally by incorporating several political-aesthetic strategies that at once situate the magazine within a radical aesthetic history and revive its strategies of resistance for the neoliberal age.

The first of these revived political aesthetics draws on the work of Harvey Kurtzman and *MAD* magazine's defiance of the conservative and authoritarian elements of 1950s American culture, which the Reagan era sought to rejuvenate. Known mainly as a juvenile satire magazine, *MAD* was in many ways also a radical political publication. For the scholar of popular culture Nathan Abrams, *MAD*'s satirical content was part of a revolutionary politics of antiauthoritarian subversion that "fulfill[ed] the function of the critic more often than did the organs of the New York intellectuals such as *Commentary*, *Dissent*, *Partisan Review*, and the *New Leader*."[23] The critic and cartoonist Robert C. Harvey goes so far as to suggest that the radical youth movements of the 1960s may have been inspired by the cultural criticism that dominated *MAD*'s pages.[24] Similarly, Spiegelman has described the influence of *MAD* on his own work in ways that tie *MAD*'s politics to its aesthetic approach: "When I was a kid, what excited me a lot was *Mad* comic books. . . . *Mad* was my introduction to satire, to questioning received opinion, and to avant-garde art."[25] For Spiegelman, *MAD*'s antiauthoritarian politics is fundamentally bound to its form and style, which would go on to shape *RAW*'s basic design: *MAD* influenced *RAW*'s title—a similarly visceral, single-word, all-caps statement—and its use of a visually striking magazine format to advance both the medium's aesthetic and its political possibilities.[26]

Importantly, *MAD*'s influence on *RAW* can be traced beyond the latter's basic format; *RAW* also employs *MAD*'s penetrating visual satire, developing its satirical tone by putting it to new political ends. As Spiegelman points out, *MAD* perfected an "arsenal of ironic techniques" that formed the cornerstone of its subversive assault on normative orthodoxy, but this satirical tone has since been either flattened out into a blanket "everything sucks" position, or co-opted by advertisers as a marketing strategy (not least by Spiegelman himself in his early commercial work).[27] Spiegelman and the artists that he promoted in *RAW* take up *MAD*'s ironic techniques, but transform them into what he calls "neo-sincerity."[28] This practice involves taking common images or characters and placing them in realistic situations, the juxtaposition revealing a darker truth underneath popular fantasies of peace and prosperity that such images are designed to evoke. As such, the techniques perfected in *MAD* are once again capable of "mak[ing] a statement that need[s] making."[29]

Unsurprisingly given his admiration of Kurtzman, Spiegelman as editor championed artists like Drew Friedman, whose piece "The Andy Griffith Show" (Vol. 1, Issue 1) employs neosincerity to expose the violent racism of America's mythic small-town 1950s. In the strip, an African American man asks for directions in the fictional town of Mayberry, only to be beaten and lynched. Friedman's pointillist caricature lends the strip a photorealist quality which at once mimics the television show and captures scenes of violence that clash with the sitcom's romantic fictions. In drawing attention to racial violence, Friedman's strip challenges the 1950s nostalgia sweeping through the Reagan era. Mark Newgarden's "Mutton Geoff" (Vol. 1, Issue 1) and "The Pep Boys" (Vol. 1, Issue 2) as well as Kim Deitch's "Duck 'N Cover" (Vol. 1, Issue 5) also disrupt the veneer of false optimism in popular comics and cartoons to counter the key tenants of Reaganite ideology: the American Dream, the correlation between hard work and success, military interventionism, and the survivability of nuclear war.

Spiegelman himself employs neosincerity in several of his own contributions to *RAW*, albeit in a slightly modified form. The "Tokyo Raw" piece in *RAW* Vol.1, Issue 7 (written with Leonard Koren, Robert Legault, and Françoise Mouly) communicates its neosincerity through both the tone of its prose and its amusingly literal illustrations. In this strip, Spiegelman evokes details of Japanese culture under the guise of explaining it to Americans; the target of his critique is America's cultural preoccupation with Japan in a way that affirms American economic and cultural superiority at a time when Japan was actually not only competing with, but also outpacing American capitalism. However, the purported Japanese features invoked in the strip in fact reflect back—through the "fun house mirror" that Spiegelman references in the introduction to the piece (itself an allusion to America's distorted self-image)—the darker parts of American culture that are often ignored or denied and that drive this kind of jingoistic competition.[30] To this end, the prose states that the Japanese are "among the most prejudiced of all the people on earth" and mocks their consumerism and obsession with useless inventions, reality television, and pledges of allegiance.[31] Of course, these are also features of American capitalism birthed in the 1950s and rejuvenated in the 1980s. The tone of mock cultural superiority highlights how prejudiced and authoritarian American culture had become under Reagan as it attempted to assert its global economic and cultural dominance.

In the same vein, "Tokyo Raw" also complains that the American occupation attempted to rectify some of the Japanese nation's strange behaviors (constructing buildings out of durable materials instead of wood and paper, so they do not have to be repeatedly demolished and rebuilt; erecting street signs to make neighborhoods more navigable), only for the Japanese to relapse into old habits once the US forces left. The tone of the prose here, combined with parodically literal illustrations like Mark Beyer's drawing of a man emptying a trashcan full of houses, reveals Americans' cultural ignorance and projects the stubbornness and superiority that supposedly characterize the Japanese back onto the reader. "Tokyo Raw" uses this acerbic sarcasm to uncover parts of American culture that directly counter the narratives of American exceptionalism proffered by Reaganite ideology. In these examples, *RAW* reinvigorates an earlier radical mode to revoice *MAD*'s own critique of 1950s authoritarianism and cultural conformity in an era when such values were being recalled as the hallmarks of American cultural identity.

The second aesthetic strategy that *RAW* consistently employs derives from Situationism and its use of détournement to articulate disaffection with US culture and politics. In much the same way that *RAW* revives and revises *MAD*'s use of irony, *RAW* takes up the Situationist International's 1960s theory of advanced capitalism, almost a decade after the SI dissolved, in order to revitalize a mode of critique targeting the capitalist culture that had penetrated US society even more deeply in the intervening years. Indeed, the 1980s mark the intensification of two key elements of Situationist critique. The first of these is consumer culture, which, bolstered by the growth of materialism and conspicuous consumption, the unregulated expansion of the free market, and an ideology of convenience and choice as replacements for freedom, came to utterly dominate US economics, politics, and culture. Situationism's vocabulary for describing ubiquitous commodity fetishism, alienation, and reification thus provided a framework for *RAW*'s critique of these elements of consumer capitalism as they were amplified across the 1980s. As noted above, Spiegelman's cover for the first issue of *RAW* draws attention to the destructive elements of neoliberal capitalism and establishes anticapitalist critique as a key tenet of the magazine's politics. This focus is carried through subsequent strips about production line labor ("Industry News and Reviews" in Vol. 1, Issue 1); standardization and convenience culture ("Four Supermarkets in Iowa" in Vol. 1, Issue 1 and "Food for Thought" in Vol. 1, Issue 3); car culture ("Automotive News" in Vol. 1, Issue 3 and "Crash" in Vol. 1, Issue 8); celebrity culture ("The Schoolboy Assassin" in Vol. 1, Issue 3); and hyperindividualism and self-interest ("Autobiography" in Vol. 1, Issue 4).

The second element of Situationism that took on a new significance in the 1980s was its theory of the spectacle in an image-saturated consumer society. Indeed, the decade saw the rise of media as a dominant cultural force, which, coupled with a move towards finance capitalism, rendered the distinction between reality and representation more difficult to discern. Reagan himself embodied this transformation as a movie star president who frequently conflated films with history to create and disseminate the version of reality he believed to be true.[32] Given this intensification of the spectacle in the 1980s, *RAW* tied its critique of a dysfunctional consumer capitalism to the penetrating influence of mass media.

Spiegelman's prose piece "Honk, Honk, It's the Bonk" (Vol. 1, Issue 2, written with David Levy) works in this vein by examining the history of entertainment news in relation to the 24-hour news cycle that accompanied the advent of cable television. "Honk, Honk" argues that audiences are overwhelmed by the incessant flow of information in this fast-paced news culture, and thus content themselves with being entertained: "Frustration, disappointment, boredom, depression and fatigue—in that passive state we no longer register information content, but settle for theatrical form."[33] Spiegelman attributes this pacification to the power of images to produce more dramatic versions of events to satisfy our expectations, thereby distorting our worldview. The title, a reference to a 1927 article from the *New York Evening Graphic*, a tabloid magazine that used composite photographs as "evidence" for its fake stories, reflects the long history of sensationalist news practices, while positioning cable news as the apex of this continuous process of spectacularization.

The power of the spectacle to recreate reality and disempower the viewer from enacting social change speaks to another key strategy of aesthetic resistance pioneered by the Situationists: détournement. Spiegelman revives this technique as a way to undermine the status quo the spectacle has helped uphold. The illustrations from *Argosy*, *Graphic*, and *Vanity Fair* that accompany "Honk, Honk" work in this way. By removing composite photographs from their original context and repurposing them to expose the disingenuous nature of news media, the illustrations are turned against themselves, as they become evidence of media manipulation rather than accurate reportage. Spiegelman also employs détournement in the "Raw Gagz" section of *RAW* Vol. 1, Issue 8—a random collection of images that were given new captions by the *RAW* editors and other artists—in order to release a transgressive social critique. As French Situationist René Viénet explains the tactic, "we bluntly impose [the images'] real truth by restoring real dialogues [by adding or altering the speech bubbles]. This operation will bring to the surface the subversive bubbles . . . formed and then dissolved in the imaginations of those who look at these images."[34]

Thus, Norma Dog's cartoon of a suburban businessman, who is reminded of the mushrooms he forgot to purchase at the grocery store when he sees a nuclear explosion on the horizon, encapsulates the acerbic tone of Situationist comic art. As such, it both ties American consumer culture to the nuclear arms race and comments on the indifference with which Americans are responding to the threat of a nuclear war. Similarly, Mark Marek's piece exposes American indifference to violence against women and the exploitation of the Global South, tying both back to the toxic aggression unleashed by masculine corporate competition. A cartoon by Joe Schwind juxtaposes grotesque images of human and animal body parts on the production line at a meatpacking plant, with the caption, "Here are people just like you now making money beyond their wildest dreams!" to reveal the brutality of Fordist production. In each of these examples, text/image relations are détourned to at once reveal the myths of the image-spectacle (economic prosperity, personal and professional fulfillment, equality, security) and harness the radical potential of the image to counter rather than reaffirm these myths.

Given Spiegelman's awareness of comics history, it follows that a number of pieces in *RAW* use détournement to also underline the way mainstream comics were used to bolster a conservative social agenda during the heyday of the Comics Code Authority. As editors, Spiegelman and Mouly opt to illustrate excerpts from Paul Boyer's book *By the Bomb's Early Light* (Vol. 1, Issue 8) with adverts for children's atomic-themed toys and comics from the 1950s, to emphasize the role that comics and cartoons played in normalizing atomic energy by encouraging young readers to trust the government's promise of a safer and brighter world through nuclear power. Spiegelman and Mouly détourne the affirmative message of these comics to reveal how they served a campaign of misinformation about the attacks on Hiroshima and Nagasaki and about the effects of the atomic bomb—a campaign that manufactured the consent of the American public, as Boyer explains. The juxtaposition of text and illustration in Boyer's piece alongside "Honk, Honk" thus critiques mainstream comics' complicity with the regime of the spectacle, while also marking *RAW* as a radical antithesis to this conservative agenda.

In this way, neosincerity and détournement are connected by a type of critical absurdity, the two techniques working together to counter the authority of the status quo. Both use irony to undermine the power of mainstream images to affirm these myths, exposing the darker truth within them. The same critique is echoed in other absurdist pieces in *RAW*, such as Francis Masse's surreal political allegories and Komar and Melamid's pop-surrealist critiques of Socialist Realism. These comics target the deranged logic of modern capitalism and Soviet-style authoritarian communism, while promoting a critical reading practice suspicious of how visual culture, and comics in particular, shape perceptions of reality in line with a conservative social agenda. Spiegelman's privileging of these tactics in his own work and in the pieces selected for *RAW* seeks to interrupt the circulation of art as a commodity or a tool of state control, and reassert it as a site of resistance that fractures the Reaganite status quo.

Third, *RAW* develops its resistant agenda by incorporating punk, an aesthetic whose visual codes are similarly tied to a critique of Reagan-era conservatism. However, if neosincerity and détournement reveal what is inauthentic about American culture, punk goes a step further by giving voice to the casualties of Reagan's tax breaks and social welfare cuts, articulating the alienation and despair of life on the margins of society. The experience that *RAW* outlines in these pieces directly contradicts the optimism of popular culture. In fact, the dark, suicidal tone of many pieces in *RAW* marks a shift away from the psychedelic hippie aesthetics of underground comix toward the no-future narratives of punk.

RAW includes multiple references to punk culture and numerous artists whose unpolished artwork draws on the aggressive "messthetics" of the punk movement—Joe Schwind's disturbing Winston Smith-style collages that mock American family values; Rod Kierkegaard's "The Schoolboy Assassin" (*RAW* Vol. 1, Issue 3) that incorporates Plasmatics frontwoman Wendy O. Williams to expose the violence and falseness of American entertainment culture; and Gary Panter's visceral Jimbo strips (first published in the punk zine *Slash*) that take on the hypocrisy of US environmental policy and the racism of the advertising industry, or his cover for *RAW* Vol. 1, Issue 3 that echoes the confrontational anger of his infamous flyer for a 1977 Screamers show. But it is Spiegelman's cover for *RAW* Vol. 1, Issue 7 that most emphatically signals this connection to the politics of punk. The cover features a décollaged face also in the vein of Winston Smith's collages, with the magazine's title written in the ransom-note style associated with punk through the artwork of Jamie Reid. Both Smith's and Reid's design languages were in turn heavily influenced by Situationism and functioned as versions of détournement, with a similar political purpose to question the conflicts and contradictions of modern capitalist society. As music journalist Jon Savage explains: "In the act of dismembering and reassembling the very images that were supposed to keep you down and ignorant, it was possible to counteract the violence of The Spectacle and to refashion the world around you."[35] Décollage at once undermines the images that uphold the regime of the spectacle and reformats them into more authentic expressions of lived experience.

Spiegelman's cover works precisely in this vein. It is composed of torn-up fragments of photorealist, Pop-art, and comic renderings of the human face, the jigsaw style of construction distorting beautiful faces from fashion magazines in order to dismantle consumerist standards of youth, beauty, and happiness. In its fragmented form, the face expresses the disconnectedness of contemporary experience imagined as a violent and deforming force on the human body, while the ransom-note lettering hints at a youth held hostage by economic decline and social conservatism. The strapline for this issue, the "Torn-Again Graphix Magazine," references both increasing social violence and the destructive energies of punk, while the play on born-again Christians positions punk as a new antireligion born from the viciousness of life in the present. While the nihilistic humor in this strapline, as well as in the strips by Panter, Schwind, and Kierkegaard, link punk to neosincerity and détournement, the anger of these aesthetic techniques evince a somewhat darker attitude.

RAW's incorporation of punk extends beyond these individual pieces; punk aesthetics permeate the magazine's overall design. As Roger Sabin notes, *RAW*'s contents pages often feature the overprints and dropouts commonly associated with punk posters and zines.[36] The effect is one of discord and decay, as the overprints create a chaotic clash of competing focal points while the dropouts convey a sense of degeneration. In this way, the contents pages evoke the

Cover of *RAW* Volume 1, Issue 7, *The Torn-Again Graphix Magazine*. Copyright © 1985 by Art Spiegelman.

same state of violent decline that punk looked to express. Similarly, the torn aesthetic on the cover of *RAW* Vol. 1, Issue 7 carries over to the issue's contents page—which includes the torn corner from another issue taped inside—to create the aggressive jigsaw format associated with punk design. Fragments of the word "seven" in different fonts on the top of the contents page create a ransom-note lettering effect and echo the free-floating typographic elements, as well as the irregularly shaped or loosely grouped blocks of text and image, common in punk flyers. The result is an overall sense of disjointedness—of an anger and violence lacking a fixed target or solution—and the disintegration of society itself via the neoliberal dismantling of the welfare state. At the same time, the ransom-note lettering expresses a kind of anonymity that speaks to the no-future nihilism of punk. Indeed, while much of punk expressed a desire to reclaim individual identity in a mass-produced, commodified world, the cut lettering intimates the impossibility of doing so, when all we have to fashion our sense of self are the words and images of consumer culture. Punk's design is also reproduced in the banner title for the *RAW* Comic Supplement in Vol. 1, Issue 5, where part of the banner (a cheery red with retro font) has been torn away to reveal the angular "RAW" in high-contrast black and white underneath. The torn aesthetic here connects to punk's desire to betray the myths of the spectacle by revealing the brutality of life under neoliberal capitalism, as the dark and jagged magazine title is exposed beneath the bright façade of traditional comics imagery.

The torn aesthetic also crops up in the *Maus* synopsis of Vol. 1, Issue 7, along with the high-contrast black-and-white color scheme of punk flyers, to help separate the plot summary from a low-resolution photograph of a dead mouse in a trap. The realism of this image counterpoises the iconic drawings from Spiegelman's memoir on the other half of the page in ways that echo the mix of styles brought together on the issue's cover. The graphic nature of the photograph recalls the violent imagery of punk posters and their desire to disturb viewers by showing what mainstream culture deems inappropriate. On one level, the photograph of the dead mouse supplements the iconicity of Spiegelman's illustrations to insist on the violence at the core of *Maus*. Indeed, while titled "A Survivor's Tale," the memoir is far from an uplifting story of escape (as a 1980s audience may have expected from a comic book on this topic).[37] The photograph of the dead mouse conjures up all those who did not survive the Holocaust, shifting the focus away from Vladek's personal story towards the horror of genocide. On another level, though, the punk style of this page links the symbol of extermination to the youth that punk spoke of and to; this generation stands in as a different sort of "vermin"—as the castoffs of an industrialized urban world at once reduced to a desperate position and rendered expendable in it. Like the mouse, this faceless generation is left to eke out a violent and brutal existence with no future.

Taken together, then, *RAW*'s punk moments reject the orderly aesthetic principles that had previously driven graphic design, favoring instead a more discordant style that reflects the anticapitalist anarchism, confusion, and anger that punk music conveyed through its speed, distorted guitars, and shouted lyrics. *RAW*'s incorporation of these design principles links its challenge to traditional comics with a larger political project aimed at dislocating the myths of American culture and expressing an alternative experience of neoliberalism as violence buried beneath the sanguine images of mainstream culture. Indeed, the rawness of punk's hostile and visually displeasing style directly links back to the magazine's title, situating the unbridled exposure of a harsh reality at the center of *RAW*'s agenda.

RAW PRODUCTION: DIY RADICALISM

RAW's oversize format and handmade elements link the magazine to yet another oppositional element in punk culture—DIY publishing. *RAW*'s odd size has been explained as a way to emphasize the visual extravagance of the magazine and as a marketing strategy that enabled Spiegelman and Mouly to promote *RAW* as a New Wave lifestyle magazine that could be sold in bookstores and at newsstands, rather than in comics stores.[38] At the same time, however, the format of the first volume also echoes the design of punk zines like *Slash* and *Search and Destroy*, which featured experimental art, literature, and political pieces. The first issue of *Re/Search* (the successor to *Search and Destroy*), for example, includes articles on the Argentine political novelist Julio Cortázar, the radical Afrofuturist Sun Ra, nuclear war, and the Situationist International. Given its similarity to these zines in content and design (though not in the quality of materials—*RAW* used high-quality paper stock rather than cheap newsprint), the oversize format also situates *RAW* within a larger history of radical political publications.

The handmade nature of the first volume of *RAW* also ties it to this history. Each of the first eight issues was hand printed and stapled in Spiegelman and Mouly's apartment by the editors and a number of volunteer artists and friends. Each issue also contains a unique element (the full-color, tipped-in image glued by hand onto the cover of Vol. 1, Issue 1 or the hand-torn cover of Vol. 1, Issue 7) or insert (the "City of Terror" bubblegum cards designed by Mark Beyer in Vol. 1, Issue 2, or the flexi disc of Reagan's speeches in Vol. 1, Issue 4). By incorporating these unique components, *RAW* aligned itself with DIY attempts to create alternative economies based on cooperation, community, and free expression rather than mass consumption and profit. The torn-off corner of the cover for *RAW* Vol. 1, Issue 7 was itself a nod to this anti-consumerist model; the sellers for the magazines had wanted to rip corner logos off the covers of previous issues to indicate the remainders,[39] so by tearing the corner off every copy of Issue 7, Spiegelman and Mouly marked them all as unsellable. This DIY approach attempted to circumvent, as much as possible, the dictates of the publishing market, instead building connections between artists through the collective publication of their work and the communal act of compiling the magazine itself. At the same time, by self-publishing *RAW*, Spiegelman and Mouly were able to break down the boundary between artist and publisher and thus dissolve any commercial hold over the material.

This emphasis on artistic control was a sensitive issue given the conditions of mainstream comics production, which remained restrictive due to the lingering influence of the CCA. Mainstream production was an almost exclusively corporate endeavor, with artists retaining only limited creative control and no ownership of their work. At a time when independent comics publishing was otherwise waning, *RAW* followed in the footsteps of the self-publishing ventures of the comix underground, its communal DIY approach enabling both artists and editors to defend their vision. By rejecting mainstream forms and styles, *RAW* was able to bypass the restrictions of the Code that colluded with market interests, and thus affirm comics as a site of resistance to capital. If the reproduction of political comics from historical publications includes *RAW* in a history of radical cartooning, then its oversize format and DIY production also tie it to contemporary underground publications that similarly integrate radical politics with avant-garde and fringe art, in an effort to carve out a space for cultural resistance against commodity capitalism by circumventing corporate systems of production and distribution.

RAW READING: NEW WAVE RADICALISM

RAW's desire to reinvigorate avant-garde art with an oppositional politics is also evident in the magazine's use of another politicized aesthetic—the New Wave style developed in the United States under the direction of Dan Friedman. Friedman was tied to the same early 1980s East Village art scene that *RAW* emerged from and that heavily influenced Spiegelman and Mouly's design preferences. New Wave typography was pioneered by the German typographic designer Wolfgang Weingart, who was himself inspired by the graphic design of Dada and surrealism, two aesthetics schools with their own radical political commitments. Friedman, one of Weingart's students in Switzerland, took this inspiration seriously and infused his design with the political ambitions of the European avant-garde. For Friedman, once the modernist aesthetic program was co-opted by corporations, it forfeited its social commitment to improving modern life.[40] Echoing the Situationist critique of postmodernity with its depthless image-commodities, Friedman envisioned New Wave design as a similar way to challenge this spectacularization of culture.

However, New Wave style works differently to neosincerity, détournement, and punk as a political aesthetic. Both neosincerity and détournement manipulate image/text relations, so that familiar images can say something different that challenges the false reality which the image in its original context sought to uphold. Similarly, punk looks to expose the reality of contemporary experience by giving form to the violence, pain, and anger that the image regime disavows. Rather than attempting to communicate a specific concept or experience that challenges the reader's acceptance of the status quo, Friedman's New Wave style works to promote a critical reading practice based on the reader's own active engagement with design.

At the core of Friedman's New Wave aesthetic was unpredictability. His style rejected the legibility of orthodox typography on the grounds that its emphasis on order, simplicity, and efficiency reduced the reader to the status of a "passive recipient."[41] To him, this legibility was also a corporate tactic that sought to entice readers into becoming consumers by reducing design to the communication of a slogan. Friedman thus eliminated grid-based arrangements in favor of inconsistent letter spacing with varying fonts, type weights, colors, and a mix of textures and gradients. In doing so, he refused the polished and predictable design principles that dominated corporate-driven graphics in favor of an anarchic aesthetic that liberated both designer and reader.

In line with Friedman's style, geometric New Wave patterns feature in the background of many strips throughout *RAW*, as do odd-sized, unusually angled or patterned text-and-image boxes, combinations of different title fonts, and loosely tracked italic titles in sans-serif fonts, including the running header that identifies the artist for each piece. The contents page for *RAW* Vol. 1, Issue 3 incorporates the canted layout common in New Wave design, with a tilt that cuts off part of the title at the top of the page. In a kind of reverse typesetting, the magazine's title is written backwards at the bottom of the page. The contents sheet for *RAW* Vol. 1, Issue 5 also includes an off-center, canted, primary text box, alongside shaded and overlaid text boxes and the non-grid arrangement of geometric shapes that characterize New Wave design; the same principles are carried through to the adverts for area businesses later in the issue. The contents page for Vol. 1, Issue 6 displays cascading snapshots of various panels from the pieces in the issue and abstract waves of shading that break with the grid format. All the contents pages use the varying fonts and line weights, geometric overlays, and dropped shadows representative of New Wave design.

Friedman's nondogmatic approach to design implies more than the freedom to break with corporate formal constraints. This unpredictability, which Friedman defines as "the ability of a design to attract or seduce you, in an intense, virtually cluttered world, into reading it in the first place,"[42] also elicits more active engagement from the reader. The abstract complexity of New Wave style requires readers to explore the design, forging their own reading paths, questioning placement, and building connections to make sense of the image. The playfulness of the New Wave style sits well with the ironic tone of *RAW*; and yet, just as with neosincerity and détournement, the playful tone is subsumed to a deeper purpose, that of fostering independent critical thought and political agency. The disorder of this style challenges the authoritarian allegiance that Reagan-era patriotism called for, stimulating a more responsive mode of reading that undermines the corporate construction of the reader as passive consumer to open up comics as a site of resistance to neoliberal capitalism.

The radical investments of New Wave design politicize those strips in *RAW* that incorporate these principles, including several by Spiegelman that seem purely formalist at first glance. On one level, "Drawn Over Two Weeks While on the Phone" (Vol. 1, Issue 1) appears to be nothing more than a formalist exploration of shape, as the story it tells—various characters in disconnected settings imagining different geometrical shapes in their thought bubbles—makes no sense. However, the strip uses the clashing lines, shapes, and patterns of New Wave design to create connections between different characters. As such, "Drawn Over Two Weeks" is about communication. Indeed, the title of the strip itself alludes to the idea of fractured communication, the "two weeks" implying multiple telephone calls perhaps to different people. In this light, the strip's theme becomes charged with the political questions embedded in its style: How should we read? How do we communicate across difference? Should we privilege similarity over difference? As a reader, what patterns do I trace and what am I overlooking in doing so? In this way, the strip can be seen as a meditation on how comics communicate meaning to their readers, and what it means to be a socially engaged and responsible reader. The same is true of Spiegelman's "One Row," again drawn in New Wave style, this time including bold, contrasting colors. Here, Spiegelman's reflections on comics form dovetail with ethical questions about the production of sympathy, the acceptance of authority, and social control. By privileging New Wave design in both his individual pieces and the larger design of *RAW*, Spiegelman once again positions radical politics at the core of *RAW*'s aesthetic identity. The complex, critical thought grounded in "disorder, originality and complexity"[43] that New Wave design promotes thereby cements *RAW*'s antiauthoritarian investments at the levels of content, form, and reception.

"One Row," from *The Raw Color Supplement* in *RAW* Volume 1, Issue 5, *The Graphix Magazine of Abstract Depressionism*. Copyright © 1983 by Art Spiegelman.

SPIEGELMAN'S COMIC POLITICS BEYOND *RAW*

Radical politics permeates *RAW* on multiple levels. The content explicitly critiques Reaganite economics and politics, while the aesthetics infused throughout the magazine further its challenge to the conservatism of the era. Both formally and thematically, the magazine seeks to weaken the power of the spectacle as a form of social control, while attempting to reinvigorate avant-garde art and to foster critical reading practices that undermine corporatized modes of engagement. Moreover, in tracing a radical comics tradition through the inclusion of historical pieces and references to earlier experimental art movements, *RAW* claims a spot in this pantheon and affirms the political potential of the medium. To this end, *RAW* highlights mainstream comics' historical role in affirming the status quo, particularly during the CCA era, which brings into sharp relief the difference between mainstream comics and those published in *RAW*.

As histories of *RAW* note,[44] to distinguish itself from the disposable commodity form of traditional American comics, *RAW* turned away from the logics of mass production towards quality, handmade production, and high-concept art. In the 1980s, however, privileging high art was far from equivalent to eschewing commercialism. The high-art world in the 1980—particularly in New York, which Howard Singerman dubbed "the art world's imperial capital"[45]—was almost completely commodified. The historical project of the avant-garde had collapsed, as art was increasingly seen in financial investment terms. Reagan's deep cuts to the National Endowment for the Arts and his argument that art needed to be more responsive to the private sector contributed to the dissolution of the avant-garde as a critical art movement and to its replacement with a new "entrepreneurial mode" of art as commerce.[46] *RAW*'s embracing of high art thus put the magazine at risk of subscribing to this neoliberal logic.

However, the entrepreneurial drive in the arts was also bound up with a need for marketability that resulted in the rejection of avant-garde practices in favor of more accessible styles that neutered art's critical potential. As Singerman argues, quoting the *October* critic Craig Owens's review of the 1982 alumni show at the California Institute of the Arts, the renewed interest in conventional painting "must be seen as part of a 'widespread' backlash against the 1960s counterculture that motivates the Neo-conservative platform for the economic and spiritual 'renewal' of the US, and which culminated in November 1980 in the election of the celebrity-commodity to the Presidency."[47] Thus despite embracing, as Bart Beaty argues, "an art-world audience slumming in the bleeding-edge margins of punk graphics,"[48] by favoring experimental aesthetics over and against stylistic conservatism, *RAW* was able to resist the market logic of the New York high-art scene and remain anchored to the marginal and oppositional graphic movements that it drew from.

Highlighting *RAW*'s radical politics and the centrality of avant-garde experimentation to its agenda opens up new ways of reading the artists that it contains, as well as new approaches to Spiegelman's own comics project, both in *RAW* and beyond. When placed next to the explicitly radical work of Sue Coe or Kiki Picasso, even Spiegelman's most abstract and seemingly apolitical strips in *RAW* reveal traces of radical politics in their content and form. Spiegelman's "Dead Dick" (Vol. 2, Issue 1), for example, at first seems to extrapolate from abstract elements in Chester Gould's *Dick Tracy* strip to produce a formal exploration of light and shadow. Closer attention reveals how Spiegelman uses this color palette to challenge the black-and-white moral landscape of the original comic and the toxic masculinity that drives it. Similarly, focusing on the intersections of form and politics exposes how Spiegelman's illustrations for "An Aborigine Among the Skyscrapers" (Vol. 1, Issue 6) reference stencil culture and the art of street protest to explore the alienation and fear a Malayan man experiences in New York, thus imbuing the story with an oppositional political tone. Even the "Two Fisted Painters" insert in *RAW* Vol. 1, Issue 1 alludes to the importance of politics in comics when the writer smashes his typewriter and dismisses his space-alien adventure styled after *Detective Comics* #395 as "escapist trash."

A focus on the intersection of style and radical politics also unlocks new frameworks for exploring Spiegelman's entire career, which has always been

Detail from "Dead Dick," *Lead Pipe Sunday*. Copyright © 1991 by Art Spiegelman.

punctuated by politically engaged work: from the influence of 1960s countercultural politics on his underground comix, his *MAD*-inspired *Garbage Pail Kids*, and his illustrations for the subversive poem *The Wild Party*, to the overtly political *In the Shadow of No Towers*, his provocative covers for the *New Yorker*, and his contribution to the 2014 *Occupy Comics* anthology, which reprises the cover of *RAW* Vol. 1, Issue 1. This return to the imagery of *RAW* uncovers a deep-seated political sensibility that Spiegelman has carried through his work for the *New Yorker* (the *Occupy* piece is a rejected *New Yorker* cover) and the persistence of this investment in the present day. Discussions of *Maus*, too, which have long been overshadowed by the graphic memoir's autobiographical framework and its narrative of trauma, would benefit from a politically radical perspective. Doing so will not only advance new avenues for engagement with Spiegelman's work, but also expand our understanding of the radical comics tradition and its legacy in the present.

Notes

1. This chapter was made possible by the generous support of the UMass Boston Healey Research Grant.

2. Paul Candler, *Raw, Boiled, and Cooked: Comics on the Verge* (San Francisco: Last Gasp, 2004), 2.

3. Roy T. Cook, "Underground and Alternative Comics," in *The Routledge Companion to Comics*, ed. Frank Bramlett, Roy T. Cook, and Aaron Meskin (New York: Routledge, 2017), 39.

4. Charles Hatfield, *Alternative Comics: An Emerging Literature* (Jackson: University Press of Mississippi, 2005), 20.

5. Beyond these short treatments, Michael Hancock's entries in *Comics Through Time*, ed. M. Keith Booker (Santa Barbara: Greenwood, 2014), 1196–98, and *Icons of the American Comic Book*, ed. Randy Duncan and Matthew J. Smith (Santa Barbara: ABC-CLIO, 2013), 592–99, offer important details about the history of the magazine. Jeet Heer's *In Love with Art: Françoise Mouly's Adventures in Comics with Art Spiegelman* (Toronto: Coach House Books, 2013) provides a more in-depth analysis of the origins and aims of *RAW* that also highlights the significance of Mouly's contribution. By far the most comprehensive history, however, is Bill Kartalopoulos, "A *RAW* History: The Magazine," *Indy Magazine*, Winter 2005.

6. Bart Beaty, *Comics versus Art* (Toronto: University of Toronto Press, 2012), 135.

7. Arie Kaplan, *From Krakow to Krypton: Jews and Comic Books* (Philadelphia: The Jewish Publication Society, 2008), 170.

8. The closest we come to a discussion of *RAW*'s politics is its brief entry in the *Encyclopedia of Social Movement Media*, where its content is described as "socially relevant works on the rightist political culture of the Reagan presidency and South Africa's apartheid regime, while also changing decent rules in some explicit imagery and language." Daniel Darland, "*RAW*," in *The Encyclopedia of Social Movement Media*, ed. John D. H. Dowling (Thousand Oaks, CA: Sage, 2011), 437.

9. See for example: Katalin Orbán, "Trauma and Visuality: Art Spiegelman's *Maus* and *In the Shadow of No Towers*," *Representations* 97, no. 1 (2007): 57–89; Laura Findlay, "*In the Shadow of*

No Towers: The Anxiety of Expression and Images of Past Trauma in Art Spiegelman's Graphic Novel," *Studies in Comics* 5, no. 1 (2014): 187–203; and Lopamudra Basu, "The Graphic Memoir in a State of Exception: Transformations of the Personal in Art Spiegelman's *In the Shadow of No Towers*," in *Drawing from Life: Memory and Subjectivity in Comic Art*, ed. Jane Tolmie (Jackson: University Press of Mississippi, 2013), 163–84. Philip Smith, *Reading Art Spiegelman* (New York: Routledge, 2016), which engages with some of Spiegelman's political commentary in *No Towers*, strongly emphasizing formal experimentation, mental health, and historical trauma in its analysis of Spiegelman's work.

10. Qtd. in Kartalopoulos, "A *RAW* History."

11. Beaty, *Comics versus Art*, 137.

12. It is important to bear in mind Mouly's role in the production of *RAW* and in determining its political sensibility. As Jeet Heer points out: "All too many journalistic and critical accounts speak of 'Art Spiegelman's *RAW* magazine' as if he did the editorial heavy lifting all by himself"—when in fact Mouly was equally involved in the design and printing of the magazine. See Heer, *In Love with Art*, 14.

13. Charles Burns, qtd. in Kartalopoulos, "A *RAW* History."

14. As the editors note, Coe's illustrations were originally inspired by a British pamphlet on Civil Defense (*RAW* Vol. 1, Issue 7: 15).

15. *RAW* Vol. 1, Issue 7: 15.

16. Masereel was raised a socialist and spent the early part of his career producing illustrations for leftist and pacifist publications; see David Beronä's "Introduction" to Masereel's *Passionate Journey: A Novel in Woodcuts* (Mineola, NY: Dover, 2007), vi. Given his explicit politics, Masereel's work was popular with socialist societies in both Europe and Latin America in the interwar period; see Patrick Frank, *Los Artistas Del Pueblo: Prints and Workers' Culture in Buenos Aires, 1917–1935* (Albuquerque: University of New Mexico Press, 2006), 48. The leader of the League of Left-Wing Writers, Lu Xun, also organized woodblock workshops based on Masereel's work in China in the early 1930s as a means of educating people about Chinese communism; see Robert Petersen, *Comics, Manga, and Graphic Novels: A History of Graphic Narratives* (Santa Barbara, CA: Praeger, 2011), 115.

17. *RAW* Vol. 1, Issue 4: 2.

18. See Art Spiegelman, "Drawing Blood: Outrageous Cartoons and the Art of Outrage," *Harper's Magazine*, June 2006: 43–52.

19. Heer, *In Love with Art*, 59.

20. Joey Cavalieri, "Jewish Mice, Bubblegum Cards, Comics Art, and Raw Possibilities: An Interview with Art Spiegelman and Francoise Mouly," *The Comics Journal* 65 (August 1981): 120.

21. The relationship between German Expressionism and leftist politics is complicated. As Peter Jelavich argues, "The majority of Expressionists leaned to the left, but the profusion of mutually hostile parties on that end of the political spectrum made it hard to find an ideological home." Peter Jelavich, "Dance of Life, Dance of Death," in *German Expressionism: The Graphic Impulse*, ed. Starr Figura (New York: MoMA, 2011), 45. However, while the movement was somewhat fractured by the divisions between the SPD, the USPD, and the KPD, as Jelavich makes clear, German Expressionists saw their art as fundamentally expressive of a new revolutionary age and of the economic woes brought on by the soaring inflation and unemployment of the interwar years.

22. *RAW* won *Print Magazine*'s regional design award three years in a row (1983–1985).

23. Nathan Abrams, "From Madness to Dysentery: *Mad*'s Other New York Intellectuals," *Journal of American Studies* 37, no. 3 (2003): 440.

24. Robert C. Harvey, *The Art of the Comic Book: An Aesthetic History* (Jackson: University Press of Mississippi, 1996), 140.

25. Qtd. in Stephen Bolhafner, "Comix as Art: The Man Behind the '*Maus*,'" *St. Louis Post-Dispatch*, 23 June 1991: 3C.

26. After almost leaving EC in 1955, Kurtzman was persuaded to stay by being given the freedom to turn *MAD* into a magazine. No longer bound by the CCA, this new design presented a "broader and more flexible platform for satire" (Harvey, *The Art of the Comic Book*, 138). In its new format, *MAD* looked more like a picture magazine than a traditional comic, its original, graphic-heavy design prefiguring *RAW*'s own innovative and politically charged format.

27. Gene Kannenberg, Jr., "A Conversation with Art Spiegelman," in *Art Spiegelman: Conversations*, ed. Joseph Witek (Jackson: University Press of Mississippi, 2007), 253.

28. Kannenberg, "A Conversation with Art Spiegelman," 253.

29. Spiegelman cites a rejected *New Yorker* cover that depicts a Muslim American family sitting down to Thanksgiving dinner, while someone throws a rock through their window, as an example of neosincerity. See Kannenberg, "A Conversation," 253. Although Spiegelman is talking about his work post-9/11 here, traces of this neosincere technique are absolutely operative in pieces that he published in *RAW*.

30. "Tokyo RAW Data," *RAW* Vol 1, Issue 7 (1985): 50.

31. "Tokyo RAW Data," 50.

32. See Michael Rogin, *Ronald Reagan, the Movie, and Other Episodes in Political Demonology* (Berkeley: University of California Press, 1987).

33. *RAW* Vol. 1, Issue 2: 12.

34. René Viénet, "The Situationists and the New Forms of Action Against Politics and Art," in *Situationist International Anthology*, ed. and trans. Ken Knabb (Berkeley, CA: Bureau of Public Secrets, 2006), 274.

35. Jon Savage, "A Punk Aesthetic," in *Punk: An Aesthetic*, ed. Johan Kugelberg and Jon Savage (New York: Rizzoli, 2012), 148.

36. Roger Sabin, *Comics, Comix, and Graphic Novels* (New York: Phaidon, 2001), 138.

37. *Maus* is often considered responsible for shifting public perception of what a comic/graphic novel could do. Yet this change in opinion was hard fought, as many thought it inappropriate for Spiegelman to tackle the Holocaust in comics form. See Ian Gordon, "Making Comics Respectable: How *Maus* Helped Redefine a Medium," in *The Rise of the American Comics Artist: Creators and Contexts*, ed. Paul Williams and James Lyons (Jackson: University Press of Mississippi, 2010), 179–93.

38. Spiegelman himself makes this point in an interview with Joey Cavalieri, "Jewish Mice," 121.

39. Kannenberg, "A Conversation," 255.

40. Peter Rea, "Reputations: Dan Friedman," (Interview), *Eye*, Autumn 1994.

41. Rea, "Reputations: Dan Friedman."

42. Rea, "Reputations: Dan Friedman."

43. Rea, "Reputations: Dan Friedman."

44. See for example Beaty, *Comics versus Art*, 135; Paul Candler, "For the Love of Comics," *Raw, Boiled and Cooked: Comics on the Verge* (San Francisco: Last Gasp, 2004), 10; and Santiago

García, *On the Graphic Novel*, trans. Bruce Campbell (Jackson: University Press of Mississippi, 2010), 125.

45. Howard Singerman, "Pictures and Positions in the 1980s," in *A Companion to Contemporary Art Since 1945*, ed. Amelia Jones (Malden, MA: Blackwell, 2006), 83.

46. Singerman, "Pictures and Positions in the 1980s," 92.

47. Qtd. in Singerman, "Pictures and Positions in the 1980s," 93.

48. Beaty, *Comics versus Art*, 134.

ART SPIEGELMAN AND 9/11

KENT WORCESTER

Tens of thousands of New Yorkers experienced the terrorist attacks of September 11, 2001, firsthand. Jeet Heer's biography of Françoise Mouly provides a vivid account of what that particular Tuesday morning felt like for Mouly and her husband, Art Spiegelman. Fourteen-year-old Nadja had just started classes at Stuyvesant High School, four blocks from the towers. Worried that debris might land on the school, the anxious parents rushed to find her. Locating her wasn't easy—the ten-story school building housed more than 3,500 students. While they searched, Spiegelman overheard a Spanish-language report from a janitor's radio saying that the Pentagon had been attacked. Then the lights went out, and the building trembled from the collapse of the South Tower. Spiegelman was sure they would all die in the school. After continuing to search for an hour and a half, they found Nadja. As they were leaving Stuyvesant, the North Tower crumbled behind them.[1]

Having located their daughter, the couple hurried over to the United Nations International School to pick up their son, Dash. As Spiegelman later told the *New York Times*: "I was willing to live through the disaster wherever it took me, as long as we were all together as a family unit."[2] By the time "the family was safely ensconced in their loft," several hours had passed.[3] Rather than watching the collapse of the Twin Towers from the relative safety of distant rooftops or closed windows, which was the experience of many thousands of tri-state-area residents, the Spiegelman/Mouly family was inside the maelstrom. As more than one journalist pointed out in post-9/11 profiles, the events of that day must have been particularly unnerving for someone whose "survivor parents" had always warned that "the world is an incredibly dangerous place and I should always be prepared to flee. . . . In that sense, the paranoids were right."[4]

In the weeks and months that followed, Spiegelman became a go-to person for reporters, broadcasters, and documentary filmmakers interested in obtaining firsthand accounts from prominent New Yorkers. Spiegelman's association

"Enduring Freedom," *New Yorker* cover, 11/26/2001. Copyright © 2001 by Art Spiegelman.

with the famous *New Yorker* cover "9/11/2001," in which "the towers were barely visible as black shadows on black, an image haunting in its somber familiarity,"[5] meant that he was part of the cultural conversation almost from the outset. Initially attributed to Spiegelman, this "graphically stunning and emotionally restrained"[6] cover art was in fact based on an idea by Spiegelman, which was then rendered by Françoise Mouly. Heer writes that when Mouly showed her editor, David Remnick, the draft image, "he asked who did it." Mouly, "driven by her desire to see the image published, didn't want to admit she'd done it—she was worried because she wasn't a 'name' artist." Accustomed "to contributing her ideas to the artists she worked with, Mouly gave Spiegelman the credit—it was his idea, after all."[7]

Their coauthored piece was well received at the time and is "now among the most famous images in the history of the *New Yorker* and one of the few lasting works of art to come out of the Twin Towers."[8] Spiegelman's covers

"Fears of July, 2002," *New Yorker* cover, 7/8/2002. Copyright © 2002 by Art Spiegelman.

for the November 26, 2001, and July 8, 2002, issues were equally topical, if not quite as minimalistic. The former shows a group of silhouetted Afghanis running toward the cooked turkeys that are being dropped off by a bomber plane. There is a magical realist quality to the imagery, since the turkeys arrive on the ground in immaculate, ready-to-eat condition. "Drop food not bombs" was the cover's Thanksgiving weekend message, but there may have been a more cynical subtext, which is that you would need to believe in miracles to think this could ever happen.

The July 8, 2002, image depicts a terrified man at home in bed on the night of July Fourth, haunted by visions of flags, fireworks, and mushroom clouds. The man and his bedroom are drawn in gray tones, while his dream offers splashes of red, white, and blue. He seems perfectly ordinary, except perhaps for his insomnia. The man's imagination conjures up something rather vivid, however. In his waking nightmare, an all-American family are in their backyard, enjoying

"Roll Up Your Sleeves, America!," *World War 3 Illustrated* #34. Copyright © 2003 by Art Spiegelman.

the fireworks. The father and son are wearing trucker caps, and the daughter has a ponytail. In the background, however, a nuclear device has detonated, and the family is about to become vaporized. The grays of the cloud will soon overpower the brighter colors, which may be why the family's picket fence resembles cemetery crosses. Behind the façade of normalcy lies the specter of untold civilian deaths.

No less startling was a piece of visual agitprop that Spiegelman came up with in late 2001 titled "Roll Up Your Sleeves, America!" The image appeared in *World War 3 Illustrated*, an irregularly published magazine of political cartooning that has provided an outlet for antimilitaristic imagery since the late 1970s. Spiegelman's cartoon depicts a brawny Uncle Sam pumping gas straight into his right arm, surrounded by SUVs and combat aircraft.[9] Here Spiegelman revisits familiar nationalist tropes and uses the contrast between shades of gray and the red, white, and blues of kitsch Americana to make a larger point about the self-mythologizing character of mainstream discourse. The bombast of the composition, along with the unabashed look of confidence on Uncle Sam's face, suggests that from the standpoint of the persuaded our national addiction to carbon, consumerism, and endless war is almost godly.

The fact that "Roll Up Your Sleeves, America!" appeared in *World War 3 Illustrated* rather than the *New Yorker* is telling. While Spiegelman was moving in one direction, the magazine was traveling in another. Spiegelman's decision to not renew his contract with the *New Yorker* in early 2003 came only a couple of weeks before the magazine's editor-in-chief, David Remnick, formally endorsed the US invasion of Iraq. Remnick spoke for many but by no means all liberals when he advanced a cautious case for preemptive intervention.[10] The fact that so many otherwise intelligent people were willing to consider supporting George W. Bush's foreign policy underscored the degree to which Spiegelman no longer felt "in harmony with American culture." As he told one interviewer, "From the time that the Twin Towers fell, it seems as if I've been living in internal exile, or like a political dissident confined to an island." Even the *New Yorker*, he said, "has not escaped this trend. [David] Remnick is unable to accept the challenge, while, on the contrary, I am more and more inclined to provocation." If he had been "content to draw harmless strips about skateboarding and shopping in Manhattan, there would have been no problem; but, now, my inner life is inflamed with much different issues." Spiegelman went on to complain that the magazine marched "to the same beat as the *New York Times* and all the other great American media that don't criticize the government for fear that the administration will take revenge by blocking their access to sources and information." He continued: "In this context, all criticism of the administration is automatically branded unpatriotic and un-American."[11]

Spiegelman's break with the *New Yorker* can be viewed as part of the cultural fallout of 9/11. As much of the country shifted right, Spiegelman pushed back, and gave voice to a perspective that was simultaneously anxious, paranoid, NYC-centric, pro arts, pro free speech, antiwar, antimilitarist, and antiterror. It was a perspective that stood in sharp contrast to those who clamored for heightened security measures, increased military spending, and preemptive warfare. It was also different from much of what was being written and said on the radical left. Spiegelman's orthogonal relationship to 9/11 discourse was underscored when Pantheon released *In the Shadow of No Towers* (2004) to widespread if not universal acclaim.[12] The book's distinctive combination of defiant secularism, morbid humor, and a "plague on both your houses" antipathy toward jihadist forces *and* the Bush administration set it apart from narratives that focused on conventional geopolitics, US war crimes, or grieving families.[13]

Spiegelman presents the paradigmatic case of the troubled artist confronting the shock of 9/11. His looming cultural presence is recorded not only in the archives of LexisNexis, but also in the growing body of academic literature on representations of 9/11.[14] A Google search of "Art Spiegelman and 9/11" yields over one hundred thousand results, including links to reviews, interviews, podcasts, blogs, videos, news stories, scholarly articles, and notices about lectures and other public events. Spiegelman's illustrations, comics, and to some extent even his distinctive, irony-filled intonations have arguably become constitutive of how 9/11 is remembered and commemorated. Certainly, the events left an impression on his own creative process. As he later told an interviewer from the Syracuse *Post-Standard*, "When I thought I would die on September 11, which I did, one of the things that was among those realizations I had was, 'Oh, schmuck. You really should have done more comics.'"[15] Or, as he confessed to Gene Kannenberg, Jr., when they shared a stage at the 2002 Small Press Expo: "In the wake of September 11, I began to think, 'OK, you've survived this particular event, and you're frittering away your time doing covers for this cake-eaters' magazine,[16] and so—you should do comics."[17]

Rather than simply take note of the historical conjuncture within which "9/11/01" and *In the Shadow of No Towers* were created and consumed, this chapter considers the extent to which Spiegelman's post-9/11 interventions were "inflamed" by explicitly political concerns. While there are well-researched accounts that acknowledge the *engagé* overtones of Spiegelman's output in this period, scholars like Hillary Chute and Ted Gournelos seem oddly reluctant to differentiate Spiegelman's approach and outlook from contending perspectives.[18] The central ambition of this chapter is to locate Spiegelman's early twenty-first-century cultural and artistic practice in the context of longstanding debates on the left, broadly defined, over liberal values, foreign policy, and religious extremism. Spiegelman has been variously described as a graphic novelist, an editor and publisher, an avant-garde artist, a historian of the comics medium, and a comics memoirist. While all of these labels are applicable, in view of his post-9/11 efforts he can also be characterized as a nonconforming political cartoonist.[19]

In brief, I argue that Spiegelman's interventions in this period were organized around three main principles: first, a robust defense of classical liberal and Enlightenment values, such as free speech, freedom of conscience, and artistic liberty; second, a refusal to downplay the magnitude and significance of 9/11 by subsuming it within larger narratives about imperialism and anti-imperialism; third, consistent opposition to both state militarism and violent extremism. These positions placed him at odds not only vis-à-vis conservatives and Republicans, but also liberal humanitarian interventionists like Remnick, who lent their support to post-9/11 military incursions in the Middle East and

Central Asia. Spiegelman's perspective was also distinct from those on the left who, in the condemnatory prose of socialist essayist Julius Jacobson, "failed to meet their elementary moral and political obligations to resoundingly condemn the hijackers and their fundamentalist mentors and trainers, to prove to the nation that they, too, mourn the victims and are in solidarity with the bereaved."[20] The key issue, in other words, may have been Spiegelman's relationship to dominant leftist narratives, rather than his similarities and differences with liberal and conservative accounts.

CULTURAL FORAYS

Images in general—not only comics and illustrations but also photography and television footage—contributed mightily to the commemorative discourse of 9/11. A few months after the WTC collapse, Jean Baudrillard noted: "What stays with us, above all else, is the sight of the images . . . Whereas we were dealing before with an uninterrupted profusion of banal images and a seamless flow of sham events, the terrorist act in New York has resuscitated both images and events."[21] The cartoon arts played an integral role in this process of resuscitation. The events of 9/11 inspired an outpouring of editorial cartoons, comic strips, minicomics, superhero stories, graphic novels, and graphic memoirs,[22] and lists of must-read 9/11 books often include comics of one type or another.[23] Titles as disparate as Jonathan Ames and Dean Haspiel's *The Alcoholic* (2009), Emmanuel Guibert, Didier Lefèvre, and Frédéric Lemercier's *The Photographer: Into War-Torn Afghanistan with Doctors Without Borders* (2009), Sid Jacobson and Ernie Colón's *The 9/11 Report: A Graphic Adaptation* (2006) and *After 9/11: America's War on Terror* (2008), Frank Miller's *Holy Terror* (2011), Ted Rall's *To Afghanistan and Back: A Graphic Travelogue* (2002), David Rees's *Get Your War On* (2008), Alissa Torres and Sungyoon Choi's *American Widow* (2008),[24] and even Marvel's fundraising anthology *Heroes* were all widely reviewed, as was *In the Shadow of No Towers*.[25] Any discussion of 9/11 and what Gilbert Seldes deemed the "popular arts"[26] would be incomplete, it seems, without due consideration of cartoons and comics, nonfiction and fiction alike.

The day's "incursion of the real into the orders of the imaginary and the symbolic"[27] left a definite mark on the comics subculture. Lower Manhattan has been at the center of commercial art in the United States since the mid-to-late nineteenth century, and scores of illustrators, cartoonists, and editors personally witnessed the collapse of the Twin Towers. Prominent newspapers placed mournful editorial cartoons on their front pages on 9/12/01 even as syndicated comic strip artists thanked emergency responders and broke the fourth wall to commiserate and grieve with their readers. Superhero and small press publishers alike brought out commemorative volumes with donations going to groups like the Red Cross. Not all of this material played it safe: In the weeks that followed, hundreds and soon tens of thousands of fans were using email attachments to get the word out about David Rees's savagely parodic War on Terror-themed clip art,[28] and the *World War 3 Illustrated* collective put out a smart and inquisitive post-9/11 issue, with contributions by Sue Coe, Fly, Peter Kuper, Josh Neufeld, Nicole Schulman, Seth Tobocman, Tom Tomorrow, and others.[29]

The fact that editorial cartoonists and superhero storytellers referenced 9/11 in their work is hardly surprising. Both genres respond to current events, albeit in different ways. More noteworthy perhaps was the newfound interest on the part of cartoonists, publishers, and readers in comics as a vehicle for journalism, memoir, and historical documentation. The emergence of nonfiction comics as a viable paraliterary category dates back to the first decade of the twentieth century, and Hillary Chute suggests that it "is not an accident that after 9/11 and the commencement of wars in Afghanistan and Iraq, there was an increase in attention to documentary experimentation."[30] Spiegelman was one of an expanding cohort of cartoonists who were making politically-minded comics that combined memoir, polemic, historical analysis, caricature, illustration, maps, and photography in this period.

For Spiegelman, the material that resonated most strongly with the 9/11 moment was old comics rather than new ones. In the pages of *In the Shadow of No Towers* he confessed that

> the only cultural artifacts that could get past my defenses to flood my eyes and brain with something other than images of burning towers were old comic strips; vital, unpretentious ephemera from the optimistic dawn of the 20th century. That they were made with so much skill and verve but never intended to last past the day they appeared in the newspaper gave them poignancy; they were just right for an end-of-the-world moment.[31]

At the same time, Spiegelman was increasingly intrigued by the formal aspects of the medium and by its ability to handle complex political and historical themes. As Joseph Witek has observed, "sequential art can explain the sequence of events so clearly. The linked but separate boxes in comics have always lent themselves to process analysis, and 'how-things-work' comics are an important subgenre of educational comic books."[32] Besides, as Spiegelman knows, the stamp of individual personality that is integral to the act of drawing can work to the advantage of the nonfiction cartoonist. As Øyvind Vågnes points out, "comics documentarism draws attention to the subjective nature of its 'handwrittenness.'" The result, he writes, "is a form of what Charles Hatfield calls 'ironic authentication,' a way of 'graphically asserting truthfulness through the admission of artifice.'"[33] Post-9/11 cartooning benefited from this "admission of artifice."

The greater visibility of comics and cartoons in this period also reflected the impact of the alternative comics movement of the 1980s and 1990s and of its multifaceted efforts to help redefine and rehabilitate the medium as a platform for thoughtful, purposive, and idiosyncratic expression. Spiegelman and Mouly are themselves key actors in this story, partly as a result of the critical success of *Maus* in the 1980s, but also by way of their coedited magazine *RAW* (1980–1991). In addition, Mouly has contributed to the project of revaluing comics through her position as the *New Yorker*'s art editor (1993–present), which under her direction has often featured cover art by cartoonists. Meanwhile, over the years, Spiegelman has given hundreds of illustrated presentations, as well as helped organize panels, workshops, and conferences on the medium's history and untapped potential. Spiegelman's capacity to leave a mark on post-9/11 discourse was connected to tectonic shifts in visual culture that he and Françoise Mouly, his closest collaborator, helped bring about.

CULTURAL POLITICS

While Spiegelman's take on 9/11 and the military and cultural conflicts that followed can be gleaned from public talks, published interviews, and his pieces for the *New Yorker* as well as smaller circulation outlets, the clearest expression of his views can be found in his 2004 project *In the Shadow of No Towers*. This thick, oversized cardboard book is divided into two parts: the first half consists of ten pages by Spiegelman, while the second showcases several fine examples of early twentieth-century cartoon art, from *The Kinder Kids* and *Hogan's Alley* to *Little Nemo in Slumberland*. Spiegelman's own pages initially appeared in foreign and small press outlets, including *Die Zeit*, *The Independent*, *The London Review of Books*, *Dead Herring Comics*, and *The Forward* as a prelude to the publication of the book itself. The final product's "pertinent and provocative"[34] juxtaposition of eventful artwork from two very different contexts came from a place of pessimism and grief, tempered by an obvious love of the comics art form. It also looks and feels unlike any other 9/11-themed book or comic. As Spiegelman revealed, "mainstream publications that had actively solicited work from me . . . fled when I offered these pages or excerpts from the series,"[35] while the book project itself was "rejected by every publisher it was brought to, which was upwards of twenty."[36]

Editors who turned down the manuscript were unlikely to have been offended by the early twentieth-century comic strip art that makes up the book's second half. If anything, they may have been charmed, as Spiegelman was, by the casual depictions of teeming cities, explosions, and madcap antics that had enthralled *fin-de-siècle* audiences. The problem was more likely to have centered around Spiegelman's own contributions, which fused neurotic confessions, traumatic memories, puns and jokes, editorial commentary, and prophecies of further violence in a way that disregarded established lines of demarcation between gut feelings and considered analysis. If Spiegelman had focused on his personal experiences—on the first page he talks about "a roar, like a waterfall . . . the air smells of death"—then the book would likely have joined the proliferating ranks of 9/11 memoirs without any fuss.

But this is not what Spiegelman was offering. Each of his pages includes pointed jabs at jihadists, conservative politicians, or both. The first page, for example, is organized around the theme of "waiting for that other shoe to drop" and refers to "New! Improved! Jihad Brand Footware—Available in finer shops near you!" Page three shows off a stunning image he designed a few weeks after 9/11—"NYC to Kids: Don't Breathe!"—with a drawing of two adorable kids wearing photo-montaged gas masks. "I even designed a poster," he tells the reader, using his *Maus* face. But "some parents protested my poster for being too shrill." At the top of the fourth page, President Bush and Vice President Cheney ride on the back of a giant bald eagle. "Let's roll!" exclaims the president, as Cheney takes a box cutter to the eagle's throat. On the next page, Spiegelman refers in passing to the "*coup d'état* in 2000," and complains about how the 2002 anniversary of 9/11 "tried to wrap a flag around my head and suffocate me!" While these images are exaggerated for political and comical effect, they are broadly indicative of the author's views. There seems to be no reason to doubt, for example, that Spiegelman regarded the outcome of the 2000 presidential election as a political takeover that was facilitated by the Supreme Court, or that he perceived Dick Cheney's behind-the-scenes machinations as inconsistent with core liberal values. From Spiegelman's vantage point, both al-Qaeda and the Republican leadership threatened democratic institutions and humanist principles.

An exceptionally bleak comic strip on the bottom of the same page, titled "Remember Those Dead and Cuddly Tower Twins," portrays Uncle Sam as a madman bent on vengeance, spraying insecticide at a bug-like Saddam Hussein. "Now iss *war*!" cackles Uncle Sam, as the Tower Twins insist, "nix, unk! Wrong bug!" The strip reminds us that the Bush administration quickly set its sights on overthrowing the Iraqi regime as well as dismantling al-Qaeda. It also highlights that Spiegelman was careful to distinguish his position from those who expressed political solidarity with authoritarian regimes that opposed US interests and forces in the Middle East. While he resisted the temptation to conflate the secular Iraqi regime with the religious fundamentalists of al-Qaeda,

"NYC to Kids: Don't Breathe!," detail from *In the Shadow of No Towers*. Copyright © 2004 by Art Spiegelman.

"Equally terrorized by al-Qaeda and by his own government," detail from *In the Shadow of No Towers*. Copyright © 2004 by Art Spiegelman.

his take on Saddam Hussein was as contemptuous as his treatment of Bush, Cheney, and bin Laden.

The book's most provocative panel appears on the second of Spiegelman's ten pages. It shows an exhausted, *Maus*-faced Spiegelman at a drawing table trying to get some rest as Osama bin Laden and George W. Bush face off at opposite ends of the table. While bin Laden hoists a scimitar tipped in blood, Bush responds with a six-shooter and the Stars and Stripes. The accompanying caption—"Equally terrorized by al-Qaeda and by his own government"—was probably enough to scare off some of the editors who passed on this unusual project.[37] The political framework implied by *In the Shadow of No Towers* may have confused some readers, too. On the one hand, Spiegelman was a critic of interventionism, whether espoused by the Bush administration or by liberal-leaning journalists, academics, and intellectuals. On the other hand, he was far more explicit in his criticisms of religiously inspired extremism and authoritarian regimes than many on the left. His position was too left-wing for conservatives and liberals, but insufficiently anti-imperialist for many leftists.

In the forgotten parlance of the mid-twentieth-century left, Spiegelman's stance vis-à-vis "al-Qaeda and . . . his own government" would be described as "third camp," meaning that it rejected both the US government (the "first camp") and its religiously motivated adversaries (the "second camp"), favoring instead a "third camp" of independent, democratic, secular, and antimilitaristically-minded individuals and groups around the world. The term "third camp" was coined by followers of the dissident Marxist writer Max Shachtman (1904–1972), who broke from the orthodox Trotskyist movement in the 1940s and argued for a wholesale rejection of both Western capitalism and Soviet communism. Shachtman and his followers were fiercely supportive of democratic rights, freedom of the press, freedom of assembly, voting rights, and freedom of conscience, and they strongly opposed censorship of the arts, whether by the government or as a result of pressure from private groups. To a remarkable extent, these are the same principles that Spiegelman advanced in his post-9/11 comics, essays, and interviews.

Operating under the guise of the Workers Party (1940–1949) and then the Independent Socialist League (1949–1957), the Shachtmanites were on the fringes of the political landscape, even though many of their ideas percolated across the wider anti-Stalinist left in the 1940s and 1950s. This is not to suggest that Spiegelman would refer to himself as a "third camper" or that he is familiar with this Cold War terminology. But anyone conversant with the minutiae of left history would recognize the echoes of Shachtmanism in Spiegelman's views during this period, from his secularism and free speech absolutism to his stance vis-à-vis militarism and religious extremism.[38]

Mourning the dead and criticizing al-Qaeda were both acceptable in the wake of 9/11, and it was also possible to raise questions about specific governmental policies. But equating democratically elected leaders with violent extremists was, and to some extent remains, a no-go area so far as the mainstream media is concerned. Many readers would have presumably agreed with one or more aspects of Spiegelman's response. Liberals would have appreciated his principled defense of free speech and artistic freedom, for example, while conservatives would have shared his profound concerns about further attacks. At the same time, few readers would have been prepared to embrace a "third camp" position that acknowledged the ongoing threat of religiously motivated violence, while opposing all forms of state-sponsored militarism. Even though writers, artists, and intellectuals on the left were for the most part horrified by what transpired on 9/11, there was a powerful inclination to frame these events in terms of larger narratives about neocolonialism, imperialism, and US war crimes. What was particularly striking about Spiegelman's approach was the extent to which it resisted the temptation to historicize and perhaps normalize non-state catastrophic violence. For Spiegelman, 9/11 was a showstopper—and he was convinced that the malignant political forces that brought down the World Trade Center would strike again.

Spiegelman's emphasis on the traumatic nature of this singular event, and on the bankruptcy of US political elites as well as their jihadist enemies, was quite different from that offered by leading figures on the international left, such as Noam Chomsky and Slavoj Žižek. As Chomsky reminded one interviewer in late 2001: "During the past several hundred years the U.S. annihilated the indigenous population (millions of people), conquered half of Mexico (in fact, the territories of indigenous peoples, but that is another matter), intervened violently in the surrounding region, conquered Hawaii and the Philippines (killing hundreds of thousands of Filipinos), and, in the past half century particularly, extended its resort to force throughout much of the world." The "number of victims is colossal," he added. "For the first time, the guns have been directed the other way. This is a massive change."[39] A few years later, Žižek lyrically described the attacks on the Twin Towers as a form of "divine violence" that erupted "in a retaliatory destructive rage."[40]

Other leftist writers offered similar talking points about the historical accumulation of injustices and the imperative of placing 9/11 within an imperialist/counterimperialist framework. The comics equivalent of this explanatory discourse was provided by Joel Andreas in his tract *Addicted to War: Why the U.S. Can't Kick Militarism*, which sold tens of thousands of copies in the aftermath of 9/11. In a chapter titled "The 'War on Terrorism,'" Andreas devoted half a page to a long quotation from Osama bin Laden, in which the terrorist figurehead "praised the September 11 attacks and called for more attacks on the United States." Andreas went on to note: "Few people anywhere in the world, including the Middle East, support bin Laden's terrorist methods. But most people in the Middle East *share his anger* at the United States." Since the "Pentagon has demonstrated time and again that its advanced weaponry can *devastate countries* targeted for attack, *leveling* basic infrastructure and *killing thousands*," it would be "*naïve* to think there would be *no retaliation*."[41]

A notable exception to approaches that sought to fold 9/11 into larger historical narratives was a lengthy polemic by Julius Jacobson that appeared in the pages of *New Politics*, an independent, "third-camp" socialist journal that was first launched in 1961.[42] In his article, titled "On Liberal and Left Responses to Bush's War on Democracy," the one-time Shachtmanite took issue with the way in which numerous writers on the left "responded dispassionately and evasively in a more or less uniform pattern," i.e., with an "opening sentence decrying September 11th as a tragedy and, then, rushed headlong into a vigorous denunciation of American imperialism for having committed an even greater number of crimes against humanity." Jacobson contrasts this approach with a call to wage "political war on two fronts." The democratic left, he argues, should not only "reveal all that is unjust and self-defeating in Washington's war without end"; it should also oppose

> the terrorist means and anti-social ends of religious fundamentalism. Such a war on two fronts is not only morally and politically mandatory, but is the only approach that can have a positive influence on a public grown embittered and anxious by 9/11 and whose support for military retaliation can never be shaken by antiwar propaganda that does not simultaneously condemn, in the strongest terms, fundamentalism's theocratic ambitions.[43]

Jacobson writes in a very different register from Spiegelman—less personal, much more declaratory, and without accompanying visuals—but the perspective advanced by *No Towers* is much closer to Jacobson's approach than to Chomsky's, Žižek's, or Andreas's. Spiegelman may not have talked about "war on two fronts," but he treats Bush and bin Laden as equally terrifying figures and condemns "fundamentalism's theocratic ambitions" with a forthrightness that nonconservative public intellectuals avoided or disdained. There is little sense in Spiegelman's book that Americans needed to appreciate where al-Qaeda was coming from, or to find a way of taking the long view. Spiegelman is antagonized by and fearful of religiously motivated terror, rather than motivated to reflect on past events. At the same time, his response is to condemn rather than applaud any sort of military buildup as well as incursions in Central Asia and the Middle East. From Spiegelman's perspective, retaliatory violence would only make things worse.

Spiegelman has continued to address public controversies in a way that reflects the perspective articulated by *No Towers*. When the Danish newspaper *Jyllands-Posten* published twelve cartoons that depicted and satirized the Prophet Muhammad in 2005, outraged Muslims organized demonstrations in over a hundred countries. In Afghanistan, a handful of anticartoon protesters died as a result of clashes with police outside the US military base in Bagram, and in Somalia a teenager was killed "when police fired in the air to disperse the protesters and set off a stampede."[44]

From the outset of the controversy, Spiegelman maintained that newspapers and magazines were obliged to reprint the twelve images, so that readers could see what the story was for themselves. "Repressing images gives them too much power," Spiegelman wrote in an essay for *Harper's Magazine*,[45] and he similarly defended the "right to insult" in a debate with Joe Sacco in the pages of the *Nation*.[46] Sacco and Spiegelman once again locked horns after the terrorist attack on the French satirical magazine *Charlie Hebdo* in 2015, in which two brothers used Kalashnikov assault rifles to kill twelve people and injure eleven others. While Sacco mourned the loss of life, he took issue with the way *Charlie Hebdo*'s contributors portrayed Muslims and Islamic culture, arguing that "when we draw a line we are often crossing one."[47] Spiegelman meanwhile advocated for reprinting the offending *Charlie Hebdo* cartoons.[48] Hillary Chute rightly notes that the "different positions of Sacco and Spiegelman . . . demonstrate the trickiness—and importance—of issues around what can be said and shown,"[49] but says nothing about the chasm between Sacco's call for greater cultural understanding and sensitivity, and Spiegelman's free speech, antiwar, antiterror orientation.

PEACE AND DEMOCRACY

In the run-up to the 2003 intervention in Iraq, an advocacy group called the Campaign for Peace and Democracy (CPD) issued a statement that was headlined: "We Oppose Both Saddam Hussein and the U.S. War on Iraq." The statement offered an explicit expression of "third-camp" principles at a time when many peace activists shied away from criticizing the Iraqi government, preferring instead to target their ire at domestic forces, and when most voters told pollsters that they supported the administration's foreign policies. "We oppose the U.S.-led war on Iraq," the Campaign's statement opened. While "Saddam Hussein is a tyrant who should be removed from power," it is "up to the Iraqi people themselves to oust Saddam Hussein, dismantle his police state regime, and democratize their country." Americans, the statement insisted, "can be of immense help in this effort—not by supporting military intervention, but by building a strong peace movement." On the other hand, an invasion will only "add to the ranks of terrorists throughout the Muslim world, and will encourage international bullies to pursue further acts of aggression."[50]

The initial signatories included Art Spiegelman, who listed "cartoonist" as his organizational affiliation. The statement was drafted in November and December 2002, published in the *Nation* in January 2003, and subsequently in the *New York Times* in February 2003. It offered a very different approach from that advanced, for example, by the A.N.S.W.E.R. coalition,[51] which organized large marches and demonstrations against the Iraq war in 2001–2005, but adopted a neutral stand toward authoritarian governments and religiously motivated terrorists, defining itself solely in opposition to US imperialism.[52]

It is not surprising that Spiegelman's name could be found on an antiwar statement—over the years he has lent his name to dozens if not hundreds of declarations and petitions, many of them having to do with free speech and open cultural expression. But he did not sign onto the Campaign's statement merely because he shared its objection to Bush's foreign policy. He signed it because its authors expressed similar views on terrorism, religious fundamentalism, and US foreign policy to those that Spiegelman himself championed in *No Towers* and indeed much of the work he generated in the months and years that followed 9/11.

Ted Gournelos has suggested that *In the Shadow of No Towers* responds "to the sincerity of trauma discourse with the ironies of the everyday." It is certainly the case that Spiegelman deploys odd juxtapositions and absurdist wordplay to remind himself and the reader that our fixed certainties are often comical and that reality itself is a messy business. But Gournelos also argues that Spiegelman's use of humor and irony serves a consciously political function—that the book's "ironic narrative rejects the rhetoric of 'heroes,' 'villains,' 'good,' and 'evil,'" and "recognizes that it makes more sense to understand the world through multiple points of view."[53] My own reading has pointed in a different direction. The book's heroes are ordinary New Yorkers who want to be able to go about their lives without interference from Republicans or terrorists; the book's villains are George W. Bush, Dick Cheney, Saddam Hussein, and Osama bin Laden. While Spiegelman's comics, post- and pre-9/11, are filled with ironic witticisms, the most striking aspect of *No Towers* is precisely the sincerity of its commitment to a perspective that is secular, intellectual, artistic, and urbane.

Notes

1. Jeet Heer, *In Love with Art: Françoise Mouly's Adventures in Comics with Art Spiegelman* (Toronto: Coach House Books, 2013), 97.

2. "A Comic-Book Response to 9/11 and its Aftermath," *New York Times*, August 7, 2004.

3. Heer, *In Love with Art*, 97.

4. Alana Newhouse, "The Paranoids Were Right," in *Art Spiegelman: Conversations*, ed. Joseph Witek (Jackson: University Press of Mississippi, 2007), 234.

5. Marita Sturken, "Memorializing Absence," in *Understanding 9/11*, ed. Craig Calhoun, Paul Price, and Ashley Timmer (New York: The New Press, 2002), 377.

6. Timothy Krause, "Covering 9/11: The *New Yorker*, Trauma Kitsch, and Popular Memory," in *Portraying 9/11: Essays on Representations in Comics, Literature, Film and Theatre*, ed. Veronique Bragard, Christophe Dony, and Warren Rosenberg (Jefferson, NC: McFarland, 2011), 12.

7. Heer, *In Love with Art*, 98–99.

8. Heer, *In Love with Art*, 98.

9. Peter Kuper and Seth Tobocman, eds., *World War 3 Illustrated: 1979–2014* (Oakland, CA: PM Press, 2014), 216.

10. See David Remnick, "Making a Case," *New Yorker*, February 3, 2003.

11. Corriere della Sera, "Art Spiegelman, Cartoonist for the *New Yorker*, Resigns in Protest at Censorship," in *Conversations*, 264.

12. Favorable reviews appeared in the *New York Times*, *The Guardian*, *Mother Jones*, *Salon*, and elsewhere, but while *Time* magazine's Andrew D. Arnold said that the book "synthesizes Art Spiegelman's incomparable talents for personal history and comix theory into a timely and unique work of art," Douglas Wolk, in the *Washington Post*, called it a "colossal wet firecracker, a trifle blown up to enormous size and heft. . . . He's venting in all directions rather than making a point, and his jokes are pure lead." See Andrew D. Arnold, "Disaster Is My Muse," *Time*, September 3, 2004; and Douglas Wolk, "Art Spiegelman's Audacious but Ultimately Leaden Take on September 11," *Washington Post*, September 12, 2004.

13. Paradigmatic examples are Sid Jacobson and Ernie Colón, *The 9/11 Report: A Graphic Adaptation* (New York: Hill and Wang, 2006); Joel Andreas, *Addicted to War: Why the U.S. Can't Kick Militarism* (Oakland, CA: AK Press, 2003); and Alissa Torres and Sungyoon Choi, *American Widow* (New York: Villard, 2008).

14. See, inter alia, *Portraying 9/11: Essays on Representations in Comics, Literature, Film and Theatre* (2011); Karen Engle, *Seeing Ghosts: 9/11 and the Visual Imagination* (Montreal: McGill-Queen's University Press, 2009); Jeffrey Melnick, *9/11 Culture* (New York: Wiley-Blackwell, 2009); David Simpson, *9/11: The Culture of Commemoration* (Chicago: University of Chicago Press, 2006); and Thomas Stubblefield, *9/11 and the Visual Culture of Disaster* (Bloomington: Indiana University Press, 2014).

15. Laura T. Ryan, "Comics as Serious Literature: Cartoonist Spiegelman Has Seen Change since Pioneering *Maus*," in *Conversations*, 304.

16. He is referring here, of course, to the *New Yorker*. The first recorded use of the term "cake-eater" is by the cartoonist Thomas "Tad" Dorgan, in his comic strip *Indoor Sports* in 1918. See Tom Dalzell, *Flappers 2 Rappers: American Youth Slang* (Mineola, NY: Dover, 2010), 17.

17. Gene Kannenberg, "A Conversation with Art Spiegelman," in *Conversations*, 239.

18. See Hillary L. Chute, *Disaster Drawn: Visual Witness, Comics, and Documentary Form* (Cambridge, Mass.: Harvard University Press, 2016); Ted Gournelos, "Laughs, Tears and Breakfast Cereals: Rethinking Trauma and Post-9/11 Politics in Art Spiegelman's *In the Shadow of No Towers*," in *A Decade of Dark Humor: How Comedy and Satire Shaped Post-9/11 America*, ed. Ted Gournelos and Viveca Greene (Jackson: University Press of Mississippi, 2011).

19. In his introductory essay for *No Towers*, Spiegelman writes: "I'd never wanted to be a political cartoonist. I work too slowly to respond to transient events while they're happening. (It took me 13 years to grapple with World War II in *Maus*!) Besides, nothing has a shorter shelf-life than angry caricatures of politicians, and I'd often harbored notions of working for posterity—notions that seemed absurd after being reminded how ephemeral even skyscrapers and democratic institutions are." Art Spiegelman, *In the Shadow of No Towers* (New York: Pantheon, 2004), n.p. Fortunately, there is no intrinsic reason why political cartooning has to "respond to transient events while they're happening," even if newspaper editorial cartooning is organized around this principle. The contemporary efflorescence of comics journalism, comics memoir, and nonfiction comics has helped to clarify and sharpen this distinction between political and editorial cartooning. See Kent Worcester, "Journalistic Comics," in *The Routledge Companion to Comics*, ed. Frank Bramlett, Roy T. Cook, and Aaron Meskin (New York: Routledge, 2016), 137–45.

20. Julius Jacobson, "On Liberal and Left Responses to Bush's War on Democracy," *New Politics* 9, no. 1 (Summer 2002).

21. Jean Baudrillard, *The Spirit of Terrorism* (New York: Verso, 2002), 26–27.

22. See Kent Worcester, "New York City, 9/11 and Comics," *Radical History Review* 111 (Fall 2011); and Kent Worcester, "Graphic Narrative and the War on Terror," in *Cultures of War in Graphic Novels*, ed. Tatiana Prorokova and Nimrod Tal (New Brunswick, NJ: Rutgers University Press, 2018).

23. See, for example, http://www.flashlightworthybooks.com/Best-Books-About-9-11/80.

24. Yves Davo suggests that Alissa Torres's "choice of graphic narration recalls the decision of Art Spiegelman in his own account of September 11, 2001, to remain as close as possible to the images he still had in his mind: 'My strips are now a slow-motion diary of what I experienced.' Torres's political struggle might have been less visible than that of Spiegelman, but her opinions resonate throughout, for example, when she criticizes someone opposed to spending money to help people via the compensation funds given to the families of the victims of the attacks. Like Spiegelman, but in a more oblique way, Alissa Torres rises up against what Joan Didion has called the 'infantilization of citizens' and thus gives to her admittedly more personal story more political overtones." While both Spiegelman and Torres refuse to disentangle the personal from the political, and lean in a social-democratic direction when it comes to public health, Spiegelman's post-9/11 work not only addresses the "infantilization of citizens" and the value of tax-funded services, but also issues of militarism, foreign policy, and terrorism, which Torres conspicuously avoids. See Yves Davo, "September 11, 2001: Witnessing History, Demythifying the Story in *American Widow*," in *Comic Books and American Cultural History*, ed. Matthew Pustz (London: Bloomsbury, 2012), 243.

25. See Jonathan Ames and Dean Haspiel, *The Alcoholic* (New York: Vertigo, 2009); Emmanuel Guibert, Didier Lefèvre, and Frédéric Lemercier, *The Photographer: Into War-Torn Afghanistan with Doctors without Borders* (New York: Macmillan, 2009); Jacobson and Colón, *The 9/11 Report*; Sid Jacobson and Ernie Colón, *After 9/11: America's War on Terror* (New York: Hill and Wang, 2008); Marvel Comics, *Heroes: The World's Greatest Superhero Creators Honor the World's Greatest Heroes* (New York: Marvel, 2002); Frank Miller's *Holy Terror* (Burbank, CA: Legendary, 2011); Ted Rall, *To Afghanistan and Back: A Graphic Travelogue* (New York: NBM, 2002); David Rees, *Get Your War On: The Definitive Account of the War on Terror* (New York: Soft Skull Press, 2008); Torres and Choi, *American Widow* (2008).

26. See Gilbert Seldes, *The Seven Lively Arts: The Classic Appraisal of the Popular Arts* (1924; Mineola, NY: Dover, 2001).

27. Stephan Packard, "Whose Side Are You On? The Allegorization of 9/11 in Marvel's *Civil War*," in *Portraying 9/11: Essays on Representations in Comics, Literature, Film and Theatre*, 45.

28. See Kent Worcester, "Get Your War On: An Interview with David Rees," *Radical Society* 30, no. 3–4 (2003): 121–26.

29. See www.ww3.nyc.

30. Chute, *Disaster Drawn*, 5.

31. Spiegelman, *In the Shadow of No Towers*, n.p.

32. Joseph Witek, *Comic Books as History: The Narrative Art of Jack Jackson, Art Spiegelman, and Harvey Pekar* (Jackson: University Press of Mississippi, 1989), 24.

33. Øyvind Vågnes, "Comics Reenactment: Joe Sacco's *Footnotes in Gaza*," in *Comics and Power: Representing and Questioning Culture, Subjects and Communities*, eds. Rikke Platz Cortsen, Erin La Cour, and Anne Magnussen (Newcastle upon Tyne: Cambridge Scholars Publishing, 2015), 159.

34. Simpson, *9/11*, 11.

35. Spiegelman, *In the Shadow of No Towers*, n.p.

36. Ryan, "Comics as Serious Literature," 303.

37. Spiegelman, *In the Shadow of No Towers*, n.p.

38. For more on Max Shachtman and the "third camp," see Peter Drucker, *Max Shachtman and His Left: A Socialist's Odyssey Through the 'American Century'* (Amherst: Humanity Books, 1993); Maurice Isserman, *If I Had a Hammer: The Death of the Old Left and the Birth of the New Left* (New York: Basic Books, 1987); Kent Worcester, "Third Camp Politics: An Interview with Phyllis and Julius Jacobson," *Left History* 18, no. 1 (2014); and Kent Worcester, "Third Camp Politics in Theory and Practice: An Interview with Joanne Landy and Thomas Harrison," *Left History* 21, no 2 (Fall/Winter 2017/2018): 9–49.

39. Noam Chomsky, *9–11* (New York: Seven Stories Press, 2001), 12.

40. Slavoj Žižek, *Violence* (New York: Picador, 2008), 179.

41. Joel Andreas, *Addicted to War*, 29–30. Emphasis in original.

42. Julius Jacobson (1922–2003) joined the Trotskyist movement as a teenager, where he met his future wife and lifelong collaborator, Phyllis Jacobson (1922–2010). He served in the US Army during World War II and after the war worked as a printer, machinist, and editor. Phyllis and Julius sided with Max Shachtman during the 1939–1940 faction fight inside the Socialist Workers Party, and contributed numerous articles and essays to the Shachtmanite press in the 1940s and 1950s. They cofounded *New Politics* in 1961 as a nonsectarian journal of leftist discussion and debate. Julius Jacobson edited *The Negro and the American Labor Movement* (New York: Doubleday, 1968) and *Soviet Communism and the Socialist Vision* (Piscataway, NJ: Transaction, 1972). Phyllis and Julius Jacobson coedited *Socialist Perspectives* (Princeton, NJ: Kaez-Cohl, 1983).

43. Jacobson, "On Liberal and Left Responses to Bush's War on Democracy," n.p.

44. Carlotta Gall, "Protests Over Cartoons of Muhammad Turn Deadly, *New York Times*, February 6, 2006.

45. Art Spiegelman, "Drawing Blood: Outrageous Cartoons and the Art of Outrage," *Harper's Magazine*, June 2006.

46. Joe Sacco and Art Spiegelman, "Only Pictures?" *Nation*, March 6, 2006.

47. Joe Sacco's position was articulated in a nonfiction comic titled "On Satire" that was first published in *The Guardian* on January 9, 2015. Art Spiegelman's views were summarized in a May 2015 interview with *Time* magazine.

48. Chute, *Disaster Drawn*, 259–60.

49. Chute, *Disaster Drawn*, 260.

50. The full CPD statement, along with the initial signatories, can be found at: http://www.cpdweb.org/stmts/1001/stmt.shtml.

51. A.N.S.W.E.R. ("Act Now to Stop War and Racism") was formed in late 2001 by members and supporters of the Workers World Party.

52. See David Corn, "Behind the Placards," *LA Weekly*, October 30, 2002.

53. Gournelos, "Laughs, Tears and Breakfast Cereals," 94–96.

Part 3

MEDIATING MEMORY

PROVISIONAL EQUANIMITY

Citation and Solace in Art Spiegelman's *In the Shadow of No Towers*

PATRICK LAWRENCE

Don DeLillo begins his novel *Falling Man* (2007) in the streets of Manhattan on the morning of September 11, 2001. We read of the unfolding catastrophe: "This was the world now. Smoke and ash came rolling down streets and turning corners, busting around corners, seismic tides of smoke, with office paper flashing past, standard sheets with cutting edge, skimming, whipping past, otherworldly things in the morning pall."[1] Unlike wide-angled journalistic accounts, by noticing these "otherworldly things in the morning pall" DeLillo focuses his readers' attention on the individual. In so doing, he signals the resonance of personal experience in public conversations about 9/11. While public documents like the *9/11 Commission Report* handled the governmental, historical, and legal aspects of memorializing 9/11, DeLillo's novel—like Jonathan Safran Foer's *Extremely Loud and Incredibly Close* (2005) and others—turns to the psychological aftereffects of the attacks on individual lives and minds.

Art Spiegelman was himself a resident of Manhattan on that day and experienced firsthand what most people were watching on TV. In Lower Manhattan on the morning of September 11, Spiegelman, his wife, and his children narrowly escaped the cloud of dust and debris described by DeLillo. In subsequent years, Spiegelman composed a graphic account of what he saw and felt that ranks among the most iconic literary chronicles of 9/11. He created a series of ten comics plates, each the size of a newspaper page, containing both narrative and nonnarrative meditations on the experience of terrorism on US soil, all infused with Spiegelman's characteristic bluntness and acerbic critique. First serialized in the German weekly *Die Zeit* before being picked up by other outlets, the plates unabashedly critique the Bush administration's policies in the run-up to the Iraq War. Alongside these polemic statements, the text also chronicles Spiegelman's personal struggle to come to terms with the events and their aftermath. *In the Shadow of No Towers* (2004) makes for a compelling companion piece to DeLillo's fictional account, in that Spiegelman's work combines the psychological elements of the personal mode with the referential specificity of history.[2]

The tension between personal memory and historical records goes beyond simple notions of subjectivity and objectivity, and it is this problematic blending of memory and history that frames Spiegelman's difficulties as he navigates his personal experience of what became a public trauma. In *Les Lieux de Mémoire*, French historian Pierre Nora describes one way of encapsulating the contrast of private and shared trauma, writing that we are now confronted "with the brutal realization of the difference between real memory—social and unviolated, exemplified in but also retained as the secret of so-called primitive or archaic societies—and history, which is how our hopelessly forgetful modern societies, propelled by change, organize the past."[3] Nora argues that modernization has created a rupture with older modes of being, especially with the ready transmission of values and traditions person-to-person. There is a deep nostalgia here for a time before the abstract chronicle of history replaced the social fabric linking personal lives to the past. Nora characterizes memory as not only intimate, but "immediate."[4] By contrast, history involves "mediation" and "distance,"[5] in the sense that it is only "indirect."[6] Contrary to Nora's nostalgia, Spiegelman sees his memories of the events as *too* direct. Seeking to avoid the intimate immediacy of a painful past, the narrating self in *No Towers* favors retreat as a therapeutic escape, and the mediation of history provides him with just the distance he needs to evade the memory of an unbearable event.[7]

In his attempt to find comfort at a time of crisis, Spiegelman turns to early twentieth-century newspaper comics as a source of models to represent what he felt and observed in millennial Manhattan. By borrowing from older modes of comics representation, he moves toward what I see as a complex, layered form of solace. However, this mode of citation also risks diminishing the specificity of the event, which many trauma theorists warn against since it encourages forgetting and limits the potential for meaningful change. *In the Shadow of No Towers* occupies an interesting paradoxical position: Spiegelman's use of citations pointing to older works delivers solace in a difficult moment, but it also works against more typical means of solace rooted in closure and willful amnesia.

IN THE SHADOW OF TRAUMA

No Towers is often read as a memoir of trauma filtered through Spiegelman's left-leaning politics and his past work on *Maus*. From this perspective, the book reveals how Spiegelman uses the comics medium to work through survivor's guilt and anxiety while trying to rescue the event from political exploitation by the Bush administration. Reading *No Towers* as a trauma narrative gives meaning to the anarchic presentation of material on the page and, as Martha Kuhlman has noted, justifies the use of multiple narrative threads.[8] Under this rubric, rather than an orderly record of the attacks, *No Towers* comes closer to what Spiegelman himself calls it: "a slow-motion diary of what [he] experienced while seeking some provisional equanimity."[9] As such, the book stages the trauma of his experience—the way it refuses to be fully resolved—by being messy, contradictory, and ambivalent.

No Towers is inflected with the sense that resolution to this kind of trauma is both elusive and possibly corrupting. In his work on trauma and representation, Dominick LaCapra highlights the possibility that recovering from trauma can feel like infidelity to the originating event:

> Those traumatized by extreme events . . . may resist working through because of what might almost be termed a fidelity to trauma. . . . Part of this feeling may be the melancholic sentiment that, in working through the past in a manner that enables survival or a reengagement with life, one is betraying those who were overwhelmed and consumed by that traumatic past.[10]

Indeed, suspicion of resolution often features in *No Towers* to remind us that reducing complex events to monolithic interpretations neglects their specificity and dilutes their transformative potential. Despite such pitfalls, I argue, Spiegelman tries to grapple with this historical moment by escaping the compulsive repetitions of trauma so that he may achieve at least some measure of personal peace.

In the period of newly ascendant sincerity following 9/11,[11] Spiegelman's weaving together of citations and references to earlier texts in the manner of high postmodernists seems surprising, though it does echo the photo/comics assemblages of *Maus*. And yet, I want to suggest that *No Towers* is only fully illuminated through a consideration of this referential practice. Such allusiveness often characterizes an epistemology of deferral and the notion that, as Jean-François Lyotard described it, "the narrative function is losing its functors, its great hero, its great dangers, its great voyages, its great goal. It is being dispersed in clouds of narrative language elements."[12] While a text may use citation to avoid the "real" by constant reference to other texts, Spiegelman's book demonstrates that citation of this kind can—under the right circumstances—strengthen, rather than weaken, our connection to the world. Spiegelman does not use citation as a way to communicate aimlessness or an erosion of meaning, but to create a sense of continuity and the awareness that despite their disruptive effects, our current times fit into common historical narratives and that the world is not, in fact, ending. In other words, even though he uses the techniques of postmodernism, Spiegelman pursues more contemporary—and less cynical—ends.

Done in this way, citation can mitigate the disorienting impact of events that defy precedent and thus come with no ready models of response. Because citation anchors our current moment to analogues in the past, it is both anathema to events like 9/11—which have been construed as one in a handful of limit events that have no parallel—and absolutely vital to reconstructing the shattered lives affected by such events.[13] Citation can take a reeling self like Spiegelman's and an exceptional historical event like the terrorist attacks of September 11 and fit them into a historical narrative that may not be neat, but is more comprehensible—at least on an emotional level, and for a limited time.

To examine how *No Towers* performs its search for "provisional equanimity," I begin with two framing moments that bookend the narrative. One passage comes from the first plate in the series, where the subtitle for a strip called "Etymological Vaudeville" reads: "Revealed: 19th century source for 21st century's dominant metaphor."[14] The strip tells the story of people waiting anxiously for their inebriated upstairs neighbor's other shoe to drop after he noisily kicked off the first one. The delayed shoe drop is a recurring motif in the text and one that encapsulates the anxiety felt by Americans (including Spiegelman) about the possibility of another attack. Reducing this fear to a hackneyed idiom the way Spiegelman does here suggests that 9/11 is profoundly knowable, in that we do have well-worn expressions for experiences of this kind. Significantly, the same passage already distills the larger aesthetic at work in *No Towers*. Looking to late nineteenth- and early twentieth-century sources, Spiegelman seeks to explain and demystify the twenty-first-century crisis that gripped the nation after 9/11. This recursive gesture of reaching far into the past for models to help address present concerns is a key aspect I will dwell on.

The other passage comes from the last plate in the series, where the caption to a large picture of dropping shoes reads: "Right after 9/11/01, while waiting for some other terrorist shoe to drop, many found comfort in poetry. Others searched for solace in old newspaper comics."[15] Importantly, when Spiegelman returns to the "21st century's dominant metaphor" at the very end of his collection, the potential for "solace" prefigures an end to the anxiety engendered by arbitrary terror strikes. The passages that follow this caption are bitter, but even at this dark moment in the text it is clear that one goal has been to find "solace" and "provisional equanimity." By aligning these moments, I want to evoke two contradictory concepts that work in concert to shape the dominant aesthetics of the book: citation and solace. The practice of citation, which in the context of postmodernism and fragmented knowledge has been thought of as a destabilizing force, is deployed here in pursuit of the relative stability of solace. In following this line of argument, I acknowledge of course that Spiegelman's move toward solace is fraught. Solace can presuppose closure, which often induces forgetting. Similarly, narrativizing trauma is often a step toward exploiting it, as Spiegelman contends was being done by George W. Bush. Nonetheless, by analyzing the referential aesthetics of *No Towers*, I explore how citational modes can be intertextual, rhizomatic, and antihierarchical, but also—if only tentatively—grounding and consoling.[16]

My argument to some extent parallels a point acknowledged by memory scholar Jennifer Cho, who suggests that Spiegelman links his experience of 9/11 with historical antecedents in order to challenge claims that the 9/11 attacks were incommensurable with prior historical events: "As he works through his own trauma of 9/11, Spiegelman remembers other catastrophic experiences . . . to highlight the cyclical nature of state violence."[17] Cho's argument then addresses this cycle, focusing especially on how identifying such cycles can inhibit the political exploitation of tragedy. Spiegelman arguably uses his own form of citation as a way to grapple with the cyclical nature of history, a task that he undertakes in the service of personal recuperation. There is also a political, communal nature to this work—and other critics, such as Cho and Karen Espiritu, point out that Spiegelman's text captures a communal trauma as much as a personal one. Cho also rightly reminds us that efforts to insert moments like 9/11 into existing historical continuums can diminish their power to change history's course, writing that Spiegelman's "decision to lump 9/11 into the collective category of national and cultural trauma empties each of these moments of their historical specificity."[18] Cho's caution is warranted; however, on some level history and individuals do move on. In the case of Spiegelman, the essential point seems to be to move on in a way that minimizes the political co-optation of grief.

Importantly, *No Towers* channels this idea by highlighting the paradoxical function of citation. On the one hand, the book undermines the notion that 9/11 changed everything, because it finds ready models for understanding the event in early newspaper culture. On the other hand, the mass of historical events loses the character of a linear progression in which each moment is a consequence of its predecessors and a predecessor of its consequences, and is characterized, instead, by its associations with otherwise unrelated phenomena. In place of linear history, we find a jumble of icons, memorials, and documents that reconstitute themselves like a recursive spiral of trauma. As Kristiaan Versluys notes: "Spiegelman interprets history as a concatenation of shocks, as a never-ending series of wounds that will not heal and keep festering."[19] This recombination of historical emblems in a tentative, chaotic format is supported by the disorganized layout of the material on the page. Because it breaks down existing ways of understanding the relationships among historical events and rearranges those events according to their use in the present, Spiegelman's practice of citation undermines the concept of fixed meaning, while creating provisional, comforting meanings in the present.

Walter Benjamin's model of historical materialism is a relevant conceptual frame here. Benjamin suggests that history is best apprehended by the subject that "grasps the constellation which his own era has formed with a definite earlier one."[20] Even more to the point: "To articulate the past historically does not mean to recognize it 'the way it really was.' . . . It means to seize hold of a memory as it flashes up at a moment of danger."[21] For Spiegelman, the moment of danger is New York in October 2001, as Americans are waiting for the other shoe to drop, and the years that follow, during which 9/11 is co-opted for political purposes. His response is to look through the documents of an earlier era and "seize hold" of what he finds there, recombining it for his own present purposes. While his repurposing of this material threatens to undermine competing historical narratives of the twentieth century, it establishes a new mooring for the twenty-first century that enables solace and meaning-making in a world that seems to resist such harmony.

REVISITING MANHATTAN WITH HAPPY HOOLIGAN AND THE KATZENJAMMER KIDS

The citations begin before one even opens the book. The cover reprises Spiegelman and Françoise Mouly's iconic *New Yorker* cover featuring black silhouettes of the Twin Towers on a nearly black field. For the book, Spiegelman adds a central color panel depicting old comics characters tumbling and falling, as well as the title of the collection. Similarly, the back cover borrows the black-on-black style of the front, but has those characters in silhouette tumbling through the air in a grim reminder of the "Falling Man" photo by Richard Drew that became such a poignant emblem of the World Trade Center attacks. This conjunction between the mute power of the "Falling Man" and the loud playfulness of the cartoons creates a dissonance that amplifies, rather than soothes, the anxiety provoked by 9/11 for both Spiegelman and the reader.

Once inside the book, we find extensive and multifaceted threads of citation. Spiegelman's appropriation of *Happy Hooligan* in the tenth plate, for example,

Cover of *In the Shadow of No Towers*. Based on the 9/24/2001 *New Yorker* cover by Art Spiegelman and Françoise Mouly. Copyright © 2004 by Art Spiegelman.

occupies over fifteen panels. In this strip, Spiegelman's narrator-persona appears in the guise of the eponymous main character, created by Frederick Burr Opper in the early twentieth century. Spiegelman recounts being asked to give an interview for a 9/11 television special, something he feels skeptical about due to the mass media exploitation of the event and what he perceives as jingoistic warmongering. Spiegelman's ironic, inappropriate responses to the interviewer, who is expecting patriotic soundbites, are recast through Happy's air of inept buffoonery. For example, in response to the prompt "the place in America where I feel most American is . . . ," Happy/Spiegelman responds "Paris, France!" with a goofy grin.[22] The older strip provides a satirical yet cheerful model for Spiegelman's refusal to conform to expectations about how the nation should deal with the trauma of 9/11.

The effect, however, is dissonant, because we know that the disconnect between expectation and action is anything but humorous for the author-figure. In George W. Bush's America, the expected answers (feeling most American at, say, Yankee Stadium) are more and more rigorously enforced while dissent is quashed. At first, Happy/Spiegelman's impishness is simply ignored, as when the production assistant assures him that they can easily edit out his statement that Shrimp Pad Thai is his favorite American food. But by the end of the sequence, Happy/Spiegelman is booted from the studio for his hapless insubordination to the dominant national narrative. In this instance and several others, the recourse to cliché does not produce solace in itself, because its orientation is primarily toward acerbic critique. And yet it reinforces the idea that 9/11 is knowable through existing phrases and tropes; this accessibility—unimaginative and misguided though it might appear—diminishes the terror of the events.

The richest of Spiegelman's comics sources in *No Towers* is *The Katzenjammer Kids*, a strip that first appeared in the 1910s and continued to be serialized for decades under this title, as well as *The Captain and the Kids*, running in both William Randolph Hearst's *New York Journal* and Joseph Pulitzer's *New York World*. Spiegelman uses characters from this strip in many guises over several pages, but the rendition of Hans and Fritz as the Twin Towers is one of the most arresting metaphors in the text. An important function that *The Katzenjammer Kids* series serves in the text is that of a stand-in for, or usurper of, Spiegelman's memories. In a panel on the second plate, Spiegelman and his wife are walking away from the towers. In the following panel, Spiegelman describes not having looked back at the explosion they heard until they saw "the face of a woman heading south."[23] He does not draw this woman, though the previous panel includes himself and Françoise in what we recognize as the text's predominantly pseudo-realistic, memoirist mode. Instead, he replaces the woman with Mama from *The Katzenjammer Kids*, shifting from thicker lines, subtler colorings, and busier panels to the stripped down, iconographic image of the cartoon character.

In addition to covering Spiegelman's memories like a comfort blanket, Hans and Fritz prove to be a provocative metaphor of the Twin Towers. In the original comics, the Kids are a source of mischief and frequently disciplined for playing pranks on Mama, The Captain, and others. Bearing this in mind, Spiegelman makes a bold statement when on plate two a version of The Captain spanks the two Kids, both represented with a burning skyscraper projecting from their heads. The Captain wears a bandage on his head in this panel, perhaps because the Kids have injured him, and we infer this is the reason for their punishment. But the bandage also looks like a turban, and The Captain's beard recalls media caricatures of the 9/11 hijackers as well as Osama bin Laden, here disciplining an obstreperous pair of misfits drawn to resemble the Twin Towers. Though the scene is hard to read with certainty, it activates a number of possible readings, including the suggestion that the United States may have provoked groups like al-Qaeda through its foreign policy in the Middle East. In this reading, evoking the naughty cartoon characters lends itself to interpretation as a critique of US provocation, wherein the attacks on the towers are punishment for American mischief abroad.

In an important later passage, however, the Kids transition from symbols of American hubris to stand-ins for New Yorkers as victims of political exploitation. In "The Tower Twins," the Twins are the unintended victims of the monomaniacal "Uncle Screwloose"—a personification of the Bush administration and a satire of that classic figure of US nationalism, Uncle Sam. This allegory of American foreign policy in the run-up to the Iraq War delivers the Kids to the misguided efforts of Uncle Screwloose, who tries to put out the fire consuming them by pouring oil on it. While the twins continue to burn, Uncle Screwloose gets distracted trying to spray some "pesky hornets" nearby. The hornets fly to safety, and Screwloose takes out his anger on a spider with the face of Saddam Hussein, which is captioned "Iraknid" and cannot fly away from his poison. Eventually, the hornets return, and Screwloose flees to a nearby cottage, gloating that the now incinerated Hans and Fritz will be left to suffer the hornets' stings. In this loosely allegorical strip, Spiegelman borrows from *The Katzenjammer Kids* to argue that the invasions in Afghanistan and Iraq neglected the true victims of the attacks and only stoked further violence. His citation choices enable political protest and offer some satisfaction for those who were critical of George W. Bush's foreign policy in the long aftermath of 9/11. And yet

Detail from "The Tower Twins," *In the Shadow of No Towers*. Copyright © 2004 by Art Spiegelman.

recalling the Kids—first created in Lower Manhattan on the verge of America's first major imperial expansion in the lead up to the Spanish-American War of 1898—also provides tentative solace by handing Spiegelman a set of manageable artistic tools under exceptional circumstances.

Comics themselves are a potent medium for protest of this kind. In *No Towers* Spiegelman points out that newspaper comics were "just right for an end-of-the-world moment,"[24] and in fact comics in general seem well suited to the kind of displacement at work here, too. As Scott McCloud suggests in *Understanding Comics*, the simplified lines and forms of comics allow readers to see characters as elastic receptacles for their own experiences. This is precisely what Spiegelman does when he "becomes" Happy Hooligan, and what happens when the Twin Towers "become" the Katzenjammer Kids. The mobility of comics signifiers—what Derek Parker Royal calls the "ability of comics to specify, and personalize, through the indeterminate"[25]—allows the medium to overwrite memory and experience, or, to put it differently, comics are ready forms for our unshaped experience.[26] Their accommodating spaces can serve as sites for our own projections as well as offer consoling icons of the past to shape current experiences of upheaval. While Spiegelman may be crafting an idiosyncratic and personal response to the attacks by turning to early newspaper comics, his efforts to gain solace through this substitution offers an intriguing model for coping with trauma.

POLITICIZING COMICS HISTORY

Rather than proffering this mode of transference uncritically, however, *In the Shadow of No Towers* analyzes its own methods of projection. Again, this self-awareness inheres in comics as a medium. In their seminal introduction to graphic narrative, Hillary Chute and Marianne DeKoven aptly contend that "the diegetical horizon of each page . . . offers graphic narrative a representational mode capable of addressing complex political and historical issues with an explicit, formal degree of self-awareness."[27] This self-reflexivity, the result of a genre that speaks to itself through its simultaneous use of visual and verbal registers, allows graphic narrative to treat history in a different way than do media that tend to obscure the artificiality of their own modes of representation. By contrast, even when depicting historical events and ostensibly telling nothing but the truth, comics remain deeply self-aware and self-reflexive.[28]

No Towers realizes these potentialities of the medium in the context of the narrator-figure's efforts to recover from his trauma. Consequently, all this destabilizing self-referentiality seems at first blush to run counter to the search for solace. Though the text is inflected with Spiegelman's manic voice and the

Detail from "Weapons of Mass Displacement," *In the Shadow of No Towers*. Copyright © 2004 by Art Spiegelman.

sense that paranoia and anxiety are irremediable effects of 9/11, *No Towers* also evinces a sense that comics and citation are stabilizing forces. For one thing, they empower and advance Spiegelman's political invective, supplying a source of strength and grounding that is perhaps parallel, though antithetical, to the widespread patriotic mobilization encouraged by the Bush administration. Additionally, as remnants of a deceptively innocent-seeming age, comics provide a partial haven from the chaos and psychological devastation of post-9/11 New York.

And yet, bitterness suffuses the end of the text, suggesting that solace has been deferred. For Spiegelman, "new traumas began competing with still-fresh wounds" as the wars in Iraq and Afghanistan and domestic curbs on civil liberties followed in the years after 9/11.[29] While Spiegelman's narrator is clearly afflicted by the mix of exploitation and neglect that 9/11 received in the national imagination, this may not be the only reason his expressive endeavor fails to result in a recovery from his trauma. The failure also has to do with the problematics of citation as a model for historicizing and recovering from trauma, due to the simultaneously familiarizing and displacing tendencies I described above. Spiegelman may seek solace in citation, but the solace that citation offers is necessarily imperfect.

Citation's logic of displacement threatens to push out the specificity of real events, as Cho and others warned. To name one example, Spiegelman's persona decries "displacement" as "America's latest craze," which caused the attack on Iraq in place of al-Qaeda and the prosecution of Martha Stewart instead of Halliburton. While the gesture of displacement can offer a recuperative approach to trauma that allows Spiegelman's character to recover from, say, the minor grief of losing his cat—by replacing that cat with one that is similar—it also has the potentially negative effect of neglecting the imperatives of remembrance and action.

The tendency to favor closure at the expense of remembrance is addressed on the final page. In the last three panels, the image of the Twin Towers fades from burning orange into darkness. The suggestion seems to be that life does continue after all, and the towers "seem to get smaller every day"[30]—receding into the shadows of the past. While the narrator is ambivalent about the retreat of 9/11 into history, the withdrawal into the past nonetheless coincides with the process of gradually lifting oneself out of grief. Still, as a counterpoint, the series ends with the ironic "Happy Anniversary" of the final panel: a sense that we have lost the opportunity to learn important lessons and that we forget at our own peril.[31]

In making sense of Spiegelman's evocation of images from the past, I want to return to LaCapra and Benjamin, both of whom address how historical narratives can be repurposed by those in the present. LaCapra explores the dense weave of relationships between fiction and nonfictive modes in historiography.[32] His approach encourages us to consider Spiegelman's text as a historical artifact—perhaps a survivor testimony—even though it does not claim strict fidelity to the facts. Benjamin expresses an ambivalence about the uses of the past that is instructive here, too. He writes: "The danger affects both the content of the tradition and its receivers. The same threat hangs over both: that of becoming a tool of the ruling classes."[33] Therefore, "the attempt must be made anew to wrest tradition away from a conformism that is about to overpower it."[34] Opposing the consolidation of power in the hands of a few, then, we must concede that the past is as liable to be repurposed for good as for ill. Even as we acknowledge the pitfalls of such borrowing, we must rededicate ourselves to the fight to ensure that the borrowing and repurposing of history will be in service of desirable ends, including both solace for survivors and loyalty to victims. This is the work Spiegelman embarks on. His citation of comics history creates links with the past to provide solace. It also helps him write his own resistive narrative which, while flattening some aspects of 9/11 and of similar events, militates against the tendency to flatten and exploit on the part of the dangerously belligerent Bush administration.

The ultimate lesson of *No Towers* is therefore an ambivalent one. Spiegelman's conflicted aesthetic choices leave us wondering about the appropriate mode for representing an event that is both personal and political, both presently traumatic and historically significant. These concerns have traditionally been memorialized in distinct media: memoirs for the personal, histories for the political. Memorials unite under national banners ahead of military operations, while polemics invigorate debate on historical precedent and the just course of action. For this reason, a hybrid medium like comics may be particularly useful, since its sharpness as a tool of contemporary commentary is matched by its variegated history. Yet *No Towers* also demonstrates that any closure must be partial. Because comics like Spiegelman's tend toward the open-ended and the dialogic, they defer the solace that they might seek, even as they search for it in complex and compelling ways. If we understand 9/11 as a moment of trauma that teases the limits of representation, then *No Towers* becomes the ideal mode for such a challenging project. While the event may ultimately resist recuperation for those who suffered most, others who suffered in more mediated ways can find solace in the weave of citation that suggests historical moments are at least somewhat knowable, that we can find partial, if not complete, "equanimity."

Spiegelman's aesthetics of citation and solace unmoors us as victims and spectators by disavowing the dominant understanding of September 11 as a unique event, and the simplified axis of victim and victor that has served to explain the period between 9/11 and the Iraq War. In its place, we are given a model of comics citation that refers us to the past, suggesting that we can rearrange the fragments of the present by provisionally empaneling the fragments of history. *In the Shadow of No Towers*, then, is a significant artifact of 9/11 and the negotiation of trauma precisely because it demonstrates the mutability of the past. The instability of accepted narratives may cause anxiety, but it also offers the opportunity to reshape the world and make it more just.

Notes

1. Don DeLillo, *Falling Man* (New York: Scribner, 2007), 3.

2. In an often-quoted line from the book's introduction that highlights the blending of the personal and broadly historical or public, Spiegelman describes how "outrunning the toxic cloud that had moments before been the north tower of the World Trade Center left [him] reeling on that faultline where World History and Personal History collide." Art Spiegelman, *In the Shadow of No Towers* (New York: Pantheon, 2004), preface.

3. Pierre Nora, "Between Memory and History: *Les Lieux de Mémoire*," *Representations* 26 (Spring 1989): 8.

4. Nora, "Between Memory," 13.

5. Nora, "Between Memory," 8.

6. Nora, "Between Memory," 13.

7. In a later passage, Nora notes a relationship between memory and trauma, addressing the more therapeutic notion that has been common since Freud, according to which reconstructing a coherent personal narrative offers a remedy to a dissociated psyche burdened by the abstractions of painful experience. He notes, however, that the placement of memory at "the heart of psychological personality with Freud" occurs simultaneously with "the historical metamorphosis of memory" and that the two are "so intimately linked that one can hardly avoid comparing them." Nora, "Between Memory": 15. In my reading of this passage, Nora suspects that the practice of privileging memory in psychology is a result of a nostalgia that comes about precisely because memory has been foreclosed and transformed into history.

8. Martha Kuhlman, "The Traumatic Temporality of Art Spiegelman's *In the Shadow of No Towers*," *The Journal of Popular Culture* 40, no. 5 (2007): 850.

9. Spiegelman, *No Towers*, preface.

10. Dominick LaCapra, *Writing History, Writing Trauma* (Baltimore: The Johns Hopkins University Press, 2001), 22.

11. The days and months following 9/11 produced a lot of speculation in popular media on whether irony was dead. In my phrasing here, I mean to invoke that sense of the death of irony and a newly refreshed currency for sincere expressions of connectedness, both in art and daily life, of which much 9/11 fiction takes part. This concept was in place before 9/11, however, and is often linked with the "New Sincerity" movement in literature and music.

12. Jean-François Lyotard, "Introduction," in *The Postmodern Condition: A Report on Knowledge*, trans. Geoff Bennington and Brian Massumi (Minneapolis: University of Minnesota Press, 1984), xxiv.

13. Evoking this sense of the incomparable, for example, Toni Morrison wrote following the attacks that she would need to "set aside all [she knew] or believe[d] about nations, wars, leaders, the governed and ungovernable" in order to speak to the dead. Toni Morrison, "The Dead of September 11," in *Trauma at Home: After 9/11*, ed. Judith Greenberg (Lincoln: University of Nebraska Press, 2003), 1. For an overview of those who describe 9/11 as a limit event and the imperative to still move ahead, see Kristiaan Versluys, *Out of the Blue* (New York: Columbia University Press, 2009), 1–3.

14. Spiegelman, *No Towers*, plate 1.

15. Spiegelman, *No Towers*, plate 10.

16. Important work has laid the foundation for my exploration of citation and solace in *No Towers*. Karen Espiritu sheds light on how Spiegelman's difficult, ongoing "labor involved in creating a graphic novel parallels the harrowing interminability not only of grief itself, but also of attempting to 'master' or understand—though *never completely*—a particularly traumatic experience." Karen Espiritu, "'Putting Grief into Boxes': Trauma and the Crisis of Democracy in Art Spiegelman's *In the Shadow of No Towers*," *The Review of Education, Pedagogy, and Cultural Studies* 28 (2006): 182. Mary Louise Penaz also mentions Spiegelman's use of newspaper characters and tropes as part of a larger destabilizing project in *No Towers*, writing, for example, that Spiegelman's references "displace the 9/11 attacks on the previous turn of the century to defamiliarize them." Mary Louise Penaz, "Drawing History: Interpretation in the Illustrated Version of the *9/11 Commission Report* and Art Spiegelman's *In the Shadow of No Towers* as Historical Biography," *a/b: Auto/Biography Studies* 24, no. 1 (Summer 2009): 107. I would argue that the opposite is true: Since Spiegelman has posited that people might have "searched for solace in old newspaper comics," it is actually possible that he makes such references precisely to *familiarize* 9/11.

17. Jennifer Cho, "Touching Pasts *In the Shadow of No Towers*: 9/11 and Art Spiegelman's Comix of Memory," in *The Popular Avant-Garde*, ed. Renée M. Silverman (New York: Rodopi, 2010), 201.

18. Cho, "Touching Pasts," 209.

19. Kristiaan Versluys, "Art Spiegelman's *In the Shadow of No Towers*: 9/11 and the Representation of Trauma," *Modern Fiction Studies* 52, no. 4 (Winter 2006): 982.

20. Walter Benjamin, "Theses on a Philosophy on History," in *Illuminations*, ed. Hannah Arendt, trans. Harry Zohn (New York: Schocken Books, 1968), 263.

21. Benjamin, "Theses on a Philosophy on History," 255.

22. Spiegelman, *No Towers*, plate 10.

23. Spiegelman, *No Towers*, plate 2.

24. Spiegelman, *No Towers*, Comics Supplement.

25. Derek Parker Royal, "Coloring America: Multi-Ethnic Engagements with Graphic Narrative," *MELUS* 32, no. 3 (Fall 2007): 9.

26. Many have found McCloud's book useful for analyzing Spiegelman's work. *In the Shadow of No Towers* also engages with the history of the medium and reinvents certain conventions of form in ways that are largely consistent with Thierry Groensteen's theories and his expectations of what kinds of things are possible, if only nascent, within the medium. See Thierry Groensteen, *The System of Comics* (Jackson: University Press of Mississippi, 2007).

27. Hillary L. Chute and Marianne DeKoven, "Introduction: Graphic Narrative," *Modern Fiction Studies* 52, no. 4 (Winter 2006): 769.

28. Andrew J. Kunka offers a compelling analysis of the relationship between historical texts and comics interpretations of them. Andrew J. Kunka, "Intertextuality and the Historical Graphic Narrative: Kyle Baker's *Nat Turner* and the Styron Controversy," *College Literature* 38, no. 3 (Summer 2011): 168–93. See also Penaz, who addresses similar issues through the lens of historical biography.

29. Spiegelman, *No Towers*, preface.

30. Spiegelman, *No Towers*, plate 10.

31. Spiegelman, *No Towers*, plate 10.

32. See, especially, the introduction to *Writing History, Writing Trauma*.

33. Benjamin, "Theses on a Philosophy of History," 255.

34. Benjamin, "Theses on a Philosophy of History," 255.

OF MICE AND MASKS

Photography as Masking in Art Spiegelman's *Maus*

LIZA FUTERMAN

The rise of social media platforms, which use unrealistic images to tell fictive truths, has resulted in the widespread belief that "the metaphorical 'death of photography' . . . seems almost an established fact."[1] While this might be the case with photographs in advertisements, social networks, and even news broadcasts, it does not usually apply to photographic representations of catastrophes on a colossal scale such as natural disasters, 9/11, or the Holocaust. These events retain their historical facticity. Those who challenge the truth-value of photographic representations of these events risk being seen to question the truth of the events themselves, an act that is unethical or, as is the case with Holocaust denial in Germany, even criminal. Writing about photographs from the Nazi concentration camps, historian Cornelia Brink notes that such images are generally "accepted as straightforward and unambiguous reality, not as a specific photographic rendering of that reality open to analysis."[2] She adds that "more than other photographs they make a moral claim to be accepted without questioning."[3] Regarding photographs of disaster or genocide, then, the prevalent belief is that photography possesses an intrinsic correspondence to reality.

In this chapter I engage with the photographs integrated in Art Spiegelman's *Maus* to argue that their incorporation in the graphic narrative probes the intrinsic documentary quality of Holocaust photography and questions our reliance on "photography's spectral power."[4] Specifically, my focus will be on the questions raised by the actual and simulated photographs in the graphic memoir. Needless to say, the photographs in *Maus* have attracted an overwhelming amount of scholarly attention. And yet, as this chapter elucidates, observing them through the prism of another graphic device—the mask—reveals a novel vantage point that might otherwise have been obscured.[5]

"How does one represent that which one knows only through representations and from an ever growing historical distance?" asks Andreas Huyssen in his essay, "Of Mice and Mimesis: Reading Spiegelman with Adorno."[6] Huyssen's question resonates throughout *Maus*, as Spiegelman confesses that his "notions" about the Holocaust "are born of a few scores of photographs and a couple of movies."[7] For Huyssen, the visual inaccessibility of past events jeopardizes the authenticity of Spiegelman's narrative. In his words: "Spiegelman accepts that the past is visually inaccessible through realistic representation: whatever strategy he might choose it is bound to be 'inauthentic.'"[8] And yet, what triggers the possibility of inauthentic narrative is precisely our familiarity with and fixation on a canonical set of photographs that promises to provide unmitigated access to the otherwise elusive past. My contention is that Spiegelman on the one hand challenges the value of photography as a direct access point to the past and on the other hand elevates the documentary quality of comics. In doing so, he invites us to approach comics with the understanding that it can provide historical evidence where other forms of representation fall short.

MASKS AND PHOTOGRAPHS AS GRAPHIC DEVICES

The presence of actual photographs in a comic book is unusual, as it interrupts the flow of the cartoons. Here, they also remind us that this is a biographical account told by a Holocaust survivor, and that the generic mice heads stand in for human faces. Though Spiegelman took the radical step of integrating actual photographs in *Maus*, his decision prompts us to wonder: Why do some photographs appear in cartoon form, as simulated photographs, while others are reproductions of real photos? I maintain that the real photos embedded in the graphic text purposefully deviate from the canon of Holocaust photography, showing the ways in which photographs like these can deceive the observer to believe that the Holocaust was not "all that bad after all," whereas comics reliably retell the atrocities of World War II. In other words, Spiegelman comments on the shortcomings of photography in authentically recording historical events, while underscoring the underrated documentary potential of the comics form.

Since *Maus* deals with the Holocaust and includes photographs in its graphic landscape, we could reasonably expect to encounter the catalogue of familiar pictures taken by British and American army photographers during the liberation of the Nazi concentration camps in 1945. However, the photographs of Vladek Spiegelman as a healthy-looking young man and the plump face of Art's brother, Richieu, are nothing like the images that "have long become part of the Western countries' collective visual memory."[9] What we have been exposed to repeatedly through documentaries, history books, and museums are photographs that portray piles of corpses, open mass graves, burning pits, sick and half-dead survivors, and other unspeakable horrors.[10]

Roland Barthes noted that "the more technology develops the diffusion of information (and notably of images), the more it provides the means of masking the constructed meaning under the appearance of the given meaning."[11] Barthes's observation recognizes the potential of the photograph to conceal reality under an artificial façade that masquerades as the ultimate reality. This idea forms a mental bridge between photography and masking, not least because it also echoes Gilles Deleuze's discussion of the mask as "the true subject of repetition." In his view, "because repetition differs in kind from representation, the repeated cannot be represented: rather it must always be signified, masked by what signifies it, itself masking what it signifies."[12] For Deleuze, then, any effort towards repetition forms an opaque mask that claims to be transparent. This mask stands for an empty signifier that appears to form a chain of signifiers, which do not mean a thing since they are limited by the opacity of the seemingly transparent mask. The removal of the mask, Deleuze asserts, could not reveal "anything except other masks."[13]

Spiegelman plays with a similar idea of masking when he draws attention to an explicit mouse mask in his comic-form introduction to *MetaMaus*. The segment is part of a fourteen-panel strip in which Spiegelman professes to answer recurring questions about his work, among them: "Why **Comics?** Why **Mice?! Why the Holocaust?!**"[14] In the opening panel, Spiegelman asserts his authorial position by addressing readers with the casual "Y' know," then explicitly comments on the mouse-mask as a visual device that conceals his human face: "It's swell to get recognition . . . but it's kinda **hard** to be seen behind a mouse mask!" Despite his evident frustration, he accepts the challenge: "I thought I'd finally try to answer as fully as I could. That way, when asked in the future, maybe I could just say . . . **NEVER AGAIN!**" The final injunction, in the given context, evokes the post-Holocaust admonition against any future anti-Semitic violence as well as the slogan of the Jewish Defense League, a militant organization founded in 1968, whose stated goal is to "protect Jews from antisemitism by whatever means necessary."[15] Yet, when read in light of Deleuze's reflections on repetition and the final frames of the introductory strip to *MetaMaus*, "Never Again" can also be seen to disavow the act of repetition itself. In this reading, the kind of repetition that purports to afford access to the past in fact merely masks its inaccessibility and underlines the profound meaninglessness of all expression in the face of disaster.

The word "again" presupposes that something has happened before, so the addition of the word "never" may be read as an attempt to prevent the infinite repetition that for Deleuze is connoted by masks. The bottom panel of this

Detail from "Intro," *MetaMaus: A Look Inside a Modern Classic,* Maus (New York: Pantheon, 2011), p. 9. Copyright © 2011 by Art Spiegelman.

two-page strip reenacts the removal of the mask, a gesture that in Deleuze's reading can only be futile. Spiegelman says, hopefully: "And maybe I could even get my damned mask off! I can't breathe in this thing!" The following panels are narrated nonverbally as we watch Spiegelman's struggle with the mask in an attempt to discard it. The only linguistic signs are a collection of semantically unintelligible sounds: "Unff! Urk! Oof! Aah!" Finally, the mask comes off, but instead of revealing Spiegelman's face, as we would expect to see in a photograph or even a drawing, what emerges is a cartoon skull—human yet unalive. Drawing a skull as the underlying face to a mask suggests that once all masks (i.e., possible meanings) have been removed, death is the only meaning that remains. Paradoxical as it might sound, masks, then, count as agents of meaning, in the sense that they provide context and framing to the face they conceal. In this way, if we regarded a photograph as a mask, we would infer that the photographed subject is ultimately meaningless unless meaning (i.e., the photo-mask) is applied to it.

MAUS IN THE AGE OF MECHANICAL REPRODUCTION

Masks are a prominent visual marker throughout *Maus* and fulfill different functions depending on context. Two recurrent mouse masks feature prominently: one that European Jews applied in order to hide their Jewishness during World War II, and another Spiegelman uses in the early stages of the second volume, where he addresses his audience directly. A third mask oftentimes goes unnoticed because of its seemingly transparent nature. This is the animal mask that prompts journalists and students to ask the perennial question: "Why Mice?" The question indicates that even though we acknowledge the characters' animalistic heads, we do not register them as being animals; we recognize their humanity and look past the mask. Unlike this semitransparent disguise, the other two types of masks are clearly marked with strings to indicate that there is something else underneath the surface.

In *MetaMaus*, Spiegelman explains the rationale for his decision to draw himself wearing a mask in the early episodes of the second volume: "*Maus I* came out before *Maus II* was finished, the success of the first book took me by surprise . . . I think that the shock of becoming celebrated, rewarded for depicting so much death, gave me the bends . . . it left me trying to burrow into a mouse hole and disappear."[16] Elisabeth Friedman seems to build directly on Spiegelman's response when she interprets the bottommost panel of the introductory strip to *MetaMaus* to signify Spiegelman's internalization of his victimized position. Friedman notes: "Once [Spiegelman] has yanked the mask off only a skull is revealed; his human face and the mouse mask have become fused."[17] Friedman's reading implies that Spiegelman's denial of his internalized identity would amount to self-annihilation. However, the context of the Q&A in which Spiegelman addresses the questions and the slippage of the mask out of the panel frame suggest that the exposed skull does not denote the internalization of a fixed identity. Rather, it can be seen as an ironic gesture that works against itself by revealing yet another mask—that of a cartoon skeleton that signifies yet another form of representation.

The bleeding of the mask out of the panel frame intimates that Spiegelman's art seeks to transcend the boundaries of the comics form and those of the mouse mask. This metanarrative functions as an authorial voice that furnishes readers with the ultimate key to the artist's work. Yet the gesture is ridiculed through the cartoon skeleton that pierces us with its hollow eyeballs, implying that underneath this mask lies another mask and so on. The mask, then, simultaneously separates the author from his textual persona and allows us to get closer to the artist, for it breaks the animal metaphor by making us aware that the animal mask hides a human face. In other words, the mask both conceals and reveals the "real" Spiegelman; or, as Deleuze would have it, removing the mask uncovers a construct as if it were "the real thing," when in fact it is only another representation. This deceptive exposure is analogous to the function photography fulfills in the graphic memoir: On the one hand, it reveals certain aspects of the past, while on the other, we are to acknowledge that these selective images are open to interpretation and therefore cannot be taken at face value. *Maus* and *MetaMaus*, as we shall see, employ the metaphor of masking to reassess our faith in the documentary function of photography.

In "The Work of Art in the Age of Mechanical Reproduction," Walter Benjamin famously argues that photography as an industrial technology accelerates the process of drawing, and he consequently defines the photographic image as an artistic product that categorically lacks the ability to document the world. With this in mind, the truth-value of *Maus* as a graphic testimony that employs both comics and photography must be challenged. And indeed, it was. Despite its historical and biographical subject matter as well as the extensive research that Spiegelman conducted in order to create a realistic account, the *New York Times* included the book in its fiction bestseller list. It was only due to Spiegelman's strong objection that Pantheon classified *Maus* as nonfiction.[18] And so the question remains: Can a visual medium that does not hold a correlation to reality still be considered trustworthy in making the past accessible to its audience?

Although Benjamin recognized the nonevidentiary quality of photography, he also acknowledged that the masses yield to the power of the photographic illusion by relying on the photograph to bridge the temporal and spatial gaps between the present and the represented past.[19] The replica of the desired object or event comes to fill in for that which is absent, with the reproduction paradoxically nurturing the illusion of accessibility. Benjamin's reflections on photography recall Deleuze's considerations regarding repetition as a type of mask: that which reveals a surface that veils nothing but other surfaces, never reaching reality's real face. In contrast to Benjamin's and Deleuze's thoughts about the truth-value of reproduction, *Maus* and *MetaMaus* ask us to view photographs as "documents of reality," which above all serve to validate the past and infuse Spiegelman's account with historical certainty.[20]

PHOTOS TO THE RESCUE: SPIEGELMAN'S PHOTOGRAPHIC TESTIMONY

Three images of real photographs are included in the graphic novel, none of which depicts the atrocities we expect to see in Holocaust photography. Instead, we are shown family portraits. The first depicts Spiegelman's mother, Anja, and the nine-year-old Art in the four-page strip entitled "Prisoner on the

Hell Planet: A Case History," which narrates the events of Anja's suicide and its aftermath. The photo, we are told, is what draws Vladek to reluctantly engage with his son's comic strip, despite his suspicion of the comics medium. The second photograph is that of Richieu, Spiegelman's elder brother, who died at the age of six under tragic circumstances and was present in Art's childhood only as a distant image from the past. As Art confesses to his wife, Françoise: "I didn't think about [Richieu] much when I was growing up . . . he was mainly a large, blurry photograph hanging in my parents' bedroom."[21] And yet Richieu's photograph is also a constant reminder of the perfect son Spiegelman could never become. Though Art feels slightly embarrassed by his "sibling rivalry with a snapshot,"[22] he cannot refrain from feeling inferior: "The photo never threw tantrums or got in any kind of trouble . . . it was an ideal kid, and I was a pain in the ass. I couldn't compete. They didn't talk about Richieu, but that photo was a kind of reproach. He'd have become a doctor, and married a wealthy Jewish girl . . . the creep."[23] In *MetaMaus*, Spiegelman explains that the decision to incorporate this photograph in *Maus* was not difficult: "The photo of Richieu hovered as a presence over my childhood," he recalls; "but I hadn't thought about it one way or another for *Maus* . . . then somehow the shape of the story came together, which included realizing that my phantom brother was a presence through not just my childhood, but now somehow still hovering in the interview moments with Vladek."[24] The portraits of Anja and Richieu have been discussed at length by Marianne Hirsch, who argues that photos "function as specters reanimating their dead subjects with indexical and iconic force," restoring "the sense of family, safety, and continuity that has been hopelessly severed" during and after the Holocaust.[25] Hirsch's reading explicitly draws on the ability of photography to preserve the ghostly presence of the dead as well as their roles in the lives of the living far beyond the moment of their erasure from the family unit.

The third intercalated photograph reflects the "hovering" of the lost child's image in Spiegelman's relationship and dialogues with his father. Vladek's own photograph appears in a section where the father elaborately explains to his son how he ended up having such a picture of himself—while in the background, on the wall between them, hangs what we assume to be Richieu's immortal reproduction. Vladek's photograph is a baffling "souvenir" of his time in the Nazi concentration camps. After the liberation of Auschwitz, Vladek had a severe case of typhus in Germany and upon recovering was told that Anja was alive and back in her hometown in Poland.[26] To quickly let her know that he, too, was alive before he undertook the lengthy journey to Poland, he wrote a letter detailing his whereabouts. To support his letter and prove to Anja that he was well, Vladek attached a photographic portrait that he had made in "a photo place what had a camp uniform—a new and clean one—to make souvenir photos."[27] The image supplies a compelling "sign" that affirms, beyond any doubt and despite what he had to endure while wearing a much dirtier version of the same uniform: "Vladek is really alive!"[28]

And yet there is irony to the statement once Vladek's souvenir photograph is considered in light of the letter attached to it, which clearly states that Vladek has just recovered from typhus—a disease that should have left some visual marks. Instead, the photograph portrays a healthy-looking young man with a "full, full face . . . probably fuller than it was before the war. This fullness was a kind of fleshing out after the years of starvation, but [it] doesn't tell you about those years of starvation."[29] Many critics, including Spiegelman himself, have commented on the performative aspect of Vladek's studio photograph. Charles Hatfield, for example, is right to observe that "the mere fact that the uniform is new, clean and well-fitted belies the seeming documentary value of the image."[30] On his arrival at Auschwitz, as Vladek tells his son, the camp guards "threw to us prisoners clothings. They never even looked on what size they threw."[31] Vladek recounts that whenever someone tried to exchange uniforms or shoes for a better fit, he would get beaten by the guards. Mandelbaum, for instance, whom Vladek knew from before the war, was a wealthy man in Poland but in Auschwitz he was "a mess. His pants were big like for 2 people, and he had not even a piece of string to make a belt. He had all day to hold them with one hand."[32] When Vladek's account and Spiegelman's comics are juxtaposed with the perfectly fitted and starched camp uniform in the studio shot, we begin to doubt the ways in which photographs can support Spiegelman's narrative.

Of course, Vladek's studio shot is a staged photograph designed to be read not as a documentary device, but as a souvenir that artificially masks the horrible reality behind the studio curtain. Hatfield observes that "Spiegelman acknowledges the deliberate, posed quality of the image, and positions it to comment subtly on his father's version of events, as Vladek slowly slips into an idealized past." For Hatfield, "The photo speaks not to the documentary truth but to what we *want* to believe. It affirms Vladek as a hero, in spite of all we know."[33] Yet in *MetaMaus* Spiegelman partially disagrees with this reading. Although aware of Vladek's posing in the "costume version of his uniform," Spiegelman insists that we "get real information" from the photograph.[34] Not only do we "find out that . . . [Vladek] was a fairly good-looking guy," we also learn something about his charismatic and self-sufficient character.[35] Spiegelman explains:

> there's . . . the jauntiness of the angle at which he carries the cap . . . And the relative high-spiritedness of the facial expression and the hat just seem[s] so at odds with the person that I'd come to know through an entire lifetime as well as through the conversations about what he had

gone through. So to be left with a photo that tells you something, but only in relation to the drawn and written telling around it, informs what you thought you knew by making you re-examine it.[36]

Spiegelman challenges our knowledge by destabilizing what we thought to be true, thus hinting at the photograph's higher authority. Simultaneously, he positions himself as the master narrator that dictates the "correct" way of reading the text. Spiegelman's own words, not unlike the photographic promise, possess the power to certify interpretations that seem to be in a constant state of flux. By arguing that the photograph reassures Vladek's wife about his condition after the war, Hatfield already privileges the evidentiary quality of photography over any other kind of representation. Had it been a sketch, a statue, or a realistic portrait painting, it would have been less convincing than a single studio photograph. When read under the guidance of Spiegelman's master narrative in *MetaMaus*, the studio shot in *Maus* speaks to the "documentary truth" by privileging the photographic power to capture information more accurately than any other medium.[37]

And yet, even though Spiegelman's metatext functions as a master narrative, I refrain from taking it at face value. I read it instead as another mask which, much like a photograph, conceals an assortment of interpretations that "unravel Spiegelman's artifice."[38] Spiegelman's constant elucidation of the mask directs our attention to the self-reflexive and performative aspects of both his narrative

Photo detail from *Maus II: A Survivor's Tale: And Here My Troubles Began* (New York: Pantheon, 1991), p. 134.

"Self-Portrait with Mouse Mask," used in both volumes of *Maus*. Copyright © 1989 by Art Spiegelman.

and his metanarrative. Hirsch notes that Vladek's photograph "*performs* the identity of the camp inmate. Vladek wears a uniform in a souvenir shop in front of what looks like a stage curtain; he is no longer in the camp but he re-enacts his inmate self even as he is trying to prove—through his ability to pose—that he survived the inmate's fate."[39] Let us turn to this closed "stage curtain" in the background and read it in juxtaposition to the open curtain of Spiegelman's study in the iconic drawing used in the blurb for *Maus*.

The open curtain in the artist's study asks the audience to visualize what lies behind the closed curtain in the studio shot. This invitation to open the curtain parallels Spiegelman's gesture, in the introductory strip to *MetaMaus*, of removing the mouse mask in order to reveal what it conceals. The implication is that were we to pull back the curtain in the background of Vladek's souvenir shot, we would see the atrocities hidden beneath the staged photograph's smooth façade. We might glimpse perhaps the Nazi guard tower looming over the artist's studio as he attempts to visualize the past through mediated representation. The irony of the call to draw back the studio curtain lies, of course, in the fact that its removal, if at all possible, would reveal just another set of canonical images (other drawings or photographs), which in turn claim to reveal certain truths while obscuring others. Spiegelman's decision to include a photograph taken in a curtained set—an image that can only be decoded as part the book's larger multimedia stage performance—clarifies his understanding of how photography and comics relate to historical reality. Specifically, *Maus* duplicates not an abstract idea of "reality" but specific photographs (of the camps, of war-torn Europe, and of the Spiegelmans) recaptioned by the graphic memoir to show that although photography may hold documentary power, this power does not extend beyond the context we assign to photos, as we reframe and empanel them through more artificial arts such as cartooning and metacartooning.

PHOTOGRAPHY'S REAL FACE

Spiegelman's *Maus* undertook the unprecedented task of recording Vladek's account of the Holocaust not through the photographic medium, but in comic book form, depicting the atrocities of World War II through drawings that portray humans as anthropomorphic animals. Spiegelman's recourse to mask-like animalistic drawings, along with his explicit visual references to masks, reveal his awareness of the drawings' potential for distortion and illusion. To avoid the peril of being perceived as unreliable, Spiegelman turns to photographs to validate his narrative. Yet, much like the Deleuzian mask that promises to reveal a hidden truth while merely exposing a palimpsest of performances, the photographs in *Maus* perform a similar function.

I want to delineate three ways in which the photographs integrated in *Maus* deliberately obscure the past and furnish viewers with a conspicuously constructed version of reality. After discussing the discrepancy between the intercalated photographs and the comics narrative in *Maus*, I turn to the skewed position of the family portraits pinned on the comic strip canvas to analyze the theatricality of photographs in *Maus*. To further illustrate my point, I focus on the closed curtain in Vladek's studio photograph and the open curtain in the autobiographical strip of Spiegelman's study, where the cartoonist sits at his desk with a pile of corpses at his feet.

Spiegelman notes that the photographs in *Maus* function as a "visual phrase" to support and stabilize the drawings, which claim to tell a reliable account "at a time when autobiographical comics weren't quite as common" and comics in general were seen to appeal primarily to the readers' imagination.[40] Ron Mann's 1988 documentary *Comic Book Confidential,* which surveys the history of the comic book medium in the United States from the 1930s to the 1980s, argues that the comic book has developed into a sophisticated medium of social criticism. This elevation also requires a rethinking of the conventional view that cartoons are an innocent means of representation incapable of communicating serious subjects to their audience. Stan Lee, former president and chairman of Marvel Comics, is featured in the film with the statement that in his later period at Marvel, he and his coworkers sought to "get stories that while imaginative still had some realism, some believability. So that the readers could relate to and believe in the stories."[41] Unlike the comic books Lee describes, *Maus* emerged from an underground that had a richer tradition of autobiographical comics, starting with Justin Green's 1972 book, *Binky Brown Meets the Holy Virgin Mary.* As such, *Maus* does not present us with an imaginative, out-of-the-Holocaust superhero plot that makes marginal use of realistic strategies. Rather, it delivers a deeply historical, autobiographical narrative based on an interview with a Holocaust survivor. And yet, this realistic narrative is delivered in a way that might appear to subvert the story's reliability—through cartooning.

It seems that in order to bestow credibility on his narrative, Spiegelman inserts photographs to support the narrated events, for—as Hatfield rightly points out—the "reliance on photographic reference is part of the drive for historiographic authority that inevitably underlines any serious depiction of the Nazi genocide." Hatfield goes on to suggest that "Spiegelman takes pains to show himself digging for corroborative references, including . . . photo-reference."[42] The decision to enlist photography makes sense on many levels. However, although Spiegelman himself expects the photographs to stabilize the truth-value of his own as well as of his father's experiences as second- and first-generation Holocaust survivors, the images end up commenting on their own context by interrupting and destabilizing the visual language of the comic strip. After all, except for Vladek's camp uniform and the context in which the three photographs are set—a graphic memoir about an Auschwitz survivor—there is absolutely nothing in these photographs to indicate their affiliation with the Holocaust.

Within the space of the book, the photographs introduce an alternative medium that on the one hand functions as a "verifier, as an immediate, incontrovertible testimony," while on the other hand the presence of the photographs and their seemingly distorted image of the Holocaust—presented via undramatic family portraits of healthy-looking individuals—threatens the trustworthiness of the account and challenges the narrative's claim for authenticity.[43] From this perspective, then, the skewed position of the photographs on the pages of the graphic memoir confirms that the new comics framework holds the power of altering the photographs' original meaning. The photos' unfixed position is signified through the visible hand that holds Anja's photograph in front of the "Prisoner" comic strip and by Vladek's tilted photograph that does not seem to fit the frame allocated for it. This wobbly status underscores the significance of context in the formation of photographic meaning. The imperfect embedding of the pictures into Spiegelman's comics comments on the practice of assigning an unnatural context to photographic images in order to reshape their meaning. Rather than shoring up the evidentiary quality of Spiegelman's narrative, the slanted photographs ultimately undermine their own reliability in a constantly shifting context.

At first glance, the portraits inserted in *Maus* are jarring simply on account of their different representational quality, but the dissonance goes further than that, as they paradoxically and substantially distort the "true story" delivered through drawings and word balloons. Unlike the picture of Anja, taken in 1958 in the United States, Richieu's and Vladek's photographs date to the war period in Europe. Richieu's portrait presents us with a well-dressed, healthy-looking, plump-cheeked boy, an image whose bonhomie clashes with the wartime photographs of children that we have been exposed to through canonical photo archives of World War II. One might argue that Richieu's photograph was taken before the war, and if he had survived the camps he may not have ended up like the starved children in the familiar photographs, but more like the happy surviving children with their tidy white shirts and dark overalls who appear in the less familiar images that can be accessed in the Yad Vashem online photo archive.[44] Still, the fact that Richieu's photograph stands in stark contrast with the atrocities that Vladek narrates cannot be overlooked, especially at those junctures in the book when his story refers explicitly to children.

A short while after Vladek and Anja had placed Richieu in the care of Anja's sister, the Germans sent more than a thousand people from the ghetto to Auschwitz. Vladek explains that most of them were children: "some only 2 or 3 years. Some kids were screaming and screaming. They couldn't stop. So the Germans swinged them by the legs against a wall . . . and they never anymore screamed. In this way the Germans treated the little ones that still had survived a little."[45] Vladek confesses he did not witness the violence himself: "This I didn't see with my own eyes, but somebody the next day told me. And I said, 'Thank God . . . *our* children are safe!'"[46] This mediation, which marks Vladek's and his first-born's absence from the scene of the crime, is what allows Vladek, and by extension Spiegelman, to retain the image of Richieu as the "beautiful boy" in the photograph.[47] Of course, having been informed of the boy's tragic end, his photograph pierces us with the understanding that the image represents what is long gone, rather than what is. Richieu's photograph thus masks the dire reality of children during the war and exposes the discrepancies between the graphic and photographic modes of representation, which in *Maus* are set in a new relation. The child's photograph challenges the absolute truth-value of photography and thereby enhances the "believability" of the (seemingly nondocumentary) storytelling mode conveyed through comics. In other words, Spiegelman paradoxically evokes the documentary power of photography to indirectly elevate the documentary value of comics. While in themselves believable, photographs are limited by their capacity to represent only a single moment in a single place, both of which are easily transformed by new framing contexts. Comics as a medium is more malleable, and even though that flexibility might inspire ways to falsify reality, it also works well as a means against falsification.

MASKED TRUTHS, FRAGMENTED HISTORIES

As I have suggested, while Spiegelman's characters within the narrative—and, we may add, readers at large—trust the photographic medium as a mode of documentation, the photographs themselves, when integrated in the graphic memoir, destabilize their own claim for authenticity. Juxtaposed with the multiple simulated photographs, the real photographs fulfill a dual and somewhat contradictory function. Not only do they, as Hatfield notes, "assert . . . the falseness of Spiegelman's drawn 'photos' throughout the text," exposing the artificiality of the comics medium as vehicle for a story about the Holocaust. They also point to the artifice of the actual photos and their inability to represent the reality of that catastrophic event.[48] It is the physical frame of the family portraits that cannot capture this reality in its entirety, and the comics around them attempt to fill in the gaps. With this observation in mind, the stack of photographs at the bottom of page 115 in *Maus II* not only "refers back to the pile of bodies as it bleeds off the page," which is what Spiegelman proposes in *MetaMaus*.[49] It also comments on the impossibility of the comics page to contain all the information that historical World War II photographs claim to encompass. The absence of a frame at the bottom of this page highlights the limitations of the photographic frame—as well as the partiality of all frames for that matter. For the frame, by definition, be it the edge of the camera lens or a comics panel, excludes as much as it includes. It's an admission of defeat

From *Maus II: A Survivor's Tale: And Here My Troubles Began* (New York: Pantheon, 1991), p. 115. Copyright © 1986, 1989, 1990, 1991 by Art Spiegelman.

on Spiegelman's part, of modesty about the completeness of his story, as well as an appeal to the reader to trust the comics medium as readily—and as cautiously—as they rely on photography in learning about the past.

Photographs are masks of past events, as they create the sense that we can visually access what may otherwise have remained unrecorded. Much like the mask that conceals the face of the actor, so does the photograph veil the face of a past that remains present yet beyond our reach. The camera's capacity to produce what Roland Barthes called "certificate[s] of presence" due to its optical indexicality invites viewers to believe in its ability to communicate the past *as it was*.[50] However, rather than simply record historical events, the photograph fragments history by "freezing . . . a moment in the past" and transmitting this frozen moment—often accompanied by words—as if it were the temporally and spatially extended event in its entirety.[51] Analyzing photographs as masks in *Maus* could, as Nea Ehrlich suggests in her work on animated documentaries, "lead to an acceptance of [photography] as a form of masking, as a surface appearance of reality," which, despite its much-touted indexical properties, cannot be an unmediated representation of reality in an absolute sense.[52] This line of thinking might help eradicate the aura of facticity attached by default to photographic representations of colossal disasters, and lead to a reexamination of other media's evidentiary power. Spiegelman takes a step in this direction by including family photos in the melancholy fabric of *Maus*, providing a powerful precedent for a documentary comics form that distinguishes itself from photographic material and takes seriously the capacity of comics to evoke the past.

Notes

1. Paul Frosh, "The Public Eye and the Citizen-Voyeur: Photography as a Performance of Power," *Social Semiotics* 11, no. 1 (2001): 43.

2. Cornelia Brink, "Secular Icons: Looking at Photographs from Nazi Concentration Camps," *History & Memory* 12, no. 1 (2000): 135.

3. Brink, "Secular Icons," 136.

4. Frosh, "The Public Eye," 43.

5. Many readings of *Maus* address Spiegelman's employment of photographs and masks at some length, yet none discusses the relationship between the two. See, among others, Marianne Hirsch, "Family Pictures: *Maus*, Mourning, and Post-Memory," *Discourse* 15, no. 2 (Winter 1992–1993): 3–29; Michael Rothberg, "'We Were Talking Jewish': Art Spiegelman's *Maus* as 'Holocaust' Production,'" *Contemporary Literature* 35, no. 4 (1994): 661–87; Hirsch, "Mourning and Postmemory," in *Family Frames: Photography, Narrative, and Postmemory* (Cambridge, Mass.: Harvard University Press, 1997), 17–40; Andreas Huyssen, "Of Mice and Mimesis: Reading Spiegelman with Adorno," *New German Critique* 80 (2000): 65–82; Jeanne C. Ewert, "Reading Visual Narrative: Art Spiegelman's *Maus*," *Narrative* 8, no. 1 (2000): 87–103; Charles Hatfield, "Irony and Self-Reflexivity in Autobiographical Comics," in *Alternative Comics: An Emerging Literature* (Jackson: University Press of Mississippi, 2005), 128–51; Lisa A. Costello,

"History and Memory in a Dialogic of 'Performative Memorialization' in Art Spiegelman's *Maus: A Survivor's Tale*," *The Journal of the Midwest Modern Language Association* 39, no. 2 (2006): 22–42; Elisabeth R. Friedman, "Spiegelman's Magic Box: *MetaMaus* and the Archive of Representation," *Studies in Comics* 3, no. 2 (2012): 275–91.

6. Andreas Huyssen, "Of Mice and Mimesis," 81.

7. Art Spiegelman and Françoise Mouly, interview by Gary Groth in *The New Comics: Interviews from the Pages of The Comics Journal*, ed. Gary Groth and Robert Fiore (New York: Berkley Books, 1988), 190.

8. Huyssen, "Of Mice and Mimesis," 76.

9. Brink, "Secular Icons," 135.

10. See for example Martin Gilbert, *Never Again: A History of the Holocaust* (London: HarperCollins, 2000); Flavio Fiorani, *A New Illustrated History of World War II: Rare and Unseen Photographs 1939–1945* (Newton Abbot: David & Charles, 2005); Donald Sommerville and Ian Westwall, *The Complete Illustrated History of the First and Second World Wars* (London: Lorenz Books, 2010).

11. Roland Barthes, "Rhetoric of the Image," in *Image Music Text*, ed. and trans. Stephen Heath (London: Fontana Press, 1977), 46.

12. Gilles Deleuze, "Introduction: Repetition and Difference," in *Difference and Repetition* (New York: Columbia University Press, 1994), 20.

13. Ibid., 19.

14. Art Spiegelman, *MetaMaus: A Look Inside a Modern Classic*, Maus (New York: Pantheon, 2011), 9.

15. On Rabbi Meir Kahane, author of the manifesto *Never Again! A Program for Survival* (1971), see Eric J. Sundquist, "Black Power, Jewish Power," in *Strangers in the Land: Blacks, Jews, Post-Holocaust America* (Cambridge, Mass.: Harvard University Press, 2009).

16. Spiegelman, *MetaMaus*, 146.

17. Friedman, "Spiegelman's Magic Box," 276.

18. Spiegelman, *MetaMaus*, 150.

19. Walter Benjamin, "The Work of Art in the Age of Mechanical Reproduction," in *Illuminations: Essays and Reflections* (New York: Schocken Books, 2007), 223.

20. Tim Dant and Graeme Gilloch, "Pictures of the Past: Benjamin and Barthes on Photography and History," *European Journal of Cultural Studies* 5, no. 1 (2002): 7.

21. Dant and Gilloch, "Pictures of the Past," 7.

22. Dant and Gilloch, "Pictures of the Past," 7.

23. Dant and Gilloch, "Pictures of the Past," 7.

24. Spiegelman, *MetaMaus*, 220.

25. Marianne Hirsch, "The Generation of Postmemory," *Poetics Today* 29, no. 1 (Spring 2008): 116.

26. Spiegelman, *Maus*, 294.

27. Spiegelman, *Maus*, 294.

28. Spiegelman, *Maus*, 294.

29. Spiegelman, *MetaMaus*, 220.

30. Hatfield, "Irony and Self-Reflexivity," 147.

31. Spiegelman, *Maus*, 186.

32. Spiegelman, *Maus*, 189.

33. Hatfield, "Irony and Self-Reflexivity," 150, original emphasis.

34. Spiegelman, *MetaMaus*, 220.

35. Spiegelman, *MetaMaus*, 220.

36. Spiegelman, *MetaMaus*, 220, 222.

37. Hatfield, "Irony and Self-Reflexivity," 150.

38. Hatfield, "Irony and Self-Reflexivity," 149.

39. Marianne Hirsch, "Family Pictures," 24.

40. Spiegelman, *MetaMaus*, 218. On the history of autobiographical comics before and after *Maus*, see Jared Gardner, "Autography's Biography, 1972–2007," *Biography* 31, no. 1 (2008): 1–26; Hillary L. Chute, *Graphic Women: Life Narrative and Contemporary Comics* (New York: Columbia University Press, 2010) as well as *Disaster Drawn: Visual Witness, Comics, and Documentary Form* (Cambridge, Mass.: Harvard University Press, 2016); Elisabeth El Refaie, *Autobiographical Comics: Life Writing in Pictures* (Jackson: University Press of Mississippi, 2012); Andrew J. Kunka, *Autobiographical Comics* (London: Bloomsbury, 2018).

41. Stan Lee in Ron Mann, *Comic Book Confidential*, 1988 (Chicago: Home Vision Entertainment, 2002), 32:50, DVD.

42. Hatfield, "Irony and Self-Reflexivity," 145–46.

43. Hatfield, "Irony and Self-Reflexivity," 150.

44. http://yadvashem.org/

45. Spiegelman, *Maus*, 110 (original ellipsis).

46. Spiegelman, *Maus*, 110.

47. Spiegelman, *Maus*, 111.

48. Hatfield, "Irony and Self-Reflexivity," 150.

49. Spiegelman, *MetaMaus*, 222.

50. Roland Barthes, *Camera Lucida: Reflections on Photography* (London: Vintage, 2000), 87.

51. Dant and Gilloch, "Pictures of the Past," 6.

52. Nea Ehrlich, "Animated Documentaries as Masking," *Animation Studies: Online Journal for Animation History and Theory* 6 (2011).

ART IMITATING LIFE

Traumatic Affect in Art Spiegelman's *Maus* and Holocaust Cinema

HARRIET EARLE

Of all the statements made on the impact of the Holocaust, Theodor Adorno's 1955 dictum that "to write poetry after Auschwitz is barbaric" counts among the most influential.[1] Much like Nietzsche's "God is dead," this striking line has suffered from inflationary overuse in contexts that seek to emphasize the absolute horror of the concentration camps. What occurred there was so unimaginable, many suggest, that it is impossible to create art in its aftermath. However, this interpretation takes Adorno's statement out of context, and Adorno himself later agreed that he was speaking hyperbolically. In his 1966 book *Negative Dialectics*, he elaborates:

> Perennial suffering has as much right to expression as a tortured man has to scream; hence it may have been wrong to say that after Auschwitz you could no longer write poems. But it is not wrong to raise the less cultural question whether after Auschwitz you can go on living—especially whether one who escaped by accident, one who by rights should have been killed, may go on living. . . . By way of atonement he will be plagued by dreams such as that he is no longer living at all, that he was sent to the ovens in 1944 and his whole existence since has been imaginary, an emanation of the insane wish of a man killed twenty years earlier.[2]

Art Spiegelman's *Maus* seeks to address Adorno's question: How *do* we create art after the atrocities of Auschwitz? I posit that Spiegelman brings together testimony and traumatic affect—the kind of emotion engendered by the intensity of trauma—to ensure that his text is both firmly rooted in personal history and able to elicit a strong emotive response in the reader. While it is impossible for a text to fully mimic the trauma of an experience—to traumatize the reader, so to speak—it is possible to induce intense emotions and to bestow on the reader part of the wider experience contained in the narrative.

In this essay, I adopt a tripartite structure to explore Spiegelman's emotional approach to his family story and, more broadly, the role of emotion in creating art after the Holocaust. First, I consider the narratives that came before *Maus* and the preexisting environment of Holocaust remembering and reflection into which Spiegelman released his graphic memoir. Specifically, I discuss *Death Mills* (1946) and *Nuit et Brouillard* (1956), two key cinematic works in this canon, to consider what influences likely played a part in the creation of *Maus*'s distinctive aesthetic. Second, I look at three aspects of *Nuit et Brouillard*—the black-and-white visuals, the iconic image of the Auschwitz gates, and the fact that violence is kept off-screen—before considering how Spiegelman uses similar techniques to convey traumatic affect. I close by asking how we can measure the legacy of Spiegelman's aesthetic of trauma in both the contemporary comics world and the wider fields of trauma art and Holocaust representation.

SPEAKING OF TRAUMA

Before discussing *Maus* in detail, I wish to return to Adorno. The shift in his understanding trauma and its relationship to "speakability" mirrors the development of trauma theory from the late 1890s to the present day. Elsewhere, I have written at length on the transformations that occurred in trauma studies across this period.[3] The founding text of trauma theory is arguably Sigmund Freud's 1896 study *The Aetiology of Hysteria*, which examines the now-defunct diagnosis of hysteria and its effect on the mental functioning of young women. Freud continued this line of inquiry with his patients until the returning servicemen of World War I caused him to reconsider his position. Observing the reactions of these men to the mental injuries inflicted by warfare and to the shock of coming home, he shifted his focus onto "war neuroses." In 1920 he published *Beyond the Pleasure Principle*, taking his earlier work on traumatic neurosis further and expanding his pool of case studies to include combat veterans.

The model of trauma studies developed from the works of Freud and his ideological descendants, including Jacques Lacan and Cathy Caruth, can be labelled the "classic model." This school of thought holds that a traumatic event is one for which the mind has no integrating coping mechanism. In the words of Anne Whitehead, "trauma . . . overwhelms the individual and resists language or representation."[4] This is one of the most problematic limitations of the classic model—the notion that trauma resists representation. The classic model suggests unrepresentability to be an axiomatic part of trauma that affects all traumatized individuals equally and without exception. In this sense, the Freudian model of trauma resonates with Adorno's first statement: Auschwitz is not speakable. The attempted utterances of survivors and the representations of nonwitnesses are of little value, because the core of the experience is lost in the creation of traumatic memory.

By recanting his earlier ideas in the longer statement discussed above, Adorno positions himself closer to contemporary trauma theory than to the classic model. In her introduction to an anthology on contemporary trauma, Michelle Balaev writes: "One result of trauma's classic conundrum removes agency from the survivor by disregarding a survivor's knowledge of the experience and the self, which restricts trauma's variability and ignores the diverse values that change over time."[5] Rather than accept the blanket definition of trauma as an unrepresentable knot in the center of one's experience, contemporary trauma theory insists that, while difficult, representation is by no means impossible. The experience itself is a personal event that may be similar to those of others, but remains in the emotional possession of the individual, who is able to access representational strategies to speak about the poignant past. This is not to say that there is no crisis of representation at the core of trauma, but to suggest that this crisis is not insurmountable, as the classic trauma model insists. More accurately, in this view, the crisis of representation refers to *how* exactly the individual represents to others an event that affected them in personal and complex ways, a formulation that diverges from the belief that the crisis is of representation per se. In light of this reworking of trauma theory, Adorno's question about living after Auschwitz becomes one of how, not if: How does the individual respond to this event, and how do they represent their experience?

Turning from Adorno's theoretical statements to Spiegelman's work, we can see how a contemporary understanding of trauma and representation manifests itself aesthetically. I suggest that Spiegelman's most important contribution to narratives of the Holocaust and family survival is not the story itself, variations of which had been told before, but his bold, almost irreverent artistic choices. *Maus* avoids moral clichés and invites the reader to participate emotionally in the recreation of both people and events. In his portrait of Vladek, Spiegelman writes a realistic, multifaceted character of greater complexity and fallibility than the long-suffering and virtuous trauma victim seen in earlier testimonial writings—such as Elie Wiesel's *Night* (especially the French translation, as opposed to the original Yiddish manuscript), Władysław Szpilman's *The Pianist* (1946), or *The Diary of Anne Frank* (1947).

While these uplifting representations now seem stereotypical, they are useful as signposts to a condition, and to show how humanity can survive under inhuman circumstances; yet they also tend to lack nuance. In contrast, Spiegelman's carefully considered personal story draws the reader into the narrative through its cautious use of affect, while also shutting us out by depicting Spiegelman's father firmly as an individual rather than an everyman. This kind of characterization has become more commonplace since the publication of *Maus*. Indeed, such characters have become easier to write as those who remember the events firsthand have aged and passed on. A morally ambiguous Jewish survivor was unlikely to be a popular character in the decades following the war, when knowledge of the Holocaust was still coming out. In recent years, narratives are changing to fit not only the available information—with the Jewish *Sonderkommandos*, "crematorium ravens"[6] who disposed of gas chamber victims, featured in films such as *The Grey Zone* (2001) and *Son of Saul* (2015)—but the facets of human nature that we know to be true.

VISUALIZING AUSCHWITZ IN *NUIT ET BROUILLARD* AND *MAUS*

The 1956 Cannes Film Festival was marked by a peculiar scandal. *Nuit et Brouillard*, Alain Resnais's thirty-two-minute documentary on the Holocaust, was banned following German protests and anxiety within the French government regarding the film's use of archival material.[7] *Nuit et Brouillard* is painful to watch, unflinching. Color footage of Auschwitz in the mid-1950s and monochrome footage of the same camp after the liberation in January 1945 are presented side by side, accompanied by a lyrical commentary by French poet and Holocaust survivor, Jean Cayrol (the translation into German was provided by another poet-survivor, Paul Celan). The film features deportations and piles of emaciated corpses; one particularly harrowing scene shows human flesh being rendered down for the making of soap. The narrator does not employ euphemism, nor does he soften the images through his descriptions.

The main reason for removing the film from the festival was to avoid anti-German sentiment following the film's release. However, as Andrew Hebard notes, the German reaction to the film was unexpected: "Within months it was being shown at film festivals and film clubs in German cities. Willy Brandt, then president of the Berlin House of Commons, came out with a statement explicitly supporting the film."[8] The German government's response, in conjunction with the growing interest in the events of the Holocaust and an overwhelming belief that they should never be allowed to happen again, led to *Nuit et Brouillard*'s firm status as a key visual document of the Holocaust and a landmark of documentary cinema. I mention it here for two reasons. First, it is one of the most influential visual works in the creation of the "Holocaust aesthetic" that Spiegelman uses in *Maus*. Second, it was one of the earliest major artworks to address the Holocaust and was met with a scandal similar to the one that befell *Maus* thirty years later.

Holocaust documentary did not start with *Nuit et Brouillard*, though Resnais's film is often spoken of with exalted fervor and has accumulated a vast array of honors and awards. The first Holocaust documentary is arguably *Death Mills* (1945), a product of the US Department of War—dissolved two years after the film's release—and a scant twenty-two minutes in length. It was intended to screen for German audiences to inform them of the atrocities of the Holocaust and was first shown in its German-language version in 1946. Unlike much of what has followed, *Death Mills* employs few narrative flourishes. As with *Nuit et Brouillard*, the camps are shown in stark images shot by their liberators. In one scene, a pair of hands sifts through a wooden tray filled with wedding bands. In another, a British Army bulldozer pushes bodies into a mass grave. Also in common with *Nuit et Brouillard* is the absence of any information on the high number of Jewish victims. This became a bone of contention for viewers of Resnais's film (as it did for readers of William Styron's *Sophie's Choice* with its Catholic protagonist), since it was felt the director was attempting to either erase or silence the impact of the genocide on the Jewish community.

Death Mills adopts a similar focus on the national, ethnic, political, and religious mix found in the camps. There are several markers in *Death Mills* that also feature in *Nuit et Brouillard*, but the tone of the two films is strikingly different. The former is clearly a product of the bureaucratic War Department, appearing cold and stark in its handling of the subject. The overarching statement of the film is: "This happened." In contrast, *Nuit et Brouillard* asks us "Who is responsible?"—with the unspoken addition: "Is it not all of us?"[9] As the novelist Jay Cantor suggests, "Resnais makes the horrible ordinary, so we might believe it; and then he makes the ordinary horrible, so that we might fear it."[10] In *Nuit et Brouillard* we can see the groundwork being laid not only for *Maus*, but for the majority of Holocaust art and representation. Indeed, as Griselda Pollock and Max Silverman write in their introduction to *Concentrationary Cinema*, *Nuit et Brouillard* is "perhaps the most influential, significant and certainly the most widely shown film on these events ever made."[11]

Some aspects of Resnais's film remain unassimilable in Spiegelman's graphic memoir. To include a narrator speaking in languid, poetic sentences, as Resnais does, may alienate the reader from the story. There is a narrator in the shape of Vladek, but his presence is more conversational and less omniscient than Cayrol's voiceover—generally more fallible and self-doubting, in keeping with the book's complicated moral stakes. Moreover, *Nuit et Brouillard* is a collection of images and explanations that render the overall experience of a place, without telling a coherent and chronological narrative with recognizable characters beyond the types that we see: the inmates, the captors, and the liberators.

In his comment on the international reception of Resnais's film, Ewout van de Knaap writes that *Nuit et Brouillard* is "based on dramatic conventions traditionally used to depict the Holocaust: in broad terms, it chronologically deals with the chain of deportation, organization and destruction."[12] We see the same markers throughout *Maus*, albeit from the reverse perspective. As the reader follows Vladek's story, he hears rumors from his friends and colleagues of German Jews being deported to ghettos (*Maus I*: 35). Further into the text, we see evidence of increased organization among the Nazis, most critically in the census taken at the Dienst Stadium (*Maus I*: 90–93). Finally, Vladek and Anja arrive at Auschwitz and a fuller picture of the true horror is revealed (*Maus I*: 159). Aside from this narrative diagram, Spiegelman adopts from *Nuit et Brouillard* not only the black-and-white visuals and the iconic architecture of Auschwitz, but he also relegates violence off the screen. I address each of the three aspects (color schemes, architecture, and violence) in order, and explain their relevance to both *Maus* and Holocaust art.

It is hardly surprising that early Holocaust documentaries and photographic records are in black and white, as such was the nature of 1940s imaging technology. However, black and white is a widely used artistic choice for Holocaust art, as demonstrated not only in *Maus* but also Steven Spielberg's award-winning film *Schindler's List* (1993) and a wide selection of comics from Dave Sim's *Judenhass* (2008) to Michel Kichka's *Second Generation: Things I Never Told My Father* (2012). This is partly because, as one critic put it, "imitating the black and white film grain of the archival footage [can effectively evoke] the celluloid memory of Holocaust history."[13] Comics in particular have fought against their reputation as a lowbrow form, ill-suited to telling serious stories. Some of this reputation has to do with their cartoonish artwork and bold, sometimes brash, colors. Removing the coloration allows stories of the Holocaust to sit apart from the bright "funnies" that came before them, and gives the narrative a different, somber feel. I would not go so far as to suggest that it lends them a documentary veracity, but the removal of color does add a level of gravitas to the work and has an immediate, striking effect on the reader, who expects color from the medium and receives monochrome instead.

In his monograph on Spiegelman, Philip Smith makes the point that "for an audience whose understanding of the Shoah has developed primarily through film and literature it is hard to imagine the Shoah as having taken place in color."[14] Smith further notes that "the use of black and white has come to signify memory, history, heritage, and identity as well as historical authenticity."[15] The black-and-white artwork in *Maus* never blurs to gray, but remains stark, in unyielding contrast to the shades of gray that attach to the moral constitution of the characters. This is noteworthy not least because Spiegelman's earlier work in *Breakdowns* (1977) and as editor of *RAW* magazine (1980 to 1991) uses

Still from *Night and Fog*, directed by Alain Resnais, 1956. Copyright © 2011 by Optimum Releasing.

bold coloration in line with the underground comix movement's spoofing of mainstream comics conventions. His post-9/11 comic *In the Shadow of No Towers* also uses color to mimic early twentieth-century newspaper funnies. The lack of color in *Maus* allows it to sit apart from Spiegelman's more distinctly humorous works.

One of the most evocative symbols of the Holocaust—and one that has become a cultural icon of atrocity and horror—is the architecture of Auschwitz, particularly its gates and observation towers. The distinctive shape of the gates and the words "Arbeit macht frei" have become a metonym for the crimes carried out inside the camp.[16] The words emblazoned on the gate have come to represent the central lie of the Final Solution: "work will set you free" suggests hope of release and the exhortation of a strong work ethic as a path to freedom. It was in *Nuit et Brouillard* that the gates were first used to demarcate the entry to the camps. Resnais even goes into some detail about the different types of architecture used in creating the towers. Film scholar Libby Saxton makes the point that "Cayrol's commentary transforms the towers from optical machines into objects of aesthetic judgment: 'alpine style, garage style, Japanese style, no style.'"[17]

Spiegelman is drawing on this aesthetic history when the gates appear in the closing pages of *Maus I*. The fact that this single image evokes an immediate, visceral response, and unlocks a vast amount of unspoken information about the experience of those who were there, helps to craft the narrative of

From *Maus I: A Survivor's Tale: My Father Bleeds History* (New York: Pantheon, 1986), p. 157. Copyright © 1973, 1980, 1981, 1982, 1982, 1984, 1985, 1986 by Art Spiegelman.

the Holocaust and negate the unspeakability often associated with it. Spiegelman deploys the image of the gates to give credence and factual weight to his account, as well as emotional resonance to Vladek's story, allowing the voices of the millions who died to resonate under the surface of the text, while maintaining a narrative focus on his family's individual experience.

In comics, where icons and visual cues are essential to the narrative, recognizable images of emotional and connotative weight can be very useful. The camp architecture certainly fits into this category. Yet there are a number of issues with using the image of the gates in this way. In *Holocaust Icons*, Oren Stier writes that the gates and the words "Arbeit macht frei" have come to represent "the entire camp system and its logic."[18] He adds that "the infamous gate at Auschwitz (and elsewhere in the concentration and death camp network) has served an emblematic function within Holocaust memorial culture for some time. Survivors and memory-tourists alike have seen it as central to their wartime or postwar Holocaust experiences, and for many it symbolizes the Shoah in its entirety."[19] And yet, despite its central position in Holocaust memory, the gate itself was largely insignificant to the camps and the prisoners themselves. In their comprehensive history of the camp, Debórah Dwork and Robert Jan van Pelt note that the gate "played no role in the Judeocide. Indeed, very few of the Jews deported to Auschwitz ever saw that gate."[20]

Spiegelman's inclusion of the gates may hint at the facile iconization of the Holocaust that works by conflating historical and memorial representations, authenticity and feeling. Whether subversively or not, both Resnais and Spiegelman situate the gates as central icons within the Holocaust aesthetic and cement their place there, despite their documented existence at the fringes of the camp's geography and the day-to-day reality of imprisonment. Of course, Spiegelman uses the loaded image of the gates to convey information quickly, but in doing so he runs the risk of making this image into an example of Holocaust kitsch. The tension is never resolved—either in the book or outside it—as the gates have become a visual metonym for Auschwitz and the Holocaust more broadly.

The final aspect of *Nuit et Brouillard* that *Maus* adopts is, as with the lack of coloration, related to the nature of the film material on which it is based. Explicit violence in both *Nuit et Brouillard* and *Maus* is kept off-screen. As most of the footage in Resnais's documentary was shot by the camp liberators, there is no direct visual record of the violence experienced by those inside. It goes without saying, then, that the violence can only be implied rather than expressly shown. In *Maus*, however, Spiegelman's decision is not based on a lack of film evidence. Spiegelman could choose to show us violence if he wished—as Pascal Croci does, to questionable effect, in his 2003 graphic novel *Auschwitz*—and he is not wary of depicting the aftermath of violence, with recurrent images of mice hanging from gallows or trees. But the animal allegory dilutes the violence of the text, while drawing on cultural touchstones that are widely recognizable, especially Western children's cartoons.

This is not to say that *Maus* does not engage with violence at all. Aside from one explicit panel showing mice being engulfed by flames, their mouths open in Munch-like screams, Spiegelman uses a range of objects as oblique cognates for violence. To begin with, the text contains a large number of labeled diagrams, including schematics of hidden bunkers (*Maus I*: 110). Presented in simplified drawings, as if by an architect or designer, the spaces are indistinguishable from the camps, especially as there is a similar drawing of Auschwitz on the back of the book itself. Yet in creating this visual link, Spiegelman makes the important point that the violence of the Holocaust was not restricted to the camps, but was felt across many levels of society and social interaction. The systemic violence of the Nazi state forced entire groups of people to live in the shadow of persecution and fear.

The fact that graphic violence in *Maus* occurs mainly off-screen, is presented obliquely, or only shown after the fact, allows the reader to engage with the text imaginatively and affectively. As comics readers, we are forced into a higher level of interaction with the text by having to move across panels. Situating violence off-page or in the panel gutters allows the reader to imagine—and in a sense to recreate—the violence, thereby distributing the burden of representation between creator and reader. It is through this investment in affect that the book's full power can be felt, despite its rejection of straightforward brutality. *Maus* absorbs key tropes from *Nuit et Brouillard* in ways that solidify their importance to both the comics form and the visual memory of the Holocaust. But Spiegelman's use of the comics medium moves beyond the technical limitations of Resnais's film, while building on aspects of the documentary that are both effective and affective.

TRAUMATIC AFFECT ON THE SCREEN AND ON THE PAGE

Both Resnais and Spiegelman use affect to draw the viewer in and evoke a response. Yet their techniques are markedly different. In *Nuit et Brouillard*, the most emotional strategy is arguably the use of archival footage presented with minimal reflection and discussion. The voiceover describes but does not explain or expound, leaving it to the viewer to make sense of the images without the added guidance of a narrator's voice. As van der Knaap writes, the "power of representation through images can be so strong that the pictures blot out the events themselves. The observation about this priority of representation above the represented leads us to the fundamental question of whether we will ever grasp the truth of historical events."[21] By the very nature of trauma, we cannot fully understand someone else's experiences without having confronted them ourselves, and even then, we may perceive them differently. If we consider Spiegelman's text not through the uniformity-demanding lens of classic trauma but through contemporary trauma theory, we cannot simply think of personal symptoms or the individual as the sole analytical framework for representation. Instead, artistic affect is a productive lens through which traumatic representation retains its individuality, while also circumventing the rigid symptomology of the classic method and acknowledging the sociocultural and historical aspects of trauma.

I have written elsewhere that "affect is at once both delightfully simple and notoriously complex."[22] For Aristotle, affect is "that which leads one's condition to become so transformed that his judgment is affected, and which is accompanied by pleasure and pain."[23] The aim of art is to imitate actions so as to provoke reactions. The work of Aristotle and later philosophers, such as William James, forms the basis of affect theory. Félix Guattari and Gilles Deleuze have expounded at great length upon the subject, writing that art is "a bloc of sensations, that is to say, a compound of percepts and affects."[24] Though their formulation directly references "art," the term can be taken to mean all artistic representation and not just the visual arts. Acknowledging Deleuze and Guattari, the theorist and artist Simon O'Sullivan insists that "you cannot read affects, you can only experience them."[25] In this view, affect must be felt rather than explored because it encapsulates the means by which a text can convey something beyond stark facts.

Writing on affect and literature, Derek Attridge suggests that literature can engage "powerfully and subtly" with human emotional response.[26] His example is a written scene in which a character is decapitated. A gory description may fail to provoke a response in the audience unless it is precisely calibrated to do so. Further examples can be found in the related film genres of horror and comedy horror: What is terrifying in one becomes amusing in the other. While the action itself may be similar, the framing is not. All sorts of production techniques are involved in creating this distinction—including soundtrack, voiceover, lighting, choice of dialogue, and choreography. In comics, the coloration, gutters, captioning, and literary style affect the way an image or scene is read, and the extent to which the representation is emotionally effective. In other words, it is the depiction of disturbing events, not their mere retelling, that holds affective power.

When Spiegelman describes Jewish toddlers being killed by Nazi soldiers, he does so to maximize the reader's emotive response. Vladek's voiceover reports matter-of-factly: "Some kids were screaming and screaming. They couldn't stop. So the Germans swinged them by the legs against a wall. And they never

From *Maus I: A Survivor's Tale: My Father Bleeds History* (New York: Pantheon, 1986), p. 108. Copyright © 1973, 1980, 1981, 1982, 1982, 1984, 1985, 1986 by Art Spiegelman.

more screamed."[27] The panel shows a German soldier from the back and a child's lower body, accompanied by a large dark "splat" on a brick wall. The following panel shows the same soldier, holding a leg, while the bloodstain is covered by Vladek's speech bubble. Attridge suggests that affect relies on form over theme: Anyone can write a gruesome or traumatic scene, but it is in the careful formal crafting that the scene becomes affective. By refusing to show the violence head-on, relying instead on partial glimpses and half-obscured events, Spiegelman asks readers to fill the gaps using their own imagination and preexisting knowledge of events. Much of this information has already been outlined in the text, so the reader can extrapolate; the rest is drawn from personal experience and understanding. We know what 'splat' normally denotes, and we can tell what is happening in the image. Paired with our knowledge—and the text's explanations—of the soldiers' violence, the image acquires its full affective weight. The starkness of the accompanying text and the alienating quality of Vladek's nonnative grammar completes this effect.

Spiegelman mobilizes the full range of comics' formal techniques to trigger a heightened emotional response and, in doing so, allows us to grasp at least a small part of the experience of trauma. Yet he is acutely aware that he cannot fully represent his father's experience of the Holocaust and he does not claim that *Maus* aims to do anything of the sort. In fact, he speaks frankly about his inability to fully recreate the story and about the limitations of the form. His alter ego in the book discusses affect in a literal sense with his psychiatrist, Paul Pavel, also a camp survivor:

> ARTIE: Some part of me doesn't want to draw or think about Auschwitz. I can't visualize it clearly and I can't BEGIN to imagine what it felt like.

PAVEL: What Auschwitz felt like? Hmm . . . how can I explain . . . ? BOO!
ARTIE: (leaping up) YIII!
PAVEL: It felt a little like THAT. But ALWAYS![28]

The interaction suggests that through Pavel, Artie comes to understand how the visceral response to trauma can be turned into artistic affect, an important representational tool for his book. Attridge reminds us that "the emotions experienced by the reader of a work of literature are real; of this there can surely be no doubt."[29] Comics in particular rely on readers' input to move the narrative forward, as readers are complicit in creating links between panels and pages as they progress through the text. These formal features of comics only enhance the intensity of traumatic affect.

Maus invites the reader to experience emotion by also showing us a series of characters who are themselves moved by the emotions of others, by past events, and by affect that travels through time. In one scene, Vladek and Artie are walking while Vladek continues to tell the story of the time he and Anja spent in a detention area in Srodula. Vladek's cousin, Haskel, a *Kombinator* (or crook), helps them to escape and find work. Haskel embodies the skewed morality and self-interest that sometimes took hold during the Holocaust. Vladek acknowledges that Haskel is a schemer, that his methods are both unconventional and morally questionable. So Haskel survives the war, using his contacts and scheming to get by, but the memory of his methods has remained with Vladek; while he does not necessarily practice them himself, many of Vladek's behaviors are influenced by the way Haskel acted. Reflecting on this section of the story, James Young suggests that "the very memory seems to stop Vladek's heart as he grabs his chest. The narrative is one thing, the heart-stopping anxiety it produces in the teller is another. Both are portrayed here—the story and the effect on the teller himself."[30] Vladek's emotional response in remembering his time with Haskel in Srodula, graphically represented on the page, links back to Artie's 'YIII!' in Pavel's office and further connects the reader to the narrative.

In reading *Maus*, we have already experienced complex and potentially uncomfortable emotions. By the time we reach this section of the book, Spiegelman is asking us to model our reactions on Vladek's—an extreme pain in the chest and an overwhelming sense of sadness and confusion. Up to this point, the text has been setting us up to feel disgust, horror, and a number of other unpleasant emotions, but there are also moments of joy and fun. In part, these responses are shaped by our cultural understanding of the Holocaust. We are supposed to feel negative emotions when confronted with this horrible event; if we do not, the implication is that something is lacking in our mental and emotional processing. The memoir is therefore carefully constructed to work with our existing feelings towards the Holocaust and to engender revulsion in us. We meet (and presumably grow to like) the young newlyweds Vladek and Anja before witnessing their part in the story of one of the most traumatic events in modern history. We are invested in their lives from the beginning and in a different way from how we relate to filmic narratives. This has to do with the heavy amount of reader participation required by the serial development of a comics narrative, while film remains a mostly passive aesthetic form with comparatively little viewer input.

Affect allows a reader who has no personal insight into a traumatic situation to connect to the wider experience through a visceral response to a particular artistic text. Of course, this is not to say the emotions that arise from engaging with affective art are the same as those experienced when engaging directly with an event. However, this is not what affective art in general—and *Maus* in particular—aims to do. Affect is channeled not only through theme, but more crucially through form. We become upset from viewing images of individuals in concentration camps, for example, because this is a typical response to such stimuli. To feel distress while reading *Maus*, however, suggests that the reader has become emotionally bound up in the form as well as the theme. As Michael Staub notes:

> *Maus* does not necessarily introduce historical materials unfamiliar to scholars or students of the Nazi genocide, nor does it add substantially to existing descriptions of the conditions concentration camp inmates experienced. What it does do is present a story of this "central trauma of the Twentieth Century" that is much more accessible to a general audience than many other accounts, because it is particularly effective at inviting emotional involvement.[31]

Spiegelman's ability to stir his readers with the complexities and nuances of his father's experiences is its greatest success; thanks to this accomplishment, "*Maus* redrew the contractual terms for depictions of the Holocaust in popular art."[32] We recognize its legacy in a number of Holocaust narratives, including Joe Kubert's *Yossel* (2003) and perhaps most notably Bernice Eisenstein's *I Was a Child of Holocaust Survivors* (2006), which shares the focus of *Maus* on the artist's parents' unspoken traumatic past. Spiegelman has also been noted as a key influence on Marjane Satrapi, creator of the award-winning memoir *Persepolis* (2000–2003) that details the author's experiences as a child during the Iranian Revolution. In ways that many of these works have emulated, in order to mobilize traumatic affect Spiegelman uses a series of palimpsests of past and present. He breaks down the usual boundaries of time to overlay memories of the past with images of the present or, more specifically, with images of how the past is remembered in the present. In the words of Lawrence Weschler, it is not a case of "whether [his] father was telling the truth, but rather, just what had he actually lived through—what did he understand of what he experienced, what did he tell of what he understood, what did [Spiegelman] understand of what he told, and what [did Spiegelman] tell? The layers begin to multiply like pane upon pane of glass."[33] In collapsing past and present into one, Spiegelman is representing the pervasiveness of trauma in Vladek's day-to-day life, while making the reader acutely aware of the conflation and emotional friction between temporal planes.

It is not only in the story-focused sections of *Maus* that Spiegelman uses traumatic affect. In the second chapter of *Maus II* (titled "Auschwitz: Time Flies"), he presents an honest and violent image of the creative process and the myriad issues that accompanied the success of *Maus I*. Spiegelman draws himself as an unkempt man in a mouse mask, sitting at his drawing table, surrounded by flies. The first four panels, uniform in size, shape, and perspective, involve Art speaking to the reader directly about his father's death and the success of *Maus I*. The fifth panel, considerably larger, shows him slumped forward on his table atop a pile of emaciated, mouse-headed corpses, with a camp watchtower visible outside the window. The final statement on the page is: "Lately I've been feeling depressed."[34] If we could ignore the corpses, this is surely an image that many creative people could relate to. The addition of the bodies and the watchtower, unequivocal symbols of the horrors of the camps, echoes the icons that despite their inaccuracies have become metonyms for the Holocaust. This does not remove the initial connection we made with Artie's ennui, which remains despite the obvious disconnect between his words in the first four panels and the bodies in the fifth—an excellent example of the "push-pull" effect I mentioned earlier. We engage because we recognize ennui and depression, but we are disconnected because we do not "know" the experiences of a second-generation survivor, just as Artie is disconnected from his father because he is not a direct survivor himself.

Despite their differences in visual representation, both *Nuit et Brouillard* and *Maus* recreate the experiences of the camps to show us the "reality" of the Holocaust. Of course, reality is a slippery, difficult term, especially when we apply the muddying filters of trauma and memory. Many images of the Holocaust have in fact become oversaturated with meaning and risk being made vacuous by sheer repetition; Spiegelman himself remains skeptical of their value. *Nuit et Brouillard*, *Death Mills*, and other works that draw heavily on contemporaneous footage rely on the authenticity of their archival sources as a truthful rendering of events. In the case of *Nuit et Brouillard*, the starkness of the images is mediated through the voiceover (written by a survivor), which places the images in the wider context of the camps, while not allowing them to lose any of their shock and horror. Embedding the same images in the more

From *Maus II: A Survivor's Tale: And Here My Troubles Began* (New York: Pantheon, 1991), p. 42. Copyright © 1986, 1989, 1990, 1991 by Art Spiegelman.

private frame of the family, for Weschler *Maus* "[sketches] a low-definition revision of the high-definition detail of the newsreel Nazis and the Holocaust footage. . . . The pictures lack detail but not depth, the low-definition medium enhancing the deep involvement of the reader."[35] Spiegelman's artistic choices give the reader a "way in"—a way for us to achieve a partial understanding of what Vladek and his family endured, through techniques that make their distress seem close and proximate, something we can (albeit only distantly) partake in. The memoir makes us feel, but also reminds us that we cannot really feel quite the same terror that its protagonists experienced—a tension that Art and the reader are painfully aware of throughout. The difficulty of feeling enough, of coming close to the original terror, compounds the emotional pressure of *Maus*, making it into a book that sets impossible affective standards which we nevertheless attempt, each time, to fulfill.

Notes

1. Theodor Adorno, "Cultural Criticism and Society," in *Prisms: Studies in Contemporary German Social Thought* (Cambridge, Mass.: MIT Press, 1955), 34.

2. Theodor Adorno, *Negative Dialectics* (London: Routledge, 1973), 362–63.

3. See Harriet Earle, *Comics, Trauma and the New Art of War* (Jackson: University Press of Mississippi, 2017).

4. Anne Whitehead, *Trauma Fiction* (Edinburgh: Edinburgh University Press, 2004), 3.

5. Michelle Balaev, ed., *Contemporary Approaches in Literary Trauma Theory* (Palgrave Macmillan: London, 2014), 6. See also Balaev, *The Nature of Trauma in American Novels* (Evanston: Northwestern University Press, 2012).

6. Primo Levi, *The Drowned and the Saved* (New York: Summit Books, 1986), 60.

7. For details on the making of the film and controversies around its aesthetic choices, see Sylvie Lindeperg, *Night and Fog: A Film in History* (Minneapolis: University of Minnesota Press, 2014).

8. Andrew Hebard, "Disruptive Histories," *New German Critique* 71 (2006): 87–113.

9. Alain Resnais's *Night and Fog*, 1955 (France: Argos Films), DVD.

10. Jay Cantor, "Death and the Image," in *Beyond Document: Essays on Nonfiction Film* (Middletown: Wesleyan University Press, 1996), 27.

11. Griselda Pollock and Max Silverman, "Introduction," in *Concentrationary Cinema: Aesthetics as Political Resistance in Alain Resnais's* Night and Fog *(1955)*, ed. Griselda Pollock and Max Silverman (New York: Berghahn Books, 2011), 2.

12. Ewout van der Knaap, *Uncovering the Holocaust: The International Reception of* Night and Fog (London: Wallflower Press, 2006), 1.

13. Thomas Doherty, "Art Spiegelman's *Maus*: Graphic Art and the Holocaust," *American Literature* 68 (1996): 72.

14. Philip Smith, *Reading Art Spiegelman* (London: Routledge, 2015), 55.

15. Smith, *Reading Art Spiegelman*, 56.

16. In a similar way, Auschwitz has become a chronotope for the Holocaust. It is a location that now stands for a larger spatial and temporal event: the systematic destruction of ethnic

and religious groups, political prisoners, and disabled persons in both camps and *impromptu* death chambers across Europe between 1941 and 1945, with earlier preparations for murder beginning as early as 1933.

17. Libby Saxton, "*Night and Fog* and the Concentrationary Gaze," in *Concentrationary Cinema*, 142.

18. Oren Stier, *Holocaust Icons: Symbolizing the Shoah in History and Memory* (New Brunswick: Rutgers University Press, 2015), 68.

19. Stier, *Holocaust Icons*, 68

20. Debórah Dwork and Robert Jan van Pelt, *Auschwitz 1270 to the Present* (London: Norton and Co., 1996), 360–61.

21. van der Knaap, *Uncovering the Holocaust*, 7.

22. Earle, *Comics, Trauma, and the New Art of War*, 42.

23. Aristotle, *The Art of Rhetoric* (London: Penguin, 1991), 6.

24. Gilles Deleuze and Félix Guattari, *What Is Philosophy?* (New York: Columbia University Press, 1994), 163.

25. Simon O'Sullivan, "The Aesthetics of Affect," *Angelaki: Journal of the Theoretical Humanities* 6 (2001): 126.

26. Derek Attridge, "Once More with Feeling: Art, Affect and Performance," *Textual Practice* 25 (2011): 340.

27. Spiegelman, *Maus I*, 108.

28. Spiegelman, *Maus II*, 46.

29. Attridge, "Once More with Feeling," 340.

30. James Young, "The Holocaust as Vicarious Past: Art Spiegelman's *Maus* and the Afterimages of History," *Critical Inquiry* 24 (1998): 682–84.

31. Michael Staub, "The Shoah Goes on and on: Remembrance and Representation in Art Spiegelman's *Maus*," *MELUS* 20 (1995): 33.

32. Doherty, "Art Spiegelman's *Maus*," 70.

33. Lawrence Weschler, "Art's Father, Vladek's Son," in *Shapinsky's Karma, Bogg's Bills, and Other True-Life Tales* (London: Penguin, 1988), 58.

34. Spiegelman, *Maus II*, 41.

35. Spiegelman, *Maus II*, 77.

Part 4

COMICS HISTORY

WHO PUBLISHED *MAUS*?

COLIN BEINEKE

In our age of relentless demystification, the text itself often remains the last mystified object, with critics naively assuming that the paperback texts that they pull from their local bookstore somehow "are" *King Lear*, or *Pride and Prejudice*, or *The Souls of Black Folk*.

—GEORGE BORNSTEIN

While countless critics have underscored the position of Art Spiegelman's *Maus* as perhaps the most seminal work of the contemporary comics canon, the manifestation of Spiegelman's text across print and digital forms remains understudied. The publication of *Maus*-as-book has been vital to its popular and critical reception. The majority of readers who encounter *Maus* do so through one of the collected editions published by Pantheon Books. As such, when critics and scholars examine *Maus*, it is almost without exception one of these editions that they cite. Unfortunately, as Hillary Chute reminds us, "few critics have noted the serialization of *Maus* prior to its publication in book volumes by Pantheon," and more significantly, "even fewer have actually analyzed the context of [*Maus*'s] appearance within *RAW*."[1] Apart from brief footnotes and asides, the original serialization of *Maus* in the pages of *RAW*—the flagship anthology of Françoise Mouly and Spiegelman's independent comics publishing house *RAW* Books and Graphics (RBG)—has indeed gone almost entirely unexamined.[2] Presented as small insert booklets or chapters stapled against the oversized pages of the magazine, the serialized *Maus*, which I am collectively calling RBG-*Maus*, differs significantly in materiality and paratextuality from its collected version, which I am calling Pantheon-*Maus*.

This question of *who* published *Maus* is fundamental. First issued serially by a small publishing house specializing in avant-garde comics, RBG-*Maus* was shaped by a convergence of aesthetic and practical concerns unique to independent publication in general and *RAW* magazine in particular. In contrast, Pantheon-*Maus*, strategically collected and redeployed as single, book-like texts by a corporatized yet well-respected publishing house, was constructed in light of commercial ambitions and a desire for literary respectability. The artistic and economic forces that fashioned these iterations of Spiegelman's text, however, are not my primary focus. Instead, I am interested in examining the aesthetic results of these processes, specifically the ways in which RBG-*Maus* offers a unique formulation and reading of Spiegelman's canonical work, one that is not available through the popular Pantheon-*Maus*.

The original serialization of *Maus* within *RAW* places the work in a unique material framework that highlights and complicates a number of formal and thematic threads in Spiegelman's narrative. Perhaps because the contents of RBG-*Maus* and Pantheon-*Maus* are largely the same, the material and paratextual signifiers key to understanding each text—in particular those of RBG-*Maus*—have been overlooked. Aaron Kashtan argues that comics scholars have traditionally "treated mediality and materiality as mere accidental features of comics or incidental devices for the transmission of meaning, and have therefore been inattentive to the ways in which materiality also shapes meaning."[3] This lack of attention to materiality is also, in part, the result of a perspective that is biased towards complete or autonomous texts. In this chapter's epigraph, George Bornstein critiques this perspective as "naïve," adding that "any particular version that we study of a text is always already a construction, one of many possible in a world of constructions."[4]

In this chapter, I contend that RBG-*Maus* and Pantheon-*Maus* constitute meaningfully distinct constructions and argue that the singular material and paratextual framings of RBG-*Maus* proffer a different—if not more complex—reading of Spiegelman's work than do the collected editions from Pantheon. The format of the *Maus* inserts and the large *RAW* pages against which they are set, what I am calling "companion pages," guide readers' engagement with the text and its themes. The insert booklets of RBG-*Maus* adopt a small physical format similar to that of a personal diary, which emphasizes the intimate nature of both Vladek's and Spiegelman's disclosures. Complementing this construction of *Maus*-as-diary, the small pages of the inserts encourage a "reading" rather than "viewing" approach to the text, a technique that Spiegelman has frequently theorized. Spiegelman also utilizes the large *RAW* companion pages to which the *Maus* inserts are attached as a space for metacommentary. These companion pages serve to guide the readers' focus towards specific thematic elements of a given chapter, on the one hand, and larger questions of Spiegelman's Holocaust representation, including a complication of the Jews-as-mice zoomorphism, on the other.

THEORIZING THE *MAUS* INSERTS

Prior to his decision to integrate *Maus* into *RAW*, Spiegelman was in talks with the Belgian comics publisher Casterman to contribute a serialized *Maus* to the house's anthology magazine, *À Suivre* (*To Be Continued*). Founded in 1978, *À Suivre* was established with the mission of serializing extended comics narratives, stories that subsequently would be collected and published as albums. Although Spiegelman ultimately elected to use *RAW* as the vehicle for *Maus*—in part because of his doubts regarding his ability to maintain the rigorous production schedule required for *À Suivre*—he nevertheless emulated the strategy underwriting the *À Suivre* approach to publication, that is, serializing with an eye towards a final book-length text.[5] (It is worth noting that had Spiegelman opted to publish with Casterman, it is unlikely that he would have had the freedom to format *Maus* as he does in *RAW*.) The companion page to which the first *Maus* insert is attached provides an imaginary rendering of the finished project: a thick red book, complete with an illustration that later served as a protodesign for the cover of Pantheon-*Maus I*. Spiegelman continued to highlight his plan for a book-length *Maus* throughout the work's serialization in *RAW*. Accompanying almost every *Maus* insert is an editorial note describing it as a portion of a "projected 200–250-page work-in-progress."[6] His desire to attain this goal served as motivation for Spiegelman's steady rate of production. Although the editorial note also asserts that "Future chapters will appear in *RAW*, on an occasional basis, as they are completed," Spiegelman managed better than the occasional *Maus* contribution.[7] Beginning with *RAW* Vol. 1, Issue 2, he consistently supplied a chapter of *Maus* for every subsequent issue of the magazine.

While varying in dimension, none of the *Maus* inserts are larger than six-by-nine-inches, a size significantly smaller than the ten-and-a-half-by-fourteen-inch pages of *RAW* itself. Compared to the higher quality, at times glossy paper on which the majority of *RAW*'s material appears, the *Maus* inserts are printed on newsprint-like, relatively flimsy paper. This strong contrast in size and material sets *Maus* apart from the rest of the *RAW* project, while also allowing Spiegelman to establish resonances between the materiality of the inserts and the narratives they contain. These resonances take a variety of forms, and before turning to my own reading of them, it is important to acknowledge one of the leading interpretations.

Having worked closely with Spiegelman to compile *MetaMaus* and its varied archival materials, Chute is perhaps the only scholar to put forth an unambiguous theory regarding the format of the *Maus* inserts. In both *MetaMaus* and her monograph *Disaster Drawn: Visual Witness, Comics, and Documentary Form*, Chute points to a collection of booklets owned by Spiegelman's parents as the

"Maus. A Survivor's Tale," first insert of serialized *Maus* in *RAW* Volume 1, Issue 2, *The Graphix Magazine for Damned Intellectuals*. Copyright © 1980 by Art Spiegelman.

inspiration for his choice of format. In *Disaster Drawn* she asserts that "The postwar booklets are the model for the format of Spiegelman's telling of his own parents' war story."[8] Produced in the years immediately following the conclusion of World War II, these booklets are "small-press pamphlets by survivors that bore witness to experiences of regular people during the war."[9] Although most are composed fully in prose, a significant number of the booklets either contain illustrations or are presented entirely as sequences of drawings. As Chute argues, "Two pamphlets in particular, which are predominately visual, both titled with simple place names of camps, had a profound effect on the would-be documentary cartoonist [Spiegelman]: *Ravensbrück* and *Auschwitz*. Anja Spiegelman had come through both camps."[10] The correlation to the *Maus* inserts, in terms of both form and content, is clear: Both sets of texts use the drawn image to represent personal narratives of the Holocaust. Further, and as I will elaborate later, the pamphlets' connection to Spiegelman's mother, Anja, may serve as an additional indicator of Spiegelman's purpose in formatting the *Maus* inserts the way he did.

In an interview with Chute for *MetaMaus*, Spiegelman describes his discovery of these pamphlets and the influence they had on the production of RBG-*Maus*[11]: "these gave me my first full and conscious realization that something enormous and devastating had hit my family. Some of those booklets actually were the models for the *Maus* booklets included in *RAW* magazine when *Maus* was presented as a work in progress. Something about their humble graphic design and printing was important to me."[12] The *Maus* inserts certainly share with the postwar booklets a "humble" mode of graphic design and printing. Spiegelman's consistent use of single or paired solid colors for the inserts' covers and the deployment of relatively cheap paper mirror the design and construction of the postwar booklets, as does his purposefully minimalist, even amateurish, style of drawing. It is fair to conclude that the *Maus* inserts may have been, at least in part, inspired by Spiegelman's decision to emulate, and thereby participate in, a more immediate and established Jewish tradition of Holocaust witnessing and testimony.

However, as Spiegelman acknowledges, when first approaching the idea of serializing *Maus* in his and Mouly's own magazine, he "didn't quite know how to make use of *Maus* in *Raw*," and that "Using *Maus* in *RAW* led to some interesting aesthetic questions, about *RAW* and about *Maus*."[13] Had Spiegelman approached RBG-*Maus* with the intention of emulating the size and shape of the postwar booklets, it is unclear why he was uncertain of how to proceed with incorporating *Maus* into *RAW*. Mouly explains that "There was a conflict, or something that we had to reconcile between the impulse behind *Maus*, which is a long book, and *RAW*."[14] This conflict involved a pair of interwoven concerns, both material and thematic. First, how to present and differentiate a serious narrative within a magazine driven by prodigious visual experimentation and formal play. Second, how to match the unique narrative of *Maus* with a complementary dimensional and material format. In other words, if *Maus* was to be a departure from the norm of *RAW*, it would require an equally specialized mode of conveyance.

It was primarily in order to answer these aesthetic challenges, I contend, that Spiegelman adopted the small insert booklet and companion page format. The decision not to utilize the oversized pages of *RAW* itself and to instead employ a much smaller canvas was inspired by Spiegelman's own theorization of comics dimensionality, wherein he aligns larger pages with visual scanning and smaller pages with narrative reading. Discussing this relationship in the context of *Maus*, Spiegelman explains:

> One interesting thing about *RAW* is that it's a large-size magazine, and therefore, almost as a result of the format, stresses the graphic element of comics strips, because its pages are very large and there's not 200 of them, but about 36. So it asks that every page be very graphically compelling. That tends to emphasize one element, the graphics, over storytelling—hopefully not at the expense of the storytelling.[15]

Following this logic, Spiegelman concluded that the large pages of *RAW* would not provide a suitable space for the type of storytelling envisaged for *Maus*. To splay *Maus* upon the oversized *RAW* pages, in Spiegelman's eyes, would have been a signal to readers that the work was meant to be appreciated primarily in visual rather than narrative terms. As he recalls, "This led to a dilemma for *Maus*, which I conceived of primarily as a comic wherein the pictures were in service of the story. I wanted very much to keep the pictures subservient to the idea. In fact, it is drawn quite small—the original for each page is about five by seven or something like that."[16] (Spiegelman drew *Maus* in the small size in which it was published rather than on a larger scale to be shrunk down, the practice typical of much comics production.) Ultimately, the smaller "pictures" that comprise the *Maus* inserts aim to emphasize its narrative.

For the first issue of *RAW*, Spiegelman tentatively employed this theory to produce a comic that relied on the same technique and format he would adopt for the *Maus* inserts. Because he was "reluctant to get started on *Maus*," Spiegelman instead drew "Two-Fisted Painters," the story of an author besieged by self-doubt and his subsequent crafting of a genre tale about the struggle between an avant-garde painter and a color-sucking alien.[17] To avoid the high cost of printing *RAW*-sized pages in full color—which Spiegelman's story required—"Two Fisted Painters" was constructed as in insert booklet and stapled into the middle of *RAW*'s first issue, a method that lowered the amount of ink required. While the *Maus* inserts would all be published in black and white, it is nevertheless clear that "Two-Fisted Painters" served as a model for the size, format, and positioning of the *Maus* inserts within *RAW*. As semiseparate booklets set against the large pages of *RAW*, the small size of both "Two-Fisted Painters" and the *Maus* inserts work to signal their shared narrative priorities.

RBG-*MAUS* AS DIARY

The *Maus* inserts not only emphasize Spiegelman's narrative interests; their intimate size and quality also demand a reading of the inserts as diary-like reproductions, stressing the autobiographic nature and personal disclosures of the work. As Spiegelman acknowledges, "Seeing these small pages of kind of doodle drawings, almost—they're rough, quick drawings—mounted together makes it seem like we found somebody's diary, and are publishing facsimiles of it."[18] While many critics have emphasized the importance of Anja's lost diaries to Spiegelman's family chronicle, few have attempted to pursue what the framing of *Maus*-as-diary itself might produce, possibly because it is the neglected materiality of RBG-*Maus* and its serial status that most immediately prompts such consideration.

Recognition of *Maus*-as-diary produces at least two major and interlacing effects on its reading: an increased sense of intimacy between reader and text and a heightened awareness of the deeply personal memories Spiegelman chooses to display publicly. When speaking further of his formatting decision, Spiegelman makes clear that the material dimensions of the inserts were purposefully shaped to induce a sense of familiarity. Mouly explains that "*Maus* couldn't be done large size. If he had started doing *Maus* for *RAW* [via the magazine's oversized pages] it would have become something else altogether in terms of the intimacy of the book [*Maus*]." Spiegelman echoes Mouly's logic, arguing: "That's why it's in this small size. *Maus* wouldn't make sense blown up to fill a *RAW*-sized page. It requires the intimacy of a smaller size."[19] Rather than being splashed at arm's length over the outsized pages of formal experimentation and bombastic illustration that define *RAW*, the *Maus* inserts require that the reader physically draw closer to the smaller pages in order to decipher their comparatively minute words, panels, and images.

This creation of a literal closeness between reader and text is figuratively enhanced by Spiegelman's decision to shape the inserts around the personal nature of his narrative, "so that it would feel more like looking at a diary, although it's a forged diary."[20] The small size and pamphlet format—along with the hand-drawn quality of the comic itself—highlights the personal nature of its contents while affording readers the constructed experience of reading a private journal. Spiegelman explains that he intended the work to "feel like a manuscript," all the more intimate for its incompleteness.[21] As a memoir of both Spiegelman and his father, Vladek, the content of *Maus* uncovers details that forge a link between the comic's form and its content. Further, since each insert resembles a private document, readers are forced to confront their own position as voyeurs and reexamine the ethics of Spiegelman's public disclosures of private material.

At multiple points throughout the narrative, the subject of the Holocaust as well as personal details Vladek shares with his son are so intimate and somber that, in a sense, their revelation to such a wide readership might be considered a violation of privacy akin to surreptitiously reading (a mass reproduction of) someone else's diary. Indeed, there are facets of his experience that Vladek explicitly desires to keep between himself and his son, and Spiegelman's conscious transgression of Vladek's wishes leads Emily Miller Budick to conclude that although "*Maus* is, without a doubt, an extraordinary artistic achievement . . . the cost of this successful course of therapy for the son—and perhaps for us the public, who share his position—is still the humiliation of the father and the exposure of secrets that the father asked the son not to tell."[22] The formatting of *Maus*-as-diary, then, serves the dual purpose of both justifying and condemning Spiegelman's violation of Vladek's privacy. Diaries are meant to be a site of intimate disclosure, yet the mass reproduction of a diary, by definition, negates this private status.

In one oft-cited moment, after relating to his son an account of the romantic relationship he developed with the sassy Lucia prior to his courting of Spiegelman's mother, Vladek requests that Art not include the story in his comic, to which Spiegelman responds with a shocked "**What?** Why not?"[23] Vladek explains that his relationship with Lucia "has nothing to do with the Holocaust!" and "isn't so proper, so respectful" to include it in the comic, concluding: "I can tell you other stories, but such private things, I don't want you should mention."[24] Although Spiegelman raises his hand in an oath-making gesture and acquiesces, "Okay, okay—I promise," he nevertheless includes the story, as well as his father's request to have the story expunged from the official narrative.[25] In violating Vladek's desire for privacy, Spiegelman breaks down the boundary between public and private, a conflict that is highlighted by the analogous tension between the diary-shaped RBG-*Maus* and its inclusion within a mass-produced publication intended for relatively wide consumption.

The construction of *Maus*-as-diary, in addition to focusing attention on the dynamics of public and private at play in the narrative, directs readers to consider how its diary-like format emphasizes Spiegelman's distress over the loss of Anja's notebooks. As a number of scholars have noted, Spiegelman's reconstruction of his family history in *Maus* may reflect his desire to restore, in part, the content of his mother's destroyed diaries. After attempting to enlist his father in a search for Anja's notebooks, Spiegelman is shocked and disgusted to find that Vladek, upon having "had a very bad day," and because the notebooks "had too many *memories*," burned them.[26] As Spiegelman scolds his father—"**Christ!** You save **tons** of worthless shit"—Vladek reveals that Anja had intended for Spiegelman to read the notebooks when "he [grew] up."[27] This proves too much for Spiegelman, who then utters the much-cited condemnation: "God **damn** you! You—you murderer! How the hell could you do such a thing!!"[28]

Spiegelman's likening of the notebooks' destruction to an act of murder might be read as a rhetorical flourish aimed to represent the depth of his anger and despair, yet a notion of diaries—in particular those of someone deceased—as a space for tangible embodiment spans the bridge between the literal and the figurative. Portions of Anja's self can be said to have been materially manifested within the pages of her notebooks, and their destruction might be seen to erase not only her physical possessions, but in a very real sense any hope Spiegelman might have had for accessing her unique selfhood and identity. While not a literal attempt to recreate Anja's lost notebooks, in crafting a "new" series of diaries (RBG-*Maus*) that relate his father's story as well as his own, Spiegelman acknowledges the ability of the diary format to capture the dynamics of memory, history, and self. Notably, in ways that doubly expound the significance of Spiegelman's decision to materially present *Maus*-as-diary, my argument complements those made by Chute regarding the relationship between the *Maus* inserts and the postwar booklets depicting survivor experiences of the two concentration camps in which Anja was incarcerated.

In addition to its material trappings, it is also the serialized nature of RBG-*Maus* that signals the work's status as a diary-like object. Nicole Stamant, one of the few scholars to take up a comparison between RBG-*Maus* and the serialization innate to the personal diary, as well as the relationship between Anja's diaries and RBG-*Maus*, argues that "Art's search for Anja's diaries resonates with his own project of self-narration over time."[29] Stamant acknowledges that even though "diaries and memoirs are two distinct genres of life writing, they share . . . the ability to be written, published, and read serially and episodically."[30] This distinction is vital. Pantheon-*Maus*, presented as either two volumes or *The Complete Maus*, is more evocative of a complete autobiography than of an ongoing diary as seen in RBG-*Maus*. As Stamant explains, "the seriality inherent in [diaries and memoirs] puts them in direct contrast to a form like autobiography, as they challenge the idea of self-representation in one volume."[31] In other words, by serializing *Maus* in *RAW*, Spiegelman succeeded in "mimicking the periodic writing of a diary" as a way to emphasize an intimate mode of self-representation.[32] In publishing portions of *Maus* as he completed them, Spiegelman was imitating the habitual pattern of daily writing central to diary composition. And although not as immediate in nature as a diary entry, the speed with which he produced each *Maus* insert did not permit Spiegelman time to significantly revise or otherwise filter his telling, lending to each insert the rawness and urgency of a diary entry.

THEORIZING THE *MAUS* COMPANION PAGES

Spiegelman pairs his *Maus*-as-diary format with an innovative use of the companion pages of *RAW* against which the inserts appear—usually single, large images that fill the page, rather than a sequence or collage of individual images. Specifically, these companion pages provide an additional site for framing and guiding readers' engagement with the narrative of *Maus*, its core concerns, and Spiegelman's attempts to represent the Holocaust, in particular the implications of Spiegelman's zoomorphic construction of Jews-as-mice. For the most part, the companion pages do not make their way into the editions of Pantheon-*Maus*, and when they do, the unique intertextual exchange they solicit in *RAW* is entirely lost. In RBG-*Maus*, each companion page is paired with a specific insert, encouraging the reader to consider the nuanced relationship between a given *RAW* page and its mated *Maus* chapter. Writing about serialized American fiction that appeared in magazines and periodicals during the latter half of the nineteenth century, Michael Lund describes a similar method of pairing contextual images with specific narrative moments, as well as the tendency of scholars to overlook the original appearance of serialized works:

> Some monthlies featured illustrations with their fiction, an element of the works' original form almost universally ignored in the paperback editions teachers use in the classroom today, as well as the books scholars refer to in their writing . . . Scholars have only begun to explore how increasingly sophisticated engravings directed readers' attention toward specific elements of novels in their first appearance.[33]

Although he describes them as illustrations, Lund also suggests that in addition to visually dramatizing individual scenes, these images further served to highlight features of the narratives themselves. It is this focusing of attention to moments in the story that defines Spiegelman's own use of companion pages.

Depending on the type of image Spiegelman chose for each companion page and insert pairing, the juxtaposition of the two generates a wide variety of resonances. Each page depicts one of three types of images: illustrations by Spiegelman, excerpted from or based on the narrative of *Maus* itself, glossy photographs depicting real-world mice, and, in one case, a sequential cartoon by nineteenth-century French protocartoonist Théophile Steinlen. The first category of images, with one notable exception, provide immediate metacommentary on the chapter with which they are paired, while the second and third image categories do not necessarily correlate with their respective inserts, instead working together to provide an ongoing complication of Spiegelman's zoomorphic representation of Jews-as-mice.

METAILLUSTRATING *MAUS*

The companion pages drawn by Spiegelman highlight central narrative or thematic concerns at play in their paired *Maus* inserts, inviting the reader to think critically about the associations the work is crafting. In the large image accompanying the second *Maus* insert—titled "The Honeymoon"—a young Vladek and Anja are pictured dancing together in celebration of their marriage. This peaceful and happy moment represents the idealized period experienced by newlyweds following their wedding, during which time the novelty of married life feels like a surreal yet ultimately transitional state. For the newlyweds, this period will hopefully never end. In stark contrast to the image of the twirling couple, the cover of the second chapter depicts a group of Jewish people travelling by train as they gaze at an unfurling Nazi flag. Within the pages of the chapter, the reader bears witness not only to the beginning stages of Vladek and Anja's marriage, but also to the earliest manifestations of Hitler's rise to power—a foreshadowing of the ghettos, incarcerations, and genocide to come. Vladek sees a publicly displayed swastika for the first time and hears terrible rumors from friends and family regarding the horrific treatment of Jews under increasing Nazi rule. Just as the honeymoon period is a transitional state that the couple nevertheless hopes will never end, the prewar period counts as a similarly liminal moment in Hitler's rise, yet one that the Jewish passengers hope will never begin. In this way, Spiegelman uses dark irony to sharpen the dissonance between the contented optimism of the honeymoon and the fearful, yet well-justified, pessimism that accompanied the ascent of the Third Reich. Vladek and Anja's relationship becomes all the more precious against the backdrop of Nazism, while the beginnings of the Holocaust take on an even darker shade when set against the blissful light of Vladek's honeymoon.

For chapter five of RBG-*Maus*, "Mouse Holes," Spiegelman appropriates a page from inside the insert to serve as its companion page. The blown-up image depicts Vladek and other Jewish fugitives hiding in the attic of a sympathetic family as Nazi soldiers invade the home and one of the Germans loudly exclaims "JUDEN RAUS!" (Jews out!). The cover of the insert portrays a similar group of Jewish refugees huddled together under blankets against a backdrop resembling a person-size mouse hole, familiar from animated cartoons such as *Tom and Jerry*. Taken together, the images heighten readers' awareness of the Nazi perception of Jews as vermin to be routed out from their hiding places. Although he places the reader in a position that shares the Nazi perspective, Spiegelman undercuts anti-Semitic ideology through a sympathetic portrayal and humanization of the Jews driven into hiding. Rather than being interchangeable, faceless vermin as conceived by the Nazis, Spiegelman's figures are individualized through their distinguishing clothing. Further, the anxious expressions on the characters' faces, along with their blanket-clad bodies—a common signifier of distress or trauma—evoke readers' empathy and identification with the refugees as humans.

MICE, RATS, AND VERMIN: SPIEGELMAN'S PROBLEMATIC ZOOMORPHISM

One of the longest-running debates in *Maus* scholarship involves the relative merits and faults of Spiegelman's figurative analogy of people-as-animals, and specifically Jews-as-mice. In his essay "On Mice and Mimesis: Reading *Maus* with Adorno," Andreas Huyssen succinctly outlines the root question facing Spiegelman's appropriation of anti-Semitic imagery:

> Another objection might be more serious: Spiegelman's image strategies problematically reproduce the Nazi image of the Jew as vermin, as rodent, as mouse. But is it simply a mimicry of racist imagery? And even if it is mimicry, does mimicry of racism invariably imply its reproduction or can such mimicry itself open up a gap, a difference that depends on who performs the miming and how?[34]

Even those who believe Spiegelman is successful in subverting racist imagery nevertheless recognize that his re-deployment of such images is a precarious move. Although she largely dismisses the objection, Marilyn Reizbaum, for instance, acknowledges that "to reproduce these images in kind is to rehearse and reinforce them."[35] My purpose here, however, is not to retread this well-worn ground, nor to offer a possible rationale for Spiegelman's problematic zoomorphism, but to examine how RBG-*Maus* paradoxically both undercuts and strengthens Spiegelman's subversive appropriation.

Spiegelman's decision to represent his Jewish characters as mice rather than rats is central to understanding his attempt at subversion. As James E. Young argues, "By adopting the mouse as allegorical image for Jews, Spiegelman is able to caricature—and thereby subvert—the Nazi image of Jews as vermin."[36] The Jewish characters in *Maus* are clearly intended to be viewed as mice, not the rats of Nazi propaganda. This purposeful swapping of rat for mouse demonstrates that although Spiegelman was re-deploying Nazi stereotypes, he was not willing to embrace the Nazi imagery wholesale and without modification: "I liked working with a metaphor that didn't work all that well though I certainly didn't want my metaphor to work as an endorsement of Nazi ideology."[37]

Whether as mice or rats, however, both representations of Jews are dehumanizing, even if our "culturally scripted responses to familiar schemas of sympathetic and antipathetic animals" identifies mice as sympathetic and rats as antipathetic.[38] The technique of zoomorphism—the depiction of people as animals—is by definition dehumanizing. So although Spiegelman's Jews-as-mice imagery might not carry with it the connotations of the Nazis' Jews-as-rats, it nevertheless, as Richard De Angelis points out, "forces the reader to share the Nazi perception of Jews as not quite human."[39] So although Spiegelman has recognized the central role of dehumanization in the Holocaust—"it [is] clear to me that this dehumanization was at the very heart of the killing project"—he nevertheless crafted *Maus* using only a slightly modified set of tools.[40]

The second and third types of companion pages—photographs of mice and a cartoon by Steinlen—provide both a clear logic for rejecting the anti-Semitic figuration of Nazi imagery and a potentially hazardous replication of its ideology. Although Spiegelman defends his Jews-as-mice zoomorphism, stating that "These images are not my images. I borrowed them from the Germans," his re-deployment of propagandistic Nazi imagery walks a fine line between subversion and reinforcement, a situation exacerbated by his use of photographic images of mice.[41] As Huyssen suggests, "Spiegelman himself draws the reader's attention to his conscious mimetic adoption of this imagery" when he uses a quotation from Hitler on the copyright page of the first *Maus* volume, leading Huyssen to conclude that "*Maus* thus gives copyright where it is due: Adolf Hitler and the Nazis."[42]

In contrast to the purposefully simplified and cartoonish—yet relatively humanizing—renderings of mice that populate his narrative, for two companion pages Spiegelman elects to forego cartooning and employ photography instead. The mice in these photographs reflect a real-world authenticity that the photographic medium is intrinsically assumed to replicate. In this sense, the mice are stripped of all human characteristics and shown as literal representations of mice-as-vermin. The contrast is clear when comparing the companion page of chapter three with that of chapter four. The photograph accompanying the third chapter of *Maus* depicts a crowded mass of mice—decidedly not the mouse characters that readers have come to identify with—closely resembling the documentary strategies of Nazi propaganda.

In particular, Spiegelman's choice of photograph recalls Fritz Hippler's infamous propaganda film *The Eternal Jew* (1940), which cuts back and forth between shots of Jewish people and masses of swarming rats. In both Spiegelman's and Hippler's representations, Jews are presented not only as non-human, but as faceless, replicated abstractions. As Harold Evans notes, this reflects one of the core tenets of anti-Semitic ideology: "[Anti-semitism's] lexicon has no word for individuality. It is fixated on group identity. It is necessarily dehumanizing when people become abstractions."[43] However, Spiegelman is aware of these implications, and—with the companion page for chapter four—works to parry their thrust.

Spiegelman invites the reader to consider the difference between his own mice and those depicted in the photographs. The mice of chapter four's companion page display distinctive human features: diverse sets of clothing, clear variations in facial structure, and upright anthropomorphic figurations. When compared to the photographic companion page of chapter three—to borrow Huyssen's observation with respect to *The Eternal Jew*—it is "clear how Spiegelman's mimetic adoption of Nazi imagery actually succeeds in reversing its implications while simultaneously keeping us aware of the humiliation and degradation of that imagery's original intention."[44] In recognizing the absurdity of ascribing to the Jewish people of *Maus* the same status suggested by the mice in the photograph and the correlating Nazi ideology, Spiegelman forces an against-the-grain reading of anti-Semitic sentiment, which ultimately undercuts its perverse logic.

The depiction of Jews-as-rats served the Nazi agenda of Jewish genocide by assigning Jews the role of vermin—a category meant to justify extermination. Visual depictions of exterminations of Jews-as-rats abounded in Nazi propaganda and were especially prominent in the cartoons of the Nazi weekly magazine *Der Stürmer*. In the photographic companion page for chapter six of RBG-*Maus*, "Mouse Trap," Spiegelman directly engages with this extermination trope by selecting the photograph of a single dead mouse caught in a Victor-brand mouse trap. Setting traps for mice is a commonplace occurrence, and in suggesting this routine action might have a connection to the Holocaust, an event anything but mundane, Spiegelman once more walks a thin line between critique and re-entrenchment of anti-Semitic ideology.

The brand depicted in the photo, Victor, is a leading producer of mouse traps worldwide, yet it is clear that Spiegelman selected the company's traps and, more specifically, its logo on the traps, for aesthetic reasons.[45] Although it appears faint in the blurry photograph, by using the negative space provided within the logo's "V," along with the addition of dotted eyes and cut-out ears, the emblem constructs a mouse-head silhouette seen from a bird's-eye view. These visual references mimic the simplicity of Spiegelman's own figurative style while also recalling the upwards-tilted heads and horrified expressions of Spiegelman's mice screaming in Auschwitz, forming hazardous links between the ideology of anti-Semitism, the supposed mundanity of extermination, and Spiegelman's own rhetorical and aesthetic techniques. With his own depiction of extermination, Spiegelman once more treads dangerously close to co-opting the visual language of anti-Semitism he is attempting to critique. Yet when

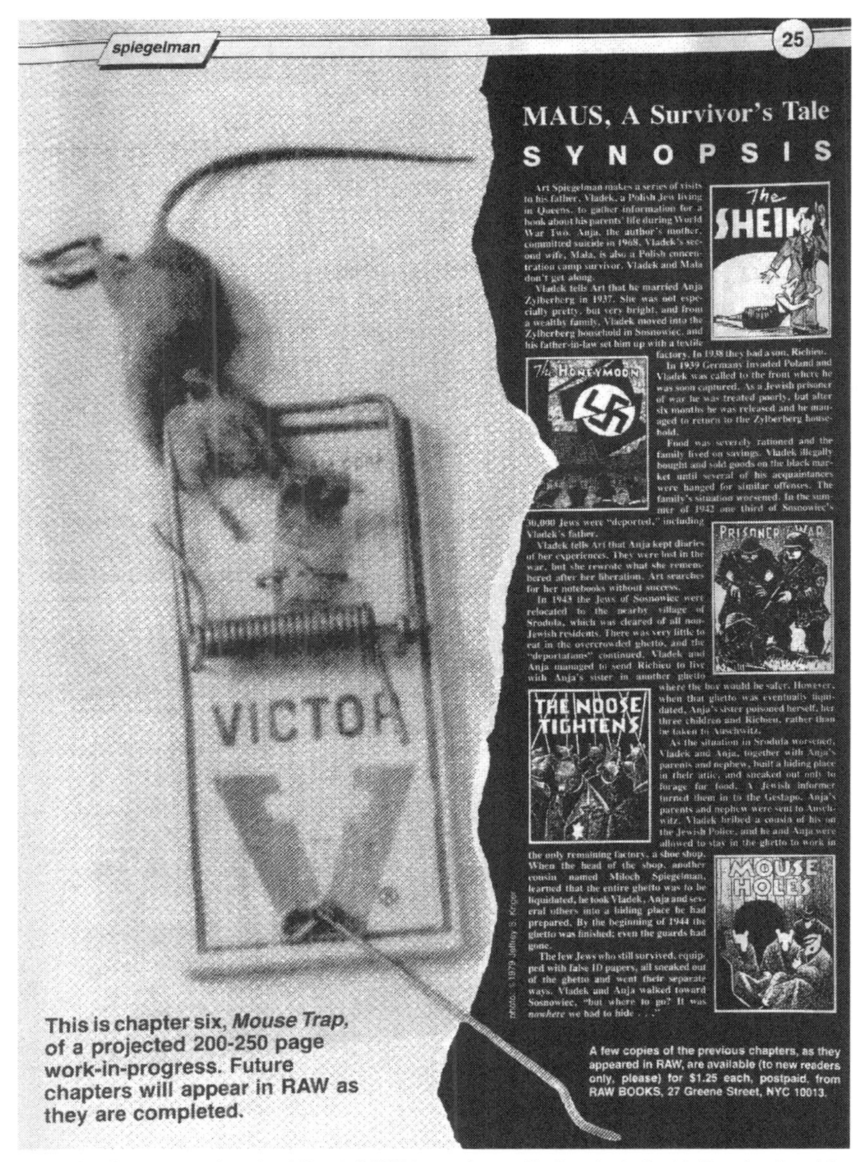
spiegelman

25

MAUS, A Survivor's Tale

SYNOPSIS

Art Spiegelman makes a series of visits to his father, Vladek, a Polish Jew living in Queens, to gather information for a book about his parents' life during World War Two. Anja, the author's mother, committed suicide in 1968. Vladek's second wife, Mala, is also a Polish concentration camp survivor. Vladek and Mala don't get along.

Vladek tells Art that he married Anja Zylberberg in 1937. She was not especially pretty, but very bright, and from a wealthy family. Vladek moved into the Zylberberg household in Sosnowiec, and his father-in-law set him up with a textile factory. In 1938 they had a son, Richieu.

In 1939 Germany invaded Poland and Vladek was called to the front where he was soon captured. As a Jewish prisoner of war he was treated poorly, but after six months he was released and he managed to return to the Zylberberg household.

Food was severely rationed and the family lived on savings. Vladek illegally bought and sold goods on the black market until several of his acquaintances were hanged for similar offenses. The family's situation worsened. In the summer of 1942 one third of Sosnowiec's 30,000 Jews were "deported," including Vladek's father.

Vladek tells Art that Anja kept diaries of her experiences. They were lost in the war, but she rewrote what she remembered after her liberation. Art searches for her notebooks without success.

In 1943 the Jews of Sosnowiec were relocated to the nearby village of Srodula, which was cleared of all non-Jewish residents. There was very little to eat in the overcrowded ghetto, and the "deportations" continued. Vladek and Anja managed to send Richieu to live with Anja's sister in another ghetto where the boy would be safer. However, when that ghetto was eventually liquidated, Anja's sister poisoned herself, her three children and Richieu, rather than be taken to Auschwitz.

As the situation in Srodula worsened, Vladek and Anja, together with Anja's parents and nephew, built a hiding place in their attic, and sneaked out only to forage for food. A Jewish informer turned them in to the Gestapo. Anja's parents and nephew were sent to Auschwitz. Vladek bribed a cousin of his on the Jewish Police, and he and Anja were allowed to stay in the ghetto to work in the only remaining factory, a shoe shop. When the head of the shop, another cousin named Miloch Spiegelman, learned that the entire ghetto was to be liquidated, he took Vladek, Anja and several others into a hiding place he had prepared. By the beginning of 1944 the ghetto was finished; even the guards had gone.

The few Jews who still survived, equipped with false ID papers, all sneaked out of the ghetto and went their separate ways. Vladek and Anja walked toward Sosnowiec, "but where to go? It was *nowhere* we had to hide . . ."

This is chapter six, *Mouse Trap*, of a projected 200-250 page work-in-progress. Future chapters will appear in RAW as they are completed.

A few copies of the previous chapters, as they appeared in RAW, are available (to new readers only, please) for $1.25 each, postpaid, from RAW BOOKS, 27 Greene Street, NYC 10013.

"Mouse Trap," sixth insert of serialized *Maus* in *RAW* Volume 1, Issue 7, *The Torn-Again Graphix Magazine*. Copyright © 1985 by Art Spiegelman.

contrasted with the humanistic portrayal of Jewish people in *Maus* and the literal, photographic representation of a mouse, Spiegelman's subversion is clear. The reader is asked to consider the contradiction between the commonplace occurrence of a mouse caught in a trap and the genocide of millions of human beings. To compare the two is absurd, and the realization that the Nazis viewed

"Mauschwitz," seventh and last insert of serialized *Maus* in *RAW* Volume 1, Issue 8, *The Graphix Aspirin for War Fever*. Copyright © 1986 by Art Spiegelman.

the two situations as one and the same emphasizes for the reader just how revolting their anti-Semitic ideology was.

For the final *Maus* insert in the first volume of *RAW*—which witnesses Vladek entering Auschwitz, or "Mauschwitz"—Spiegelman departs from both photographs and his own cartoon renderings to appropriate one of Steinlen's numerous "cat study" cartoons as a companion image. The intertextual relationship between this sequence and the ideology Spiegelman is attempting to subvert highlights the fact that the Nazi regime not only incarcerated and murdered, but also systematically tortured and tormented prisoners. Steinlen, a French cartoonist and anarcho-socialist, was a great admirer of cats who produced a series of sequential cartoon studies depicting them in various modes of play. The original purpose of Steinlen's studies was to capture the movement and elegance of cats-in-motion, while also providing his audience with whimsical recreations of the popular pet.

However, being aware of the cat and mouse analogy in *Maus*, the reader cannot view Steinlen's depiction of the hunting game as anything but vindictive. Indeed, it is difficult not to infuse the trio of cats with a malicious consciousness akin to that of the Germans/cats in the pages of *Maus*. The single mouse of Steinlen's study begins the sequence caged—as Vladek himself is consigned to Auschwitz in the accompanying chapter of *Maus*—while the cats work together as a highly regimented unit, mirroring each other's movements and stances. The last image of the sequence, a close-up of a single cat's open-clawed paw covering the dead (or soon to be dead) mouse, drives home the somberness of the encounter and the harsh reality of the game being played. Read alongside *Maus*, Steinlen's playful cartoon takes on sinister tones and anti-Semitic implications, while *Maus* is in turn enriched by Steinlen's piece with a characterization of the Nazis as callous tormentors who disregarded the humanity of Jews, viewing them as nothing more than disposable vermin and "playthings."

NOTES ON PANTHEON-*MAUS*

By way of conclusion, I want to briefly discuss how the presentation of Pantheon-*Maus* as a complete commercial work influenced the text's reception. Pantheon's publication of *Maus I* in 1986 was not incongruous with the house's extant catalog, nor entirely unprecedented within its institutional history. Founded in 1942 by the Jewish-German immigrants Kurt and Helen Wolff, Pantheon marked the American continuation of Kurt Wolff's agenda to publish works of literary and political distinction—an impulse that consequently secured Pantheon's status as a prestige publisher of highbrow fiction, theory, and criticism, as well as cultural, political, and social commentary. As far as I am aware, no mention has been made in scholarship on *Maus* that the Jewish founders of the publishing house which would subsequently issue one of the most significant contemporary works of art concerning the Holocaust had themselves fled from Germany to escape fascism and genocide.

Were it not for its publication by Pantheon, it is questionable whether *Maus* would have garnered such extensive and continued attention, bolstered by the widespread distribution, consistent availability, and respectability afforded by the prestigious press. As Robert Hutton cleverly observes, "It is hard to imagine the Pulitzer judges trawling through comic book stores looking for self-published masterpieces—it was the social capital and means of distribution that Pantheon provided which allowed *Maus* to find its way into the hands of the literati."[46] As RBG-*Maus*, Spiegelman's work was relatively obscure, but as Pantheon-*Maus* it was able to reach an audience outside the confines of the comics world. Pantheon's large-scale publication of *Maus* and, just as significantly, the house's ability to keep the work in constant and affordable circulation has permitted Pantheon-*Maus* to be widely adopted in classrooms and accessed by a general readership.

A canonical book or comic cannot exist without significant distribution and continued availability, and Pantheon provided the infrastructure that allowed *Maus* to accomplish both, while also lending it respectability and prestige. Compared to RBG-*Maus*, Pantheon-*Maus* fashions itself as a paperback novel, while nevertheless recalling the long form Spiegelman foresaw and explicitly mentioned alongside the first installment of *Maus*. And indeed, Pantheon-*Maus* lacks most of the intertextual formatting present in RBG-*Maus*. In the process of reshaping *Maus* for a literary market and readership, Pantheon removed the comic memoir from its more subversive iteration within *RAW* and presented it as a holistic piece of (ostensible) literature.

This is regrettable. Stripped of the original's more explicit provocations, specifically through the loss of the *RAW* companion pages, Pantheon-*Maus* can be viewed as an expurgated, or even derivative, version of RBG-*Maus*. On the one hand, it is to be expected that Pantheon would err on the side of caution. The house was already taking a substantial risk in publishing *Maus*, which at the time was considered controversial by default in both form and content. On the other hand, having already opened the door to such challenging material, it is surprising that Pantheon did not go all in, backing Spiegelman in his high-wire balancing act between an outright condemnation of Third Reich ideology and the subtle co-optation of its imagery.

With the expanded dimensions of the digest format—so that it might rest on bookshelves alongside respectable prose works—Pantheon-*Maus* is deprived of RBG-*Maus*'s connotations of diary materiality. Consequently, the explicit link to Anja's diaries, the relationship to the postwar Polish pamphlets, and, perhaps most significantly, the facilitation of a more intimate engagement with the text are all lost between RBG-*Maus* and its conversion to Pantheon-*Maus*. The answer to the question, then, of who published *Maus* is, of course, both *RAW* Books and Graphics and Pantheon Books. As suggested by George Bornstein in the epigraph to this chapter, however, neither iteration can really count itself as the definitive *Maus*: Such a notion is intangible, while texts are materially embodied. Each material manifestation of *Maus* offers readers a different mode of engaging with the complexities of Spiegelman's contemporary classic.

Notes

1. Hillary Chute, *Disaster Drawn: Visual Witness, Comics, and Documentary Form* (Cambridge, Mass.: Harvard University Press, 2016), 169.

2. Given the hyper-canonicity of *Maus*, it is certainly surprising that—as far as I am aware—Chute is alone in having attempted to examine *Maus* in the context of its shape and placement within *RAW*. This may be explained in part by the scarcity of the magazine's issues, which not only had relatively small print runs but have become an in-demand collector's item. It is also possible, however, that for many scholars and students of Spiegelman's text, Pantheon-*Maus* serves as a more than adequate object for their theoretical and critical purposes, and that there is simply no need to turn to what may be considered its gestational phase in *RAW*.

3. Aaron Kashtan. "My Mother was a Typewriter: *Fun Home* and the Importance of Materiality in Comics Studies," *Journal of Graphic Novels and Comics* 4, no. 1 (2011): 92.

4. George Bornstein, *Material Modernism: The Politics of the Page* (Cambridge: Cambridge University Press, 2001), 5.

5. *Maus* is unique in *RAW* in terms of both its seriality and Spiegelman's conceptualization of its "final" or collected form. With minor exceptions, *RAW* was not designed, as was *À Suivre*, to serve as an outlet for serial narratives. However, Spiegelman considered the presence of *Maus* in *RAW* as vital to the magazine's mission of demonstrating the plastic capabilities of the comics form. For him, *Maus* served as an example of the ability of comics to address serious subject matter through a layered and sustained narrative. As he explains, "it was necessary to have something like *Maus* in *Raw* to keep the book balanced in terms of what possibilities are open for comics." In other words, while *RAW* specialized in presenting highly visual and formal comics of the avant-garde, these types of works alone did not present an argument for the ability of comics to engage serious topics or constitute lengthy narratives. See Gary Groth et al., "Slaughter on Greene Street: Art Spiegelman and Françoise Mouly Talk about *RAW*," in *Art Spiegelman: Conversations*, ed. Joseph Witek (Jackson: University Press of Mississippi, 2007), 40.

6. Bill Kartalopoulos, "A *RAW* History," *Indy Magazine*, Winter 2005.

7. Kartalopoulos, "A *RAW* History."

8. Chute, *Disaster Drawn*, 169.

9. Chute, *Disaster Drawn*, 164.

10. Chute, *Disaster Drawn*, 165.

11. As far as I have been able to discover, this is the first time that Spiegelman specifically and publicly alludes to his parents' postwar booklets as key inspiration in formatting the *Maus* inserts. In all other public interviews and discussions of the inserts since the early eighties, Spiegelman and Mouly have acknowledged other aesthetic challenges and goals as prompting the small insert booklets. In other words, the postwar booklets are a connection and influence which Spiegelman—as far as I am aware—did not stress before his conversation with Chute.

12. Art Spiegelman, *MetaMaus: A Look Inside the Modern Classic,* Maus (New York: Pantheon, 2011), 15–16.

13. Kartalopoulos, "A *RAW* History."

14. Kartalopoulos, "A *RAW* History."

15. Kartalopoulos, "A *RAW* History."

16. Kartalopoulos, "A *RAW* History."

17. Kartalopoulos, "A *RAW* History."

18. Brian Tucker, "Interview with Art Spiegelman," in *Art Spiegelman: Conversations*, ed. Joseph Witek (Jackson: University Press of Mississippi, 2007), 216.

19. Kartalopoulos, "A *RAW* History."

20. "'MetaMaus': The Story Behind Spiegelman's Classic." National Public Radio. October 5, 2011.

21. "'MetaMaus': The Story."

22. Emily Miller Budick, "Forced Confessions: The Case of Art Spiegelman's *Maus*," *Prooftexts* 21, no. 3 (2001): 387.

23. Art Spiegelman, *Maus: My Father Bleeds History* (New York: Pantheon, 1986), 25.

24. Spiegelman, *Maus: My Father Bleeds History*, 25.

25. Spiegelman, *Maus: My Father Bleeds History*, 25.

26. Spiegelman, *Maus: My Father Bleeds History*, 161.

27. Spiegelman, *Maus: My Father Bleeds History*, 161.

28. Spiegelman, *Maus: My Father Bleeds History*, 161.

29. Nicole Stamant, "'Too Meta to Live': The Materiality of Seriality from Art Spiegelman's 'Maus' to *MetaMaus*," in *Serial Memoir: Archiving American Lives* (London: Palgrave Macmillan, 2014), 108.

30. Stamant, "'Too Meta to Live': The Materiality of Seriality," 108.

31. Stamant, "'Too Meta to Live': The Materiality of Seriality," 108.

32. Stamant, "'Too Meta to Live': The Materiality of Seriality," 108.

33. Michael Lund, *America's Continuing Story: An Introduction to Serial Fiction* (Detroit: Wayne State University Press, 1992), 18. My emphasis.

34. Andreas Huyssen, "Of Mice and Mimesis: Reading Spiegelman with Adorno," *New German Critique* 81 (2000): 74.

35. Marilyn Reizbaum, "Surviving on Cat and *Maus*: Art Spiegelman's Holocaust Tale," *Mapping Jewish Identities*, ed. Laurence Silberstein (New York: New York University Press, 2000), 125.

36. James E. Young, "The Holocaust as Vicarious Past: Art Spiegelman's 'Maus' and the Afterimages of History," *Critical Inquiry* 24, no. 3 (1998): 690.

37. Spiegelman, *MetaMaus*, 118.

38. Suzanne Keen, "Fast Tracks to Narrative Empathy: Anthropomorphism and Dehumanization in Graphic Narratives," *SubStance* 40, no. 1 (2011): 136–37.

39. Richard De Angelis, "Of Mice and Vermin: Animals as Absent Referent in Art Spiegelman's *Maus*," *International Journal of Comic Art* 7, no. 1 (2005): 230.

40. Spiegelman, *MetaMaus*, 115.

41. J. Stephan Bolhafner, "Art for Art's Sake: Spiegelman Speaks on *RAW*'s Past, Present and Future," Steve's Reads, October 1991, http://bolhafner.com/stevesreads/ispieg2.html

42. Huyssen, "Of Mice and Mimesis," 75.

43. Harold Evans, foreword to *A Convenient Hatred: The History of Anti-Semitism*, ed. Phyllis Goldstein (Brookline, Mass.: Facing History and Ourselves, 2012), ix.

44. Huyssen, "Of Mice and Mimesis," 75.

45. Considered in this context, Victor recalls the Third Reich's greeting of "hail victory," the direct translation of "Sieg Heil."

46. Robert Hutton, "A Mouse in the Bookstore: *Maus* and the Publishing Industry," *South Central Review* 32, no. 3 (2015): 34–35.

ELLIS ISLAND ART

Art Spiegelman's Place in the History of Immigration Comics

CARA KOEHLER

SPIEGELMAN AND IMMIGRATION

"Sometimes, I think I would like to emigrate to Europe," Art Spiegelman remarked in 2003. "Seeing that in America they won't even let me smoke," he added, "the temptation is very great."[1] This is the blunt-but-lovable, chain-smoking comics legend that shall accompany us in this chapter—the Artist as an Old(er) %@&*!, whose jests are usually thinly veiled jabs at the miserable state of politics and culture, and whose later body of work might best be summed up by the motto "laughing on the outside, crying on the inside."[2] And it is this smoking, mouse-masked persona that we find at the center of his 2009 cartoon titled "The St. Louis Refugee Ship Blues" that appears to be a beacon—or smoke signal, if you will—of Spiegelman's preoccupation with immigration and borders which, though present throughout his career, has manifested itself more concretely in his cartoons from the last two decades.[3] Spiegelman demonstrated in "The St. Louis Refugee Ship Blues," and even more vividly three years later in his contributions to JR's *The Ghosts of Ellis Island*, that the American immigrant experience is deeply embedded in the history of comics, an art form whose pedigree, visibility, and reception Spiegelman is credited to have almost single-handedly transformed.[4]

Spiegelman's "Refugee Ship Blues" cartoon was published in a *Washington Post* issue commemorating the day in 1939 when over 900 Jewish refugees fleeing Germany were denied entry into Cuba and the United States. Unsurprisingly, Spiegelman's contribution had an ulterior agenda. While lamenting the "Voyage of the Damned," he takes to task both the American people and

Detail from "The St. Louis Refugee Ship Blues," *Washington Post* op-ed feature, 6/20/2009. Copyright © 2009 by Art Spiegelman.

American cartoonists of that era for their "failure of moral imagination . . . of *empathy*."[5] Spiegelman's mouse persona then walks us through a selection of cartoon responses to the tragedy, rating them from worst to best, and adding a sepia-toned panel of his own to the mix: a sketch of Lady Liberty handing out orange jumpsuits to "huddled masses" of immigrants. The text overlay cites figures from *Human Rights First Online* regarding asylum seekers who have been detained in prisonlike conditions by the Department of Homeland Security. Spiegelman uses this opportunity to remind audiences that it is the duty of cartoonists to "say the right thing" when nobody else has the gall to do so. Indeed, in one of the final panels, his alter ego holds as a model a copy of Barry Blitt's 2008 *New Yorker* cover (of the Obamas giving dap), which Spiegelman publicly defended along with his own controversial 1993 cover "The Kiss."[6] After all, the ability of cartoons to codify and satirize the oddities of contemporary culture is what drew Spiegelman to the medium in the first place.[7]

More than a defense of the First Amendment, "Refugee Ship Blues" feels especially personal given that Spiegelman, son of immigrants to the United States, has dusted off his mouse persona for this strip, thereby linking the refugee subject matter to his personal biography as immigrant, Jew, and victim—a "Prisoner on the Hell Planet" that was or still is America. Subtle early traces of the vision that informs the refugee ship strip are found in a panel of "Hell Planet" depicting the lifeless body of Spiegelman's mother in the bathtub. Spiegelman revisits this trope of an immigrant body set against a wet emptiness in one panel from *The Ghosts of Ellis Island* titled "Island of Tears . . . ," in which the naked and infirm immigrant named Leile floats in her own prison, a bathtub inside the Ellis Island's hospital quarantine. Indeed, in *The Ghosts of Ellis Island*, Spiegelman revisits a number of tropes he introduced in "Refugee Ship Blues": the timely image of the Statue of Liberty blocking the passage of immigrants; a collage of digitized comics archives and photographs; and his own cartoon panels alongside ample personal commentary. Conspicuously absent from *The Ghosts of Ellis Island* is Spiegelman's trademark persona—the cigarette-smoking mouse on a soapbox—suggesting that this is Spiegelman's least self-conscious book-size work yet.

In three major book-length publications as author and illustrator—*Maus*, *In the Shadow of No Towers*, and *The Ghosts of Ellis Island*—Spiegelman deconstructs historic events that help correct a misconception of America as an immigrant-friendly nation: World War II, the attacks of September 11, 2001, and the passage of twelve million immigrants through New York's Ellis Island between 1892 and 1924. The related significance of side projects such as editing *Si Lewen's Parade* or "The St. Louis Refugee Ship Blues" should not be underestimated, as they, too, give a voice to the disenfranchised and the wartime dead. Taken together, these projects convey the haunting echoes of America's history of newcomers. Within this framework, Spiegelman's illustrations for the *Ellis Island* project have a twofold purpose: to negotiate the alienation of immigrant arrival; and to enable the comics themselves qua literary form to comment on their own status as a new and suspicious European import.

It is worth remembering that Spiegelman harbors an attachment to Europe that goes beyond its smoker-friendly culture and the bond forged by his marriage to French-born Françoise Mouly. This attachment deserves a closer look, given its considerable impact on Spiegelman's life as an artist and public figure. His cultural affinity to Europe can be found in his art's subject matter, such as the fate of European immigrants to the United States in the aftermath of the Holocaust; in his mission at *RAW* magazine to expose American readers to the "vital work of established cartoonists around the world" and especially from Europe[8]; and of course in his Polish-Jewish-American lineage.[9] It is a wonder that Spiegelman and Mouly have yet to pack up and emigrate to

Europe, considering his outspoken disdain for many aspects of American society—including censorship in the arts, which led to his resignation at the *New Yorker*—and the direct ways in which his later works (*In the Shadow of No Towers*; *The Ghosts of Ellis Island*) confront America's forever rotten relationship with foreigners.

Spiegelman's love-hate attachment to America is what his later comics capture best and makes Spiegelman's art richer, more idiosyncratic. The duality of his personal identity informs the hybrid style he has practiced and championed throughout his career. As a result, his creations bridge the gulf between another set of borders: those that separate cartooning and literature.[10] This tension became especially evident in the wake of *Maus* and its critical as well as commercial success. Spiegelman teeters back and forth along the tenuous binary of what he calls the "vulgar" and "genteel" impulses of cartooning, a "tug" he could be on either side of.[11] This border-play across geographic and artistic demarcations has come to define both the art and the man. Spiegelman himself has not always been comfortable with, or even sure how to articulate, his place in the history of literature, let alone the history of immigration comics. This chapter aims to clarify his place in the latter.

I contend here that because Spiegelman's artwork obsessively transgresses lines and borders, both political and aesthetic, his role in the history of comics should be seen as that of a champion for immigrants' respect and appreciation of their own art. In other words, while scholars continue to call Spiegelman *the* transformative figure of American comics, we would be rewarded by gently turning our attention away from the more famous projects that confirm his literary prowess to look at some of the equally interesting, below-the-radar projects he has taken up since the turn of the millennium, and which suggest a benevolent impulse behind all the smoke and sarcasm. His quieter projects paint a broader picture of how Spiegelman prognosticated in his comics a new wave of xenophobic American attitudes towards both immigrants and provocative art—two equally alien challenges to the political status quo.

IMMIGRANT MODERNISMS

Joseph Witek, Bart Beaty, and Benjamin Woo have explained Spiegelman's role in comics history by invoking Pierre Bourdieu's model of cultural production. Spiegelman has produced works that appeal to a mass public (Topps comics; *Maus*), but has always also addressed a niche readership (with *RAW* and *Arcade*). Much in the same vein, comics as a medium is "brimming with anxiety about the high/low divide, mass culture, and aesthetic elitism" in ways that parallel the literary and aesthetic modernism of the early twentieth century.[12]

A recognizable New York personality with a broken-record scrutiny of (and disregard for) political correctness and what Bourdieu calls "cultural capital," Spiegelman "moves seamlessly form the 'high' to the 'low' in comics because he knows the truth about his art form: The borders are bull."[13] His artwork negotiates lines and borders, both political and aesthetic. Often the two go hand in hand, in that the artistic transgressions he seeks are inseparable from incursions into foreign cultures.

One of Spiegelman and Mouly's original goals with *RAW* was to make available in the United States the free license that comics in Europe were taking. Around a third of the artists in *RAW* were European, while the remainder comprised both "high art" cartoonists and work that simply fit "the sensibility of the magazine."[14] Spiegelman and Mouly have spent a large portion of their careers working toward a creative acculturation of comics arts and an appreciation of comics artists "as disparate as Rodolphe Töpffer and the anonymous pornographers of the Tijuana Bibles."[15] In doing so, they have opened up America's cultural borders to outside influences, even though they made little effort to reach the mainstream. If anything, steps were taken—already with *RAW* magazine—to avoid reaching the masses, as Mouly explains in a 1980 interview: "We think that we have queer enough—strange enough—taste and we're not in touch with the masses. . . . We certainly don't expect that this magazine will ever have a mass audience."[16] For such a household name, it is surprising just how much of Spiegelman's work has taken shape out of the limelight, be it through publishing obscure international artists in *RAW*, the collaboration with JR on *The Ghosts of Ellis Island* that was only thinly documented in the press, or a very personal quest around the same time to immortalize the wordless graphic narrative *The Parade* by the political refugee and immigrant Si Lewen.[17]

The Parade was crafted in the modernist period, but, as Spiegelman points out, it evaded the kitsch and irony of formal experimentation: "It doesn't feel contrived, it feels just like a very pure wail of poem or song . . . and it really got to the heart of something that one can do with pictures, which is tell something that can resonate across language and cultures."[18] Lewen's biography is not irrelevant to this assessment. Lewen's personal friendship with Spiegelman, a Polish-Jewish artist like himself, led Spiegelman to eulogize Lewen in the August 2016 edition of *Harper's Magazine*, shortly after Lewen had passed away.[19] Spiegelman recounts Lewen's journey as a young immigrant in precise, almost clinical detail, using language that recalls two illustrations published a year earlier in *The Ghosts of Ellis Island*: "Island of Tears . . ." and "Island of Hope."

Spiegelman's Lewen project had begun as early as 2013, predating his collaboration with JR on *The Ghosts of Ellis Island*. In a poetic turn, then, he went from curating the work of an immigrant artist thirty years his senior to collaborating with a French artist thirty years his junior on a project that narrates the plight of immigrants. Spiegelman begins his 2016 eulogy in *Harper's Magazine* by invoking the "ghost" of Si Lewen hanging in his studio—a painting from the 2008–2015 series by the late artist, which depicts a half-smiling ghostly figure in black-and-white tones.[20] This friendly ghost and the friendship with Lewen seem to have stirred some sediments of Spiegelman's own past, as he reveals in a 2017 interview with Anthony Audi.[21] Spiegelman recalls that Lewen came to dislike art as a commodity and endured financial hardship as a result. While JR may embody Lewen's "art for all / art for free" ethos, he has done so with great success year after year. In working with JR, then, Spiegelman is able to produce art that retains its integrity while at the same time reaching a mass audience.

Spiegelman's high-wire acts echo the formal battles of modernism in more ways than by cultivating a mere disregard of popular approval. In the pre-*Maus* era, comics endured the same kind of criticism that disparaged modernist art: "Once considered corrupted hybrids of purer forms," Harry Backlund of the *Paris Review* reminds us, "comics now claim proximity to a kind of fundamental language."[22] The nomenclature here—"corrupted hybrids"—recalls the early twentieth-century eugenics movement in the United States, which influenced the deeply racist Immigration Act of 1924 barring Jewish, Italian, and other immigrants deemed "inferior" from entering the country. Recent comics scholarship, notably by Charles Hatfield, has framed the inherent diversity of comics in affirmative terms, speaking to the symbolic power of the immigrant as subject. In Hatfield's formulation, "comics can be a complex means of communication and are always characterized by a plurality of messages. They are heterogeneous in form, involving the co-presence and interaction of various codes."[23] Terms like "complex," "plurality," and "heterogeneous" hint at the hybridity that runs through so many comic strips in the form of immigrant characters confronted with their complex, dual status.

Spiegelman's most immigrant-focused work to date, *The Ghosts of Ellis Island*, is set inside the hospital and quarantine buildings that millions of immigrants passed through on their way to the United States. The photo/comics collage captures the contiguity of contemporary anti-immigrant sentiment with the nativist politics of the past, best encapsulated in a now-infamous, antimodernist tenet from the twentieth-century art critic Royal Cortissoz:

> There is something in the art situation analogous to what has been so long going on in our racial melting pot. The United States is invaded by aliens, thousands of whom constitute so many acute perils to the health of the body politic. Modernism is of precisely the same heterogeneous *alien* origin and is imperiling the republic of art in the same way. It began, as our excessive immigration began, in an insidiously plausible

> manner. . . . These movements have been promoted by types not yet fitted for their first papers in aesthetic naturalization—the makers of true *Ellis Island Art*.[24]

In the unwittingly powerful phrase "Ellis Island Art," Cortissoz conflates the "heterogeneous" spirit of the movement with a sickness not unlike the kind immigrants purportedly brought over with them on their journey to the United States. His objection, importantly, lay not so much with the cultural heritage of modernist artists or even with their subject matter, but rather with the unconventional form of their creations.[25]

In the early decades of the twentieth century, comics art and immigration shared a stigma of lowbrow crudeness aptly epitomized by the stage on which JR and Spiegelman's visual palimpsest is arranged: the 750-bed hospital complex where people with infectious diseases were, too, corralled and contained as a threat to the nation's health. JR's contribution to *The Ghosts of Ellis Island* asks visitors to come face to face with the mysteries of silent, frozen-in-time, life-size photographs of immigrants who suffered disease and stigma inside and outside the walls of the hospital. Spiegelman's artwork flouts the disgust and disdain for the foreign body-politic articulated by Cortissoz. Together, Spiegelman and JR resist classification through different means, but in their goal—to implicate us, our place in the story, and thereby expose "the humanity we may have overlooked"[26]—they are united.

COMICS AS IMMIGRANT ART

Spiegelman himself, a first-generation immigrant, and Mouly, who emigrated to the United States in the 1970s, are poster children for the comics subculture that attracts artists and publics on the fringes of society, from impoverished *fin-de-siècle* immigrants to bohemian émigrés of the twenty-first century. These fringe artists in turn create fringe figures who negotiate tenuous borders within and beyond the panels, from Chris Ware's *Jimmy Corrigan* to Alan Moore and David Gibbons's *Watchmen*. Hatfield has noted that by the 1970s, the pedagogical value of comics was already taking hold among US audiences, but comics' accessibility and relatively basic vocabulary—their modernist "exchange between poetic and everyday speech"[27]—allowed them to become informal educational tools about a century earlier. For one, Richard Felton Outcault's *Hogan's Alley* sketched out the "look" of the immigrant (or more generally othered) experience. The Yellow Kid, Outcault's emblematic figure, was essentially a crude, bald man-child—a hybrid figure that Chris Ware would conspicuously modernize through the figure of Jimmy Corrigan a century or so later—who stood out as much for his oversize yellow t-shirt as for his English use—a "marginally intelligible pidgin jumble of ethnic clichés," to quote David Hajdu.[28] Immigrants thus appear as both subjects and creators who embrace their so-called crudeness and hybridity in the service of their art.

Like the immigrants who passed through Ellis Island, the graphic medium arrived in America by way of Europe. Spiegelman explicitly refers to comics art as possessing a "European patrimony . . . a life that came before," which he credits to the works of Swiss artist Rodolphe Töpffer.[29] In the same 2012 interview, he dismisses the widespread notion that the birth of comics coincides with the conception of *The Yellow Kid*. The difference, he feels, is that Outcault's newspaper drawings in fact marked the rise of comics as merchandised consumer products, as opposed to vehicles of the avant-garde. At first, this impulse to align comics with a revered European pedigree is puzzling for someone like Spiegelman, who has always reveled in the gritty side of American comics history, rather than in its mainstream legitimization. Spiegelman's wish to distance himself and the comics medium from its origins in mass journalism is a phenomenon David M. Ball has likewise observed. This "desire to disassociate," Ball contends, is what "makes graphic narratives so thoroughly, persistently modernist."[30] And yet the vaudeville and vulgar side to *The Yellow Kid* was key in hooking linguistically challenged immigrant readers, or, as Ball more subtly puts it, "served first as a boon to mass readership."[31] Somewhat against the grain of Spiegelman's only oblique acknowledgement of the immigrant's role in the popularization and later in the cultural acceptance of comics arts, I argue for a more nuanced inquiry into comics' indebtedness to the immigration story.

Through the idiom of sequential, usually captioned images, the comics medium has time and again proven its ability to create new morphologies that transcend language barriers. In fact, when nonnative speakers of English accounted for roughly forty percent of the population of late nineteenth-century New York City, Outcault's *Hogan's Alley* found an ideal audience for its Yellow Kid.[32] William Randolph Hearst III noted that the celebrity of *The Yellow Kid* and similar cartoons derived from the fact that newspaper readers might ignore the piece of a columnist they dislike, but "nobody can ignore the pictures. You notice. You can't look away."[33] The slumdog-*cum*-Irish immigrant would remain one of America's most iconic cartoon figures until the debut of Superman in 1938, who soon became the world's most recognizable "alien." In 1959 France, the adventures of *Astérix*, revolving around the globetrotter and defender of his native land of Gaul, was inaugurated by cartoonists René Goscinny and Albert Uderzo.

Migrant iconography was also at the heart of a 2013 art exhibition in Paris titled *Comics and Immigration: 1913–2013*, which featured over one hundred immigration-themed works of comics art. The curator, Hélène Bouillon of the

National Museum of Immigration History, quipped that "the whole history of comic books is the history of immigration."[34] Immigration has also been a shared experience of the artists behind many of these popular comics, including first-generation immigrants such as Jerry Siegel, Joe Schuster, Will Eisner, and Marjane Satrapi. Immigration as a theme in comics experienced a paradigm shift with the publication of *Maus* and continues to haunt subsequent comics and graphic novels such as Joe Sacco's *Palestine* (1993–1995), Marjane Satrapi's *Persepolis* (2000), Shaun Tan's *The Arrival* (2006), or Jérôme Ruillier's *The Strange* (2016).

As much as *Maus* may have inspired Tan, Spiegelman and JR's *The Ghosts of Ellis Island* is in turn indebted to *The Arrival*, a wordless graphic narrative that depicts one family's immigrant experience. Tan's Art Nouveau drawing style more closely resembles the clean lines of Chris Ware and Winsor McCay, as opposed to the "ratty" lines Spiegelman employs in *Maus*, and yet Tan's direct inspiration for *The Arrival* was in fact Ellis Island: "A lot of my 'inspirational images' blu-tacked to the walls of my studio were old photographs of immigrant processing at Ellis Island, visual notes that provided underlying concepts, mood and atmosphere behind many scenes that appear in the book."[35] In this engagement with Ellis Island photographs—sketching from them and reworking their impact into comics language—JR, Spiegelman, and Tan find a common catalyst for their work. Together they have crafted new frames for immigrant narratives, be they on the crisp pages of a paperback or on crumbling, ragged walls. In *The Ghosts of Ellis Island*, JR also used real photographs of Ellis Island immigrants, which he enlarged to achieve an even more haunting, lifelike quality. In ways that duplicate collages in *Maus* and "Refugee Ship Blues," Spiegelman's *Ghosts* comic strip "Island of Tears . . ." incorporates a real photograph, this time of a trachoma-infected eye side by side with drawings of an immigrant woman from Russia reported to have suffered from the disease. Spiegelman supplies documentary evidence of the suffering this woman experienced, without confronting readers with too much realism—the photograph of the actual woman—though the reality of the illness is painfully implied.

Bill Blackbeard suggests it was photography, in fact, that inspired early American cartoonists to engage with the plight of immigrants in the first place: Outcault's *Hogan's Alley* gained popularity contemporaneously with the publication of Jacob Riis's *How the Other Half Lives* (1890), which depicted New York City's slum tenements and the mostly immigrant population living there.[36] Making "fun" of (or out of) social problems like poverty, immigration, or illness is where American comics got their start. Blackbeard specifically notes that when *Life* magazine cartoonist Michael Angelo Wolff "sensitively depicted" New York's scruffy street children, it was impossible to ignore his "deeply felt concern" for the human beings represented.[37] The difference, however, between turn-of-the-century cartoonists and someone like Spiegelman rests in their authorial self-image. For Blackbeard, there is no way to be sure how slum cartoonists truly felt: When interviewed they spoke only anecdotally, revealing nothing about the ethical elements of their work, insisting instead on their entertainment value.[38] In contrast, the desire to "bring to life"—in a caring, humane way—the people who once occupied the Ellis Island Hospital complex was the unabashed impetus behind the exhibit "Unframed—Ellis Island" and the resulting *Ghosts*.[39]

SPIEGELMAN, JR, AND THE SOCIAL WORK OF COMICS

Around 2014, Spiegelman's work entered a retrospective phase. He oversaw the publication of *Co-Mix*, an overview of his career in cartooning; he debuted his audiovisual tour *WORDLESS!*, a tribute to the earliest graphic novels; and he created four major drawings for *The Ghosts of Ellis Island*, an ode to America's past immigrants. All three projects juxtapose history with the present in a gesture that can be traced back to Spiegelman's work on *Maus*—at once the record of "the greatest cataclysm of the 20th century" and the narrative of a single survivor.[40] *Co-Mix: A Retrospective of Comic, Graphics, and Scraps* looks back at 50-odd years of Spiegelman's mostly uncollected material while *WORDLESS!* exposes the public to the hushed beauty of early twentieth-century woodcut novels. Similarly, in *The Ghosts of Ellis Island*, Spiegelman underscores the hybridity of his medium by engaging with the quiet ruins of America's once teeming gateway. All the while he ropes in the present moment to highlight the legacies of past migration history on America's ethnic and racial makeup in the early twenty-first century. In this chapter, *Ghosts* will be of primary interest because it best juxtaposes, textually and formally, the past and present plight of immigrants, and does so in ways that yoke together other Spiegelman projects (reissuing Lewen's *Parade*; the "Refugee Ship Blues" strip) in which the cartoonist used his art to make pointed sociopolitical statements.

The *Ghosts* project and the creative force behind it, French-Tunisian artist JR, were given due accolades in the media, culminating in a summons from art dealer Jeffrey Deitch for a new project titled *SO CLOSE*, for which in 2018 JR took his Ellis Island photo-posters and melded them with those of Syrian refugees. "He is one of the rare artists to combine artistic innovation with political engagement," Deitch wrote. "JR's unique community-based approach to the creation and experience of art has inspired and engaged people who had never before connected with contemporary art."[41] Deitch's words ring a bell to those who remember the media praise of Spiegelman's *Maus* upon the publication of its first volume in 1986.

JR and Spiegelman have been inspired by contested, marginal, historically complex, and politically loaded canvases—for Spiegelman, the trauma of the Nazi concentration camps; for JR, the border fence between Palestine and Israel in his *Face 2 Face* project, or the favelas of Rio de Janeiro in *Women Are Heroes*.[42] JR's black-and-white "flyposts" are provocative, but they never come across as snide social critiques.[43] He gives photographs an ample scale and a context outside the usual frame of a single image, thereby allowing his subjects to acquire a pulse and emotional depth. His flyposts are meant to be seen and felt, yet never glorified. (JR famously disappears as soon as media buzz begins to build around his projects, leaving the art and the people it affects or represents to speak for themselves.) In his own words, JR "take[s] the names and above all the faces of people that live in the margins of society and give[s] them back their individuality," while at the same time refusing to reveal his own name, since doing so would only distract from his subjects and the meaning of his work.[44]

Spiegelman's subject matter is very much in accord with JR's: borders, thresholds, personal suffering—made palpable for the everyman—and faceless masses; is there a more haunting panel in *Maus* than the crowd of Jewish mice in their prison garb, facing down the reader, showing how racism is easier when one denies an individual's humanity? What Spiegelman adds to what JR already does is crucial. As the widely-known author of *Maus* and some of the most Hebdo-esque *New Yorker* covers, he is the American standard-bearer for how aesthetics that goad the public can spark a shift in social perception. In other words, Spiegelman embodies a sea change in the acceptance of mass visual art.[45] In her book *Social Works*, performance studies scholar Shannon Jackson looks at publicly situated locales where "aesthetic and social provocations coincide."[46] JR's art is placed within a public monument, prompting a "perceptual shift" of that space and its subjects, to borrow Jackson's term. She writes: "But if the aesthetic mélange shifts perspective, then we also need frames that show the social stakes of that perceptual shift. . . . When the pace slows . . . or when collision cannot be avoided, we register the contingency of the 'ground' that supports our everyday acts of self-figuration."[47] Thus when JR takes his immigrant subjects out of their original photographic "frames" and gives them a new context—in a discomposing anachronism—the audience's perception of their contiguity with our current era becomes more acute. Something slightly different occurs when Spiegelman draws cartoons on the color-drained pages of *Ghosts*. This is yet another set of "frames that show the social stakes" of shifting perspectives. The vibrant hues interrupt our expectations and jerk us out of the moment, forcing us to pay close attention to what is being shown. In this sense, JR's and Spiegelman's art can both be considered immigrant "social works," to invoke Jackson's doubly connoted book title.

Aside from the subject matter of *Ghosts*, Spiegelman's formal choices for his cartoon inserts also act as a pacemaker for the photobook and serve a practical purpose by dictating how much time is spent on a single panel.[48] This pacing is especially helpful considering the ability of the drawings to mirror the unique temporality at work in the book, as it goes back in time to resurrect ghostlike stories that must stay with us. Additionally, with comics panels or indeed a photograph of empty rooms, there is an implicit invitation for the reader to fill in the gaps—to recover what lies before, after, or beyond the immediate present of the page or panel. This request for readers to put in the effort to decode the image is not only the animating principle behind comics as a medium, it also befits JR's larger project titled *Unframed*, which likewise relies on audience "collusion" (JR asks permission to put up his artwork on public or privately owned buildings) and later on audience involvement (to help display posters, or speak to the media about them) to complete his narrative.[49] When Spiegelman and Mouly discussed in a 1982 interview the extent to which comics art is a "temporal medium," they were touching on an idea that Brian Tucker would flesh out in 2009, namely that "the image [in sequential art, i.e., comics] is no longer restricted to 'the single moment of time' that Lessing identifies as visual art's primary limitation; it becomes a narrative element."[50]

Together, in *The Ghosts of Ellis Island*, Spiegelman and JR have crafted a new narrative of social justice and commemoration in the abandoned hospitals of Ellis Island by decoding each other's work. The presence of the long departed, however, can only be understood by first engaging with the overpowering absence on the page. The book confronts us with an unaltered photograph of an empty room, then, as we turn the page (sometimes forward, sometimes back), we see the room come to life with one of Spiegelman's illustrations, or one of JR's photo installations. The ghosts of the immigrants are all the more present through their disappearing act: flip the page, and they are gone. In an interview with *Slate* France, JR explains that while stories of immigration were the artistic stimulus for the project, they were never an endpoint:

> At Ellis Island, I honored history, context, location and archival photos but I'm currently working with Art Spiegelman on a book that will more clearly span a bridge between past and present immigration. I think that by integrating both comics and drawing, we will be able to compare today's images with the walls of yesterday and show that, ultimately, it [the past] is not so distant from us.[51]

The relation between JR's and Spiegelman's images duplicates that between words and drawings in a book of comics. JR's photographic work creates a tone, an atmosphere, to which Spiegelman attaches explosive, moodily drawn "captions." During his *WORDLESS!* tour, Spiegelman shared with the crowd a sentiment that speaks to his impulse to "vandalize" JR's Ellis Island compositions: "Picture stories ask us to make meaning out of abstractions, using both sides of our brain, and as you focus on and decode the images, you're left with that holy-shit flash of recognition as the pictures take on meaning."[52] In a brilliant role reversal, JR—a famous guerrilla street artist—provides the private property (literally the walls of a protected national landmark) on which Spiegelman "tags" cartoon panels and pencil drawings (albeit only inside the sanctioned pages of an art book).

While JR's meticulously pasted portraits keep the immigrants immobile, literally stuck in their past, tucked into corners, trapped behind windowpanes, or glued to the floor, Spiegelman's "throw up"-style illustrations (to use graffiti terminology) replicate the hostile emotions that the stranded and disillusioned foreigners are likely to have experienced. Spiegelman no doubt left his images deliberately unpolished, as he has noted in the past how a scribbled effect matches the "immediacy and the urgent sign" of the thing represented.[53] Hatfield agrees that the "raw gestural qualities of a drawing"—a style associated with *Maus*, but pioneered by Gary Panter—act as a "record of physical activity" rather than signaling a drawing's "iconic or referential function."[54] Spiegelman's quivery drawings, in other words, leave readers with an "I WAS HERE" effect, which suits the overall goal of the *Ghosts* project: to provide a "record of physical activity" of the individuals who passed through.

SPIEGELMAN'S ELLIS ISLAND

If Spiegelman recognizes the irony in working on a project with Ellis Island as its centerpiece, when his past copyright feud involved a certain Jewish mouse washing up on the shore of Ellis Island, he has not said as much.[55] When he spoke of Steven Spielberg's "mindless, fashionable, self-congratulatory, patriotic fervor" for planning to release the film *An American Tail* on the centennial of the Statue of Liberty, Spiegelman revealed, as an aside, that what bothered him most were the historical inaccuracies: "if you were being true to the initial metaphor, in depicting the way things really were in 1940, you would have to strand mice people off the coast of Cuba, *drowning*, because it is precisely the case that at that point, the time of their greatest need, mice people were being denied entry into the U.S."[56]

Spiegelman returned some twenty years later to the question of historical accuracy (and to his own brand of mindful, self-effacing, unpatriotic satire) to draw a cartoon commemorating the very event he describes above, but does not name: the refusal in 1939 of both Cuba and the United States to admit the

European Jewish refugees on board the St. Louis on the eve of World War II. Spiegelman recalls—with both his "St. Louis Refugee Ship Blues" cartoon and *Ghosts*—his outburst in 1986 which scoffed at the idea that the Statue of Liberty could truly be the symbolic equivalent of a warm welcome for immigrants. To call the panels predictive of the Trump era immigration policies would be both fitting and an oversimplification. Spiegelman has, for years, drawn our attention to underlying racial hostility in America and he has been committed to disturbing the cordial, sentimentalized history of ethnic and racial homogenization in the United States. He begins this effort in *Ghosts* by disrupting even the placid, introspective visual provocations of his collaborator, JR.

After the foreword to *The Ghosts of Ellis Island*, the first image that confronts us is the photograph of a snow-covered trash heap at Ellis Hospital, taken through a shattered window. The final image, titled "A Warm Welcome," shows the Statue of Liberty, mouth aflame, sticking her neck through another shattered window, disturbing the "peace" created at the beginning of the book. Here, Spiegelman harkens back to comics' "architectural approach to a page" by using a design he also employs in *Maus*, one that involves the cinematic trick of drawing the viewer's eye through a window to "see" things differently.[57] In the early image of the broken window, the jagged edges and point of view from behind the pane recall the project's larger title—*Unframed*—and sets the mood of the photobook: quiet entrapment, as if inside a room insulated by a blanket of snow, preventing both sounds and bodies from escaping. We are about to see images that begin as carefully composed, neatly framed portraits of rooms and corridors, before they merge with unframed portraits of the immigrants who once inhabited the halls, but now occupy their walls. While JR's immigrants remain within the boundaries in which they are placed, it is Spiegelman's depiction of a wrathful, red-eyed Lady Liberty, the symbol of national pride in freedom, that transgresses the borders of the frame to generate anxiety among the newcomers.

On the pages of *Ghosts*, the imagery of eyes is the subconscious red thread weaving between JR and Spiegelman's contributions. Eyes in fact feature as a highly prominent motif throughout much of JR's collaborative work, from his *Women Are Heroes* project in Rio de Janeiro to the *Inside Out Project* with Lakota Native Americans; from his collaboration with Chinese artist Liu Bolin to his Berlin murals with Italian artist Blu.[58] At the January 2018 Grammy Awards, Irish band U2 performed a pro-immigration ballad on a stage in the Hudson River, with Ellis Island and the Statue of Liberty in the background. The stage was covered in JR's recognizable flyposters of eyes, which stared back at viewers as Bono shouted, "Blessed are the shithole countries, for they gave us the American Dream"—disparaging President Trump's similarly worded diplomatic gaffe from earlier that month.[59] Spiegelman's illustrations in *Ghosts*

"A Warm Welcome," *The Ghosts of Ellis Island* (Bologna, Italy: Damiani, 2015), p. 102–3. Copyright © 2015 by Art Spiegelman.

breathe similar fire in ways that foreshadow how the situation of immigrants would become much worse under the Trump administration. For Spiegelman, the eyes he draws in *Ghosts* may recall a "baseline dread that runs through so much of his work," which, as Anthony Audi rightly argues, "no longer strikes [us] as neurotic, but, alas, as clear-eyed and prescient" in light of everything we have witnessed since the attacks on the World Trade Center—a war on terrorism but also on cultural pluralism.[60]

The title of Spiegelman's first drawing, "The Old Colossus," riffs on the "huddled masses" of immigrants evoked in Emma Lazarus's 1883 sonnet, "The New Colossus." Here, the Statue of Liberty rises from the depths of an inky stairwell, through which the powder-blue, ghostly outlines of immigrants are filing. Lady Liberty's "lamp," as in Lazarus's poem, does not illuminate a "golden door" but an upward climb, a waiting line with no clear beginning or end. This gloomy effigy sets the tone for the next three drawings, which capture the tears, the hope, and the less-than-warm welcome that immigrants, past and present, experience. With Spiegelman's final piece, "A Warm Welcome," the Statue of Liberty turns on a group of contemporary immigrant subjects, something hitherto missing from JR's murals, to highlight how emblems like the Statue of Liberty hold precious little of the cultural connotations they once

"The Old Colossus," *The Ghosts of Ellis Island* (Bologna, Italy: Damiani, 2015), 20–21. Copyright © 2015 by Art Spiegelman.

did. In fact, the self-aware, doodled quality of the drawing itself summons up both the pettiness of nativist Americans who conveniently forget the country's immigrant histories, and more interestingly also the immediacy of cartoons as "a kind of mother tongue, a language that one falls back to instinctively and one that recaptures the earliest experience of trying to make sense of the world."[61] What Jeet Heer underlines here, when speaking about the comics medium, is that even though Spiegelman and Mouly have helped transform comics from "a children's art form" to "an adult literature," they have not attempted to erase the rawness of the earliest human impulses for creativity.[62] In other ways, Spiegelman's Statue of Liberty cartoon in *Ghosts* also recalls the September 15, 1997, *New Yorker* cover by Robert Sikoryak titled *The Last Salute*. A tribute to Princess Diana following her untimely death, the waxy, crayon-like texture of the image is not particularly refined, yet its elementary technique effectively conveys a genuine emotionality.[63]

JR's 2015 short film *Ellis*, starring Robert De Niro and scripted by Academy-Award-winning screenwriter Eric Roth, presents through photographs, drawings, and minimal voiceover "the forgotten story of those immigrants who built America while questioning about those who currently seek the same opportunities and safety in this country and other parts of the world."[64] Although the film paints a melancholy, mournful picture focused on the poetry of immigrant life, in *Ghosts* it is Spiegelman's drawings that do much of the "questioning." I return for a moment to his most inflammatory illustration, "A Warm Welcome," because it proves how one artist's sober, almost impartial vision can be polemicized by a more outspoken peer. Spiegelman transforms the culturally charged space of Ellis Island into a ready canvas for a *RAW*-like parody of Lady Liberty and the Land of the "Free." The facetiously warm welcome might just as well reference the tentative embrace that comics have received from the art world at large, seeing as their aesthetic hybridity renders them neither simply a visual nor a literary form.[65]

The statue of Emma Lazarus's 1883 poem no longer "glows world-wide welcome"; her once "mild eyes" now bulge and bleed, an image Spiegelman repeats in another illustration to the book.[66] The drawing in question, titled "Island of Tears . . . ," depicts a family of Russian immigrants undergoing a medical exam, "including the scary trachoma inspection." The panels recall a series of snapshot-like panels in Tan's *The Arrival*: eyes, ears, tongue, and heart are all examined with no textual commentary at all. The silence underscores one of the greatest hurdles for all immigrants after their health inspection—the challenge of communication. When the sounds and signs they used to make sense of the world dissolve, the vulnerability and loneliness of the newly arrived are felt all the more deeply.

Ellis Island, as we know, was not intended to be a barrier for all immigrants, and indeed the third of Spiegelman's four illustrations, titled "Island of Hope!" resists all-out doom and gloom to illustrate that some passengers were, in fact, able to escape their temporary entrapment at the gates of New York City. Using an excerpt from a 1908 *New York Times* article, Spiegelman unearths the scandalous human-interest story of Mary Johnson (or rather, Frank Woodhull), a crossdresser who disguised himself as a woman in order to find gainful employment. Johnson/Woodhull endured a short stay in the Ellis Island Hospital, and it is in this setting that Spiegelman draws them shaving their face. (Woodhull was eventually—miraculously—welcomed to the United States as a free *man* a short time later.) The backdrop for Woodhull's story is the same bathroom that provided the background to "Island of Tears. . . ." The bathtub where deported trachoma patient Leile Kwarczinsky was shown—red-eyed, blind, bathing—is now covered up with text and almost unrecognizable. Spiegelman emphasizes here the passage of time and the transient, dual nature of the rooms in the hospital; for some immigrants, these walls spelled freedom while for others, death and sadness. Though both figures are depicted in the textured crayon colors of a child's drawing, their stories do not fail to move the reader.

To paraphrase Scott McCloud, the act of abstracting images through cartooning is not about eliminating detail, but rather turning the focus onto more specific or unusual details.[67] Spiegelman broadens our capacity to imagine immigration by defamiliarizing the real stories of immigrants (the blind Russian mother at Ellis Island, the man who posed as a woman) with cartoons whose colors and textures look nothing like a photograph (as JRs images do), yet retain a legibility that fosters empathy for the immigrant experience at the margins of society. Precisely because they do not harmonize with JR's austere photographs, Spiegelman's bright scribbles impress upon readers the urgency to confront the many shades of tragedy and brands of bigotry at the heart of US immigration history.

Spiegelman's *In the Shadow of No Towers* captured the anti-immigrant *zeitgeist* of America in the wake of 9/11 by using broadsheet-size pages that recalled late nineteenth-century newspapers, an era whose xenophobia parallels present-day nativist sentiments. Today's Mexicans and Muslims are the Chinese, Irish, or Italians—the "Yellow Kids"—of the past. In *The Ghosts of Ellis Island*, Spiegelman revisits the past a second time, swapping out the broadsheet for the solemnly photographed rooms of the Ellis Island Hospital. The bleak walls demanded a new tone from Spiegelman, one that steps away from his sardonic persona in *No Towers* and demonstrates a more muted approach which, on the one hand, honors JR's commission to "graffiti" his photo-narrative, and on the other enlists the mongrel art of comics to expose the artificiality of aesthetic and cultural purism.

This chapter set out to elucidate Spiegelman's place in the history of immigration comics, a position that only becomes clear when the smoke of his celebrity and mainstream, prize-winning work dissipates. His quieter immigration-themed comics occupy the silence around the topic of justice for the victims of US border politics, regardless of whether the topic was or is trending in the news media. Knowing how immigrants and minorities were often shut out of respectable fields in art, and how censorship in America affected both comics (in mid-twentieth century) and his own art (at the *New Yorker*), it appears that Spiegelman's mission is to keep cartooning a border-crossing, or rather border-bridging practice.[68] The duality of Spiegelman's identity as a Jewish American artist not only informs the Holocaust-themed *Maus* and the hybrid style its author has practiced throughout his career. More than that, *Ghosts* also shows that Spiegelman's own immigrant sensibility allows him to straddle the gulf between two new sets of borders, in addition to the boundary of comics and literature: those that separate cartooning from documentary arts like photography, and those between art and social activism.

Notes

1. Art Spiegelman, "Art Spiegelman, Cartoonist for the *New Yorker*, Resigns in Protest at Censorship," interview by *Corriere della Sera*, in *Art Spiegelman: Conversations*, ed. Joseph Witek (Jackson: University Press of Mississippi), 265–66.

2. Art Spiegelman, "Art Spiegelman: If It Walks Like a Fascist . . . ," interview by Anthony Audi, *Literary Hub Online*, March 22, 2017.

3. Art Spiegelman, "The St. Louis Refugee Ship Blues," *Washington Post Online*, 2009.

4. JR and Art Spiegelman, *The Ghosts of Ellis Island* (Bologna, Italy: Damiani, 2015).

5. Art Spiegelman, "The St. Louis Refugee Ship Blues," emphasis in original.

6. Art Spiegelman, "Art Spiegelman Defends 'New Yorker' Obama Cover," interview by Farai Chideya, *NPR*, July 15, 2008, audio, 6:51. Spiegelman felt "this [Barry Blitt cover] is cartooning working at its best in the sense that it's functioning as a vaccine, you know? Like most vaccines, it has to take some of the toxin and inject it into you in order to make you strong enough to resist it."

7. Art Spiegelman, *MetaMaus: A Look Inside a Modern Classic,* Maus (London: Viking, 2011), 190.

8. Joseph Witek, "Introduction," in *Art Spiegelman: Conversations*, ed. Joseph Witek (Jackson: University Press of Mississippi, 2007), x.

9. In *MetaMaus*, Spiegelman hints at an early trauma concerning his own immigration story: He shows his parents visa documents and discusses at length the process of name changing as part of his and their cultural assimilation into America (17–18). Like the Jews in *Maus,* who wear either the pig or the mouse mask depending on social necessity, Spiegelman's biography is rooted in the precarious juggling act of hybrid identities.

10. See Witek, "Introduction," xiii; Bart Beaty and Benjamin Woo, "*Maus* by Art Spiegelman?," in *The Greatest Comic Book of All Time* (New York: Palgrave Macmillan, 2016), 18.

11. Andrea Juno, "Art Spiegelman," in *Conversations*, 165.

12. Daniel Worden, "The Politics of Comics: Popular Modernism, Abstraction, and Experimentation," *Literature Compass* 12, no. 2 (2015): 61; David M. Ball, "Comics Against Themselves: Chris Ware's Graphic Narratives as Literature," in *Rise of the American Comics Artist: Creators and Contexts*, ed. Paul Williams and James Lyons (Jackson: University Press of Mississippi), 105.

13. Michael Cavna, "Art Spiegelman Speaks Out For the 'Wordless' Cartoonist," *Washington Post Online,* October 16, 2014.

14. Dean Mullaney, "*RAW* Magazine: An Interview with Art Spiegelman and Françoise Mouly," in *Conversations*, 23.

15. Witek, "Introduction," x.

16. Mullaney, "*RAW* Magazine," 29.

17. *Si Lewen's Parade*, with an introduction by Art Spiegelman (New York: Abrams, 2016).

18. Art Spiegelman, "If It Walks."

19. Art Spiegelman, "A Sigh and a Salute," *Harper's Online*, August 2016, 1–5.

20. Spiegelman, "A Sigh and a Salute," 1.

21. Spiegelman, "If It Walks."

22. Harry Backlund, "The Silent Treatment," *The Paris Review online*, February 13, 2014.

23. Charles Hatfield, *Alternative Comics: An Emerging Literature* (Jackson: University Press of Mississippi, 2005), 36.

24. Royal Cortissoz, *American Artists* (New York: Charles Scriber and Sons, 1923), 18. Emphasis mine.

25. Lauren Kroiz, *Creative Composites: Modernism, Race, and the Stieglitz Circle* (Berkeley: University of California Press, 2012), 1.

26. Jane Rosenthal, foreword to *The Ghosts of Ellis Island*, 6.

27. Hatfield, *Alternative Comics*, 35.

28. David Hajdu, *The Ten-Cent Plague: The Great Comic-Book Scare and How It Changed America* (New York: Farrar, Straus and Giroux, 2008), 10.

29. lacitebd, "Rodolphe Töpffer et le Yellow Kid par Art Spiegelman," YouTube video, 2:41, October 25, 2012.

30. Ball, "Comics Against Themselves," 103–23.

31. lacitebd, "Rodolphe Töpffer et le Yellow Kid par Art Spiegelman"; Ball, "Comics Against Themselves," 106.

32. Hajdu, *The Ten-Cent Plague*, 25; See also Joanna Davis-McElligatt, "Confronting the Intersection of Race, Immigration, and Representation in Chris Ware's Comics," in *The Comics of Chris Ware: Drawing Is a Way of Thinking*, ed. David M. Ball and Martha B. Kuhlman (Jackson: University Press of Mississippi, 2010), 136–37.

33. William Randolph Hearst III, foreword to *R. F. Outcault's the Yellow Kid: A Centennial Celebration of the Kid Who Started the Comics* (Northampton, MA: Kitchen Sink Press, 1995), 15.

34. Thomas Adamson, "Superman and Asterix Have More in Common Than You'd Think," *theJournal.ie*, October 20, 2013.

35. Hatfield, *Alternative Comics*, 61; Shaun Tan, "Comments on *The Arrival*," Shauntan.net.

36. Bill Blackbeard, "Coming Events: R. F. Outcault and the first Newspaper Comics," in *R. F. Outcault's the Yellow Kid: A Centennial Celebration of the Kid Who Started the Comics* (Northampton, MA: Kitchen Sink Press, 1995), 21.

37. Bill Blackbeard, "Laughing on the Outside: The Slum Kids of M.A. Wolff," in *R. F. Outcault's the Yellow Kid*, 18.

38. Blackbeard, "Laughing on the Outside," 18.

39. Janis Callela, introduction to *The Ghosts of Ellis Island*, 15.

40. Jon Niccum, "Art Spiegelman's 'Wordless' Makes for an Atypical Tour," *Kansas City Star*, October 17, 2014.

41. Sarah Cascone, "The Artist JR Will Plaster the Facade of This Year's Armory Show with the Faces of Immigrants," *Artnet news*, February 7, 2018.

42. "The Man Who Pasted the Favelas: 5 Reasons to Follow Street Artist JR," *Christie's online*, October 15, 2015.

43. Marie Salomé Peyronnel, "JR à Ellis Island: 'Quand je colle, je ne livre pas de message avec,'" *Slate.fr.*, November 28, 2017.

44. Bertie Ferdman, "Urban Dramaturgy: The Global Art Project of JR," *AJ: A Journal of Performance and Art* 34, no. 3 (September 2012): 15, 12.

45. Witek, "Introduction," xii.

46. Shannon Jackson, *Social Works: Performing Art, Supporting Publics* (New York: Routledge, 2011), 5.

47. Jackson, *Social Works*, 5–6.

48. Douglas Wolk, *Reading Comics* (New York: Da Capo Press, 2007), 128.

49. Hatfield, *Alternative Comics*, 35–36.

50. Gary Groth, Kim Thompson, and Joey Cavalieri, "Slaughter on Greene Street: Art Spiegelman and Françoise Mouly Talk about *RAW*," in *Conversations*, 55; Brian Tucker, "Gotthold Ephraim Lessing's Laocoön and the Lessons of Comics," in *Teaching the Graphic Novel*, ed. Stephen E. Tabachnick (New York: MLA, 2009), 31.

51. Peyronnel, "JR à Ellis Island." Translation mine.

52. Backlund, "The Silent Treatment."

53. Michael Silverblatt, "The Cultural Relief of Art Spiegelman," in *Conversations*, 131.

54. Hatfield, *Alternative Comics*, 61.

55. Spiegelman was distraught when in 1986, he read that Steven Spielberg planned to produce a film about a family of Jewish mice and call it *An American Tail*. Spiegelman's own forthcoming *Maus* was subtitled *A Survivor's Tale*, yet another similarity he just could not let go of. Eventually *Maus* came out before the film (in two parts) but not before Spiegelman went "sleepless for nights on end." R. Crumb laughed off the fiasco, calling Spiegelman (good-naturedly) an egomaniac for even caring (Weschler in Witek, 72–73).

56. Lawrence Weschler, "Art's Father, Vladek's Son," 1986, in *Conversations*, 72–73. Emphasis in the original.

57. Spiegelman, *MetaMaus*, 167.

58. *JR-art.net*, "Collaborations," "Lakota Project."

59. Alexandra Schwartz, "The Artist JR Lifts a Mexican Child Over the Border Wall," *New Yorker Online*, September 11, 2017. Indeed, the 'eye' symbolism grows even stronger in light of JR's publicity-stunt art: a picnic at the border wall to Mexico in Baja, California, where people shared a meal around the 'eyes' of a Dreamer, pasted to the ground.

60. Spiegelman, "If It Walks."

61. Jeet Heer, *In Love with Art* (Toronto: Coach House Books, 2013), 115.

62. Heer, *In Love with Art*, 114.

63. Heer, *In Love with Art*, 92, 112.

64. *JR-art.net*, "Ellis film," video, 1:55, http://www.jr-art.net/videos/ellis-trailer

65. See Worden, "The Politics of Comics," 59.

66. Emma Lazarus, "The New Colossus," *Poetry Foundation*, https://www.poetryfoundation.org/poems/46550/the-new-colossus.

67. Scott McCloud, *Understanding Comics: The Invisible Art* (New York: HarperCollins, 1993), 30.

68. Alex Abad-Santos, "The Insane History of How American Paranoia Ruined and Censored Comic Books," *Vox online*, March 13, 2015. In the Golden Age of comics, roughly 1930s–1950s, "the people producing comic books at the time—illustrators, writers, creatives—were often immigrants and minorities who were shut out of more respected fields of publishing in one way or another."

ART SPIEGELMAN'S FAUSTIAN BARGAIN

TOON Books and the Invention of Comics for Kids

LEE KONSTANTINOU

BEYOND THE *BILDUNGSROMAN* DISCOURSE OF COMICS HISTORY

In 2012, the satirical newspaper the *Onion* published a short article entitled "Comics Not Just for Kids Anymore, Reports 85,000th Mainstream News Story."[1] "Though comics have long been considered a favorite pastime of children and teenagers," the satirical article observes, "the continued popularity of comic books and movies for adults proves the genre isn't just for kids anymore, bold national news outlets reported." The *Onion* here invokes a clichéd journalistic discourse that has, since the mid-1980s, celebrated the growing popularity and changing character of comics. The inaugural instance of this discourse was Ken Tucker's 1985 review of *Maus* in the *New York Times*. Tucker held up *Maus* as an example of a new wave of post-countercultural comics that might "expand the very notion of what a comic strip can do, to make intelligent readers reconsider—and reject—the widespread notion of, in Mr. Spiegelman's phrase, 'comics-as-kid-culture.'"[2] Since Tucker's pioneering article, journalists have often reached for the same narrative frame when writing about new cartoonists who they think merit attention. Examples are legion.[3] The *Onion* spoof mocks the continual rediscovery of the obvious: that cartoonists have been making comics for adults, telling stories about adult subjects, and expanding the formal range of the medium for decades. At the same time, the *Onion* also clarifies that journalistic celebrations of comics as adult fare do not necessarily *elevate* the status of the medium—but might instead be a backhanded way of deprecating it.

As Christopher Pizzino has observed in *Arresting Development*, cultural celebrations of comics continue to insist that for every good or worthy comic there is a vast library of bad or worthless counterexamples.[4] Within this discourse, a bad comic does not have the same relation to its medium as, say, a bad novel. In Pizzino's view, all bad comics are thought to reflect on an essential childishness of comics, whereas all good comics become the exception that proves the rule. This is why journalists are able again and again to rediscover the new maturation of comics—85,000 times, as the *Onion* quips. At this rate, comics will never grow up. More, as Pizzino documents, these arguments implicitly associate artistic worthlessness with childhood and artistic achievement with adulthood. They associate certain genres (superhero narrative, science fiction, fantasy) with child readers and other genres (memoir, realism, metafiction) with adults. And they personify media, speaking as if comics *as such* could be characterized as mature or immature, adult or childlike. Similar assumptions are evident even in Scott McCloud's defense of the medium in *Understanding Comics*: "Sure, I realized that comic books were usually crude, poorly-drawn, semiliterate, cheap disposable kiddie fare—but, they don't have to be!"[5] McCloud personifies comics, describing it as a childlike medium whose growth has been stunted or stalled, and he suggests that the maturation of comics will be signaled by the age of the people who read them. This is a clear example of what Pizzino calls the "Bildungsroman discourse" of comics criticism.[6]

Pizzino does much to clarify the problems with this discourse, yet he often seems to suggest that it is only journalists, critics, and mainstream cultural gatekeepers who make use of these tropes. Cartoonists, in his view, only register the low cultural status of their medium through an artistic practice Pizzino names "autoclasm," a self-deprecating, reflexive style of cartooning that uses the resources of comics to dramatize its precarious cultural status. But many cartoonists who mean to promote comics have, I would argue, also often embraced the *bildungsroman* discourse Pizzino condemns; like McCloud, they have claimed that after a long period of childishness, comics has finally "grown up." As Marc Singer shows in *Breaking the Frames*, many prominent cartoonists celebrate realism and autobiography as serious genres, over and against childish science fiction and superhero stories.[7] And more than any other cartoonist, it is Art Spiegelman himself who has promoted this *bildungsroman* discourse. Ken Tucker was, after all, quoting Spiegelman when he found in *Maus* evidence that comics was finally growing up. In Spiegelman's view, undermining the hegemony of the "comics-as-kid-culture" narrative was a necessary step if *Maus* was to find a wider audience beyond the pages of *RAW*.

It is hard to argue that Spiegelman did anything other than succeed. He found the audience he sought. If a comics canon can be said to exist, *Maus* (1980–1991) has a secure place on the list. The memoir won a special Pulitzer in 1992 after the publication of its second volume, and it has appeared on myriad syllabi, supporting curricula focused on Holocaust education, comics and the graphic novel, as well as life writing and the memoir. *Maus*'s success has arguably not only elevated Spiegelman but has created a new audience for comics. It, moreover, secured a niche for comics at publishing imprints such as Pantheon and opened up space on the shelves of traditional book retailers such as Barnes & Noble and Borders. Yet Spiegelman has expressed anxieties about his success, often describing the elevation of his medium as the product of a "Faustian deal."[8] "[T]he medium gets tainted by its aspirations toward legitimacy," he worries, "and I was part of the taint."[9] Success might lead cartoonists to start "making [comics and graphic novels] so they can be used in schools. . . . I think that leads to a different kind of work—designing them for an audience of academics."[10] At the same time, Spiegelman admits he is "proud that *Maus* is being used as a canonical text," conceding that "not only bad stuff . . . happens in classrooms."[11]

Keeping Spiegelman's ambivalence in mind, we are better equipped to understand one of the surprising ways the cartoonist has followed the success of *Maus*. Alongside his decades-long fight to elevate comics, Spiegelman began creating and advocating for children's comics. He authored two book-length children's comics—*Open Me . . . I'm a Dog!* (1997) and *Jack and the Box* (2008)—and along with Françoise Mouly, he edited *The TOON Treasury of Classic Children's Comics*. Mouly and Spiegelman also edited three volumes of the *Little Lit* anthology series (2000–2003), which showcases comics for children by a range of cartoonists and illustrators, including Spiegelman, whose "Prince Rooster" (2000) inaugurated the series. Neatly reversing the commonplace that comics are not just for kids anymore, the back cover of the first *Little Lit* volume insists that "COMICS" are "not just for Grown-Ups Anymore!"[12] Mouly also founded a publishing house dedicated to publishing comics for kids. Launched in 2008, TOON Books describes itself as making available "the first high-quality comics designed for children ages three and up."[13] The books they print have been "vetted by educators to ensure that the language and the narratives will nurture young minds."[14] The publisher of Spiegelman's *Jack and the Box* and two dozen other books, TOON advertises itself as "combin[ing] its high-quality, award-winning comics with a rigorous genre study aligned to the Common Core State Standards [CCSS] for Reading, Writing, and Speaking & Listening."[15] TOON's "Comics Genre Study" set, sold directly to primary school teachers, even comes with a two-hundred-page curriculum guide, *TOON into Comics: Genre Study for Reading and Writing*, which promises to be "CCSS Aligned" for Grades 1 through 3. Far from shy away from the classroom, then, TOON writes the very lesson plans through which its books ought to be taught.

And yet, even as it invites integration into the classroom, *TOON into Comics* seems to equivocate on the question of *why* comics should become part of the curriculum. The genre study guide promises, first, that reading comics can lead to improved capacities with grapheme-based literacy. "Comics are a gateway drug to literacy," Spiegelman is quoted as saying.[16] But the teaching materials also treat reading comics as an end in itself. It is the "world of comics" that students are ultimately being trained to enjoy, not comics as a means toward some other end.[17] The equivocation between comics as *means* and as *end* suffuses the guidebook. In this equivocation, we glimpse again a version of Spiegelman's "Faustian bargain" with the museum and the school. If Spiegelman was so unsure about this bargain, why did he turn to creating comics explicitly designed for the classroom? Why revive or even strengthen the association between childhood and comics? How does creating "high-quality" comics for kids help advance Spiegelman's aim of securing the future of comics? This chapter argues that Spiegelman's turn to children's comics does not break with his broader mission. Instead, creating comics-for-kids is, from Spiegelman's perspective, the next logical step of the necessary-if-problematic bargain he struck with the culture's gatekeepers. To support this claim, the chapter offers readings of Spiegelman's *Jack and the Box*, *Open Me . . . I'm a Dog!*, and "Prince Rooster."

These texts not only reward close reading but, I would argue, are knowingly designed to be legible through a practice of comics-specific close reading. Analyzing Spiegelman's children's comics will allow me to develop three related claims. First, making comics for kids serves much the same function as declaring that comics are not just for kids. In rhetorically constructing a category of "children's comics," Spiegelman hopes to rescue comics as such from its association with childhood by suggesting that there is a more general category containing both adult and children's comics. My second claim is that this category of comics as such depends upon a concept of "comics literacy"—that is, a set of reading protocols that every comics reader needs to learn. Comics for kids, Spiegelman implies, should train children to become adult readers of comics. To make such training possible, Spiegelman invents a new type of comics: children's-comics-qua-children's comics. While children have read comics since the birth of the medium, and cartoonists have always created comics for children, never before has a cartoonist created comics meant to be part of an educational curriculum whose end is reading adult comics. My final claim is that advocates of "comics literacy" join a broader educational campaign to celebrate "visual literacy," "multiliteracies," and "multimodal literacies." Celebrations of multimodal literacy, I briefly conclude, elevate modernist values such as "autonomy" and "medium-specificity," but also cannot avoid thinking of these values instrumentally. This is the cultural contradiction that, I argue, lies at the heart of Spiegelman's ongoing struggle to find a non-Faustian way to legitimate, nourish, and protect comics in the twenty-first century.

TOON BOOKS AND ART SPIEGELMAN'S COMICS FOR KIDS

TOON Books' mission statement recounts a familiar story of US comics history, a version of events that has been described as the "tribal myth" of the medium.[18] It's a tale of persecution followed by a slow struggle to win back critical and public recognition. In this telling, the 1954 United States Senate Subcommittee on Juvenile Delinquency becomes the defining traumatic moment in the history of the medium. Following the direction of the respected liberal psychiatrist and anti-comics crusader Fredric Wertham, the Subcommittee's witch hunt crippled the medium in its cradle, forcing the industry to police itself by creating the Comics Code, delaying by decades the full flourishing of comics. In the wake of this primal trauma, the story goes, cartoonists and fans faced half a century of reparative efforts, working tirelessly to justify their beloved art form to an indifferent or hostile public. The history of post-Code comics, in this narrative, becomes the history of different ways in which cartoonists have sought to make comics for adult audiences. When *MAD* ruthlessly criticized all sources of adult authority, it did so in the name of a higher maturity or understanding of the world. When underground luminaries such as R. Crumb took an interest in violent, sexually explicit, and politically abrasive comics, they were creating works that were, by definition, not for kids. Indeed, the cover of the first issue of *Zap Comix* announced that it was "For Adult Intellectuals Only."[19] The reference to "Adult Intellectuals" is (just as much as the debunking tone of *MAD*) highly ironic, but parents of the era would certainly not have approved of *Zap*.

When Spiegelman and his collaborators sought to transcend the underground, they did so by taking seriously the notion that comics might, indeed, be created for adults. The cover of Spiegelman's 2008 reprint of *Breakdowns*, in fact, announces that it is for "Adults Only!" In "Cracking Jokes," a comics-essay published in *Arcade* in 1975 and reprinted in *Breakdowns*, Spiegelman gives a psychoanalytic account of the origin and function of humor. His narrator is an aggressive jack-in-the-box who wears a jester's cap tipped with penises. In the opening panel, the side of the jack-in-the-box reads: "The child's jack-in-the-box provides a potent example of the joke in its primitive form. A momentarily threatening surprise proves itself to be harmless. The child learns to master its fears through laughter."[20] This panel exemplifies the most "primitive" (i.e., childlike) form of a joke. Spiegelman subsequently elaborates a progression of figures—the fool, the jester, the circus clown—each of whom masks the fundamental aggression of humor in increasingly sophisticated ways. This deconstructive comics-essay explores variations of a joke about a man who believes he is dead. Unable to convince him that he is, in fact, alive, his family sends him to a shrink. The psychiatrist, who resembles Freud, tells the man to look into a mirror and repeat the phrase "Dead men don't bleed" for three hours. Afterwards, the shrink pricks the man's finger and asks him, "What does *that* prove?" The man delivers the punchline: "Dead men do bleed!" After presenting this simple version of the joke, Spiegelman's narrator changes elements of the joke—exploring what might happen if the psychiatrist becomes the butt of the joke, if the gender of the man and the shrink were changed, if the joke's latent violence were made manifest, and so on. The comics-essay culminates with a page and a half of identical images of the man in front of the mirror, repeating "Dead men don't bleed!"

"Cracking Jokes" plainly undermines the authority of the psychiatrist figure, and the absurdist conclusion of the comic in some ways deflates its pedagogical function. But the comic cannot help but also be genuinely instructive—and *instructional*. As Scott McCloud explains, extolling the power of Spiegelman's comics-essay, "This single, four-page comic was an entire *college course*."[21] McCloud's comment suggests that the content of this "college course" is not only the psychoanalytic theory of humor but also the power of comics as a vehicle of education and exposition. Spiegelman wants to break the association between comics and the crude form of humor represented by the jack-in-the-box, and he wants to demonstrate that comics is supremely well suited to the most

From "Cracking Jokes," first published in *Arcade, the Comics Revue* No. 1. Copyright © 1975 by Art Spiegelman.

advanced forms of analysis, exposition, and storytelling. If "Cracking Jokes" is an advanced education in the power of comics, a sort of "college course" or master class on the medium, many cartoonists working in the mode of the graphic novel have, in one way or another, attended Spiegelman U, and many of the landmarks of the graphic memoir seem, like Spiegelman's strip, tailored to the classroom. Children or young adults might indeed read comics such as Joe Sacco's *Palestine*, Alison Bechdel's *Are You My Mother?*, or Chris Ware's *Building Stories*, but they are more likely to have such difficult and metafictional texts assigned to them in a university course than to read them unprompted.

But TOON suggests that attending Spiegelman U came at a cost. Sure, cartoonists may have succeeded in attracting older audiences, but TOON worries that "as the medium grew up, kids got left behind."[22] TOON represents itself as part of a fourth wave of reparation and healing in the aftermath of the Comics Code. After the underground, the avant-garde of the 1970s and 1980s, and the graphic novel, TOON argues that it is time to make sure kids have access to "high-quality" comics. As with previous defenses of comics, the development of "kid's comics" concedes much to those who once opposed the medium. That is, the new genre does not challenge historical critiques of comics—but reinforces them. TOON does not so much seek to ignore Wertham's analysis as answer his charges, showing that comics can be good for you after all. Specifically, Spiegelman and Mouly hope to counteract the claim that comics damages the development of literacy, a central charge of Wertham's attack. In his Subcommittee testimony, for example, the psychiatrist claimed, "we have found *all* comic books have a very bad effect on teaching the youngest children the proper reading technique, to learn to read from left to right. The balloon print pattern prevents that. So many children, we say they read comic books, *they don't read comic books at all*."[23]

In *Seduction of the Innocent*, Wertham argues that "comic books are death on reading" and that comics "interfere with [the formation of] proper reading habits."[24] As Bart Beaty has suggested, Wertham's anticomics views did not only indict horror comics.[25] Rather, they blamed the *form* of comics for destroying literacy. Some midcentury academics agreed. In an amusing article published in the *Australasian Journal of Optometry*, for example, Matthew Luckiesh and Frank K. Moss suggested that the illegibility of poorly printed comics posed a special threat to literacy. "Comic books represent a great step backward in safeguarding the eyesight of children," they conclude.[26] Such verdicts notwithstanding, refereed scholarship of the era was more divided about the effects of comics than is remembered. Even so, though it did invoke expert authority, the anticomics movement had little serious interest in scouring the era's scholarly literature on comics. Why, then, did comics as such become an object of parental opprobrium? What was the real fear behind the midcentury anticomics panic?

I would argue that what was at stake was the integrity of the institution of childhood. Many scholars agree that the development of print culture in the Renaissance and mass literacy in the nineteenth century created the modern version of childhood. That is, literacy "created a new and lasting dark age for the young and illiterate," removing children from the adult world and creating new zones of cognitive privacy for adults.[27] Literacy is, on this view, foundational to the very possibility of modern childhood. After the Renaissance, childhood was correlated with illiteracy, and full adult citizenship required full literacy. If becoming an adult meant learning to decode text, might comics not threaten the parent-regulated transition from one developmental stage to the next? Amy Kiste Nyberg suggests that another part of what was at stake in the anticomics movement was the proper regulation of children's leisure time.[28] As an article in *Catholic World* argued during the height of anticomics hysteria, parents who allowed children to read comics felt they had "lost control" of their children's moral development. Kids who wasted leisure time reading comics had not been "taught to use their leisure for work as well as play."[29]

This same fear is evident in more highbrow quarters. An essay by the literary critic Robert Warshow, for example, describes the discomfort his son's identification as an "E. C. Fan-Addict" causes him. Though he is critical of Wertham, Warshow ultimately complains that "for many thousands of children comic books, whether 'bad' or 'good,' represent virtually their only contact with culture."[30] For *Catholic World* and Warshow alike, comics threatens to crowd out more enriching forms of leisure. It is always tempting to read this midcentury moment as an unenlightened era of moral panic. But these parents arguably exhibited more or less the same worry that has inspired recent pundits such as Neil Postman to conclude that the era of electronic media might result in the "disappearance" of childhood as such.[31] For those invested in maintaining a received distinction between childhood and adulthood, the growing popularity of comics and electronic media alike may portend the arrival of a postliterate world.

Though few parents seem to be worried about comics today—and concerns that childhood might disappear are arguably (and in my view) wildly overstated—librarians, cartoonists, and comics advocates have nonetheless tried to reassure parents and teachers that comics can be a steppingstone to literacy. In some ways, TOON and Spiegelman's *Jack and the Box* join this chorus of reassuring voices. But *Jack and the Box* does more than claim that comics might help kids learn how to read. The book also dramatizes the notion that reading comics might require a special type of literacy, and it expresses a hope that reading comics might become an end in itself. The book's cover declares that it is "[a] first comic for brand-new readers," and the back cover promises to "bring new readers to the pleasures of COMICS." The cover copy is strategically ambiguous, playing on two possible understandings of what a "reader" is. On the front cover, the "reader" seems sometimes to be the reader of grapheme-based texts. On the back, however, it is comics itself, in all caps, that the new reader will learn to appreciate. Spiegelman's book therefore promotes not only literacy but also comics literacy, that is, the competency to read comics as such. In order to realize this second purpose, Spiegelman's 32-page book offers something like a training gym for the new comics reader.

Given Spiegelman's long history of creating formally complex and metafictional comics, it should not be a surprise to learn that *Jack and the Box* is a highly reflexive text that rewards close attention, and that the book is partly in dialogue with his earliest experiments (especially "Cracking Jokes," which also features a jack-in-the-box character). The plot is straightforward: Jack is a humanoid rabbit whose parents—also rabbits—give him a "silly toy," a terrifying jack-in-the-box.[32] Jack plays with the box for a while but after he calls the box a "bad toy," the jack-in-the-box insists, "I am a silly toy."[33] The jack-in-the-box, whose name is Zach, escapes from its box, introduces Jack to another character, Mack, contained in Zach's hat, and releases a flock of ducks into Jack's bedroom. The flock breaks a lamp, which Mack ultimately replaces, and the toys all go into hiding again before Jack's parents return. At the level of content, Spiegelman figures Zach (the jack-in-the-box) as the art form of comics, casting Jack (the rabbit) into the role of the comics reader, who is charged with the task of gaining the ability to open, enter, and in a sense read the box. Playing with the box becomes an allegory of mastering comics. At a formal level, the box becomes an example of what I would call a "subpanel." A subpanel is an element of a panel that itself has an empaneling function.

In *Comics and Sequential Art*, Will Eisner describes the panel as a means by which cartoonists "secure control of the reader's attention and dictate the sequence in which the reader will follow the narrative."[34] As a conventional (rather than technical) device, the panel can easily become "part of the story."[35] In many cases, panels are made to resemble a "structural element" of a scene—such as a window, a door, or cave entrance.[36] Such structural panels have the capacity to draw attention to the "interplay between the contained space and the 'non-space' (the gutter) between the panels."[37] Building on Eisner's description, I would argue that Zach's box—in its capacity as a panel within a panel—serves two related functions. First, as I have already suggested, it is an embedded metacomic, a comic within the comic. Second, it draws the young reader's attention to the primary panels within which the subpanel is embedded. That is, the young reader is meant to become aware of the narrative convention of using panels.

To achieve this end, Spiegelman has Zach's box increasingly affect the arrangement of the book's primary panels. When Zack first leaps out of his

Detail from *Jack and the Box* (New York: TOON Books, 2008), p. 11. Copyright © 2008 by Art Spiegelman.

box, the pale teal background color shifts, for the first time, to an angle. Indeed, whenever Zack escapes the box, background panels start shifting from their conventional orientations. Eventually, these solid colored panels begin giving off action lines, suggesting that the panels within which Jack and his box are embedded are themselves sorts of boxes, on par with Zach's box. By the end of the book, after Zach has escaped from his box, the box entirely disappears from view. Jack is no longer merely playing with Zach's box but has, in a sense, entered the box, though some panels show Jack standing in the gutter outside the boundaries of the panels, almost making it seem as if Jack were in a gallery space looking at large paintings on a white wall. Still, the final pages blend the panel's borders with the edges of the page, inviting the young reader to understand the book we are holding is the physical corollary to Jack's box. The reader becomes a version of Jack, who is holding a version of Zach's box (the book). Child readers not only have their attention manipulated by panels; they are trained to see the artistic form which enacts that manipulation. Just as Jack masters his box, so too must the child reader master *Jack and the Box*.

Spiegelman employs a similar homology in *Open Me! . . . I'm a Dog!* Though it is more of an illustrated book than a work of comics, the book nonetheless invites child readers to become aware of the physical object they are holding, and to recognize that what they are holding is in fact the titular dog. The book tells the story of a dog who gets lost in an enchanted wood and undergoes a series of transformations at the hands of various magical creatures. After

Detail from *Jack and the Box* (New York: TOON Books, 2008), p. 23. Copyright © 2008 by Art Spiegelman.

metamorphosing into a human shepherd and a frog, the dog is transformed into a book by an evil wizard. The drama of the book involves not only recounting how the dog becomes a book, but also convincing the (presumably skeptical) child reader to recognize the book as a dog. "I'm sure *you*, of all people, could see past the wizard's curse," the dog-book beseeches us.[38] "Just believe me," it concludes. "I AM a dog."[39]

At the level of plot, *Open Me . . . I'm a Dog!* perhaps offers a veiled commentary on the history of comics. Here, the evil wizard's curse, which we might read as Wertham's condemnation of comics as such, becomes the very terms of legibility of the art form itself. Like the dog-book, the contemporary graphic novel becomes what it is, not despite Wertham's curse but because of it. Though we might worry that the dog's plight is tragic, our task as readers is nonetheless to recognize that the wizard's curse has not been disabling after all. What the dog-book is asking for is not to be transformed back into a biological dog, but to have us recognize it as a dog (one we happen to own) despite the fact that it will never again be a biological being. We cannot reverse the wizard's curse—only see past it. At the level of form, Spiegelman's dog-book invites the young reader to subordinate the dog's different adventures to the whole of the dog-book itself, of which its different adventures are merely parts. Unlike *Jack and the Box, Open Me . . . I'm a Dog!* does not specifically train readers to recognize the conventions of comics storytelling, but it does emphasize that readers must not only look at the subject matter of a page, but also notice the layout and physical dimensions of any illustrated book. We must learn that the book-object itself can become an active element of the artist's craft—and be an object worthy of analysis and interpretation.

Finally, Spiegelman's children's comics do not only make an argument about how child readers should read comics. They also allegorically offer advice to readers on how to manage their social identity as comics readers as they grow up. In "Prince Rooster," the inaugural comic of the *Little Lit* anthology, Spiegelman teaches the child reader how to become an adult reader of comics in a world that devalues and stigmatizes the medium. At first, "Prince Rooster" might seem less obviously to be a metacommentary on comics than Spiegelman's other work for kids, but I will suggest that this short parable comments on the *bildungsroman* discourse that I discussed above. Spiegelman's parable tells the tale of a young prince who is convinced that he is a rooster—and will not accept that he is a human. Despite copious evidence to the contrary, he steadfastly refuses his father's attempts to convince him otherwise. One day, an old man comes to the castle and promises a solution. "If you want to help someone who is stuck in the mud you sometimes have to get your feet muddy," the old man says.[40] When the king gives the old man an opportunity to help his son, the old man strips naked and tells the prince he is also a rooster, and slowly reintroduces various human practices into the prince's life. The old man finally lets the young prince in on a secret: "You can dress like a man, eat like a man, and act like a man but *still* really be a rooster!"[41] The story concludes with the prince growing up to be "a fine man, and in time . . . a good and wise king," though he still, "when he was all alone," crows at the rising sun.[42]

This story is, at one level, an amusing commentary on the process of accommodating yourself to adult life. The traditional *bildungsroman* requires a protagonist to compromise with the demands of adulthood and social responsibility. The ironic fantasy of this parable is, by contrast, that you might accept the responsibilities of adulthood without compromising your childlike proclivities. You can act in every way like a man without ever conceding that you are a man. At the same time, the prince's capitulation to his father's demands (walking upright, wearing clothes, eating human food) also sometimes seems to signal the prince's bad faith. As the old man suggests, walking upright or wearing clothes is indeed more comfortable. Why would the prince not want to enjoy the trappings of his wealth and power? Whatever the prince's motivation, the story's end might be regarded as wistful or tragic. After all, it is only when he is alone that the new king feels comfortable behaving like a rooster. It is not too far of a stretch, I hope, to suggest that the adult fan of comics faces a similar challenge in navigating a machinery of legitimation that, as Pizzino suggests, has not yet fully embraced the medium. So, though "Prince Rooster" appears in an anthology explicitly aimed at children, perhaps it is training readers to preserve supposedly childish interests into an adult world that will not support or nourish those interests. That is, like *Jack and the Box* and *Open Me . . . I'm a Dog!*, "Prince Rooster" arguably addresses itself to the child reader of comics who will, one day, become an adult reader of comics.

COMICS AND MODERNIST AUTONOMY

In all three cases, Spiegelman trains the child reader to recognize the autonomy of comics. *Jack and the Box* renders comics legible as comics by suggesting that comics is defined by the juxtaposition of discrete but interrelated panels. The newly enlightened child recognizes how the boxlike panels within the book are an active part of a larger whole. Indeed, TOON's *Genre Guide* instructs teachers to "[t]ell students: 'Comics are built around the idea that single panel illustrations *do not stand alone*.'"[43] In *Open Me . . . I'm a Dog!*, the child must learn that the book and the page stand between her and a represented scene; the reader is thus trained to recognize that the book is an active part of the artist's craft and an object worthy of interpretation. Finally, "Prince Rooster" does not offer any particular lessons about comics as an art form. Instead, it offers an amusing parable that shows the child reader of comics a way of securing herself against an adult world that is still not entirely accepting of the art form. All told, we might take Spiegelman and TOON to be promoting a modernist understanding of comics. Indeed, scholars such as David M. Ball and Daniel Worden have suggested that many contemporary cartoonists have embraced modernist priorities in their bid for wider cultural recognition, and Worden especially has highlighted artists who "emphasize the abstract aesthetics and autonomous form of comics" as part of that bid.[44]

We can trace the idea of medium-specificity back to Gotthold Ephraim Lessing's *Laocoön: An Essay on the Limits of Painting and Poetry*, but in its modernist version the doctrine is most often associated with the art critic Clement Greenberg, who defined medium-specificity as "the unique and proper area of competence of each art" and who celebrated artists for their rigorous explorations of these unique and proper competences.[45] Of course, modernist autonomy has long been an object of criticism, if not outright scorn. Andrew Goldstone notes that claims of autonomy are often regarded as "the most hopelessly deluded aspect of modernism."[46] Furthermore, many have pointed out that the equation of modernism with the doctrine of medium-specificity does not keep faith with the praxis of actual modernists; medium-specificity is, if anything, a relatively late formulation of modernist aesthetics.[47] Finally, we might be surprised that Spiegelman's children's comics invoke an idea of modernist autonomy because, as the other essays in this collection make plain,

Spiegelman has often embraced multimodal and mixed art forms, collaborating with dancers, writers, photographers, and musicians. He seems to be anything but a proponent of artistic purity. Indeed, he once coined the term "commix" to emphasize the mixed quality of his preferred art form.[48]

Yet Spiegelman's children's comics nonetheless seem committed to the idea that comics is a unique formal language that requires special training to appreciate. Indeed, we might go so far as to suggest that some notion of modernist purity or medium-specificity is a necessary precursor to the possibility of multimodal experimentation. After all, only media that are distinct can subsequently be mixed or hybridized. And some notion of comics autonomy is arguably necessary to render advocacy for comics legible in the first place. If comics is not a coherent and autonomous practice, what would you be advocating for anyway? Attempting to answer the medium-specific critiques of parents and educators, many cartoonists have chosen to defend their work in medium-specific terms. The notion that comics is a special type of autonomous language is, I would argue, part of a larger critical and cultural conversation about what is called "visual literacy," "multiliteracy," and "multimodal literacies." This set of related ideas holds that grapheme- and even language-based forms of literacy are a narrow slice of the forms of "reading" we need to learn to navigate the contemporary world.

I do not have the space to fully document the historical development of this view, but the most prominent text promoting it is the manifesto of the New London Group. The manifesto explains that it's important to teach "multiliteracies," in part because learning to read images will prepare the student for the post-Fordist workplace. In an age of "post-Fordism" or "fast capitalism," which demands "commitment, responsibility, and motivation" from workers, in an era when workplaces require "well-rounded workers who are flexible enough to be able to do complex and integrated work," educators must ask how literacy education contributes to "a productive working life."[49] That is, the New London Group suggests that multimodal literacies are a vital skill that the child will need to learn to navigate a neoliberal world of work. To be clear, I do not mean to suggest that teaching multimodal literacies promotes neoliberalism, but the context of neoliberalism does illuminate the reason Spiegelman might feel a need to invoke the idea of aesthetic autonomy. After all, the modernist artist is often held up as the idealized sort of worker in the flexible, network-driven capitalism of the twenty-first century. The ideology of modernism is, today, a valued resource for the worker, and it informs the activities of some contemporary corporate firms.[50] The autonomous artist is, for many, the very model of what the intrinsically motivated worker looks like. This, finally, is the context in which TOON has struck a new Faustian bargain to nurture comics for a new century. It may be that the young prince of "Prince Rooster," who donned the protective coloration of crown and scepter, but maintained a subversive commitment to crowing at the rising sun, has discovered, at last, that his rooster-like habits were, in fact, the very qualities of good kingship—qualities widely celebrated across the land.

I shall conclude by suggesting that Spiegelman's reconstruction of a paradoxical version of modernist autonomy—autonomy with a role to play in the economy—participates in a broader cultural movement of artists who want to move beyond postmodern aesthetics toward a neoliberal aesthetics of "neo-sincerity." The term is Spiegelman's. Speaking of the first volume of *Little Lit*, Spiegelman recalls, "When I was a kid, *Mad* magazine was salvation. Everybody's lying to you—that was their message. It was so well heard that an entire generation has become so ironic that it's almost catatonic." Now, Spiegelman suggests, we are moving toward an era of "neo-sincerity, which is sincerity built on a thorough grounding in irony, but that allows one to actually make a statement about what one believes in."[51] I have written elsewhere about artistic attempts to move beyond postmodern irony and cynicism.[52] Spiegelman's version of this project notably does not posit that neosincere artists will overcome irony, but that they must build their sincere commitments atop "a thorough grounding in irony." The era of the Comics Code would represent the moment of the old sincerity. Indeed, however cynical an exercise the Code was for corporate comics producers, the rationale for creating it was to protect morals. By contrast, *MAD*, the underground, and Spiegelman's pre-*Maus* formalism represent a long period of scalding irony: that is, a systematic effort on the part of cartoonists to demolish the hypocritical moralism of the Code.

MAD meant to teach children that no authority could be trusted. The underground, embodied in the work of artists such as R. Crumb, sought to violate all taboos, norms, and constraints. Spiegelman's metafictional comics in *Arcade* and *RAW* interrogated the medium-specific language of comics in order to deconstruct the conventions that glued the medium together. In the age of neosincerity, however, Spiegelman's children's comics return to the project of protecting and educating young minds—but with a difference. What is different, I have sought to show, is that it is now the comic book that is the means of morally uplifting the child. If today we are told that comics are not just for kids, Spiegelman's reply is to agree—by showing what comics written for kids should be. When, on the back cover of *Jack and the Box*, Spiegelman promises to "apply his out-of-the-box thinking to a book that has all the surprise and bounce of a Jack-in-the-box," we should not only read this phrase as a pun but also as a sincere promise. After all, who can deny that such out-of-the-box thinking plays well with contemporary educational institutions that are ultimately charged with preparing kids for the fast-paced, image-saturated world of contemporary work? Recalling the terms of the midcentury anticomics movement, we might ask: What parent concerned with the project of regulating her child's leisure time would have reason to complain, if her child became a Fan-Addict of Art Spiegelman?

Notes

1. "Comics Not Just for Kids Anymore, Reports 85,000th Mainstream News Story," *The Onion*, July 10, 2012, https://entertainment.theonion.com/comics-not-just-for-kids-anymore-reports-85-000th-main-1819573609.

2. Ken Tucker, "Cats, Mice and History—The Avant-Garde of the Comic Strip," *New York Times*, May 26, 1985.

3. See, for example, Ray Sawhill, "The Comic Book (Gulp!) Grows Up," *Newsweek*, January 18, 1988; Len Strazewski, "Comics Fantasyland Brought to Earth by Some Serious Issues," *Advertising Age*, July 7, 1986; Joe Queenan, "Drawing on the Dark Side," *New York Times*, April 30, 1989, sec. 6; Charles McGrath, "Not Funnies," *New York Times*, July 11, 2004, sec. Magazine, https://www.nytimes.com/2004/07/11/magazine/not-funnies.html.

4. Christopher Pizzino, *Arresting Development: Comics at the Boundaries of Literature* (Austin: University of Texas Press, 2016).

5. Scott McCloud, *Understanding Comics: The Invisible Art* (New York: William Morrow Paperbacks, 1994), 3.

6. Pizzino, *Arresting Development*, 21–45.

7. Marc Singer, *Breaking the Frames: Populism and Prestige in Comics Studies* (Austin: University of Texas Press, 2019), esp. Chapter 4, 127–52.

8. See, for example, Joseph Witek, ed., *Art Spiegelman: Conversations* (Jackson: University Press of Mississippi, 2007), 239–40. W. J. T. Mitchell and Art Spiegelman, "Public Conversation: What the %$#! Happened to Comics?," *Critical Inquiry* 40, no. 3 (2014): 21.

9. Mitchell and Spiegelman, "Public Conversation," 21.

10. Mitchell and Spiegelman, 21.

11. Mitchell and Spiegelman, 21.

12. Art Spiegelman and Françoise Mouly, ed., *Little Lit: Folklore and Fairy Tale Funnies* (New York: RAW Junior, 2000), back cover.

13. Françoise Mouly and Art Spiegelman, "Our TOON Books Mission," TOON Books, accessed October 30, 2018, http://www.toon-books.com/our-mission.html.

14. Mouly and Spiegelman, "Our TOON Books Mission."

15. "Toon into Comics: Genre Study for Reading and Writing (CCSS Aligned! Grades 1–3)," TOON Books, accessed October 30, 2018, http://www.toon-books.com/comics-genre-study.html.

16. Suzanne Simons, *Toon into Comics: Genre Study for Reading and Writing* (New York: RAW Junior, 2013), 6.

17. Simons, *Toon into Comics*, 6.

18. Catherine Yronwode, qtd. in James E. Reibman, "Fredric Wertham: A Social Psychiatrist Characterizes Crime Comic Books and Media Violence as Public Health Issues," in *Pulp Demons: International Dimensions of the Postwar Anti-comics Campaign*, ed. John A. Lent (Madison, NJ: Fairleigh Dickinson University Press), 254.

19. R. Crumb, *Zap Comix*, no. 1 (1968), cover.

20. Art Spiegelman, "Cracking Jokes: A Brief Inquiry into Various Aspects of Humor," in *Breakdowns: Portrait of the Artist as a Young %@&*!* (New York: Pantheon, 2008), 39.

21. Joe Fassler, "Scott McCloud and the Necessity of Humor," *The Atlantic*, February 4, 2015. My emphasis.

22. Mouly and Spiegelman, "Our TOON Books Mission."

23. United States Senate Subcommittee on Juvenile Delinquency, *Juvenile Delinquency (Comic Books): Hearings before the Senate Subcommittee on Juvenile Delinquency*, 83rd Congress, 2nd sess., April 21–22 and June 4, 1954. My emphasis.

24. Fredric Wertham, *Seduction of the Innocent* (New York: Rinehart & Company, 1954), 121.

25. Bart Beaty, *Fredric Wertham and the Critique of Mass Culture* (Jackson: University Press of Mississippi, 2005), 140.

26. Quoted in Amy Kiste Nyberg, *Seal of Approval: The History of the Comics Code* (Jackson: University Press of Mississippi, 1998), 11. Nyberg offers a helpful overview of anticomics scholarship of the era, and she concludes that "critics exaggerated the [negative] effects of comics" (11).

27. Joshua Meyrowitz, *No Sense of Place: The Impact of Electronic Media on Social Behavior* (New York: Oxford University Press, 1986), 264.

28. Nyberg, *Seal of Approval*, 12.

29. Nyberg, *Seal of Approval*, 12.

30. Robert Warshow, "Paul, the Horror Comics, and Dr. Wertham," in *The Immediate Experience: Movies, Comics, Theatre and Other Aspects of Popular Culture* (Cambridge, Mass.: Harvard University Press, 2001), 72.

31. Neil Postman, *The Disappearance of Childhood* (New York: Vintage, 1994), 13.

32. Art Spiegelman, *Jack and the Box* (New York: TOON Books, 2008), 7.

33. Spiegelman, *Jack and the Box*, 15.

34. Will Eisner, *Comics and Sequential Art: Principles and Practices from the Legendary Cartoonist* (New York: W. W. Norton & Company, 2008), 40.

35. Eisner, *Comics and Sequential Art*, 46.

36. Eisner, *Comics and Sequential Art*, 49.

37. Eisner, *Comics and Sequential Art*, 49.

38. Art Spiegelman, *Open Me . . . I'm a Dog!* (New York: HarperCollins, 1997), 28.

39. Spiegelman, *Open Me . . . I'm a Dog!*, 28.

40. Art Spiegelman, "Prince Rooster," in *Little Lit: Folklore and Fairy Tale Funnies* (New York: RAW Junior, 2000), 10.

41. Spiegelman, "Prince Rooster," 12.

42. Spiegelman, "Prince Rooster," 12.

43. "Toon into Comics," 84.

44. Daniel Worden, "The Politics of Comics: Popular Modernism, Abstraction, and Experimentation," *Literature Compass* 12, no. 2 (2015): 63. For his part, David M. Ball persuasively argues that "contemporary graphic narratives' characteristic ambivalence about their status as popular cultural productions repeats modernist anxieties about literary value that reemerge precisely at the moment graphic narratives are bidding for literary respectability." David M. Ball, "Comics Against Themselves: Chris Ware's Graphic Narratives as Literature," in *The Rise of the American Comics Artist: Creators and Contexts*, ed. Paul Williams and James Lyons (Jackson: University Press of Mississippi, 2010), 103. I would argue that emphasizing the autonomy of comics is one tactic for making this bid for respectability.

45. Clement Greenberg, "Modernist Painting," in *The Collected Essays and Criticism, Volume 4: Modernism with a Vengeance, 1957–1969*, ed. John O'Brian (Chicago: University of Chicago Press, 1995), 86.

46. Andrew Goldstone, *Fictions of Autonomy: Modernism from Wilde to de Man*, 1. edition (New York: Oxford University Press, 2013), 1.

47. Andrew E. McNamara and Toni Ross, "An Interview with Jacques Rancière: On Medium-Specificity and Discipline Crossovers in Modern Art," *Australian and New Zealand Journal of Art* 8 (2007): 86. Fredric Jameson offers an even more extreme claim, suggesting that Clement Greenberg is a figure who "more than any other can be credited as having invented the ideology of modernism full-blown and out of whole cloth." Fredric Jameson, *A Singular Modernity: Essay on the Ontology of the Present* (London: Verso, 2002), 169.

48. Art Spiegelman, "Commix: An Idiosyncratic Historical and Aesthetic Overview," *Print* 42, no. 6 (1988): 61–73, 195–96.

49. The New London Group, "A Pedagogy of Multiliteracies: Designing Social Futures," in *Multiliteracies: Literacy Learning and the Design of Social Futures*, ed. Bill Cope and Mary Kalantzis (London: Routledge, 2000), 19.

50. On the way neoliberal economic theory celebrates the worker as a sort of autonomous artist, see Luc Boltanski and Eve Chiapello, *The New Spirit of Capitalism*, trans. Gregory Elliott, Reprint edition (London: Verso, 2018); and Sarah Brouillette, *Literature and the Creative Economy* (Stanford: Stanford University Press, 2014).

51. Witek, *Conversations*, 228.

52. Lee Konstantinou, *Cool Characters: Irony and American Fiction* (Cambridge, Mass.: Harvard University Press, 2016). For a discussion of what he calls New Sincerity, see Adam Kelly, "David Foster Wallace and the New Sincerity in American Fiction," in *Consider David Foster Wallace: Critical Essays*, ed. David Hering (Los Angeles/Austin: SSMG Press, 2010), 131–46; Adam Kelly, "The New Sincerity," in *Postmodern/Postwar-and After: Rethinking American Literature*, ed. Jason Gladstone, Andrew Hoberek, and Daniel Worden (Iowa City, IA: University of Iowa Press, 2016), 197–208.

APPENDIX: ART SPIEGELMAN'S PRIMARY WORKS

"Abstract Thought is a Warm Puppy." *New Yorker*, v. 75, no. 46 (Feb. 14, 2000): 61–63. [comic strip on the retirement of Charles Schulz].

"Ace Hole Midget Detective." 6 p. in *Short Order Comix*, no. 2 (1974).

"Alienation Blues." 1 p. in *Short Order Comix*, no. 1 (1973).

"And Now a Word from Our Sponsor ('In Vitro Veritas')" / Marc Caro; translation by Françoise Mouly & Art Spiegelman; lettering by Paul Karasik. *RAW*, v. 2, no. 3 (1991): 204–5.

"And Now, on the Big Screen . . ." *New Yorker* (May 24, 1999): 81. [*Star Wars* and real-world violence cartoon]

Arcade, the Comics Revue. Berkeley, Calif.: Print Mint, 1975–1976. ill.; 27 cm., v. 1, no. 1 (Spring 1975)—v. 1, no. 7 (Fall 1976). Edited by A. Spiegelman and B. Griffith.

"Art Spiegelman On His Decision to Withdraw Work from The Masters Exhibit on Its NY/NJ Stop." *Comics Reporter* (September 18, 2006).

"As the Mind Reels/A Soap Opera." 4 p. in *Arcade, the Comics Revue*, no. 4 (Winter 1975).

"Ballbuster: Bernard Krigstein's Life Between the Panels." *New Yorker* (July 22, 2002): 72–74.

Barefoot Gen: Out of the Ashes / by Keiji Nakazawa; English translation and production by Project Gen; foreword by Art Spiegelman. Philadelphia: New Society Publishers, 1994. 268 p.: ill.; 21 cm.

"The Basket Case" / Jacques Tardi; translated by Robert Legault, Kim Thompson, Françoise Mouly & Art Spiegelman; lettering by Paul Karasik. *RAW*, v. 2, no. 2 (1990): 13–36.

Be a Nose! Three Sketchbooks. San Francisco: McSweeney's, 2009. 3 vols.: chiefly ill.; 16 × 21 cm + 1 pamphlet [14 p.: ill (some col.); 21 cm].

"Beau and Eros." Cover of the *New Yorker*, v. 73, no. 25 (Aug. 25 & Sept. 1, 1997).

"Big Broadcast of 1952" (Space Age Confidential) / J. Hoberman, illustrated by Art Spiegelman. 1 p. text in *Arcade, the Comics Revue*, no. 6 (Summer 1976).

"Birth of the Comics." *New Yorker*, v. 70, no. 43 (Dec. 26, 1994/Jan. 2, 1995): 106–7.

Breakdowns: From Maus to Now: An Anthology of Strips. New York: Belier Press, 1977. 42 p.: ill. (some col.); 36 cm.

Breakdowns: Portrait of the Artist as a Young %@?!* New York: Pantheon, 2008. unpag.: ill.

"Brief Encounter." Cover of the *New Yorker*, v. 70, no. 30 (Sept. 26, 1994).

"The Bungle Family, 1924–1925: George Tuthill." *The Comics Journal*, no. 210 (Feb. 1999): 36. (The Top 100 English-Language Comics of the Century, no. 99)

The Cabbie / Marti Riera; introduction by Art Spiegelman; translated from the Spanish by Jeff Lisle; edited by Bernd Metz. New York: Catalan Communications, 1987. 79 p.: ill.; 28 cm. Translation of: *Taxista*.

"Centerfold Manifesto" / Griffith, "Skeeter" Spiegelman, Schenkman. 2 p. in *Short Order Comix*, no. 1 (1973).

"Classifieds of '96." Cover of the *New Yorker*, v. 72, no. 12 (May 20, 1996).

"Comics Are to Art What Yiddish Is to Language." *Forward* (Aug. 12, 2002). [Will Eisner tribute]

Comix, Essays, Graphics and Scraps: From Maus to Now to Maus to Now = Comics, Essays, Grafiken und Fragmente: from Maus to Now to Maus to Now. Sellerio Editore-La Centrale dell'Arte, 1999. 103 p.: col. Ill.; 34 cm. (A *RAW* Book) Exhibition catalog designed by *RAW* Books and Graphics to accompany La Centrale Dell'Arte's traveling exhibition of Spiegelman's work: "Comix, Drawings & Sketches (from Maus to Now to Maus to Now)." Introduction by J. Hoberman. Parallel texts in English and German; translation by Jutta Hohe.

"Commix: An Idiosyncratic Historical and Aesthetic Overview." *Print*, v. 42, no. 6 (1988): 61–73, 195–96.

The Complete Maus. CD-ROM. New York: Voyager, 1994.

The Complete Maus. New York: Pantheon, 1997. 295 p.: ill; 24 cm.

The Complete Color Polly & Her Pals / Cliff Sterrett; edited and with an introduction by Rick Marschall. Abington, PA: Remco Worldservice Books; Princeton, WI: Kitchen Sink Press, 1990-, col. ill.; 34 cm. Vol. 1 (1926–1927), includes foreword by Art Spiegelman.

Contribution to "Cartoonists on Cartooning": *The Comics Journal* Special Edition, no. 1 (Winter 2002): 100.

"Couple." *RAW*, v. 1, no. 5 (1983): 6.

"Cracking Jokes." 3 p. in *Arcade, the Comics Revue*, no. 1 (Spring 1975).

"Day at the Circuits." 1 p. (back cover) in *Arcade, the Comics Revue*, no. 2 (Summer 1975).

"Dead Dick." *RAW*, v. 2, no. 1 (1989): 26.

"Discussion Panel: Bande Dessinée" / edited by Scott Nybakken. *The Comics Journal*, no. 149 (Mar. 1992): 66–80. Panel with Art Spiegelman, Jerome Charyn, Jacques de Loustal, Robert Hughes, and Maurice Horn, with Jules Feiffer from the audience, introduced by Marcel Gutwirth and Annie Cohen-Solal.

"Don't Get Around Much Anymore." 1 p. in *Short Order Comix*, no. 2 (1974).

"Drawn Over Two Weeks While On the Phone." *RAW*, v. 1, no. 1 (Fall 1980): 27.

Dr. Seuss Goes to War: The World War II Editorial Cartoons of Theodor Seuss Geisel / Richard H. Minear. New York: New Press, 1999. 272 p.: ill.; 24 cm. Published in cooperation with the Dr. Seuss Collection at the University of California at San Diego. Introduction by Art Spiegelman.

"Duchamp Is Our Misfortune." *New Yorker*, v. 78, no. 4 (Mar. 25, 2002): 104.

"The Evolution of Xmas." *New Yorker* (Dec. 20, 1999): 69.

"An Examination of 'Master Race'" / by John Benson, David Kasakove and Art Spiegelman. *Squa Tront*, no. 6 (1975): 41–47.

"Eyeballs for Breakfast." 1 p. in *Roxy Funnies*, no. 1 (1972).

"A Family Movie." *New Yorker* (Sept. 4, 2000): 62–63.

"Family Values." Cover of the *New Yorker*, v. 72, no. 9 (Apr. 22, 1996).

"Farsighted." Cover of the *New Yorker*, v. 73, no. 32 (Oct. 20 & 27, 1997).

"Fatty's Fatal Fling" / Al Flooglebuckle (i.e., Art Spiegelman). 8 p. in *Sleazy Scandals of the Silver Screen* (S.F., Calif.: Cartoonists Co-op Press, 1974).

"Fears of July, 2002." Cover of the *New Yorker*, v. 78, no. 18 (July 8, 2002).

"A Flash of Insight, a Cloud of Dust and a Hearty Hi-Yo Silver." 3 p. in *Witzend*, no. 2 (1967).

"Forms Stretched to Their Limits: What Kind of Person Could Have Dreamed Up Plastic Man?" *New Yorker*, v. 75, no. 8 (Apr. 19, 1999): 76–85.

"41 Shots, 10 Cents." Cover of the *New Yorker*, v. 75, no. 2 (Mar. 9, 1999).

Four Sketchbooks and a Table of Useful Information. S.F., Cal.: D. Donahue; dist. by Apex Novelties, 1973. 48 p.: chiefly ill.; 19 cm. Contents: Bill Griffith. Art Spiegelman. Spain. Justin Green.

Funny Aminals. No. 1. S.F., Calif.: Apex Novelties, 1972. 32 p.: ill.; 26 cm. Underground comics by Robert Crumb, Shary Flenniken, Justin Green, Bill Griffith, Jay Lynch, Michael McMillan and Art Spiegelman.

"Getting in Touch with my Inner Racist." *Mother Jones*, v. 22, no. 5 (Sept./Oct. 1997): 52–53.

"Gloomy Toons." *New York Times*, 27 December 1992. [*Flood* by Eric Drooker, review].

"The Guns of September." Cover of the *New Yorker*, v. 69, no. 29 (Sept. 13, 1993).

"A Hand Job" (Real Dream). *Arcade, the Comics Revue*, no. 1 (Spring 1975): 32.

Harvey Kurtzman's Jungle Book, or, Up from the Apes! (and Right Back Down). Princeton, WI: Kitchen Sink Press, 1988. xii, 140 p.: ill.; 28 cm. Introduction by Art Spiegelman.

"Henry Foulbite: His Lucky Day." 1 p. in *Mondo Snarfo*, no. 1 (1978).

"H.K. (R.I.P.)." *New Yorker* (March 29, 1993). [strip on Harvey Kurtzman's influence]

"Honk! Honk! It's the Bonk! History as Soap Opera, the News as Entertainment" / by David Levy and Art Spiegelman. *RAW*, v. 1, no. 2 (1980): 12–16.

"Horton Hears a Heil." *New Yorker* (July 12, 1999): 62–63. [on Dr. Seuss' WWII political cartoons].

How to Draw Art for Comic Books: Lessons from the Masters: Corben, Elder, Foster, Kane, Kubert, Kurtzman, Raymond, Spiegelman, Sprang, Williamson / by James Van Hise. Las Vegas, NV: Pioneer Books, 1989. 158 p.: ill.; 28 cm.

"I Didn't Raise My Boy to Be a Soldier." Cover of the *New Yorker*, v. 69, no. 19 (June 28, 1993).

"I Had a Dream . . ." Cover of the *Nation* (Jan. 29, 2001).

"In the Dumps" / Maurice Sendak, Art Spiegelman. *New Yorker*, v. 69, no. 31 (Sept. 27, 1993): 80–81.

"In the Shadow of No Towers." *Forward* (Sept. 6, 2002) and *LA Weekly* (September 13/19, 2002); *Forward* (Oct. 4, 2002): 20; *Forward* (Nov. 1, 2002): 22; *Forward* (Dec. 6, 2002): 18; *Forward* (April 11, 2003): 20; *Forward* (Jan. 3, 2003): 18; *Forward* (Feb. 7): 18.

In the Shadow of No Towers. New York: Pantheon, 2004. unpag.: col. ill.; 38 cm.

"In the Temple of Cartoon Gods." Back cover of *Legal Action Comics*, v. 1 (New York: Dirty Danny Legal Defense Fund, 2001).

"In Their Own Image." Cover of the *New Yorker*, v. 78, no. 16 (June 17 & 24, 2002).

It Was a Dark and Silly Night . . . / edited by Art Spiegelman & Françoise Mouly. New York: HarperCollins Publishers, 2003. 48 p.: col. ill.; 34 cm.

Jack and the Box. New York: TOON Books, 2008. 32 p.: col. ill.; 16 × 24 cm.

Jack Cole and Plastic Man: Forms Stretched to their Limits / by Art Spiegelman and Chip Kidd. San Francisco: Chronicle Books, 2001. 1 v.: col. ill.; 26 cm.

"Jailbreak Hotel" / by Marc Caro; rewrite by Paul Karasik and Art Spiegelman; lettering by Paul Karasik. *RAW*, v. 1, no. 8 (1986): 4–5.

"A Jew in Rostock." *New Yorker*, v. 68, no. 42 (Dec. 7, 1992): 119–21.

Jimbo: Adventures in Paradise / Gary Panter; edited & designed by Art Spiegelman & Françoise Mouly. New York: Pantheon, 1988. 88 p.: ill.; 31 cm.

"Just a Piece o' Shit!" / Skeeter Grant (Art Spiegelman). 4 p. in *Short Order Comix*, no. 1 (1973).

"Krigstein: A Eulogy by Art Spiegelman." *The Comics Journal*, no. 134 (February 1990): 13.

"Life Had Been Tough" / by Jacques Tardi; translation by F.M. & a.s; lettering by Phil Felix. *RAW*, vol. 1, no. 4 (1982): 38.

Little Lit: Folklore & Fairy Tale Funnies / edited by Art Spiegelman & Françoise Mouly. New York: HarperCollins, 2000. 64 p.: col. ill.; 34 cm.

"Little Signs of Passion." 3 p. in *Young Lust*, no. 4 (1974).

"Love's Body." 1 p. in *Young Lust*, no. 1 (1971).

"The Low Road." Cover of the *New Yorker*, v. 74, no. 1 (Feb. 16, 1998).

"Lunch Breaks." Cover of the *New Yorker*, v. 74, no. 11 (May 11, 1998).

"Lusty Little Laffs." 1 p. in *Young Lust*, no. 3 (1972).

"The Malpractice Suite" (Nervous Rex). 2 p. in *Arcade, the Comics Revue*, no. 6 (Summer 1976).

"'M' is for the Many Things She Gave Me." Cover of the *New Yorker*, v. 69, no. 12 (May 10, 1993).

"Manhattan" / Jacques Tardi; translation A. Spiegelman & F. Mouly; lettering by John Workman. *RAW*, v. 1, no. 1 (Fall 1980): 7–14.

"Marcel, the Little White Man of Iwindo" / Jacques Loustal; translation by Françoise Mouly & Art Spiegelman; lettering by Tomas Bunk. *RAW*, v. 2, no. 3 (1991): 9–11.

Maus: A Survivor's Tale. 1: My Father Bleeds History. New York: Pantheon, 1986. 159 p.: ill.; 23 cm.

Maus: A Survivor's Tale. 2: And Here My Troubles Began. New York: Pantheon, 1991. 136 p.: ill.; 24 cm.

MetaMaus: A Look Inside a Modern Classic, Maus. New York: Pantheon, 2011. 299 p.: ill (some col.); 24 cm + DVD.

"Mightier than the Sorehead: Drawing Pens and Politics." *Nation*, v. 258, no. 2 (Jan. 17, 1994): 45.

"My Heart Skipped a Beat for a Meat-Beating Fiend!" / J. Cutrate. 3 p. in *Bizarre Sex*, no. 2 (Sept. 1977).

The Narrative Corpse: A Chain-Story by 69 Artists! / edited by Art Spiegelman and R. Sikoryak. Richmond, VA: Raw Books; Gates of Heck, 1995. 19 p.: ill.; 42 × 23cm.

"Nature vs. Nurture." *New Yorker*, v. 73, no. 36 (Sept. 8, 1997): 75. [comic strip on child rearing]

"The New Normal." *TV Guide* (Dec. 22, 2001): 7.

"New ork Journal" [sic]. 1 p. in *Arcade, the Comics Revue*, no. 3 (Fall 1975).

"News R Us." Cover of the *New Yorker*, v. 71, no. 27 (Sept. 11, 1995).

"9/11/01." Cover of the *New Yorker*, v. 77, no. 28 (Sept. 24, 2001).

"Nursery Rhymes for Those Who Just Can't Get with the Program." *New Yorker*, v. 77, no. 2 (Mar. 5, 2001): 106.

"One Row." *RAW*, v. 1, no. 5 (1983). (*The RAW Comic Supplement*): 41. 1 tier.

Open Me . . . I'm a Dog! New York: HarperCollins, 1997. 30 p.: col. ill.; 19 cm.

"Open-Minded Mayor." Cover of the *New Yorker*, v. 75, no. 30 (Oct. 11, 1999).

"Out Like a Lamb." Cover of the *New Yorker*, v. 76, no. 2 (Mar. 6, 2000).

"Overrated & Underrated: Comic Strip." *American Heritage* (May/June 1998): 47–48.

"Oy! We Got Dem Inauguration Day Blues Again!" *New Yorker* (Jan. 17, 2005): 98.

"Pigs, Be Not Proud." *New York Times* (Nov. 8, 1992). [review of *Little Pig* by Akumal Ramachander]

"The Plastic Arts." Cover of the *New Yorker*, v. 75, no. 8 (Apr. 19, 1999).

"Pluto's Retreat: That Hot After Hours Club where the Comic-Strip Crowd Cools Out." 1 p. in *Bizarre Sex*, no. 8 (Mar. 1980).

"Po-Po Comics." S. and C. Minor. 2 p. in *Bijou Funnies*, no. 2 (1972, c1969).

"Poems from the Booby Hatch." 1 p. in *Bijou Funnies*, no. 2 (1972, c1969).

"Portrait of the Artist as a Young %@?*!" *Virginia Quarterly Review*, v. 81, no. 4 (Fall 2005).

"Private Lives." Cover of the *New Yorker* (Aug. 24 & 31, 1998).

"Prisoner on the Hell Planet." 4 p. in *Short Order Comix*, no. 1 (1973).

"A Problem of Taxonomy." *New York Times* (Dec. 29, 1991). [letter]

"Projunior Learns to Draw" / an entwining of talents by Art Spiegelman and Justin Green. 3 p. in Don Dohler's *Pro Junior*, no. 1 (1971).

"Public Baths" / Baru; translation by F.M. & a.s.; lettering by R. Sikoryak. *RAW*, v. 2, no. 1 (1989): 171–74.

"A Race of Racers" / by Francis Masse; translation by Nikki Matheson, Paul Karasik, F.M. & a.s.; lettering by Paul Karasik. *RAW*, v. 1, no. 4 (1982): 7–18.

RAW, Vol. 2, #1 / edited by Art Spiegelman and Françoise Mouly. New York: Penguin, 1989.

RAW, Vol. 2, #2 / edited by Art Spiegelman and Françoise Mouly. New York: Penguin, 1990.

Read Yourself Raw: Pages from the Rare First Three Issues of the Comics Magazine for Damned Intellectuals / edited by Art Spiegelman and Françoise Mouly. New York: Pantheon, 1987. 89 p.: ill.; 36 cm.

"Real Dream." 1 p. in *Arcade, the Comics Revue*, no. 2 (Summer 1975).

"Real Dream." Back cover of *Short Order Comix*, no. 2 (1974); *AARGH!* (Northampton, England: Mad Love, 1988): 40.

Roach Killer / Tardi-Legrand; with an introduction by Art Spiegelman; translation by Randy & Jean-Marc Lofficier. New York: Nantier Beall Minoustchine, 1992. 60 p.: ill.; 28 cm.

"The Round Table." *Wonderworld*, v. 3, no. 1 (Aug. 1973): 28, 31. Letters to the editor from Charlie Roberts, Lee Roberts, George Metzger, Dan Gheno, Art Spiegelman, Joe Brancatelli, Bernie Zuber, Jim Jones, Larry Johnson, Kermit Long, Glenn Goggin, and Mort Walker.

"Skeeter Grant" / by Skeeter Grant (Art Spiegelman). 1 p. in *Short Order Comix*, no. 1 (1973).

"Skeeter Grant's Skinless Perkins" (Zip-a-Tunes and Moiré Melodies). 1 p. in *Short Order Comix*, no. 1 (1973).

Skin Deep: Tales of Doomed Romance / Charles Burns; edited by Art Spiegelman and R. Sikoryak; designed by Dale Crain and Art Spiegelman. New York: Penguin, 1992. 86 p.: ill.; 30 cm.

"A Slice of Life with Art and Françoise" / Art Spiegelman (and Françoise). 1 tier in *Snarf*, no. 8 (Oct. 1978).

"The Slithery Slibb." 1 p. in *Bijou Funnies*, no. 2 (1972, c1969).

"Snow Smoking." Cover of the *New Yorker*, v. 71, no. 44 (Jan. 15, 1996).

"Spiegelman Previews *Wild Party*." *The Comics Journal*, no. 172 (Nov. 1994): 30–31.

"The Squinks." 1 p. in *Bijou Funnies*, no. 7 (1972).

"The St. Louis Refugee Ship Blues: Art Spiegelman Recounts a Sad Story 70 Years Later." *Washington Post* (June 21, 2009).

"Star Drek"/ Al Floogleman (i.e., Art Spiegelman). 1 p. in *Sleazy Scandals of the Silver Screen* (S.F., Calif.: Cartoonists Co-op Press, 1974). Back cover.

Strange Stories for Strange Kids / edited by Art Spiegelman & Françoise Mouly. New York: HarperCollins, 2001. 64 p.: col. ill.; 34 cm. (Little Lit)

"The Sub-Teen Snatch Snatch" (The Viper) / Skeeter Grant (i.e., Art Spiegelman). 6 p. in *Real Pulp Comics*, no. 2 (Jan. 1973).

"The Technophobe." *New Yorker* (Dec. 6, 1999): 111.

"The Tenth Muse." Cover of the *New Yorker*, v. 77, no. 31 (Oct. 15, 2001).

"Theology of the Tax Cut." Cover of the *New Yorker*, v. 71, no. 8 (Apr. 17, 1995).

Tijuana Bibles: Art and Wit in America's Forbidden Funnies, 1930s–1950s / compiled by Bob Adelman; introductory essay by Art Spiegelman; commentary by Richard Merkin; essay by Madeline Kripke; photography, Bob Adelman and Michael Macioce. New York: Simon & Schuster Editions, 1997. 160 p.: ill.; 24 x 31 cm.

The TOON Treasury of Classic Children's Comics / Art Spiegelman and Françoise Mouly. New York: Abrams ComicArts, 2009. 350 p.: col. ill.; 30 cm.

"Tour de France" / by Baru; translation by Deborah Bonner, Françoise Mouly and Art Spiegelman; lettering by Tomas Bunk; grey tones by Steven Guarnaccia. *RAW*, v. 1, no. 8 (1986): 68–77.

"Track Zero" / by Francis Masse; translation by F.M. & a.s.; lettering by Paul Karasik. *RAW*, v. 1, no. 5 (1983): 50.

"Two-Fisted Painters." Center insert, 12 p. in *RAW*, v. 1, no. 1 (Fall 1980).

"Two in the Balcony: The Mouseum of Natural History" / Francis Masse; translation by Joachim Neugroshol, Françoise Mouly & Art Spiegelman; lettering by Paul Karasik. *RAW*, v. 2, no. 3 (1991): 4–8.

"Unveiled." Cover of the *New Yorker*, v. 70, no. 36 (Nov. 7, 1994).

"Valentine's Day." Cover of the *New Yorker*, v. 68, no. 52 (Feb. 15, 1993).

"Villie Vetback Visits the City" (The Viper). 5 p. in *Bijou Funnies*, no. 7 (1972).

Warts and All / Drew Friedman and Josh Alan Friedman; edited and designed by Art Spiegelman, R. Sikoryak, and Françoise Mouly. New York: Penguin, 1990. 1 v.: ill.; 19 × 21 cm.

"We Could Get Any Artist ta Draw Us!"* (Nard n' Pat) *Jayzey Lynch's Nard n' Pat*, no. 1 (1974): 21–24. Guest artists: Skip Williamson, Justin Green, Art Spiegelman, Harvey Kurtzman, Robert Crumb, Gilbert Shelton, Robert Williams, Spain, S. Clay Wilson, Dave Sheridan, Denis Kitchen, Pete Poplaski, Kim Deitch, Evert Geradts, Trina, Rich Corben, Willy Murphy, and Bill Griffith.

"What's Next." Cover of the *New Yorker* (Oct. 26 & Nov. 2, 1998).

"What's Wrong with Comics?" *Heavy Metal*, v. 6, no. 12 (Mar. 1983): 4–8. (Dossier) Respondents: Lou Stathis, Will Eisner, Dan Steffan, Kim Thompson, Ted White, Robert Greenberger, John Workman, Mary Wilshire, Walt Simonson, Byron Preiss, Rod Kierkegaard Jr., Howard Cruse, Art Spiegelman, Bhob Stewart, Harvey Kurtzman, and Pete Hamill.

"When Grisly Horror Is a Family Value." *New York Times* (Sept. 29, 1996). [Charles Addams exhibit]

Whole Grains: A Book of Quotations / co-edited with Bob Schneider. New York: Douglas Links, 1973. 159 p.; 26 cm.

"The Wild Party." *New Yorker* (June 27, 1994).

The Wild Party: The Lost Classic / by Joseph Moncure March; drawings by Art Spiegelman. New York: Pantheon, 1994. 110 p.: ill.; 23 cm.

"Winter Fiction." Cover of the *New Yorker* (Dec. 28, 1998–Jan. 4, 1999).

"Without Trumpets!" 2 p. in *Roxy Funnies*, no. 1 (1972).

"Words, Worth a Thousand." *New Yorker* (Feb. 20/27): 196–99. [strip on the New York Public Library]

Writers Dreaming/Dreamers Writing: 25 Writers Discuss Dreams and the Creative Process / interviewed by Naomi Epel. New York: Carol Southern Books, 1993. 292 p.: ill.; 22 cm. Participants include Clive Barker, Stephen King, Anne Rice, Maurice Sendak, Art Spiegelman.

"Written on the Wind" / Lorenzo Mattotti and Toni Capuozzo; translation by Eduardo Kaplan & Art Spiegelman; lettering by Paul Karasik. *RAW*, v. 2, no. 3 (1991): 116–17.

X / pictures by Sue Coe; text by Sue Coe with Art Spiegelman; "concurrent events" by Judith Moore; edited by Françoise Mouly and Art Spiegelman; design by Françoise Mouly. New York: *RAW* Books and Graphics, 1986. 32 p.: col. ill.; 24 cm. (Raw One-Shot; no. 6)

"Zephyr" / Lorenzo Mattotti; text by Kramsky; translation by Kim Thompson, Lilia Ambrosi, F.M. & a.s.; lettering by Susan Moore. *RAW*, v. 2, no. 1 (1989): 115–22.

ABOUT THE CONTRIBUTORS

GEORGIANA BANITA is an associate professor of North American Literature and Culture at the University of Bamberg. She is the author of *Plotting Justice: Narrative Ethics and Literary Culture after 9/11* (Nebraska, 2012) and coeditor of *Electoral Cultures: American Democracy and Choice* (Heidelberg, 2015). She is currently completing a monograph on wordless comics and starting a new project on modernism and comics art, a first section of which appeared in 2021 as "*Maus*, Modernism, and the Mass Ornament" in *Modernism/modernity.*

COLIN BEINEKE is a professor of English at the Savannah College of Art and Design, where he teaches courses in the liberal arts and sequential arts programs. His research focuses on the intersection of aesthetics and editorial praxis within contemporary comics publishing houses, as well as the formal and cultural associations between comics and other art forms. His writings on comics have appeared in venues including *ImageText*, *INKS: The Journal of the Comics Studies Society*, *The Los Angeles Review of Books*, and *The International Journal of Comic Art.*

HARRIET EARLE is a lecturer in English at Sheffield Hallam University. She is the author of *Comics, Trauma, and the New Art of War* (Mississippi, 2017). She has recently published articles in *The Journal of Popular Culture* and *Film International*. Currently, her research interests include American comics and popular culture, representations of violence, protest narratives, and biopolitics.

ARIELA FREEDMAN is a professor at the Liberal Arts College, Concordia University, Montreal. She is the author of *Death, Men and Modernism* (Routledge, 2003), the novels *Arabic for Beginners* (LLP, 2017) and *A Joy to be Hidden* (LLP, 2019), and numerous articles on modernism, trauma, and comics. She holds a grant from the Social Sciences and Humanities Research Council for her current project on comics and the representation of pain.

LIZA FUTERMAN is the founder, CEO, and artistic director of the School of Human Thought & HeArtivism, a social enterprise that explores artistic expression and experiential learning. In 2013, she graduated with a master's degree in History of Art and Visual Culture from the University of Oxford. She is a social entrepreneur, dancer, poet, and the author of the graphic medicine novel *Keeper of the Clouds*. In 2016, she delivered her first TEDx talk on her doctoral research at the University of Toronto, which examines arts-based methods for communication with people living with Alzheimer's. She is currently working on a book about experiential anatomy and somatic dance practices.

SHAWN GILMORE is a senior lecturer at the University of Illinois, Urbana-Champaign, where he teaches a range of courses on comics, prose, popular culture, critical theory, and professional writing. His research and publication interests include comics and graphic narratives, modernisms and postmodernisms, media franchises, narratology, fiction across media, space, geography, maps, architecture, and academic labor.

SARAH HAMBLIN is an associate professor of Cinema Studies and English at the University of Massachusetts Boston. Her current research focuses on global art cinema and graphic literatures, emphasizing the relationships between aesthetics, affect, and radical politics. Her work has appeared in *Cultural Politics*, *Cinema Journal*, *English Language Notes*, and *Black Camera*, and she is currently completing a book manuscript on global revolutionary filmmaking in the 1960s.

CARA KOEHLER is a doctoral candidate at the University of Bamberg and the recipient of a prestigious doctoral grant from The German Academic Scholarship Foundation. Before moving to Germany, she studied English literature and French at DePaul University, Chicago. Her dissertation, *Seven Deadly Habits in Film Noir: Cinema, Addiction, and Postwar America*, examines the aesthetics and politics of substance abuse in classical American film noir. Other research interests include American visual culture, film studies, the graphic novel, and teen culture.

LEE KONSTANTINOU is an associate professor of English at the University of Maryland, College Park. He wrote the novel *Pop Apocalypse* (Ecco/HarperCollins, 2009), the literary history *Cool Characters: Irony and American Fiction* (Harvard, 2016), and *The Last Samurai Reread* (Columbia University Press, 2022). With Samuel Cohen, he coedited *The Legacy of David Foster Wallace* (Iowa, 2012).

PATRICK LAWRENCE is an assistant professor of English at the University of South Carolina, Lancaster. His research links obscenity discourses surrounding artistic production with American political culture. His current book project, *Obscene Gestures: Counter-Narratives of Sex and Race in the Twentieth Century*, reconsiders the divergent afterlives of cultural texts that depict taboo subjects during the late twentieth century. He has also published articles in *Mosaic*, *Asian American Literature: Discourses and Pedagogies*, and *Intertexts*.

PHILIP SMITH is a professor of English at Savannah College of Art and Design. He earned his doctoral degree from Loughborough University. He the author of *Reading Art Spiegelman* (Routledge, 2018) and his work has been published in, among others, *Studies in Comics*, *The Journal of Graphic Novels and Comics*, *The Journal of Popular Culture*, and *Image [&] Narrative*.

KENT WORCESTER is a professor of political science at Marymount Manhattan College. His books include *C.L.R. James: A Political Biography* (SUNY, 1996), *A Comics Studies Reader* (Mississippi, 2009, coedited with Jeet Heer), *The Superhero Reader* (Mississippi, 2013, coedited with Charles Hatfield and Jeet Heer), and *Silent Agitators: Comic Art from the Pages of New Politics* (New Politics, 2016).

INDEX

Page numbers in **bold** refer to illustrations.

"Aborigine Among the Skyscrapers, An" (A. Spiegelman), 150
Abrams, Nathan, 137
Abrams Books, 24
"Ace Hole, Midget Detective" (A. Spiegelman), 11, 24, 49, 56–58, **57**, 60, 65n28, 74
Addicted to War (Andreas), 168
Adorno, Theodor W., 38, 65n20, 210–12
Aetiology of Hysteria, The (Freud), 211
affect, 39, 210–13, 219–26
Afghanistan, 103, 162, 169, 185, 187
After 9/11 (S. Jacobson and Colón), 161
Agamben, Giorgio, 98
Alcoholic, The (Ames and Haspiel), 161
"Alienation Blues" (A. Spiegelman), 90
"Alliteration" (Gorcey), 60
al-Qaeda, 122, 164, 166–67, 169, 185, 187
amblyopia, 31
American Tale, An, 15, 32, 263, 271n55
American Widow (Torres and Choi), 161
Ames, Jonathan, 161
Andreas, Joel, 168
"Andy Griffith Show, The" (Drew Friedman), 137
Ann-Margret, 51, 52
anti-Semitism, 41n40, 77, 118, 122–24, **122**, 194, 241–44, 246–47
anxieties, 55, 97, 129, 134–35, 179–80, 182, 186, 189, 213, 222, 254, 264, 274, 288n44
Appel, Alfred, 68
appropriation, 31, 82, 182, 241–42, 246
Arcade, 4, 7, 9–10, 13, 33, 50, 54, 58–59, 62, 74, 90, 117, 254, 276, **277**, 286
Arcades Project, The (Benjamin), 54, 64, 65n20
architecture, 29, 215–16, 218–19, 264
Arendt, Hannah, 19
Are You My Mother? (Bechdel), 278
Aristotle, 220
Arnold, Andrew D., 172n12
Arresting Development (Pizzino), 273
Arrival, The (Tan), 259, 267
art: fine, 30–31, 38, 112; high, 58, 61–62, 70–71, 124, 129, 149–50; high versus low distinction, 4, 28, 56, 59, 61–62, 68–69, 71, 75, 80, 82, 116–18, 254–55; low, 62, 112, 120, 124, 215, 257, 273
"Art as Technique" (Shklovsky), 30
Artforum, 50, 61
Art Spiegelman, Traits de Mémoire, 18
Astérix (Goscinny and Uderzo), 258
"As the Mind Reels" (A. Spiegelman), 11
À Suivre, 27, 233, 249n5
Attridge, Derek, 220, 222
Audi, Anthony, 256, 265
Auerbach, Erich, 53
Auric, Georges, 70
Auschwitz, 16, 29, 87, 100–101, 198–99, 203–4, 210–19, 221–22, 226n16, 244, 246–47. *See also* concentration camps
Auschwitz (Croci), 218
Auster, Paul, 19, 106n24
authenticity, 39, 193, 204, 205, 215, 218, 224, 243

autobiography and memoir, 15, 18, 28, 34–36, 39, 49, 74, 80, 86, 97–98, 100, 102, 129, 144, 151, 164, 179, 184, 188, 197, 202–3, 205, 222, 237, 239, 273–74
Autobiography of Alice B. Toklas, The (Stein), 56
"Auto-destructo" (A. Spiegelman), 92–93
avant-garde, 3, 28–29, 32, 38, 43n64, 60, 69–70, 72, 96, 106n26, 128–30, 136–37, 146, 149–50, 160, 231, 236, 249n5, 258, 278
Avedon, Richard, 19

Backlund, Harry, 72, 256
"Back to the Front" (Masereel), 133
Bacon, Francis, 78
Balaev, Michelle, 212
Ball, David M., 107n50, 113, 258, 284, 288n44
Ballet Intime, 72
Ballet Russes, 72
Bambi, 58
Barks, Carl, 30
"Baron Desert, The" (A. Spiegelman), 90
Barry, Lynda, 129
Barthes, Roland, 194, 207
Bateman, H. M., 69
Baudrillard, Jean, 161
Be a Nose! (A. Spiegelman), 18
Beaty, Bart, 36, 129–30, 149, 254, 278
Bechdel, Alison, 32, 278
Beckett, Samuel, 88, 96–97
Belier Press, 115, 119
Bell, Clive, 71, 82
Benjamin, Walter, 54, 64, 65n20, 182, 188, 197
Benson, John, 55
Betty Boop, 32
Beyer, Mark, 41n40, 129, 138, 145
Beyond the Pleasure Principle (Freud), 211
bildungsroman discourse, 273, 283
Binky Brown Meets the Holy Virgin Mary (Green), 30, 203
bin Laden, Osama, 166, 168–69, 171, 185
Blackbeard, Bill, 259–60
Blitt, Barry, 43n58, 252, 269n6
Bloomberg, Michael, 80
Blown Covers (Mouly), 95
Blu, 264
Bo Bo Bolinski (Crumb), 52–53, 105n8
Bolin, Liu, 264
Bolm, Adolph, 72
Bono, 264
Bornstein, George, 231, 232, 248
Bouillon, Hélène, 258
Bourdieu, Pierre, 254–55
Boyer, Paul, 60, 136, 141
Brakhage, Stan, 32
Brandt, Willy, 213
Breakdowns (A. Spiegelman), 7, 11–14, **12**, 30, 36–37, 40, 49, **51**, 54–55, **57**, 58–59, 65n22, 74, 92–95, 105n2, 111, 115, 117, 122, 129, 215, 276
Breaking the Frames (Singer), 273
Brink, Cornelia, 192
Broadway Boogie Woogie, 71
Brown, MK, 33
Brown, Tina, 19
Bruce, Lenny, 116
Buchenwald, 24. *See also* concentration camps
Budick, Emily Miller, 238
Building Stories (Ware), 278
Bukowski, Charles, 59, 62
Burns, Charles, 14, 22, 33, 42n41, 129, 131, 136
Burroughs, William S., 74
Busch, Wilhelm, 29
Bush, George W., 21–22, 159, 164, 166, 169, 171, 177, 179, 181, 184–85, 187, 188
By the Bomb's Early Light (Boyer), 60, 141

Cain, James M., 30
Calloway, Cab, 32
Campaign for Peace and Democracy (CPD), 170–71, 174n50
Caniff, Milton, 30, 72
Cantor, Jay, 214
capitalism, 38, 130–31, 134, 138–39, 141–42, 144, 146–47, 167, 285
Captain and the Kids, The. See *Katzenjammer Kids, The*
Carload O'Comics (Crumb), 11
Carnal Knowledge, 51
Caro, Marc, 60
Carpenter, John Alden, 72–73

Carter, Jimmy, 134
Caruth, Cathy, 211
"Cats" (Steinlen), 132
Cayrol, Jean, 213–14, 216
Celan, Paul, 213
censorship, 26, 78, 97, 121, 133, 167, 254, 268
Chagall, Marc, 103
Chambers, Ross, 30
Chandler, Raymond, 30
Charlie Hebdo attack, 37, 104, 122, 170
Cheney, Dick, 164, 166, 171
Chinitz, David E., 83n9
Cho, Jennifer, 181, 187
Choat, Gilbert, 55
Choi, Sungyoon, 161
Chomsky, Noam, 168
Chute, Hillary, 52, 58, 119, 160, 162, 170, 186, 231, 233–35, 239, 249n2, 249n11
Cioran, Emil, 134
citation, 68, 178–82, 185–89
closure, 54, 178, 181, 188–89
Clowes, David, 43n64
Cocteau, Jean, 29
Coe, Sue, 20, 42n41, 129, 131, 132, 150, 162
Cold War, 134, 136, 167
Cole, Jack, 20, 29
Coleridge, Samuel Taylor, 59, 62
Colón, Ernie, 161
Comedian Harmonists, 32
Comic Book Confidential, 42n50, 203
comics: adult, 30, 39, 129, 272–76, 283–84; alternative, 74, 112–13, 118, 124, 128–30, 163; autobiographical, 203; children's, 22, 39, 73, 272–87; commercial, 88, 92, 130; culture, 28, 58, 128–29; history, 33; language of, 33–34, 53, 87, 95, 102, 286; Muslim and Islamic, 170; radical, 130; underground, 9–11, 14, 28, 36, 38, 52, 56, 58–59, 65n23, 70, 88, 95, 111–20, 124–25, 126n5, 128–30, 141, 146, 151, 203, 216, 276, 278, 286; wordless, 87–89, 92, 102–5, 105n8, 107n47
Comics and Immigration: 1913–2013 exhibition, 258
Comics and Sequential Art (Eisner), 280
Comics Code Authority, 29, 58, 66n34, 114–15, 141, 145–46, 149, 153n26, 276, 278, 286
"Comics 101" lecture, 28, 34
"Comic Strip" (Drew Friedman), 131
Co-Mix (A. Spiegelman), 24, 74, 111, 124, 160
Comix, Essays, Graphics & Scraps (A. Spiegelman), 17, 116
communism, 141, 152n16, 167
Complete Maus, The. See *Maus* (A. Spiegelman)
Complete Mr. Infinity, The (A. Spiegelman), 11
Concentrationary Cinema (Pollock and Silverman), 214
concentration camps, 6, 8, 20–22, 44n97, 96, 98, 101, 192–93, 198, 201–4, 210, 214, 218–19, 223–24, 227n16, 235, 239, 261. *See also individual names*
Considering Maus (Geis), 35
constructivism, 31
copyright, 8, 9, 146, 243, 263
Cortázar, Julio, 145
Cortissoz, Royal, 256–57
cosmopolitanism, 69, 73–81, 105
"Cracking Jokes" (A. Spiegelman), 11, 276–78, **277**, 280
Croci, Pascal, 218
Crow, Thomas, 28
Crumb, R., 9, 11, 30, 33, 42n58, 44n95, 52–53, 59, 64n11, 65n23, 105n8, 112–16, 124, 126n3, 271n55, 276, 286
Cuba, 251, 263
Cubism, 52–53, 58, 82, 86, 105n2
culture, 4, 7, 28, 34–36, 38–40, 49, 59, 66n42, 68, 70–72, 80, 112–14, 116–20, 124–25, 130–32, 136–39, 141, 144, 146, 156, 159–63, 170–71, 181, 210, 216, 219, 222, 251–55, 258, 265, 267–68, 269n9, 272–73, 275–76, 284–86; capitalist, 139; comics, 28, 58, 128–29; commodity, 131, 136; conservativism, 136; consumer, 7, 139–40, 144; convenience, 139; counter, 10, 114, 126n5, 149, 151, 272; criticism, 137; entertainment, 142; heritage, 257; high, 24, 27, 69–70; hippie, 9; Holocaust memorial, 218; image, 130; immigrant, 81; industry, 27; Japanese, 138; Jewish, 34; literary, 36; low, 69; mass, 254; political, 151n8, 163–70; popular, 8, 32, 62, 71, 83n9, 141, 288n44; power, 83n9; print, 279; production, 254; punk, 141, 145;

subculture, 9, 161, 257; underground, 70; visual, 28, 35–36, 141, 163; whorehouse, 68, 73

Dada, 43n79, 55, 146
Dark Knight Returns, The (Miller), 119
Davis, Jack, 6
Davis, Miles, 68
Davis, Stuart, 133
Davo, Yves, 173n24
"Day at the Circuits" (A. Spiegelman), 11
DC Comics, 128
"Dead Dick" (A. Spiegelman), 150, **150**
Dead Have the Same Skin, The (Vian), 93–94, **94**
Dead Meat (Coe), 42n40
De Angelis, Richard, 243
Death Mills, 211, 214, 224
Deitch, Jeffrey, 260
Deitch, Kim, 60, 138
DeKoven, Marianne, 186
Deleuze, Gilles, 194–97, 202, 220
DeLillo, Don, 36, 177–78
deMause, Lloyd, 132
DeNiro, Robert, 266
depression, 36, 96–97, 134, 140, 224
Der Sturm, 77
Der Stürmer, 244
Destruction of the European Jews, The (Hillberg), 16
détournement, 140–42, 146–47
Devlin, Tom, 74
Diaghilev, Serge, 72
Diana, Princess, 266
Diary of Anne Frank, The (Frank), 212
Diaz, Aaron, 125
Dick, Philip K., 30
Dick Tracy (Gould), 6, 150
Didion, Joan, 173n24
Die Zeit, 21, 163, 177
Dirks, Rudolph, 72
Disaster Drawn (Chute), 233–34
Disney, Walt, 117
DIY publishing, 145–46
Dog, Norma, 140
"Don't Get Around Much Anymore" (A. Spiegelman), 5, 10, 49–54, **51**, 56, 64n1, 64n9, 93
Doré, Gustave, 29, 129
Dorfman, Ariel, 119
Dorgan, Thomas "Tad," 172n16
Doury, Pascal, 60, 128, 133
"Drawing the Line" (A. Spiegelman), 120, **120**
Drawn & Quarterly, 115, 123, 126n5
"Drawn Over Two Weeks While on the Phone" (A. Spiegelman), 92, 148
"Drawn to Death" (A. Spiegelman), 26
Dreams of a Rarebit Fiend (McCay), 29
Dresden Codak (Diaz), 125
Drew, Richard, 182
drugs, 8, 9, 19, 117
"Duck 'N Cover" (K. Deitch), 138
Dvořák, Antonin, 70
Dwork, Debórah, 218

East Village Other, 6
economics, 28, 62, 113, 115, 132, 134, 136, 138–40, 142, 149, 152n21, 232, 289n50
Ed Head (A. Spiegelman), 27
Ehrlich, Nea, 207
Eichmann, Adolf, 19, 95
Eisenstein, Bernice, 53, 223
Eisner, Will, 8, 29, 53, 65n13, 259, 280
Eliot, T. S., 70, 75, 83n9, 88
Ellis, 266
Ellis Island, 253, 257–60, 262–68
Emmaüs (Trondheim), 120
Encyclopedia of Social Movement Media (Dowling), 151n8
"Enduring Freedom" (A. Spiegelman), **156**
erasure, 82, 198, 214, 239
Espiritu, Karen, 181, 190n16
Eternal Jew, The, 243–44
"Etymological Vaudeville" (A. Spiegelman), 180
Evans, Harold, 243
"Every Dog Has Its Day" (A. Spiegelman), 13
existentialism, 30, 96, 134
expressionism, 3, 32, 74–77, 88, 93, 97, 102; German Expressionism, 43n79, 132, 135, 152n21

Extremely Loud and Incredibly Close (Foer), 177

Falling Man (DeLillo), 36, 177
"Falling Man" (Drew), 182
Family Frames (Hirsch), 36
"Family That Lays Together Stays Together, The" (Crumb), 124
Faulkner, William, 30, 55, 91
"Fears of July, 2002" (A. Spiegelman), **157**
Feininger, Lionel, 29
Ferris, Emil, 32
"First Amendment Fundamentalist" (A. Spiegelman), 121, 124
First Gulf War. *See* Gulf War
Fitzgerald, F. Scott, 70, 74
"Flash of Insight, a Cloud of Dust and a Hearty Hi-yo Silver, A" (A. Spiegelman), 90, **91**
Fly, 162
Foer, Jonathan Safran, 111, 177
"Food for Thought" (Mouly), 131
"Form and Content" (A. Spiegelman), 30
"41 Shots, 10 Cents" (A. Spiegelman), 95
Frahm, Ole, 46n125
framing, 195, 205, 220, 226, 232, 237, 240, 256, 259, 261, 272
Freud, Sigmund, 189n7, 211–12, 277
Friedman, Dan, 146–47
Friedman, Drew, 60, 131, 137
Friedman, Elizabeth, 196
Fritz the Cat (Crumb), 30
Frost, Robert, 75
Funny Aminals (Crumb), 10, **10**, 65n23

Gaiman, Neil, **121**
Garbage Pail Kids, The (A. Spiegelman), 7, 151
gatekeeping, 3, 113–14, 273, 275
Gehr, Ernie, 32
Geis, Deborah, 35, 45n115
Gelman, Woody, 6–7
Gerard, Charley, 82
Gershwin, George, 80, 82
"Gertie the Dinosaur" (animated short), 72
Get Your War On (Rees), 161
Ghosts of Ellis Island, The (JR and A. Spiegelman), 23, 39, 251, 253–57, 259–68, **265**, **266**
Gibbons, Dave, 119, 257
Goldberg, Rube, 72, 92–93, 117
Goldstone, Andrew, 284
Gopnik, Adam, 61
Gorcey, Leo, 60
Goscinny, René, 258
Gould, Chester, 6, 29, 62, 117, 150
Gournelos, Ted, 160, 171
graphic novels, 3–4, 13, 83, 88, 102, 105n8, 113, 119, 278, 282, 288n44
Green, Justin, 9, 30, 59, 203
Greenberg, Clement, 284, 289n47
Grey Zone, The, 213
Griffith, Bill, 4, 9–10, 58–59, 112, 117
Groensteen, Thierry, 191n26
Gross, Milt, 32, 69, 105n8, 129
Grosz, George, 8, 18
Guattari, Félix, 220
Guernica, 58, 60
Guggenheim Fellowship, 16, 28, 64, 119
Guibert, Emmanuel, 161
Gulf War, 18
"Guns of September" (A. Spiegelman), 95
Guston, Philip, 24
gutters, 30–31, 99, 219–20, 280–81

Hajdu, David, 258
Halbwachs, Maurice, 35
Hamblin, Sarah, 38
Hamilton, Ronnie, 6
Hammer Museum, 17, 66n54
Hammett, Dashiell, 30
Hamshahri, 122–23, **122**
Handler, Daniel (Lemony Snicket), 22
Hanks, Fletcher, 129
"Hapless Hooligan in 'Still Moving,'" 23, 68, 73
Happy Hooligan (Opper), 68, 103, 182–86
Harper's Magazine, 75, 122, 169, 255–56
Harvey, Robert C., 137
Haspiel, Dean, 161
Hatfield, Charles, 112–13, 162, 199–200, 203, 205, 256–57, 263

Hearst, William Randolph, 29, 184, 258
Hebard, Andrew, 213
Heer, Jeet, 8, 28, 60, 71, 74, 134, 152n12, 155–56, 266
Hefner, Hugh, 27
Heidegger and "the Jews" (Lyotard), 107n34
Here (McGuire), 16, 112
Heroes (Marvel anthology), 161
Herriman, George, 29, 62, 72, 82, 116, 129
Hershfield, Harry, 29
"High & Low" exhibition, 28, 50, 61–62, **63**, 66n54–55
"High Art Lowdown," 61–62, **63**
High Times, 13
Hillberg, Raul, 16
Hippler, Fritz, 243
Hirsch, Marianne, 36, 198, 201
Hitler, Adolf, 241, 243
Hogan's Alley (Outcault), 163, 257–59
Holocaust, 3, 8, 13–16, 18, 27, 34–36, 39–40, 45n125, 88, 95, 97, 100–101, 107n45, 117, 119, 144, 153n37, 192–94, 197–98, 202–5, 210–26, 226n16, 232, 235, 238, 240–41, 243–44, 247, 253, 268, 274
Holocaust, The (TV series), 44n97
Holocaust Icons (Stier), 218
Holocaust of Texts, The (Hungerford), 36
Holy Terror (Miller), 161
"Hommages Posthumes" (Jarry), 132–33
"Honk, Honk, It's the Bonk" (A. Spiegelman), 139–41
Hopper, Edward, 31
"How a Mosquito Operates" (animated short), 72
How the Other Half Lives (Riis), 259
How to Read Donald Duck (Dorfman and Mattelart), 119
Hungerford, Amy, 36
Hussein, Saddam, 166, 170, 171, 185
Hutton, Robert, 247
Huxley, Aldous, 91
Huyssen, Andreas, 193, 242–44
hypotaxis, 53

"Ice and Fire" (Frost), 75
identity, 36, 40, 124, 144, 196, 201, 215, 239, 254, 269n9; aesthetic, 148; cosmopolitan, 81; cultural, 139; group, 244; Jewish American, 268; LGBTQ+, 113; masked, 46n125; politics, 34; racial, 82; social, 283
immigrants and immigration, 39, 81, 251–68, 271n68
I'm Supposed to Protect You from All This (N. Spiegelman), 31
Indoor Sports (Dorgan), 172n16
Inside Out Project (JR), 264
In the Shadow of No Towers (A. Spiegelman), 21–22, 36, 40, 50, 68–69, 80–81, 103, **104**, 111, 120, 124, 127n34, 129, 151, 152n9, 159–64, **165**, 166, **166**, 169, 171, 172n19, 177–89, **183**, **185**, **187**, 190n16, 191n26, 216, 253–54, 268
Iraq, 18, 103, 159, 162, 164, 170, 177, 185, 187, 189
irony, 95, 139, 141, 160, 171, 190n11, 199, 202, 241, 255, 263, 286
I Was a Child of Holocaust Survivors (Eisenstein), 223

Jack and the Box (A. Spiegelman), 22, 274–75, 279–82, **281**, **282**, 284, 286
Jack Cole and Plastic Man (A. Spiegelman), 20
Jackson, Shannon, 261
Jacobs, Ken, 32, 44n99
Jacobson, Julius, 161, 168–69, 174n42
Jacobson, Phyllis, 174n42
Jacobson, Sid, 161
James, C. L. R., 71
Jameson, Fredric, 289n47
Jarry, Alfred, 26, 29, 132–33
Jazz in Black and White (Gerard), 82
Jazz Modernism (Appel), 68
jazz music, 32, 38, 44n95, 68–83, 94
Jelavich, Peter, 152n21
Jewish American literature. *See* literature: Jewish American
Jewish Defense League, 194
Jewish Forward, The, 16
Jewish Museum, **25**
Jews, 5, 8, 15–16, 31–32, 34–35, 39, 45n120, 93, 97–99, 116, 118, 123, 196, 198, 213–15, 218, 220, 232, 235, 240–45, 247, 251, 253, 255–56, 261, 263–64, 268, 269n9, 271n55

Jimbo (Panter), 42n41, 60, 142
Jimmy Corrigan (Ware), 257
Joel M. Cavior Award for Jewish Writing, 15
Johnson, Mary (Frank Woodhull), 267
Johnston, Phillip, 24, 26, 68–69, 72–74, 102, 106n26
Jones, Spike, 106n26
Joyce, James, 17, 55, 117
Joyce, William, 22, 30
JR, 23, 39, 251, 255–57, 259–66, 268, 271n59
Judenhass (Sim), 215
juxtaposition, 49–50, 52–54, 58–59, 62–63, 137, 140–41, 163, 171, 201, 205, 240, 260, 284
Jyllands-Posten, 169

Kafka, Franz, 30, 88
Kahn, Douglas, 133
Kannenberg, Gene, Jr., 160
Kantor, Alfred, 43n60
Kaplan, Arie, 129
Kashtan, Aaron, 232
Katchor, Ben, 33, 42n41, 60, 129
Katzenjammer Kids, The (Dirks), 29, 39, 103, 182–86
Kawamura, Yosuke, 129
Keaton, Buster, 32
Kelly, Mike, 58
Kertész, Imre, 16
Kichka, Michel, 215
Kidd, Chip, 20
Kierkegaard, Rod, 142
Kinder Kids, The, 163
Kiš, Danilo, 16
Kitchen Sink Press, 9
Knockabout, 126n5
Komar, Vitaly, 128, 141
Kominsky-Crumb, Aline, 33, 59
Koren, Leonard, 138
Kościelniak, Mieczyslaw, 43n60
Krazy Kat (Herriman), 62, 72–73, 82, 116
Krigstein, Bernard, 8, 30–31, 33
Kubert, Joe, 223
"Kubla Khan" (Coleridge), 59
Kuhlman, Martha, 179
Kunka, Andrew J., 191n28
Kuper, Peter, 162
Kurtzman, Harvey, 8, 9, 20, 29, 32, 40, 137, 153n26
Kwarczinsky, Leile, 267

Lacan, Jacques, 211
LaCapra, Dominick, 179, 188
La mémoire collective (Halbwachs), 35
Lang, Fritz, 32
Langer, Lawrence, 36
language, 22, 33–34, 40, 53, 75, 77, 82, 87–88, 90, 92–93, 95–97, 100, 102–3, 105, 142, 151n8, 179, 203, 211, 244, 255–56, 258–59, 266, 274, 285–86
Lanzmann, Claude, 32, 95
Laocoön (Lessing), 284
L'Assiette au Beurre, 26
Lawrence, Patrick, 38–39
Lay, Carol, 129
Lazarus, Emma, 265, 267
Lead Pipe Sunday (A. Spiegelman), **150**
League of Left-Wing Writers, 152n16
Lee, Stan, 203
Lefèvre, Didier, 161
Legault, Robert, 138
Lemercier, Frédéric, 161
Les Demoiselles d'Avignon, 56
Les Lieux de Mémoire (Nora), 178
Lessing, Gotthold Ephraim, 262, 284
Levine, Michael, 96
Levy, David, 139
Lewen, Si, 24, 40, 69, 102, 255–56, 260
Library of America, 24, 69, 102
Lichtenstein, Roy, 62
Life in Ink, A (A. Spiegelman), 26
Life Is Beautiful, 32
Life magazine, 8, 51, 52, 259
literacy, 278–80; comics, 37, 275, 280; multiliteracies, 275, 285; multimodal, 275, 285; visual, 275, 285
literature, 5, 11, 14, 30, 68, 96, 107n50, 113, 145, 160, 190n11, 215, 220, 222, 248, 254, 268, 278; adult, 266; graphic, 129; high, 91; Holocaust, 46; Jewish American, 35; pictorial, 36; postmodern, 34
Little Lit anthology series, 22, 274, 283, 286

Little Nemo in Slumberland (McCay), 29, 56, 163
"Little Signs of Passion" (A. Spiegelman), 11
"Living with Contradictions" (Tillman), 131
Long Island Post, 6
Looney Tunes, 73
Lovecraft, H. P., 59, 62
"Love Song of J. Alfred Prufrock, The" (Eliot), 75
Luckiesh, Matthew, 278
Lund, Michael, 240
Lynch, David, 40
Lynch, Jay, 6
Lyons, James, 112
Lyotard, Jean-François, 107n34, 179

MacDowell Medal, 40
Maddocks, Melvin, 51–52
MAD magazine, 6, 7, 59, 66n37, 88, 137–38, 151, 153n26, 276, 286
Magritte, René, 61
"Making *Maus*" exhibition, 16
"Malpractice Suite, The" (A. Spiegelman), 11, 30
Manchin, James, 7
manga, 14, 129
"Manhattan" (Beyer), 41n40
Mann, Ron, 203
March, Joseph Moncure, 68–69, 74–77, 82, 127n25
Marek, Mark, 140
marginalization, 4, 39, 113, 150, 261
Mariscal, Javier, 128
Marsalis, Wynton, 73, 82
Marvel Comics, 9, 28, 33, 65n28, 128, 161, 203
Masereel, Frans, 69, 75, 102, 132–33, 152n16
masks and masking, 39, 46n125, 192–207, 207n5, 251, 269n9
Masse, Francis, 141
Masses, The, 133
"Master Race" (Krigstein), 8
"Masters of American Comics" exhibition, 17, 66n54
materialism, 136, 139, 182
materiality, 231–33, 237, 248
Mattelart, Armand, 119
Maus, 3–5, 8, 9–22, **10**, 26–40, 42n53, 43n64, 45n113, 45n115, 45n125, 49–50, 60, 63–64, 65n23, 67n56, 67n60, 68–69, 74, 84n34, 86, 88, 95–103, 107n45, 111–13, 116, 118–20, 127n25, 127n28, 128–29, 144, 151, 153n37, 163–64, 166, 172n19, 179, 192–207, **201**, 207n5, 210–26, 231–48, **234**, 249n2, 249n5, 249n11, 253–54, 259–61, 263–64, 268, 269n9, 271n55, 272–74; *Maus I*, 16–17, 42n50, 66n43, 74, **99**, 100, 106n23, 119, 122, 196, 216, **217**, **221**, 224, 243, 247; *Maus II*, 16–17, 63, 64, 74, 95–96, 106n23, 196, **200**, 205, **206**, 224, **225**, 274; Pantheon-*Maus*, 17, 231–33, 239–40, 247–48, 249n2; RBG-*Maus*, 231–32, **234**, 235, 237–42, 244, **245**, **246**, 248
Max and Moritz (Busch), 29
McCay, Winsor, 29, 33, 56, 72, 117, 129, 259
McCloud, Scott, 30, 53–54, 68, 186, 191n26, 267, 273, 277
McGuire, Richard, 16, 22, 112
McSweeney's, 18
Melamid, Alexander, 128, 141
memory, 15, 35–36, 44n97, 46n125, 107n34, 164, 178, 182, 184, 186, 189n7, 218, 222–23; visual, 193, 219, 224, 239
"Memory Hole" (A. Spiegelman), 7
metacommentary, 232, 240, 283
MetaMaus (A. Spiegelman), 24, 67n61, 111, 119, 122, **122**, 194, **195**, 196–202, 205, 233, 235, 269n9
Meulen, Ever, 128
Michaels, Walter Benn, 118
Microscopic Septet, 106n26
Middle East, 18, 21, 160, 164, 168–69, 185
militarism, 81, 160, 167–68, 173n24
Miller, Frank, 119, 161
Miró, Joan, 61
Modern Art in the Common Culture (Crow), 28
modernism, 8, 17–18, 30, 32–33, 38, 40, 49–56, 58, 60–64, 65n13–14, 69–74, 86–88, 91, 102–3, 105, 146, 254–58, 275, 284–87, 288n44, 289n47
Modigliani, Amedeo, 52, 56
Mondrian, Piet, 8, 71

Moore, Alan, 119, 257
Morgan, Rex, 117
Morrison, Toni, 40, 190n13
Morton, Jelly Roll, 44n95
Moss, Frank K., 278
Mouly, Françoise, 4, 11, 13–14, 18–20, 22, 24, 26, 28–29, 31, 33, 42n41, 58–60, 86, 95, 97, 103–5, 105n8, 115, 128, 130–34, 138, 141, 145, 152n12, 155–56, 163, 177, 182, **183**, 184, 198, 231, 235, 237, 249n11, 253, 255, 257, 262, 266, 274, 278
Munch, Edvard, 93–94, 117, 219
Muñoz, José, 128
Museum of Contemporary Art, 17, 66–67n54
Museum of Modern Art (MOMA), 16, 28, 50, 52, 60–64, **63**, 66–67nn54–55, 119
Museum of Modern Art (Paris), 31
Music Survives!, The, 106n26
Muslims, 21, 153n29, 169–70, 268
"Mutton Geoff" (Newgarden), 138
"My Sweetie Went Away," 78

Nabokov, Vladimir, 30
Nasty Tales, 112
Nation, The, **120**, 124, 170
National Book Critics Circle Award, 15, 64, 119
nationalism, 18, 81, 185
National Lampoon, 59
Nazis, 3, 21–22, 31–32, 96, 116, 192–93, 198, 202–3, 215, 219–20, 223, 226, 241–47, 261
Negative Dialectics (Adorno), 210
neo-sincerity, 137, 286
Neufeld, Josh, 162
"New Colossus, The" (Lazarus), 265
Newgarden, Mark, 129, 138
New London Group, 285
New Politics, 168, 174n42
New Statesman, 120–21, **121**
New Wave style, 130, 145–48, 254
New York, New York, 6–8, 10–14, 80–81, 112, 149–50, 155, 159, 161, 171, 177, 182–87, 253, 255, 258–59, 267
New York City I, 71
New Yorker, 4, 18–22, **21**, 24, 28, 31–33, 38, 42n58, 61, 94–95, 103, 105n8, 106n26, 112–13, 119, 122–25, **123**, **125**, 151, 153n29, 156–59, **156**, **157**, 163, 172n16, 182, **183**, 252, 254, 261, 266, 268
New York Journal, 29, 184
New York Public Library, 42n53
New York Times, **25**, 42n47, 113, 155, 159, 170, 197, 267, 272
New York Times Book Review, 15, 119
New York Trilogy (Auster), 106n24
New York World, 184
Nietzsche, Friedrich, 210
Night (Wiesel), 212
Night and Fog, 8, 39, **216**, 226n7
"9/11/01" (A. Spiegelman), 160
9/11 Commission Report, 177
9/11 Report, The (S. Jacobson and Colón), 161
9/11 terrorist attacks, 18–22, 26, 36, 38, 80–81, 155–71, 173n24, 177–89, 190n11, 190n13, 190n16, 192, 216, 253, 265, 268
Nixon, Richard, 24, 130
noir, 30, 56, 74, 93, 132
Noomin, Diane, 33
Nora, Pierre, 178, 189n7
nostalgia, 38, 69, 80–82, 131, 136, 138, 178, 189n7
Nückel, Otto, 69
nuclear technology, 131–32, 134–36, 138, 140–41, 145, 158
Nuit et Brouillard, 210, 213–19, 224
Nyberg, Amy Kiste, 279, 288n26

Obama, Barack, 43n58, 252
Occupy Comics, 151
Oliveros, Chris, 74
"One Row" (A. Spiegelman), 148, **148**
Onion, The, 272–73
"On Satire" (Sacco), 174n47
Open Me . . . I'm a Dog! (A. Spiegelman), 111, 274–75, 281–82, 284
Opper, Frederick Burr, 68, 182
oppression, 95, 131
O'Sullivan, Simon, 220
Outcault, Richard Felton, 257–59
Owens, Craig, 149
Oz, 112
Ozick, Cynthia, 35

Palestine (Sacco), 259, 278
Palmer, Amanda, **121**
Panter, Gary, 14, 28, 33, 60, 129, 142, 263
Pantheon Books, 15, 16–17, 21, 32–33, 39, 115, 119, 159, 197, 231, 247–48, 274
Parade, The (Lewen), 24, 102, 255, 260
paratextuality, 231–32
Paris Review, 72, 256
Parks, Van Dyke, 26
Passionate Journey, A (Masereel), 75
Patterson, David, 95
Patriot Act, 21
Pavel, Paul, 15, 96–97, 221–22
Pekar, Harvey, 43n64, 118
Penaz, Mary Louise, 190n16
Penguin Books, 22, 33, 66n43, 119
"Pep Boys, The" (Newgarden), 138
Perec, Georges, 103
Persepolis (Satrapi), 223, 259
Peterson, Robert S., 71
Photographer, The (Guibert et al.), 161
photography, 39, 117, 192–207, 207n5, 243–46, 253, 256, 259, 261–62, 264, 266, 268
Pianist, The (Szpilman), 212
Picasso, Kiki, 60, 128, 150
Picasso, Loulou, 128
Picasso, Pablo, 52–53, 55–56, 58, 62, 67n58, 86, 117
Pilobolus Dance Theater, 23, 68, 72
Pipe Dreams, **89**
Pizzino, Christopher, 273, 283
Plasmatics, 142
"Plastic Arts, The" (A. Spiegelman), **21**
Plastic Man (Cole), 20
"*Playboy* Funnies," 114
Playboy magazine, 9, 13, 20, 27
PM, 133
Poiré, Emmanuel (Caran D'Ache), 41n40, 129
Poland, 3, 6, 14, 118, 198–99
politics, 4, 18–20, 30–31, 34, 38–39, 60, 80, 97, 111, 114, 118, 123–24, 129–34, 136–37, 139, 141–42, 144–51, 151n8, 152n12, 152n16, 152n21, 153n26, 160–71, 173n24, 179, 181–82, 185–89, 214, 227n16, 247, 251, 254–57, 260–61, 268, 276
Pollack, Howard, 73
Pollock, Griselda, 214
Pollock, Jackson, 31
Porkopolis (Coe), 42n40
Portrait of Gertrude Stein (P. Picasso), 53, 62, 67n58
Postman, Neil, 279
postmodernism, 28, 30, 34–35, 45n115, 46n125, 107n32, 146, 179–81, 286
Pound, Ezra, 55
"Prince Rooster" (A. Spiegelman), 274–75, 283–86
Print Magazine, 152n22
Print Mint, 9, 52
"Prisoner on the Hell Planet" (A. Spiegelman), 5, 10, 11–12, 15, 30, 93, 97, 111, 129, 197–98, 204, 253
Projects: Art Spiegelman, 63–64
Proust, Marcel, 30, 55
Psst . . . ! magazine, 41n40
psychoanalysis, 36, 40, 105, 238, 276–77
Pulitzer, Joseph, 184
Pulitzer Prize, 3, 37, 49, 64, 119, 129, 248, 273
punk, 141–46, 149
Pussey! (Clowes), 43n64

Queneau, Raymond, 11, 103

race and racism, 19–20, 31, 39, 44n99, 70–71, 77, 81–83, 83n9, 94, 103, 114–16, 118, 122, 124, 127n25, 131, 137–38, 142, 242, 256, 260–61, 264
radicalism, 19, 71, 130–48
Rall, Ted, 44n102, 161
Rare and Extraordinary History of Holy Russia, The (Doré), 29
Rasula, Jed, 69–70, 82
RAW Books and Graphics, 13, 33, 231, 248
RAW Junior, 22
RAW magazine, 4, 7, 11–15, 19–20, 22, 26–29, 31–33, 38–40, 42n40, 44n95, 50, 58–59, 64, 66n42, 74, 107n49, 112, 115, 117–20, 128–51, 151n8, 152n12, 152n22, 153n26, 153n29, 163, 215, 231–33, 235–37, 240, 248, 249n2, 249n5, 253–55, 267, 273, 286; Vol. 1, 129, 131, 132–38, **136**, 140, 142–45, **143**, 147–48,

148, 150, 233, **234**, **245**, 246, **246**; Vol. 2, 33, 119, 150
RAW One-Shots, 13
Reading Art Spiegelman (Smith), 36
Read Yourself RAW (A. Spiegelman), 59, 67n56, 119
Reagan, Ronald, 38, 130–34, 136–39, 141, 145, 147, 149, 151n8
Reagan's America (deMause), 132
"Real Dream" (A. Spiegelman), 93
Reclining Nude (Modigliani), 52, 56
"Red Flowers" (Tsuge), 14
Rees, David, 161, 162
Reid, Jamie, 142
Reizbaum, Marilyn, 242
religion, 87, 136, 142, 160, 164, 167–71, 214, 227n16. *See also specific religions*
"Remember Those Dead and Cuddly Tower Twins" (A. Spiegelman), 164
Remnick, David, 18–20, 112, 156, 159–60
representation, 24, 34–36, 39, 43n64, 44n99, 61, 81, 100, 113, 132–33, 139, 160, 178–79, 186, 189, 192–94, 196–97, 200, 202–5, 207, 211–12, 214, 218–22, 224, 232, 239–40, 243, 245
Re/Search, 145
Resist! (Mouly and N. Spiegelman), 104
resistance, 100, 112, 130, 136, 140–41, 146–47
Resnais, Alain, 8, 39, 213–16, **216**, 218–19
Rhapsody in Blue, 80
Richter, Gerhard, 45n125
Riis, Jacob, 259
Rites of Spring, The, 72
Rodriguez, Manuel "Spain," 9, 59
Rogers, Boody, 129
"Roll Up Your Sleeves, America!" (A. Spiegelman), 158–59, **158**
Rostock, 20. *See also* concentration camps
Roth, Eric, 266
Roth, Philip, 35
Royal, Derek Parker, 186
Ruillier, Jérôme, 259
Rund, Jeff, 11
Russian Formalism, 30

Sabin, Roger, 112, 114–15, 142
Sacco, Joe, 20, 169–70, 174n47, 259, 278
Samba, Chéri, 128
Sampayo, Carlos, 128
San Francisco, California, 9–11
San Francisco Bulletin, 69
San Francisco *Oracle*, 9
Sartre, Jean-Paul, 96
Satrapi, Marjane, 32, 34, 113, 223, 259
Savage, Jon, 142
Saxton, Libby, 216
Schindler's List, 15, 32, 36, 44n97, 215
Schneider, Bob, 11
"Schoolboy Assassin, The" (Kierkegaard), 142
Schulman, Nicole, 162
Schulz, Charles, 40
Schuster, Joe, 259
Schwind, Joe, 140, 142
Scott, Raymond, 73
Scream, The (Munch), 93–94
Screamers, 142
Screw, 9
Search and Destroy, 145
Second Generation (Kichka), 215
Seduction of the Innocent (Wertham), 278
Seldes, Gilbert, 70–71, 82, 161
"Self-Portrait with Mouse Mask" (A. Spiegelman), **201**
Sendak, Maurice, 22
September 11 terrorist attacks. *See* 9/11 terrorist attacks
"Set-Up, The" (March), 77
Seurat, Georges, 31
Seven Lively Arts, The (Seldes), 70–71
Severin, John, 6
Shachtman, Max, 167–68, 174n42
"Shaping Thought" (A. Spiegelman), **23**, 24
Shklovsky, Viktor, 30, 37, 44n84
Shoah, 32, 95
Short Order Comix, 50, 54, 58; *#1*, 10; *#2*, 50, **51**, 56, **57**
Siegel, Jerry, 259
Sikoryak, Robert, 266
silence, 38, 87–89, 92, 95–105, 107n34
Silverman, Max, 214
Sim, Dave, 215
Simplicissimus, 26
Singer, Marc, 34, 273

Singerman, Howard, 149
Situationist International, 139–40, 142, 145–46
Six Nudes with Baguettes (Crumb et al.), 20
"Skeeter Grant" (A. Spiegelman), 90
Slash, 142, 145
"Slice of Life, A" (A. Spiegelman and Mouly), 86
Smith, Bessie, 78, 82
Smith, Philip, 36–37, 215
Smith, Winston, 142
social class, 81, 131–32, 135–36, 188
Social Works (Jackson), 261
solace, 178, 180–82, 184–89, 190n16
Son of Saul, 213
Sontag, Susan, 38, 86–88, 104–5
Sophie's Choice (Styron), 16, 214
Sorel, Edward, 19
spectacle, 77, 92, 103, 139–42, 144, 149
Spiegelman, Anja, 6, 11–13, 16, 21, 29–30, 97–100, 105, 197–98, 200, 204, 215, 222–23, 234–35, 241, 249n11, 253; death, 8, 11, 19, 29, 41n29, 87, 97, 198; diaries, 96–98, 237–39, 248
Spiegelman, Art: as children's book author, 3, 22, 39, 111, 272–87; as comic book historian, 29, 35, 38–39, 111, 160; as editor, 3–4, 10–11, 13–14, 33, 40, 49–50, 54, 58–60, 63, 69, 88, 111, 118, 125, 130–33, 136–37, 141, 152n12, 215; hospitalization of, 19, 34, 41n29, 90; working style of, 26–27
Spiegelman, Dashiell, 16, 18, 22, 155, 177
Spiegelman, Mala, 101
Spiegelman, Nadja, 16, 18, 24, 28, 31, 104, 155, 177
Spiegelman, Richieu, 97, 101, 193, 198, 204, 205
Spiegelman, Vladek, 5, 6, 8, 12–13, 16–18, 21–22, 29, 36, 43n64, 44n97, 63, 95–101, 105, 118, 144, 193, 198–205, 212–15, 218, 220–24, 226, 232, 234, 237–39, 241, 246–47, 249n11
Spielberg, Steven, 15, 32, 215, 263, 271n55
Stallings, Carl, 73
Stamant, Nicole, 239
Stanford Friedman, Susan, 54
Staub, Michael, 223
Stein, Gertrude, 30, 56
Steinberg, Saul, 31
Steinlen, Théophile Alexandre (Jean Caillou), 132, 240, 243, 246–47
stereotypes, 77–78, 116, 121, 124, 131, 212, 242
Sterne, Laurence, 30
Stevens, Wallace, 55
Stier, Oren, 218
"St. Louis Refugee Ship Blues, The" (A. Spiegelman), 251, **252**, 253, 259–60, 264
Storr, Robert, 63
Strange, The (Ruillier), 259
Stravinsky, Igor, 55, 72
Styron, William, 16, 214
subversion, 38, 62, 111–12, 115, 137, 140, 203, 242–43, 245–46, 248, 286
Sugiura, Shigeru, 129
suicide, 8, 11, 20, 29, 34, 41n29, 87, 94, 97, 134–36, 198
Sun Ra, 145
SUNY Binghamton (Harpur College), 8, 28
"Super Colored Guy" (Artie X and Hamilton), 6
Superman, 258
surrealism, 26, 56, 90, 94, 117, 132, 141, 146
Swarte, Joost, 13, 33, 60, 128
Szpilman, Władysław, 212

Tan, Shaun, 259, 267
Tardi, Jacques, 128
terrorism, 18, 103, 168, 171, 173n24, 177, 265. See also *Charlie Hebdo* attack; 9/11 terrorist attacks
Testament, The (Wiesel), 95
"Theodore Death Head" (Doury), 133
therapy, 15, 105, 238. *See also* psychoanalysis
third camp, 167–68, 170
"This Little Piggy Went to Market" (Coe), 131
Tijuana bibles, 77, 88, 255
Tillman, Lynne, 131
Time magazine, 9
To Afghanistan and Back (Rall), 161
Tobocman, Seth, 162
"'Tokyo Raw" (Koren et al.), 14, 138
Tomorrow, Tom, 162
TOON Books, 22–23, 272–87
TOON into Comics, 274–75, 284

TOON Treasury of Classic Children's Comics, The (A. Spiegelman and Mouly), 274
Töpffer, Rodolphe, 26, 29, 34, 82, 255, 258
Topps Chewing Gum Company, 6–8, 114, 254
Torres, Alissa, 161, 173n24
"Tower Twins, The" (A. Spiegelman), 185, **185**
toxic masculinity, 131, 140, 150
transgression, 38, 113–16, 118–25, 140, 238, 254–55, 264
trauma, 3, 15–16, 19, 21, 36, 38, 103, 129, 134, 151, 164, 168, 171, 178–82, 184, 186–89, 189n7, 190n16, 210–26, 242, 261, 269n9, 276
Trip to the Bottom of the World, A (Viva), 22
Trondheim, Lewis, 120
Trump, Donald, 24, 43n58, 104, 264–65
Tsuge, Yoshiharu, 14, 129
Tucker, Brian, 262
Tucker, Ken, 119, 272–73
"Two Fisted Painters" (A. Spiegelman), 150, 236
Tyler, Andrew, 131

Uderzo, Albert, 258
Understanding Comics (McCloud), 30, 53, 186, 273
Uneeda Comix, 52
Unframed project, 260, 262, 264
Updike, John, 19
U2, 264

Vågnes, Øyvind, 162
"Valentine's Day" (A. Spiegelman), 123–24, **123**
van de Knaap, Ewout, 215, 219
Vanity Fair, 19, 140
van Pelt, Robert Jan, 218
Varnedoe, Kirk, 61
Versluys, Kristiaan, 181
Vian, Boris, 19, 93–94, **94**, 106n23
Viénet, René, 140
Village Voice, The, 44n97, 44n102
violence, 12, 31, 39, 56, 58, 74–75, 77–78, 90, 95, 100–101, 103, 114–15, 117–18, 124, 127n25, 135–38, 140, 142–44, 146, 160, 164, 167–69, 181, 185, 194, 204, 211, 215, 218–19, 221, 224, 276–77
Viper Vicar of Vice, Villainy, and Vickedness, The (A. Spiegelman), 11, 65n22
visual parataxis, 49–50, 53–55, 58, 60, 62, 64, 65n14
Viva, Frank, 22

Wacky Packages (A. Spiegelman), 7, 95
Ward, Lynd, 24, 69, 88, 102–3
Ware, Chris, 14, 22, 32–33, 60, 101, 107n47, 107n50, 112, 129, 257, 259, 278
Warhol, Andy, 32
Warshow, Robert, 279
Washington Post, 251, **252**
"Wasteland, The" (Eliot), 70, 75
Watchmen (Moore and Gibbons), 119, 257
"Weapons of Mass Displacement" (A. Spiegelman), **187**
Weingart, Wolfgang, 146
Weirdo magazine, 33, 126n5
Wertham, Fredric, 114, 276, 278–79, 282
Weschler, Lawrence, 5, 27, 223, 226
Whitehead, Anne, 211
Whole Grains (A. Spiegelman and Schneider), 11
Wiesel, Elie, 95, 212
Wild Party, The (A. Spiegelman), 68–69, 74–76, **76**, **79**, 80–81, 111, 127n25, 151
"Wild Party, The" (March), 74, 76–80, 82
Williams, Paul, 112
Williams, Wendy O., 142
"Willie Wetback, Boy Immigrant" (A. Spiegelman), 65n22
Wilson, S. Clay, 9, 59
Wimmen's Comics Collective, 33
Winds of War, The (Wouk), 51–52
Witek, Joseph, 37, 117, 162, 254
Wolff, Helen, 247
Wolff, Kurt, 247
Wolff, Michael Angelo, 259
Wolfreys, Julian, 113–14
Wolk, Douglas, 120, 172n12
Wolverton, Basil, 129
Women Are Heroes project, 261, 264
Woo, Benjamin, 36, 254
Wood, Michael, 75–77, 80
Wood, Wally, 6, 88, 90

woodcuts, 24, 29, 31, 38, 56, 69, 75–76, 88, 102, 107n49, 260
Woodford, Jack, 117
Woodhull, Frank (Mary Johnson), 267
Worden, Daniel, 284
WORDLESS!, 23–24, **23**, 26, 68–69, 71–74, 82–83, 102, 260, 263
wordless comics. *See* comics: wordless
Work and Turn (A. Spiegelman), 13
World War II, 13, 21, 52, 172, 174n42, 193, 196, 202, 204–5, 234, 253, 264
World War 3 Illustrated, 129, 158–59, **158**, 162
Wouk, Herman, 51–52

X (Coe), 42n41
xenophobia, 20, 39, 268
Xun, Lu, 152n16

Yellow Kid, The (Outcault), 257–58
Yossel (Kubert), 223
Young, Art, 24
Young, James E., 63, 222, 242
Young, Murat Bernard "Chic," 92
Yumura, Teruhiko, 129

Zap Comix, 9, 112, 276
Zippy the Pinhead, 9
Žižek, Slavoj, 168

Made in the USA
Las Vegas, NV
20 February 2024